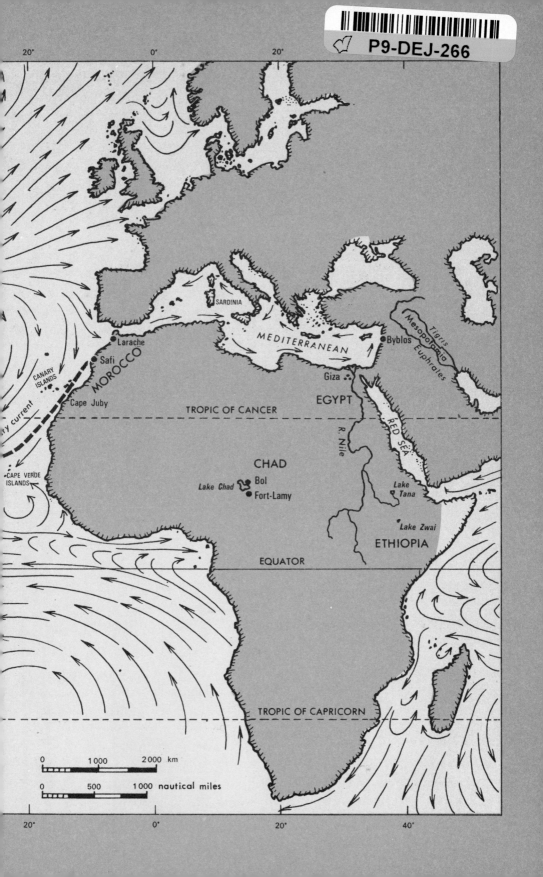

20°   0°   20°

MEDITERRANEAN

SARDINIA

Tigris
Mesopotamia
Euphrates

Larache
Safi
MOROCCO

Byblos

Giza

EGYPT

CANARY
ISLANDS

Cape Juby

TROPIC OF CANCER

R. Nile

RED SEA

CHAD

Lake Chad Bol
Fort-Lamy

*Lake
Tana*

CAPE VERDE
ISLANDS

Lake Zwai

ETHIOPIA

EQUATOR

TROPIC OF CAPRICORN

0   1000   2000 km

0   500   1000 nautical miles

20°   0°   20°   40°

THE RA EXPEDITIONS

By Thor Heyerdahl

KON-TIKI
AMERICAN INDIANS IN THE PACIFIC
AKU-AKU
SEA ROUTES TO POLYNESIA
THE RA EXPEDITIONS

With Edwin N. Ferdon

THE ARCHAEOLOGY OF EASTER ISLAND (2 VOLS.)

Thor Heyerdahl

THE RA EXPEDITIONS

Translated by Patricia Crampton

DOUBLEDAY & COMPANY, INC., GARDEN CITY, NEW YORK
1971

To Yvonne

Contents

Illustrations

THE RA EXPEDITIONS

Chapter One

ONE RIDDLE, TWO ANSWERS AND NO SOLUTION

A REED flutters in the wind.

We break it off.

It floats. It can bear a frog.

Two hundred thousand reeds flutter in the wind. A whole meadow billows like a green cornfield along the shore.

We cut it down. We tie it into bundles, like great corn sheaves. The bundles float. We go on board. A Russian, an African, a Mexican, an Egyptian, an American, an Italian, and myself a Norwegian, with a monkey and a lot of clucking hens. We are off to America. We are in Egypt. It's blowing sand, it's dry and hot, it's the Sahara.

Abdullah assures me that the reeds will float. I tell him that America is a long way off. He does not think people like black skins in America, but I assure him he is wrong. He does not know where America is, but we will get there in any case, if the wind is blowing that way. We will be safe on the reeds as long as the ropes hold. As long as the ropes hold, he says. Will the ropes hold?

I felt someone shaking me by the shoulder and woke up. It was Abdullah. "It's three o'clock," he said. "We are starting work again." The sun was baking inside the hot tent canvas. I sat up and peered through a gap in the door opening. The dry heat and blinding sunshine of the Sahara thrust at me from outside. Sun, sun, sun. A sun-soaked expanse of sand met the bluest thing God has created, a cloudless desert sky unfolding in the afternoon sunshine above a world of golden-gray sand.

A row of three large and two small pyramids were set like shark's teeth against the arch of sky. They had stood so, motionless and unchanging, since the time when men were part of nature and built in accord with nature. And in front of them, down in the shallow depression, lay something timeless, built yesterday, built ten thousand years ago: a boat in the desert sand, a sort of Noah's ark stranded in the wilderness of the Sahara, far from surf and seaweed. Two camels stood beside it, chewing. What were they chewing? Trimmings from the boat itself, perhaps, "the paper boat." It was built of papyrus. The golden reeds were lashed together in bundles taking the form of a ship with prow and sternpost which stood out against the blue sky like a recumbent crescent moon.

Abdullah was already on his way down there. And two coal-black Budumas in fluttering white robes were clambering on board, while Egyptians in colorful garments dragged up fresh bundles of papyrus reed. There was work to be done. "Bot! Bot!" shouted Abdullah. "More reeds!" I staggered out onto the hot sand as if I had awakened from a thousand-year sleep. After all, they were working for me, it was I who had conceived the absurd idea of reviving a boatbuilder's art that the Pharaoh Cheops and his genera-tion were already beginning to abandon at the time they ordered the building of those mighty forms, the pyramids which now stood there like a solid mountain range, hiding our timeless shipyard from the twentieth-century maelstrom whirling in Cairo's hectic city streets down in the green Nile Valley on the other side.

Our world, outside the tents, was bare sand. Hot sand, pyramids, more sand, and huge stacks of sun-dried reeds, brittle, combustible papyrus reeds, which the men were dragging over to the licorice skinned boatbuilders who sat on the crescent moon, tightening rope lashings with the aid of hands, teeth and naked feet. They were building a boat—a papyrus boat. A *kadáy* they called it in their Buduma tongue, and they knew what they were building. Busy fin-gers and teeth strapped the loops round the reeds as only experts could. "A paper boat," said the people at the Papyrus Institute down in the Nile Valley. For there they soaked these reeds in water and beat them into a crisp paper, to show tourists and scientists the material on which the world's most ancient scholars had painted their hieroglyphic memoirs.

A papyrus reed is a soft, sappy flower stem. A child can bend and crush it. When dry, it snaps like a matchstick and burns like paper. On the ground in front of me lay a tinder-dry papyrus reed, savagely screwed and fractured into a zigzag tangle. It had been thrown there in the morning by an indignant old Arab who mangled it between his fingers before flinging it away from him on the sand, spitting after it and pointing scornfully. "That thing," he said, "that wouldn't even hold a nail; it's only a reed, and how could you fix masts to a thing like that?" The old man was a canny boat-builder who had taken the bus up from Port Said to conclude a contract for masts and rigging for the vessel we were building. He was so outraged that he took the next bus back to the coast. Were we trying to make fun of an honest craftsman, or were the men of today completely ignorant of what was needed to build a decent boat? It was no good explaining to him that many boats of reed were painted on the walls of the ancient burial chambers out here in the desert. After all, he said, these tombs also contain paintings of men with the heads of birds and serpents with wings. Anyone could see that a reed was a soft stalk in which neither nails nor screws could find a grip. Material for a haystack. A paper boat. Thanks for the return ticket.

What now? Boats must have masts. Our three black friends from Lake Chad in the heart of Africa declared that the boatbuilder was an idiot; he could never have seen a proper *kaday*, because they were always made from these reeds. On the other hand, they had never seen masts on a *kaday*, and what did we want with one? If people wanted to cross the water they used paddles. Lake Chad was large, the sea could not be larger, they claimed. Stoically unperturbed, they continued to lash the bundles of papyrus together. That was their specialty. The Arab from Port Said was an ignorant bluffer who had never seen a *kaday*.

I went up to the tent again and dug out of the portfolio the sketches and photographs of ancient Egyptian boat models and wall paintings. True, there were, of course, no spikes in the papyrus boats. The mast was fixed to the reeds in a very special way. A thick, wide footplate was made fast with rope on top of the reed bundles where the mast was to stand, and it was stepped into this solid block of wood and secured with rope. I pushed the drawings aside and lay down on my back on a heap of ropes and canvas stacked along one wall of the tent. It was cooler here and I could think. What was I really taking on, and what reason had I to think that such a craft could be used outside the Nile Delta? I admitted to myself that the suspicion was based as much on intuition as on concrete facts.

At the time when I decided to build the *Kon-Tiki* raft of balsa logs, my reasoning had been quite different. True enough, I had never seen a piece of balsa wood then and never sailed a boat, let alone a raft, but I had had a theory, solid scientific evidence and a logical conclusion. This time I had none. Before I ventured to set sail with *Kon-Tiki*, I had already accumulated enough material to fill a very bulky manuscript with evidence proving to my own satisfaction that an offshot of the oldest civilization in Peru had reached the Polynesian Islands before any voyagers had reached the East Pacific out of Asia. The balsa raft was considered the nearest thing to a boat known in ancient Peru, and I therefore concluded that it had to be seaworthy. How else could the ancient Peruvians have come across to Polynesia? I had no other reason to trust the abilities of a balsa raft. But the conclusion held good.

This time things were different. I had no theory that the ancient Egyptians had carried their civilization to distant islands or continents. There *were* many others who believed so and argued that the Egyptian pyramid-builders had brought cultural inspiration to tropical America long before Columbus. I had no such theory: I had never found any conclusive evidence favoring it, but neither had I found any evidence to the contrary. Besides, pyramids were built in Mesopotamia also. I was fascinated by the problem, but in no position to see any tenable solution. Science lacked too many pieces of the jigsaw puzzle. Anyone seriously looking for a possible connection between the ancient cultures of Egypt and Mexico could not avoid finding very serious stumbling stones: wide gaps in the chronology, inexplicable contradictions, and an ocean gap ten thousand times wider than the Nile.

For water travel the ancient Egyptians originally had only bundle boats made of papyrus reed. Later they made themselves long wooden ships of planks, dovetailed and sewn together, vulnerable in a heavy sea, but eminently suited to all kinds of transport and trading on the calm waters of the Nile. A few hundred yards from the tent where I lay, at the foot of the Pyramid of Cheops, my Egyptian friend Ahmed Joseph was busy piecing together one of the magnificent wooden ships of the Pharaoh Cheops. Archaeologists had recently discovered that a large ship lay buried on each side of this large pyramid; four ships in all were lying there, hermetically preserved. They lay in deep, airtight chambers, covered with enormous stone slabs. Only one pit had been opened so far, revealing hundreds of thick sections of cedarwood planking piled in stacks, as fresh as when they were buried over 4600 years ago—some 2700 years before Christ. Now, Egypt's chief curator, Ahmed Joseph, was busy threading new rope through all the thousands of small holes where the ship had once been held together by hemp. The result was a ship over 140 feet long, so perfectly streamlined and elegant that the Vikings had not built anything more graceful or larger when some millennia later they began to sail the high seas.

There was only one essential difference between the two types of ship: the Viking ships were built to bear the brunt of the ocean rollers, while Cheops' ship was built for pomp and ceremony on the placid Nile. Wear and tear on the wood where the ropes had chafed furrows showed that Cheops' ship had been in proper use, and had not been just a "solar-ship" built solely for the Pharaoh's last voyage. Yet the streamlined hull would have collapsed on its first encounter with ocean waves. This was truly amazing. The exquisite lines of the ship were specialized to perfection for true ocean voyaging. Its gracefully curved hull with elegantly upthrust and extremely high bow and stern had all the characteristic features found only in seagoing vessels, specially shaped to ride breakers and towering waves. Here was something to puzzle over. Perhaps the real key to an unsolved mystery. A Pharaoh, living on the calm shores of the Nile nearly five thousand years ago, had built a boat which in practice could stand up only to the peaceful ripples of the river, yet he had built it on architectonic lines which the world's leading seafaring nations never surpassed. He had built his frail river boat to a pattern created by shipbuilders from people with a long, solid tradition of sailing on the open sea.

Then one could begin to guess. There were only two possibilities. Either this seagoing, streamlined shape had been developed locally by Egyptian seafarers of the same brilliant generations which had already evolved the arts of writing and pyramid building, the science of mummification, cranial surgery and astronomy; or else the Pharaoh's shipwrights had been trained abroad. There are facts that point to the latter. No cedars grow in Egypt. The material of which Cheops' ship was built came from the cedar forests of Lebanon. Lebanon was the home of the Phoenicians, experienced shipbuilders who sailed the whole of the Mediterranean and even part of the Atlantic with their ships. Their principal port, Byblos, the oldest known city in the world, imported papyrus from Egypt because Byblos was a center of book production in ancient times (hence the word Byblos, or Bible, which means book). There were lively trade relations between Egypt and Byblos at the time the Pyramid of Cheops was built, so Cheops' shipbuilders might have copied their specialized design abroad. Maybe.

The trouble is, however, we know little or nothing about the appearance of Phoenician wooden ships. All we can say with certainty is that they can scarcely have been papyriform, that is, built on the lines of a papyrus boat, since the Phoenicians imported papyrus from Egypt because it did not grow in Lebanon. This is just where the problem arises. The Pharaoh Cheops' ship was papyriform, and all the other large wooden ships depicted from Pharaonic times in Egypt were also papyriform; they all had the older papyrus boat as their direct model. This is noteworthy, for it was precisely this model, built of papyrus, which had all the seagoing ship's characteristics, with prow and stern soaring upward, higher than a Viking ship, to ride out breakers and high seas, not to contend with little ripples on the Nile. It was the papyrus ship that had been the prototype ship, not the other way round. The design of the papyrus ship was already fully developed when the first Pharaohs were entombed along the Nile. They had their mythical ancestors, the gods, painted on the walls of their tombs as standing on papyrus ships. Sun-god and bird-headed men, the legendary forefathers of the first Pharaoh, are not portrayed as passengers on Phoenician wooden ships, nor on rafts or flat river barges, but on upswept papyrus ships of the type the Pharaoh Cheops' boatbuilders faithfully copied, even to the sharply incurved stern, with the calyx shape of the papyrus flower at its tip.

In order to build a ship as the Egyptians did at the dawn of Mediterranean culture, one needs neither an ax nor a carpenter's skill, but a knife to cut reeds and some rope. That was what my African friends Mussa, Omar and Abdullah were now doing, down there near the foot of the pyramids of Cheops, Chephren and Men-kaw-ra. We had chosen our buildingsite in the desert sand, and they were building a papyrus boat of the same design as the ancient ships painted on the walls of the tombs around us here.

Why? What was I trying to prove? Nothing. I did not want to prove anything. I wanted to learn something. I wanted to find out if it was true, as the experts believed, that the Phoenicians had to come to the Nile to gather the papyrus, because the Egyptians themselves were unable to sail their reed boats outside the Nile Delta. I wanted to find out if the ancient Egyptians had originally been able boatbuilders and seafarers, before they settled down along the Nile to become sculptors, Pharaohs and mummies. I wanted to find out if a reed boat could withstand a sea voyage of 250 miles, the distance from Egypt to Lebanon. I wanted to find out if a reed boat would be able to sail even farther, even from one continent to another. I wanted to find out if a reed boat could make the journey to America.

Why? Because no one knows who was the first person to reach America. Columbus, most school books say. But Columbus did not discover America. He rediscovered America. Columbus was an extremely capable and courageous man, who sailed out into the unknown because he was convinced that the world was round, and that he would not tumble over the edge. Columbus marks a turning point in history; he changed the way of life of a whole world, gave birth to mighty nations and was responsible for the growth of skyscrapers where only bushes and scrub had grown before. But he did not discover America. He was the first to show the rest of the world the way to America, but he only arrived there in the year A.D. 1492.

When was America discovered? Nobody knows. The first man to set foot on American soil had no method of calculating time.

He had no calendar. He could not write. His geographical concepts were too limited for him to realize that he had reached a new continent hitherto untrodden by man.

The first representative of *homo sapiens* to go ashore in America was a homeless, nomadic hunter and fisherman who spent his life, as his forefathers had, roaming the frozen coasts of Arctic Siberia, until one fine day he found himself on the eastern shore of the ice-covered Bering Strait, without suspecting that only the wild beasts had roved here before him. We do not know if the discoverer of America came walking across frozen water, or paddling with his crude fishing tackle in a frail craft along the naked shore of tundra and snowdrifts. All we know is that the first man to die on American soil was probably born in Arctic Asia. We also know that the discoverer of America was ignorant of agriculture and architecture, metal and weaving; that he clothed himself in the skin of wild animals or pounded bark; and that his weapons and tools were of bones and stone, because he was still a pure Stone Age man.

Science does not yet know for certain when the descendants of the first discoverers of America began to spread southward through Alaska and down through the whole of North, Central and South America. Some believe that the settlement of the New World began about fifteen thousand years before Christ. Others maintain with equal conviction that this time span should be doubled at least. All agree, however, that the first step into America was taken in the Arctic North by unorganized flocks of savages whose numerous descendants were to become known to the present world as the wide variety of aboriginal American Indians.

The narrow gap between Arctic Asia and Alaska was always open for man to cross, and many recent discoveries indicate that primitive family groups continued to move back and forth in both directions between Siberia and Alaska. The Aleutian chain of islands and the Japan Current to the south also provided a bridge for those who had seagoing vessels. Inside America, from Alaska in the north to Tierra del Fuego in the south, the rising generations settled in igloos, in wigwams, in leaf huts and in caves, for as man moved southward he was to encounter every variety of climate and nature. Through intermarriage in isolated groups and through new migrations and mixing, a long chain of highly distinctive Indian tribes began to develop inside America. Not only did they differ strikingly from one another in facial type and body build, but they spoke quite unrelated languages and evolved completely different ways of life.

Then came Columbus. On October 12, 1492, he landed on San Salvador in the West Indies with his standard and his cross, and in his wake followed Cortés, Pizarro and all the other Spanish conquistadores. No one can ever deprive Columbus of the glory of having flung open the doors of America to all these peoples who had not already struggled in across the Arctic ice. But we Europeans easily forget that there were thousands of non-European people waiting to receive him on land. And on the mainland, behind the islands where he had landed, great empires with high cultural achievement were seemingly prepared for a visit from across the sea. Their scholars told the Spaniards that white-skinned, bearded men had come over the sea once before, bringing with them all the secrets of civilization. The arrival of the Spaniards caused surprise neither in Mexico nor in Peru; they were not received as "discoverers" but as voyagers repeating an ocean crossing held to have been achieved long before by culture bearers who had come to their forefathers at the dawn of traditional history.

And it was certainly true that this part of America was no longer inhabited by primitive hunters and fishermen, such as those who had originally made their way down from the ice fields of Siberia. In those far from stimulating tropical zones, where the trade winds and the mighty ocean current from Africa had carried the Spaniards themselves ashore, they were met by learned men who themselves produced paper books and taught history, astronomy and medicine. Among the natives who received them were true scholars who could read and write, with a system of their own. They had organized schools and astronomical observatories. Their mathematical astronomical and geographical knowledge was so astonishing that they had worked out the movements of important celestial bodies with maximum accuracy, calculated the positions of the equator, the ecliptic and the tropics, and were able to distinguish between the fixed stars and the planets. Their complicated calendar system was more accurate than the one used in Europe in Columbus' day and they began their precise chronology, the Mayan year 0, with the year 3113 B.C., by our calendar. Their physicians mummified eminent people with professional skill where the climate allowed preservation, and like the ancient Egyptians they performed trepanning, or true cranial surgery, without killing the patient, an operation unknown to European surgeons until several generations after Columbus.

Scribe and layman lived together in planned urban societies, with streets, paved roads, aqueducts and sewers, market places, sports grounds, schools and palaces. The urban population lived neither in tents, nor in leaf huts; they manufactured bricks of sun-dried clay mixed with straw, using the same formula as in the adobe of Mesopotamia and Egypt, and built proper houses of two or more stories lined out in regular city plan. The grander structures had halls with colonnades to support the roof, and the walls were decorated with reliefs and artistic frescoes painted in beautiful and durable colors. The loom was in common use and spinning and weaving had reached such a perfection that the Spaniards were shown tapestries and cloaks which in technical accomplishment and skillful composition surpassed anything to be seen in Europe. Professional potters made jars and dishes, jugs and mugs and ceramic models of people and animals involved in all sorts of activities, with an expertise equal to, if not surpassing, the best that the classical cultures of the Old World had been able to produce. And the gold and silver work of the local jewelers, with filigree and inlay, was so highly developed, both technically and artistically, that the Spaniards drew their swords, losing all self-control and conscience in their ecstasy at what they had "discovered." Stepped pyramids of breathtaking magnitude, pillared temples, and the gigantic monolithic monuments of priest-kings towered over the adobe roofs, while regular roads, man-made waterways, and large suspension bridges set their stamp on the landscape. Countless artificially irrigated and terraced fields bulged with varieties of root crops, cereals, vegetables, fruit, medicinal herbs and other cultivated plants. Even the cotton plant had been refined from its lintless and unusable wild state and was professionally cultivated in huge fields as a lint-bearing species. Both wool and cotton were spun, dyed and woven, and sometimes with thinner thread and finer mesh than any fabric ever produced in Europe prior to the twentieth century.

The Spaniards first thought they had circumnavigated the world and reached some of the amazing civilizations of distant India. All the people who received them, irrespective of physical type or cultural standing, were therefore termed "Indians," a name to survive forever in European languages even when the Spaniards knew the mistake they had made and realized they had run into a new world.

Who discovered whom? Those who were standing on the shore watching the ships arrive from beyond the eastern horizon, or those who were standing on the decks spotting people ashore as land emerged from the western haze? Informed of the Spaniards' arrival by his organized scouts and messengers, the priest-king was carried to receive the newcomers in his elegant litter with fan and parasol. He, too, like the arriving Spaniards, had bewildered preconceived ideas as to whom he was to meet. The mighty priest-king, like his entire people, was convinced that he himself was descended from the sun through bearded white men, just like those who were now repeating their visit to his country. The occasion called for celebration. His musicians played on flute and trumpet, beat drums and rang silver bells. He came with his bodyguard and a standing army of many thousands of men. His scouts had found a handful of Spaniards coming ashore and making their way across country toward the capital.

Precisely the same thing happened in the Aztec's mighty kingdom of Mexico as subsequently in the gigantic empire of the Incas in South America. A small handful of Spaniards with white skins and beards vanquished those huge empires virtually without firing a shot, simply because the scribes and priests on the shores where they landed had either hieroglyphic records or verbal religious traditions which stated that white men with beards had brought the gifts of civilization to their forefathers before they eventually passed on to foreign regions with their teaching, promising to return. All American Indian tribes were beardless. They could not grow hair on their chin. This peculiar feature was common to all descendants of the golden-brown stock who had filtered in from the Arctic north. But the Spaniards, when they were "discovered" by the Indians on land, were bearded and white-skinned like the culture heroes of all local tradition. Although a mere handful, they were therefore warmly welcomed back both to Mexico and Peru by the mightiest absolute monarchs of medieval time.

Great culture centers had once been strung like a row of beads from the Aztec and Maya kingdoms in the north to the Inca kingdom in the south, yet never outside this central area which abounded in the legends about the arrivals of white and bearded men. Aboriginal American civilization never spread beyond the tropic zones to those parts of America where the climate has stimulated men in our day to great enterprise and industry. The rest of the world caught only a brief glimpse of the New World's great civilizations before they collapsed and disappeared almost as abruptly as they had become known. The curtain that Christopher Columbus drew aside for his contemporaries was quickly pulled across again by his successors. Only a few decades passed before America's pulsating civilizations crumbled in ruins, ceased to function, and partly by annihilation, partly by integration, took new forms that make it easy for us Europeans to believe that everything positive, everything which smacks of culture, is due to ourselves, while any exotic, murky aspects are the heritage of the pre-Columbian era. We gained this impression because the gold-hungry conquistadores, with the Cross for alibi, were so quick to draw the curtain again for their massacres, before anyone had fully realized what had been found on the other side of the globe.

What had really happened in Mexico and Peru before Columbus and his followers turned up in America? Was the ignorant Stone Age man from the Arctic tundra alone responsible for planting the seeds of all that the Spaniards found? Or were there other roads to ancient America? Had man mixed blood in America before Columbus, like in every other corner of the world? Had descendants of barbarians from Arctic Asia received voyagers who landed in the Gulf of Mexico in the morning of time, when civilization also spread from Africa and Asia Minor up to the coasts of barbaric Europe?

This was precisely the question. And the answer was no. Obviously no. Probably no. Or possibly. . . . I felt a coil of rope grinding into my back and sat up a little uneasily in the tent. Possibly. . . . The question tormented me. I settled myself more comfortably on the ropes. I could see no solution. It was no use pondering. I was simply thinking the same thoughts all over again. If the ancient civilizations of America had developed locally in Mexico or Peru, the archaeologists should be able to trace the sites where gradual development had taken place. But wherever a center of civilization was found in Mexico or Peru, excavations proved that it had arrived in fully mature form, developing local variants later on. There was no clear beginning to be found anywhere. So the answer should be obvious: Importation. If civilization, begun suddenly without local evolution, it must have been imported. Infiltration from overseas. Obviously. The only trouble was that at the time when the great civilizations were beginning to flourish in the New World, some centuries before Christ if present theories hold good, a couple of thousand years had passed since corresponding culture had ceased to exist in Egypt. So the answer was not obvious at all. We were stuck.

Then why build a papyrus boat? My thoughts floated away again, *via* America, right out into the Pacific. There I was on my home ground. It was there that I had devoted all my time to research and field work. I had been visiting Egypt simply as a tourist when I saw the first wall paintings of reed boats in the Valley of Kings four years earlier. I had recognized the type of boat at once. It was of the same general type that the pyramid builders in northern Peru had painted on their ceramic pots when their civilization flourished in South America, long before Polynesia was inhabited. The largest reed boats in Peru were depicted as two-deckers. Quantities of water jars and other cargo were painted in on the lower deck, as well as rows of little people, and on the upper deck the earthly representative of the sun-god, the priest-king usually stood larger than all his companions, surrounded by bird-headed men who were often hauling on ropes to help the reed boat through the water. The tomb paintings in Egypt also portrayed the sun-god's earthly representative, the priest-king known as the Pharaoh, like an imposing giant on his reed boat, surrounded by miniature people, while the same mythical men with bird heads towed the reed boat through the water.

Reed boats and bird-headed men seemed to go together, for some inexplicable reason. For we had found them far out in the Pacific Ocean too, on Easter Island, where the sun-god's mask, the reed boats with sails, and men with bird heads formed an inseparable trio among the wall paintings and reliefs in the ancient ceremonial village of Orongo, with its solar observatory. Easter Island, Peru, Egypt. These strange parallels could hardly have been found farther apart. They could hardly furnish better proof that men must have arrived independently at the same things in widely separated places. What was even more strange was that the aboriginal people of Easter Island called the sun *ra*. *Ra* was the name for the sun on all the hundreds of Polynesian Islands, so it could be no mere accident. *Ra* was also the name for the sun in ancient Egypt. No word was more important to the ancient Egyptian religion than *Ra*, the sun, the sun-god, ancestor of the Pharaohs. The one who sailed reed boats, with an entourage of bird-headed men. Giant monolithic statues as high as houses had been erected in honor of the sun-god's earthly priest-kings on Easter Island, in Peru and in ancient Egypt. And in all three places, solid rock had been sliced up like cheese into blocks as big as railroad cars and fitted together in stepped pyramids designed on an astronomical basis according to the movements of the sun. All in honor of the common ancestor, the sun, *ra*. Was there some connection, or was it just coincidence?

Centuries ago, when sail still ruled the sea, it was usual to assume that the ancient civilized people were capable of almost unlimited movement. After all, Magellan, Captain Cook and many others had sailed round the world once or twice with only the wind to help them, so why not? But then we invented the propeller and the jet, and as the world grew smaller and smaller for rising generations, we began to get the idea that it must have been larger and larger going back through the ages, until in the days before Columbus it must have been endless, and before that the oceans were impassable.

The year 1492 has a magical effect on us all. It was then that Columbus sailed to America. It was then that the world first became round. Before that time, the earth had been flat. The sea had been flat also, so that everything that floated on the currents and winds must necessarily have tumbled off the edge. Actually, we know today that the world was round also before Columbus, but it was somehow not completely round, more like a hat where anything that went far enough out on the ocean currents would fall off at the brim.

Nothing could float over the abyss and into the unknown before 1492, not even a reed. After Columbus had made our planet round, however, nothing tumbled over the edge. Anything with buoyancy that followed the natural current from Africa would land on the other side, on the new coasts that had turned up, either on the islands where Columbus himself had landed, or on the long tropical coast just behind. Columbus sailed over, a sort of St. Peter, with the keys to the New World. After him came caravels by the hundreds, and other small sailing vessels in their thousands. Twentieth-century adventurers keep on every year to cross the Atlantic by dinghy, rowboat, fifteen-foot sailing craft, rubber raft, amphibian jeep and kayak.

Columbus patented the Atlantic. Before him, America could only be reached on bare feet, or in moccasins, across the endless snow-covered ice that stretches along the Siberian wasteland in the bitter cold of the Arctic. Up there no one could plant cotton or build towns of brick houses. On that point everyone agrees. But how then did the fur-clad Arctic migrants get the idea of cultivating cotton to be spun into thread and woven into garments when they moved down into the drowsy climate of the tropics? One should think that in the warm jungle leaves and bark cloth might have served their need. And why did they hit on the idea, down in the sedative torrid zone, that they should mix straw with clay and mold regular building bricks so that they could live in proper houses like in the Old World? Here agreement ends. Here the schism begins among those who have been looking for the answers to the puzzle.

One of the last theorists who quite unreservedly let the peoples of antiquity sail round the world was the Englishman Percy Smith. He observed that the ancient cultures of Mexico and Peru had so many special features in common with the civilization of ancient Egypt that there must have been some form of transoceanic contact. When he also discovered the same remarkable similarities on Easter Island and other Polynesian groups nearest to the Peruvian coast, he reached for his ruler and his flat world map and drew a line from Egypt via the Red Sea, the Indian Ocean and the Pacific, all the way to Polynesia and South America. That, he wrote, was how the sun-worshipers reached America. Via Easter Island.

Others consulted a round globe and shook their heads. A voyage from Egypt to Easter Island was meaningless. Easter Island was closer to Egypt by way of America than by way of India. The round globe shows the Pacific alone as a complete hemisphere that extends over half the circumference of the world. If Egyptians had sailed twenty-five hundred miles eastward, they would barely have reached India, and would still have exactly half the world left in order to reach Easter Island. On the other hand, if ancient South Americans had sailed twenty-five hundred miles westward from their coast, they would have passed Easter Island. With the *Kon-Tiki* raft built on the ancient Inca model, we traveled forty-three hundred miles westward from the coast of South America and passed Easter Island halfway through our voyage.

Easter Island. The world's loneliest inhabited island. It lay off the open coast of Peru, not off the Nile Delta. Easter Island. On this sea-girt lump of lava almost a thousand abandoned stone colossi in human shape raised their heads mutely to the sky when Europeans eventually reached those shores and "discovered" the island in 1722. "Easter Island" we call it, because a Dutchman sailing from South America stumbled upon it on Easter Sunday. "The Navel of the World" was what the Polynesians called it when they landed there in dugout canoes a few centuries earlier and found the little island already inhabited by still older seafarers who carved on the chests of some of their stone giants large representations of reed boats with masts and sails. These sickle-shaped reed boats were also painted on the stone walls of Easter Island's oldest ceremonial village to-gether with sun symbols and mythical men with bird heads. It was at the same ceremonial site that the sun, locally known as *ra*, was observed and worshiped, and the entire population of the island was united in an annual bird-man cult, swimming to offshore bird islets, supported by small reed boats. This custom survived until mission-aries put a stop to it with the introduction of Christianity in 1868.

Reed boats on Easter Island. At this my thoughts stopped turn-ing. One thing was quite clear. It was there that reed boats began for me. Yet perhaps it was here, geographically speaking, that the history of reed boats had finally come to an end.

I had indeed seen reed boats long before I went to Easter Island. We had used them on Lake Titicaca in the high Andes when I was there studying the South American monoliths of human form which had been abandoned in the plains around the great inland sea. I had been impressed by the carrying capacity of these vessels, which had once been used to ferry huge blocks weighing many tons across the lake to the ruined city of Tiahuanaco. But I had regarded this peculiar type of bundle boat mainly as a curiosity. Like every-one else who had read the history of the Inca empire, I knew that these reed boats on Lake Titicaca were simply the surviving remnants of a pre-Columbian watercraft, which had been in general use all along the Pacific coast of Peru when the Spaniards landed. In fact, at that time they were still seen as far north as Mexico and what be-came known as California. The smallest of these reed vessels was shaped like a curved elephant tusk and could bear no more than one man, supporting his chest on it while swimming. The biggest the Spaniards saw each had a crew of twelve; tied together in pairs such vessels were strong enough to help the colonists transport cattle and horses by sea. In Peru the reed boat went back as far as the balsa log raft; as far, in fact, as the earliest pre-Inca civilization, because the first pyramid-builders on the coast of Peru, the Mochica people, seldom failed to include seagoing reed boats in their versatile pictorial art.

When I decided to build the *Kon-Tiki* raft I had a choice. Three types of seagoing vessel had been used in the ancient Inca empire. Rafts of balsa logs usually brought from the jungles of Ecuador; reed boats made of totora, a reed that grew wild in the mountain lakes and was cultivated by irrigation along the entire Pacific desert coast; and pontoon floats made of two big inflated sealskin bags joined together with cross bars in the form of a plow.

I had no difficulty in making my choice. The air was inclined to escape from the inflated sealskin pontoons when they had been at sea for days on end, and the Indians had to swim alongside and blow them up at regular intervals. They did not tempt me very much. I had no particular faith in the reed boats either. One usually thinks of reeds and straw as exceptionally fragile, delicate things. One clings to them, figuratively, when all else has failed. One does not put to sea on flower stalks of one's own free will. So I thought then. And everyone else agreed. If we were to go, then we were to go on the balsa-wood raft, a solid platform of light, untrimmed timber. And so we did. The balsa-log raft was tried and found amaz-ingly seaworthy. And so the reed boat was discarded and forgotten —for the time being.

Chapter Two

WHY A REED BOAT?

IT WAS on Easter Island. The surf was breaking on the eastern shore. Four old brothers, their skin wrinkled like tobacco leaves, trotted down the beach and into the breakers, carrying a small, banana-shaped craft between them. The sun was dancing on the blue ocean waves and painting the banana boat with gold. The four nimble old men pushed the vessel out between the foaming crests and jumped on board, paddles whirling, just in time to send the boat through the froth of a retreating breaker. Hoop-la! Like a see-saw it rocked over the next rising breaker, and the next, and then it was out among the rollers on the open sea. It was just as dry inside as before the breakers had surged over it. All the water that had showered on board had run out again in the same instant through a thousand fissures in the bottom. There were no sides to the boat, no hollow hull; the four men sitting on the flat deck were, in fact, sitting on top of the thick bottom. Fore and aft, the raft boat curved up in snout-shaped points, the better to ride the seas. It rode them like a golden swan.

This was in 1955, the first time for a hundred years that a reed boat of this type had put out to sea from Easter Island. It had been made by the elders of the island, who wanted to show us a type of boat made by their ancestors for sea fishing. It was a miniature of the larger vessels in the illustrations from the island's bygone golden age; but it was large by comparison with the tusk-shaped one-man boats, *pora*, which the islanders had used in their bird-man contests. It was a solemn moment for the natives of Easter Island when they saw the four old fishermen paddling out of the open inlet in a boat they all knew so well from their fathers' tales, a boat that meant to them what the *Mayflower* means to the average American, or the Viking ship to us in the north. The little craft slithered over the wave like an air bed with the crew perched on top, still dry, up and down, over and round the waves, no matter which side they came from. As the four brown bodies in the golden boat rounded the point where we were busy re-erecting the first of all Easter Island's overthrown giant statues, more than one of the old people on land whispered with shining eyes that the island's dead past was about to be resurrected.

To me, however, it was a vessel once used far beyond the eastern horizon which had been resurrected. There was a striking similarity here to the boats I had seen on Lake Titicaca, and a still greater similarity to the crescent-shaped reed boats of pre-Inca times that the old Mochica people had so often portrayed in their realistic ceramic art on the Pacific coast. The water flowing round our legs on this beach came straight from that very coast. I myself had drifted past here by raft on these eternally flowing masses of water. The suspicion was born. The same boat united by the same flow of water.

Up in the crater of the extinct volcano Rano Raraku, six men were sinking a twenty-five-foot steel bore into the edge of the marsh. Round about us, high in the crater walls, lay many unfinished stone giants bearing witness to the sculptor's suddenly interrupted work. Some were completed in every detail except for their backs which were still firmly embedded in the rock as part of the crater wall itself. They lay with closed eyes and hands flexed on their stomachs, petrified in a giant's version of the Sleeping Beauty. Others had been hacked free and raised on end to give the sculptors a chance to complete the rugged back, which was to be made arched, slim and elegant like the rest of the giant. These standing figures were scattered at random round about the rock galleries, some covered up to the chin by silt from the quarries. Thin lips compressed, they craned in all directions, as if critically appraising what these six little dwarfs of flesh and blood were up to, with their steel bore, down there on the brink of the crater lake.

The long steel spike sank inch by inch into the soggy mud. Rain and a thousand years of sludge had changed the bottom of the deep, dead crater into a glassy blue lake where the sky was mirrored. Small, white trade-wind clouds seemed to be drifting across the surface and disappearing into the green reeds in an eternal procession from east to west. Three such rain-filled crater lakes encircled by tall reeds were the only water supply available on Easter Island. Here the islanders had fetched their drinking water since the days when they had burned down the primeval forest and changed the wooded landscape into one of open grass and bracken slopes, where all the brooks gradually seeped down into the porous lava floor and vanished.

The mud we extracted with the long bore had much to tell us about this early destruction. At the tip of the long steel rod was a revolving blade and a small cavity with a lid that opened to allow the chamber to fill with mud, clay or sand, according to what lay in the depths we wanted to study. The deeper we bored, the further we delved into the past. The swamp edge was like a closed book, with the first page at the bottom and the last on top. At the lowest level there was nothing but solidified lava and volcanic fall-out from the days when Easter Island rose fire-spitting from the ocean floor. Above this sterile bottom layer, clay and mud had begun to ooze down from the weathered crater rim of the dead volcano, and as time had passed, the layers of mud farther up began to contain more and more hermetically preserved flower dust, pollen. By studying the stratification of different kinds of pollen, a professional pollen expert could tell us the order in which different species of grass, fern, bush or tree had spread to the new-born island, carried by the current, the wind, birds and finally man. Every plant has its own characteristic form of pollen. Seen under the microscope they resemble fantastic fruits and berries of the most extraordinary shapes and patterns.

A detective hides behind many names: some call themselves paleobotanists and thus escape common people's curiosity. They are the ones who sort out pollen grains with the same thoroughness as others identify fingerprints. We tamped our small pats of soil down in numbered tubes of glass, for delivery to just such a vegetable detective agency in Stockholm. That was how we came to know a little about things that had happened in Easter Island's forgotten past, a little about where they had come from, those first, mysterious sculptors who raised their gigantic monuments on the island, unobserved under the cover of the darkness of history.

The pollen borings revealed a secret. The European "discoverers" found this island barren and naked, with mere savages living amid fields of sweet potatoes, abandoned quarries and giant monuments from a forgotten past. Yet the pollen now revealed that the island had originally been wooded, and that swaying palms had covered what are now arid cones and crater walls. In the midst of this virgin greenery skilled stonemasons landed long before the Europeans knew the Pacific. These masons set fire to the woods. Smoke and particles of soot from their burnings rained down upon the lakes in the dead volcanoes and were deposited at the bottom together with the last pollen from palms and forest trees. The trees suddenly began to vanish. The newcomers burned down the forest to clear space for large fields of the American sweet potato, which was their staple diet. They wanted clearings for their stone houses, and for large temple plazas with stepped pyramidal platforms of giant dressed blocks resembling the religious structures of ancient Peru and the mastabas of Egypt. They destroyed the palms and tore turf and earth away from the volcanic slopes to gain access to the solid rock which their expert sculptors converted into smooth building blocks and monolithic statues of deceased priest-kings. The trees that fell were ignored as building material, for the first settlers of Easter Island were accustomed to working with rock and not timber. Stone was their traditional raw material; single blocks as heavy as six, eight or ten elephants and as high as houses were transported from one end of the island to the other, raised on end as monoliths, or hoisted on top of one another and meticulously fitted into sun-oriented megalithic walls, the like of which the world has never seen except in Peru and Mexico, and among the ancient Mediterranean sun-worshipers handling stone in the very same manner on the opposite side of the globe.

The detectives digging into our pats of soil had more to tell.

Not only had the early settlers destroyed Easter Island's natural vegetation, but they had partly replaced the exterminated species with cultivated plants that could only have traveled across the ocean in the care of human beings. The strictly American sweet potato had been brought to Easter Island and neighboring Polynesia from Peru before Columbus reached America. We had known this before. The Easter Islanders call it *kumara*, the name given to the same plant throughout Polynesia and among the aboriginal population in vast areas of the ancient Inca empire. But in our pats of earth there were remnants of another plant which was of greater importance to a seafaring nation.

The reed. The totora reed.

The uppermost layers of mud, after the forest had been burned down, were yellow with destroyed pollen from totora reeds, mingled with a network of tough shreds from the reed stalks. Huge quantities of decayed reed fibers formed a floating mat over most of the crater lake. Down to the layers containing the rain of ash which marked the coming of man, the pollen of only one other water plant was mingled in the sludge. Below that, before man's arrival, there was no pollen from fresh-water plants. Before the stone sculptors came, nothing grew in Easter Island's crater lakes; they lay open; the extinct volcanoes were filled with clear rain water.

Here were clues for a detective: fingerprints in the mud. That the two fresh-water plants had been brought by sailors across the sea was easy to understand. Both were useful species; one a principal building material, the other a medicinal plant. Neither was a species which could have been transplanted by ocean currents, birds or wind. They generate only by new shoots from their suckers. In order to become established in three fresh-water lakes inside deep volcanoes on lonely Easter Island, they must have been planted as living bulbs brought dry across the salt ocean. And now we were on the right trail. For both plants belonged to species which grew nowhere else in the world except the American continent. The totora reed, *Scirpus tatora*, was one of the most important used by the aboriginal population all along the desert coast of the Inca empire. The coastal peoples of Peru cultivated it in irrigated swamps and used it to make large and small reed boats, house roofs, mats, baskets and rope. The second imported water plant, *Polygonum acuminatum*, was used by the South American Indians as a medicine. Both plants served precisely the same purpose in the Inca empire as among the inhabitants of Easter Island.

With a piece of the light, sun-dried totora reed in my hand I stood watching the four old Polynesians bobbing about on the wavetops out on the open sea, as nonchalantly as they would trot round on horseback ashore on their rocky island. I had known for a long time that one of the great mysteries of Pacific botany was how this American fresh-water plant came to grow down in the three crater lakes hidden away on the world's loneliest inhabited island. Here was one simple solution. Perhaps those old voyagers from Peru had not reached the Pacific islands with balsa rafts alone. Perhaps a second of their three old forms of watercraft had gone with them across the ocean. Perhaps they had imported the practice of building reed boats as well, and even living tubers, so that they could continue the old tradition with identical material.

As we dragged the crescent-shaped reed boat up the beach I was no longer in any doubt that the Easter Islanders had inherited the art of building these remarkable vessels from the old pyramid-builders in Peru.

Five years later I was sitting round a large table with the leading Pacific archaeologists gathered for a world congress at the University of Hawaii in Honolulu. Five years had passed before the diversified material from the excavations on Easter Island had been analyzed by colleagues who were specialists in different branches of science. Skeletons and stone tools, blood samples, pollen and carbon from hearths and bonfires, all had their tale to tell to the scientific detectives whose task it was to find out what had happened on the loneliest island in the world long before Columbus reached America, and thus opened the road for the Europeans into the Pacific.

Our results from the Easter Island expedition had been presented by my collaborators at the congress. Those of us seated around the large table were ready to sign a scientific document, a resolution. The text declared that South America, together with Southeast Asia and its adjacent islands, represented the main homelands of the ancient peoples and cultures on the Pacific islands. I had nothing against signing. Indeed, it was to call attention to the possibilities of such mixed settlement that I had sailed from Peru to the islands on a balsa raft. This bilateral origin of Polynesian culture was what I had suspected, long before the *Kon-Tiki* voyage, when I was living for a year as a Polynesian among Polynesians on the lonely island of Fatuhiva in the Marquesas group, where the surf pounded on the east coasts, and clouds and seas, day and night, came scudding and rolling in the same direction from South America. The resolution was read out to the three thousand Pacific scholars participating in the plenum meeting and unanimously approved. I left the Tenth Pacific Science Congress with a mandate to promote further excavations on those of the Pacific islands which were facing South America, and the South American coast was formally included for the first time in the areas of concern to oceanic archaeology. The gateway between Peru and Polynesia was left open, the Pacific had acquired two sides even in retrospect to pre-Columbian times.

The reed boat, however, sank into oblivion once more. Then came the moment when it was dragged back into the limelight in a totally unexpected way and from a totally unexpected quarter. A well-known anthropologist at the University of California pointed out in the professional journal *American Antiquity* (January 1966) that the reed boats of ancient Peru resembled the reed boats of ancient Egypt. And, he said, the two ancient cultures bore a striking resemblance to each other in more ways than one. The article contained a list of sixty special features, of a quite unusual nature and restricted world distribution, which were characteristic of the ancient cultures of the eastern Mediterranean (with Mesopotamia and Egypt) and pre-Columbian Peru. The reed boat was only one of sixty different items on the list.

Now it is usual in science to interpret a single cultural feature, or even two or three, which crops up in the same form in widely separate areas, as a matter of coincidence, a result of independent evolution along parallel lines. Human beings are so alike all over the world that it is natural for them to have similar notions. But if a really varied and numerous array of similarities or indentities occurs and these are of such a specialized nature that no equivalents are found outside two clearly defined geographical areas, then one must be aware of the possibility of some former contact between these two cultural centers. The list of sixty specific cultural parallels was a textbook example of the latter category. It therefore sounded the alarm: tread warily. So I was not alone in my astonishment. Not because the list was impressive and thought-provoking. It certainly was. But because it had been drawn up by an isolationist. The author was known as one of the most zealous advocates of the theory defending a total isolation of America before Columbus: only the ice in the north could have provided a passage for human beings. Nevertheless, he had now produced a list which Percy Smith and his old school of diffusionists would have envied: sixty specialized cultural parallels between ancient Peru and Egypt.

This list could provoke conclusions. It was, in fact, intended to do so. The author of the article concluded that, since Egypt is in eastern Africa and Peru in western America, there are two continents and a whole Atlantic Ocean between them. Two cultures both of which used reeds for boatbuilding could not have had contact across such distances. A reed boat cannot traverse an ocean. Accordingly the sixty cultural parallels must have arisen independently of each other; they could not for practical reasons have been the result of a human voyage. The lesson to the reader: diffusionists, those who believe that America received inspiration from across the sea before 1492, must stop nosing around after cultural parallels, because it is hereby demonstrated that such parallels prove nothing.

The diffusionists reacted vigorously. They could not swallow the reasoning. They remained convinced that Middle America with Peru had received some early impetus from across the sea. But which sea? And by what ships? They could not agree. The waves of discussion refused to subside. The answer had not yet been given.

In the same year the organizers of the Thirty-seventh International Congress of Americanists summoned representatives of the two contending doctrines to a scientific duel. Every other year this congress assembles scholars from all over the world who specialize in America's aboriginal population. This time it was held in Argentina and I had been asked to invite speakers to a symposium for and against transoceanic contact with America before Columbus.

The meeting was in session. The doors were closed. The author of the sixty points of resemblance was invited, but did not show up. But the diffusionists who believed in contact attended in strength, with speakers from four continents. The isolationists were also present in strength, but only in the audience. Their tactic was usually to let the others speak and then shoot down their arguments. They had always stayed on the defensive, deliberately leaving the burden of proof on anyone suspecting that America could have been reached by sea before Columbus. The diffusionists never lacked arguments, but they always lacked proof. Therefore, said the isolationists, the oceans had not been crossed.

The Icelandic sagas, written down in detail by Viking historians long before Columbus, were one of the themes for discussion. No one could deny that Norwegian Vikings had settled Iceland and later the whole southwestern coast of Greenland, where they had lived continuously for nearly five hundred years before Columbus hoisted sail. They had left behind the ruins of countless farmsteads, graveyards, sixteen churches, two monasteries and an episcopal residence that kept in touch with the papal throne via regular sea communications with Norway. This pre-Columbian colony on Greenland paid taxes to the king of Norway.

The distance across the North Atlantic from Norway to the Norse settlements in Greenland was as great as the distance across the South Atlantic from Africa to Brazil. It was only a negligible jump of some two hundred miles further west from Greenland to the coast of the American mainland, but it was this last hop that had not been made, said the isolationists.

It had been made, said the written text in the ancient Viking sagas. Bjarni Herjolfsson was recorded as the first to make the full Atlantic crossing as his ship went astray in a fog. But instead of landing on the long, unknown coastline he had discovered in the far west, he put about and returned to the colony in nearby Greenland. His ship was bought by Leif Ericsson, the son of Greenland's discoverer, Eric the Red, who in about the year 1002 set sail with thirty-five men for the reported coastline southwest from the colony in Greenland. Leif and his men were the first to set foot on the new coast, which they named Vinland, and there they built houses and spent the winter before returning home to Greenland. His brother, Thorvald Ericsson, made the crossing next year and settled in Leif's deserted houses with his people. Two years later, on a voyage of discovery along the wooded coasts of this new continent, he was killed by an arrow in a fight with the natives. His thirty men buried him in Vinland and sailed home to Greenland.

Thorfinn Karlsefne and his wife Gudrid were the next to make the journey, with two ships and a large number of people. Eric the Red's daughter Freydis was with them, and this time the emigrants took cattle along. Gudrid gave birth to her son Snorri in their newly built home in Vinland, but steadily increasing attacks by large numbers of Indians, *Skraelings*, made life in the new land intolerable so that in the end the colonists left their farms, after bloody losses, and went home to Greenland and Europe. The handwritten sagas were crammed with prosaic facts. Coasts and travel routes were described in detail. There could be no doubt about it. The Vikings really had discovered Vinland and tried to settle the new country, in the first ten or fifteen years after the year 1000.

But where was Vinland? How can we know that Vinland was America? This is what the isolationists had been asking for years. And now came the sensation. The congress was given proof.

At Lanse aux Meadows on the northern tip of Newfoundland proof had been found showing beyond doubt that the Vikings had landed and attempted a brief settlement about the year 1000. The embankments from a cluster of house foundations in typical Viking style had been discovered, well preserved under the turf. The charred fragments of wood had been dated and the results checked ten times over by a series of radiocarbon analysis. The houses had been inhabited at the very period, about A.D. 1000, referred to in the Viking sagas. No American Indians had known iron before Columbus. And here were remnants of iron nails from doors, and bog-iron from a primitive smithy. The Indians in the north could not weave. And under the turf was a typical Norse spinning wheel of soapstone.

The discovery was made by the noted Norwegian expert on Greenland, Helge Ingstad, who had hit upon the site through a practical geographical appraisal of the old Icelandic records; and the excavations were led by his wife, the archaeologist, Anne Stine Ingstad, with the aid of leading American colleagues. These were sober scientific facts. No one could protest. No one tried to raise any more objections. The Vikings had been in Newfoundland. They had reached America by crossing the Atlantic, and recorded the events before anyone else. But, said the isolationists, they had come and gone without leaving any traces other than a few grassy mounds. Their visit had had no bearing on the course of history. The savage Indians in the north had driven them out and their own ancestral way of life had not been influenced. According to the sagas the Vikings had given them no more than a few strips of red cloth before fights and slaughter put a stop to further trading.

The Vikings never got a lasting foothold in America. Still, America had at least been reached, both from east and west, in the Arctic north, before Columbus crossed in the tropical latitudes.

But in the tropical belt the isolationists won the battle. And this was the main battlefield. No one could present tangible proof of landings in Mexico before the Spaniards. The written records made by Mexico's aboriginal scribes were taken even less seriously than the sagas of the Vikings. Their tales about the landings of white and bearded men before Columbus could not be proven. The diffusionists' mustering of ever more cultural parallels was as easily repulsed as before. Cultural affinities on two sides of an ocean were interesting observations but not proofs. Apart from the Viking visit in the far north, the isolationists remained unshattered on their sea-girt island when the duel was over. Two large oceans defended their position. One important argument seemed clearly in their favor. An ocean crossing required a seaworthy craft, like those of the Vikings. If anybody had sailed across from Africa and acquired such a strong foothold in America that they taught the Indians to build with bricks and write on paper, then the least one could expect was that they should also have taught them how to build seagoing vessels. No mariners could cross the Atlantic with architects and astronomers capable of building pyramids without also bringing their own shipbuilding traditions with them. At least 2700 years before Christ, the Egyptians had learned to build properly framed wooden ships, with hollow hulls and decks and cabins of trimmed planks, but the idea of a ship's hull built of planks had never reached the Indians. In the whole of America before Columbus, no one had learned to build vessels other than reed boats, rafts, various kinds of pontoon floats and canoes made of skin or dug-out tree trunks. That was a fact which could not be disputed. Columbus and his companions introduced the art of true shipbuilding to the New World. Nobody before him.

Reed boats and rafts. Here they were again. The balsa raft had been proven seaworthy, but it could only set sail *away* from America, for before the Spaniards came the balsa tree had grown in no other part of the world. But the reed, reeds of different types, grew everywhere, not least on the Nile and in Asia Minor, where boats were built from reeds, like in America.

"Yvonne, we must return to the Andes and take a second look at the American reed boats," I said to my wife. The Ingstads came with us, to witness that the Vikings were not the only ones who could build elegant vessels. On the day the congress closed, we climbed into an aircraft for La Paz in Bolivia, and next day we were up by sky-blue Lake Titicaca on the roof of the world, 12,500 feet above sea level, surrounded by snow-covered peaks that soared still another 6000 to 9000 feet higher into clear space. Behind us on the plateau lay the ruins of South America's mightiest pre-Inca capital, the old cultural center of Tiahuanaco, with the devastated Akapana pyramid, megalithic walls and gigantic statues of unknown priest-kings carved in stone.

In the strong breeze out on the lake some Aymara Indians maneuvered to and fro as they fished. At a distance one could see only the wind-filled sails. Tattered canvas had been hoisted on most of the boats, but a few had stuck to tradition and hoisted a big mat of golden totora reed on two straddling masts joined at the top. Three of them steered straight for us, sailing flat out, and soon we could see the Indians in their rainbow striped stocking caps looking out from behind the sail, while the shape of the boat itself appeared above the waves. Glorious. They were expertly built. Each reed was placed with maximum precision to achieve perfect symmetry and streamlined elegance, while the bundles were so tightly lashed that they looked like inflated pontoons or gilded logs bent into a clog-shaped peak fore and aft. They cut through the water at high speed and ran right up to the shore in a clearing between the reeds, where they were driven firmly aground in the mud. The Indians waded ashore with their catch of fish.

Boats of this distinctive type are still built in their hundreds on every side of this enormous inland sea. They were built exactly in

this way by the Aymara and Quechua Indians' fathers and grand-
fathers. This is exactly how they had looked four hundred years
ago also when the Spaniards came to this lake and discovered
Tiahuanaco's deserted ruins with their stepped platforms, pyramid
and stone colossi, abandoned vestiges which according to consistent
traditions among the primitive Aymara Indians were not the work
of their own ancestors. They firmly believed the spectacular con-
structions to have been left since the morning of time by the
viracocha people. These were described as white men with beards,
whose priest-King was Con-Ticci-Viracocha, the sun's representative
on earth. At the outset, the *viracocha* people had settled on the
Island of the Sun out in Lake Titicaca. Legend has it that it was
they who built the first reed boats. The white and bearded men,
it was claimed, had come forth in a flotilla of reed boats when first
appearing to the local Indians who at the time were ignorant of
sun worship, architecture, and agriculture. These legends, which the
Spaniards wrote down four hundred years ago are still alive among
the lakeside Indians. Many times I was addressed as *Viracocha*,
still the word for "white man."

I did not know what to believe. Again, I was filled with admiration as I gazed at the enormous blocks, weighing fifty to a
hundred tons, carved to perfection and fitted together to a fraction
of a millimeter, while down on the lake the elegant reed boats plied
the waves today as they had when ferrying the giant blocks from
Kapia, the extinct volcano miles away over on the opposite shore.
There was no reason to doubt that modern science is right in
suspecting that this vanished civilization was somehow connected
with the other ancient American cultural centers that European
discoverers found abandoned and overgrown, strung through the
tropical jungles from Mexico all the way down to this wind-blown
highland plateau. Before the giant pre-Inca structures of Tiahuanaco
tumbled into ruins, this had been the capital of one of the world's
mightiest empires, with an influence covering all of present Peru and
adjacent parts of Ecuador, Bolivia, Chile, Brazil, and the Argentine.
A coastline of at least fifteen hundred miles was under the influence
of the art and religion radiating from the empire's inland capital at
the mountain lake, and this vast coastline was washed, then as now,
by the mighty ocean current that carried our *Kon-Tiki* raft straight

to Polynesia. Ceramic sherds of Coast Tiahuanaco origin have been excavated on the Galapagos Islands, six hundred miles offshore, and the oldest statues encountered below the soil on Easter Island closely follow Tiahuanaco prototypes. Like the reed boats. There could be no doubt that the original Easter Island culture was but one of the many branches of this expansive pre-Inca civilization, perhaps the very last off-shoot.

But where were the roots? Here in America? Or on the other side of the Atlantic? Who were right, the isolationists or the diffusionists? At the congress none of them had seemed convincing. As chairman of the symposium I had taken a neutral stand. But I was certain of one thing. Both isolationists and diffusionists underestimated the qualities of the ancient Tiahuanaco boat. The reed boat would not have held its own against four hundred years of European cultural contact had it been an inferior craft.

True enough, plank-built ships were known on only one side of the Atlantic. But reed vessels were known on both sides. After all, this was one of the sixty points of resemblance. The art of building reed boats was an ancient heritage both in Egypt and Peru. Only in those two places? No. And this was where I had discovered a tiny crack in the logic. Reed boats were not quite as isolated as some of the other fifty-nine points of resemblance on the list. Scarcely anyone had bothered to study their earlier distribution. But I had noticed one or two things. For instance, they had been in use also in Mesopotamia, on various Mediterranean islands, on the Atlantic coast of Morocco below Gibraltar, and in ancient Mexico as well. The jump from Morocco to Mexico was not as startlingly absurd as the distance between the farthest points, Egypt and Peru.

I decided to build a reed boat.

Chapter Three

TO THE INDIANS
IN THE CACTUS FOREST

THE COAST. A glimpse of the sea between giant cacti. A make-believe world. Feeling very small, I tilted my head back to look up at the tops of the green, spiky, giant cacti that towered above me like organ pipes and huge candelabra in a world of swollen, overfed vegetation. Overfed and overgrown. And yet the ground I was walking on was nothing but a bone-dry crust of hard-baked, barren sand, without grass or flowers except for red and yellow ones peeping out between spiny tufts on the sinews of the cactus giants themselves. This was the cactus world. On the ground between the giants stood, lay and swarmed all manner of spiky plants, globular, sausage-shaped, articulated. In the evening sunlight some looked like silhouettes of dishes and cutlery superimposed in a fantastic state of equilibrium, others like worn-out shoe soles bristling with nails, bent ends of barbed wire, or long, waving cat's tails. This was a still and silent forest. Not even a rustle from the leaves of the gnarled iron trees that stood here and there, writhing as if to avoid the prickles on their ubiquitous neighbors.

A desert hare leaped noiselessly among the cactus shadows in the evening sun, pricked up its long ears, and glanced about before it bounded off again and disappeared. Crossing the hare's path a tiny striped chipmunk came scurrying along at a tremendous rate, stopped dead with its tail in the air, and bowled on again like a little bristling ball through the fairy-tale wood. On the highest fork of a three-branched candelabra plant, towering over all the rest, an eagle sat motionless. It did not stir until I was close against the trunk. Then it spread silent wings and glided smoothly away over the enchanted wood. The eagle was not moving: it was the forest and me that were sliding backward, as the bird hung against the vault of sky before disappearing from view. The perfect silence was only interrupted when I moved my own feet. I could hear the leather sole cracking the earth crust, breaking through into invisible cavities dug in the sand by rats, snakes and other desert vermin.

Then I caught a faint sound, faint but with the same effect as a lion's loud roar of menace. It sounded like a half-empty matchbox being gently shaken. This was a warning note of hypnotic terror, in a sort of nature's Esperanto. One had no need to have seen a rattlesnake before in order to jump aside at this unobtrusive sound. Tongue darting, eyes glittering, tail tip slightly raised and twitching, the beast lay rattling its tail, ready to strike. The dry rattle, like a set of plastic rings on the light tail tip, was quivering with fury, and in the hope of leaving the field victorious I looked around desperately for a stick or branch. But just here there was nothing but cactus, with fleshy, thorny branches that simply snapped like cucumber when I struck out at the slithering, supple creature. Finally, a shriveled, fibrous skeleton of a dead cactus proved hard enough to knock the rattlesnake senseless, and before it regained consciousness the victory was won, even if the tail end of the dead body went on quivering and rattling for a long time afterward.

We were supposed to be hunting for boatbuilders in this cactus country. There was not a single tree we could climb to spy out the way. My Mexican friend, Ramon Bravo, had disappeared into the cactus wood to the left in the hope of finding a rocky outcrop with a view, while his wife Angelica and our friend German sat in the Jeep down in the valley. For the twentieth time at least, we had lost the wheel tracks we were following. Now, from where I was standing, I caught my first glimpse of the sea. The lookout point was marked by a living monument of a cactus, shaped like Neptune's own trident, with a trunk so thick that I could hide behind it. This was where the eagle had perched. From up there it must have been able to see

Captions for the following four pages

1. *Reed boat* of Easter Island, where the author's interest in reed boats began. The island's enigmatic giant statues were carved by seafarers who planted the South American fresh-water reed in the crater lakes and built reed boats of the type found in Peru.

2, 3, 4, 5. *Reed boats* were once in use from Mesopotamia to the Atlantic coast of Morocco. They have survived to the present day on Lake Chad in the African interior (2 left) on Lake Zwai in Ethiopia (3 above) on Lake Tana at the source of the Nile (4 middle) and in Sardinia in the Mediterranean (5 below).

6. *In Mexico* reed boats were once in use both at sea and on inland lakes. The last to survive were used by the Seris Indians in the Gulf of California. (Above)

7. *Lake Titicaca* in Bolivia and Peru has the world's best reed boats today. Large reed ships used to sail along the shores of the Inca kingdom. (Below)

8. *The world's oldest reed boat models* from Egyptian mummy tombs, examined by the author in Cairo Museum. (Above)

9. *Tomb reliefs in Egypt* show that the custom of gathering papyrus reeds to build boats goes back to the earliest dawn of civilization. (Below)

10. *Boatbuilders in ancient Egypt* bound papyrus reeds together with strong hemp rope. Some were black-haired, others fair. (Above)

11. *Naval action on the Nile.* The papyrus boats were loaded with cages of ducks, baskets of food and jars of drink. (Below)

12. *A noble and his wife* in the cabin on board a papyrus boat, served by a royal butler, while an ordinary seaman, portrayed normal size, steers with the double steering oar. (Above)

13. *Cattle freighting on the Nile.* The herdsman's rolled-up papyrus tent made an effective life belt. (Below)

14. *Sailing skills* were extraordinarily advanced in Egypt almost five thousand years ago. The mast was straddled, with steps.

great stretches of coast and those savage red mountain peaks inland, through which we had been lurching before the wheel tracks branched off and vanished into the cactus forest. I could see only a silver flash of sunlight on shining water, and blue-tinged mountains far away on the other side. That was enough to set our course. So the four of us jolted on through the enchanted wood, trying to make haste before the sun sank.

Suddenly the cactus forest opened up, giving way to low ever-green scrub, and there, just before us, lay the sea, with small, rippling waves and a wide, virgin beach. Five straining black whale-backs came bursting through the surface of the water, as if heading straight for us, and as they dived and disappeared a shower of glittering small fry shot up in front of them, cascading out of the water. Close inshore they seethed and sparkled for a moment before they, too, scattered and disappeared.

This was nature unadulterated. Before us lay the Gulf of Cali-fornia and behind us on all sides stretched the Sonora desert. The bare blue mountains ranged on the other side were the Mexican desert peninsula of *Baja California*, Lower California, some six hun-dred miles long. We would have to back out of the scrub and into the cactus wood again, for there was not a single hut and no trace of human life to be seen along the shore. We had to go farther up the gulf.

And just as the sun sank behind the line of mountains on the other side and the sea began to turn black, there it was in front of us, the Indian village. One could hardly say that this last surviving remnant of the once powerful Seris tribe had been converted to a romantic architecture by its encounter with the white man and his culture. Half a score of families, some sixty adults and children, had settled here in the sand on barren Punta Chueca, where the head of each family had built a tiny little shack of corrugated iron and tarred paper. Inside there was scarcely room to lie full length on the sandy floor. The building materials and the scrap heaps against the back walls, or broken glass and empty tins, were the result of the sale of turtles, which the Indians caught alive and kept crawling round in a pen at the water's edge.

The Indians did not react noticeably to our arrival. Most of them went on with what they were doing, sitting in small groups or walking calmly around between the huts in a medley of colorful headbands, home-made ornaments and long, gaudy raiment in gypsy style. Each man had a long, black pigtail hanging down to the small of the back. The women's faces were painted with lines and spots in symmetrical patterns, barbarically attractive and timeless. An age-old fashion that may suddenly crop up again in our own oversophis-ticated world as the very latest thing. A not unattractive woman in an ankle-length skirt sat surrounded by others grinding natural colors with oil in small pots, while another one had acquired an ordinary lipstick that lent itself admirably to drawing vertical lines on the chin. She beckoned authoritatively to Ramon's wife, who had been watching spellbound. Now she had to sit down on the sand and have her face painted in the same pattern. An aged gaffer and a flock of children had joined us, and Ramon was soon recognized. The children sped off like arrows to the farthest hut to fetch Chuchu with all his family. He had been Ramon's interpreter and guide the last time he had been here, filming seal and other animals in the gulf. Now at last there was universal recognition and rejoicing.

Ramon had brought a friend who wanted to see their reed boats? But there were no Seris Indians building *askam* nowadays. The one Ramon had seen two years ago? That was the last they had made. Not even the other Seris villages farther north used *askam* today, since the government had helped every village to buy a wooden boat with an outboard motor. A little naked boy disappeared like a streak and came running delightedly back with a small toy. It was a torpedo boat made of yellow plastic.

Night fell about us. We were lent some cardboard cartons which we folded up under ourselves before lying down to sleep on the floor in a fishing-tackle shed. All night long the Indians kept up their monotonous, incomprehensible chatter. I was drowsily aware of them every time I turned over. They were sitting round small heaps of embers, debating, until they crept to bed an hour or so be-fore we all got up as the stars were beginning to fade.

Before the sun had yet begun to redden the tall cactus crowns, the four of us sat, surrounded by a few Indians, looking out over the peaceful gulf. No one spoke. We just sat. Chuchu rose slowly and ambled down to the silent beach, where he threw out a little round net. With two casts he pulled in four fine fish. Two tiny boys with three-pronged throwing spears doubled the catch in an instant. That was food enough. Everyone sat. It looked as if nothing more was going to happen that day.

"Will you build an *askam* for me?" I asked circumspectly.

"*Mucho trabajo*," they all responded in chorus. "A lot of work." This was about the sum of their vocabulary in Spanish. For anything else they needed an interpreter. Chuchu acted as intermediary.

"You will be paid," I promised. "In goods or pesos."

"*Mucho trabajo*," they repeated simply.

The offer increased. Silence. It increased again.

"It is a long way to the reeds," said Chuchu, stalling.

"We will come with you," I replied, and rose to my feet.

Four Indians stood up. They were willing to go. Chuchu, with two brothers and a nephew. Only the eldest brother, Caitano, knew where the reeds were. They grew by a lake on Isla Tiburon, Shark Island, whose rugged outlines we could just make out in the sunrise on the other side of the sound.

The government's outboard motor came into service. Soon we were bucking away over the ripples toward the distant horizon. I was surprised that there were no reeds nearer than this.

"They are fresh-water reeds," Caitano explained. "They cannot grow on the seashore by the desert here. It is a long way to the fresh-water lake."

Shark Island, with its savage mountains, loomed out of the sea. It is not a small island. With a surface area of nearly four hundred square miles, it appears even in world maps. As we jumped ashore on a white sandy beach we found ourselves on the edge of a broad plain, thickly grown with low bushes and scattered cactus trees, between us and the dawn-flushed mountains inland. A single *berrendo* deer, with a great spread of antlers on its lifted head, stood motionless on the beach, staring. Out came the cameras, stealthily, to immortalize the beast before it took off. Still it did not move, and we crept nearer. Nearer. I went ahead and was included in the picture. Caution was indicated. The deer began to move. Slowly. It strode forward proudly and deliberately, bent its head and butted me in the stomach with friendly determination, an antler in each of my armpits. I tried in vain to push the deer away so that we could get a decent picture; but no, it intended to be immortalized

like this, and all my pushing and shoving, all my efforts to withdraw from this humiliating position were useless. The friendly deer
simply followed, now forward, now back, close enough to hold me
between its horns without goring and without wishing me any harm.
It was a ridiculous situation. Not until the deer had been scratched
on the neck and behind the ears was it sufficiently astonished to
lift its head and stand staring, wide-eyed, while I backed slowly
toward the two-legged company with whom I had come ashore.

We dragged the boat well up on the sand and began our walk
across the level ground. I was expecting at any moment to see the
reed-grown inland lake. But no, there was only dry sand here and we
had to struggle through a labyrinth of low evergreens, thorn scrub
and scattered cactus. No path. No trace of anything but deer, hare,
lizards, snakes and rodents. Shark Island had been uninhabited by
human beings since the last Seris Indians were compulsorily evacu-
ated to the mainland, some time in Caitano's childhood. We plodded
and trudged, right, left, straight ahead, wherever openings appeared
in the rugged terrain, but always heading generally inland toward
the mountains.

"Where is the lake?" we asked in turns.

"Over there," Caitano replied each time, pointing with his nose
without lifting a hand. We walked and we walked. Gradually a vast
stretch of land lay between us and the sea. The mountains came
closer. Soon we were standing at their foot. Half the day had passed,
the sun was blazing straight down on our heads, and we were without
water or provisions.

"Where is the lake? I'm thirsty," muttered German.

"Over there," repeated Caitano, pointing his nose upward. We
began to clamber over the stony scree that ran down a cleft in the red
mountainside. Up to now we had seen only lizards and hares, but here
startled mountain sheep and deer began to run the rocky shelves
around us. They were anything but eager to give us the sort of welcome we had had from our lonely friend down on the beach. Once or
twice I came upon broken potsherds of Indian manufacture. Indians
must once have stumbled down here with their water supply from
the lake. Higher and higher. Incredible that any lake could lie up
here in the steep, arid mountain wall where only cactus grew now.

Then Caitano stopped. This time he pointed with his whole

hand. We were standing on some huge, tumbled boulders, looking out over a rocky canyon. High up on the opposite wall the bare red rock split in a side canyon leading up to a little bowl-shaped plateau, and up there the sun was shining on a lush green patch, more fertile and lusher in its light spring-green color than any cactus or desert plant. Reeds!

The lowland, with the plain and the sea in the distance, was already far behind us. Weary and parched, we hurried over the rocks, looking forward only to throwing ourselves into the mountain lake and gulping down great draughts of water. I noticed a few rock shelters half-buttressed with crude stone masonry. Human beings had once been busy here. Reaching at last the tall green luxuriance, Caitano seized his knife and cut his way into it, until his brown back, with the black pigtail of hair, disappeared in the reeds, which reached high above our heads. I hurried after him.

"Where is the lake?" I asked when I caught up, standing inside the greensward. We could not see further than an arm's length away. He stood gazing at the ground under his toes and pointed straight down with his nose. Black, moist earth mold. The rest of us pressed forward, wanting to push farther in to see the lake. Caitano crawled hesitantly into a dark tunnel made in the reeds by animals who came there to drink. The tunnel ended in a sort of overgrown cavern formed by the reeds, so large that there was room for everyone if we huddled together. Here the ground was obviously swampy. Mossy stones felt like cold fungus, and in the midst of them was a shallow pool smaller than a washbasin and completely covered with green spirogyra. I was about to lower my seat into it to cool myself when a suspicion struck me and I stopped without touching the water.

"Where is the lake?" I asked.

"There," replied Caitano, pointing to the exact spot where I had been about to sit.

No one had anything to say. We all suddenly felt desperately thirsty as the promised lake faded away like a mirage. We gingerly fished up the floating greenery below our feet and filtered barely enough water through our closed fingers for everyone to wet their dry throats. Then we smeared the remaining dregs over our hot bodies and squelched our feet in the mud to exploit the last drop of moisture.

In spite of everything, it was incredibly cool and comfortable inside this shady green nest and life was suddenly marvelous and attractive. It is the great contrasts that give the greatest pleasure; a little slush and shade after the grueling walk made us feel better than a champagne reception after a bus ride. The Indians squinted at the section of sun that could just be glimpsed through the thick roof of reeds above us. They were thinking of the long walk home, and two of them crawled out with their big knives and began to slice the longest stalks off at the root while the rest of us lay for a while dozing idly.

There was something to be learned from this walk. I had assumed, like most other scientists, that it was natural for the Seris Indians to build reed boats. We had assumed that they did so because it was difficult to find wood in the Sonora desert, while the coast was presumably thick with reeds. And now the reality had turned out to be quite different. The Seris Indians had not built reed boats because they had easy access to reeds. On the contrary, they had made their way right up here into the mountains to find a minute trickle of fresh water where they could plant reeds to provide the raw material for their boats. If building reed boats had not been a tradition brought by their ancestors from elsewhere, or learned from visiting sailors, they would never have thought of trailing up to this pool to gather reeds for boatbuilding. They would certainly have made the framework of the boat from the branches of the sturdy iron tree and covered it with animal skins. Sealskin was ideal for kayak building, and the rocks on the south coast of Shark Island were covered with seals. The Seris Indians had learned to build reed boats from someone who came from an area where reed was common. From whom?

Soon we were on our way down the mountainside, the four Indians in front, each with his big bundle of bound reeds over his shoulder, the rest of us following with the camera tripods and equipment. As we scrambled down I noticed that the Indians had dropped a reed here and there. Down on the level ground the Indians began to scatter, and soon we found ourselves in front, with them following. So that we should not go astray before the sun sank behind the mountains, I searched for the tracks we had made and followed them zigzag fashion, while the Indians insisted on bringing up the rear. After all, they had the heaviest burdens to cope with, even if it did seem to me that they had shrunk a bit during the descent from the mountain.

The sun was just going down as we regained the boat. We knew we would see the light of the campfires on Punta Chueca after dark, so we waited patiently for the four Indians. One after another, they appeared padding silently onto the beach. Chuchu came last, smiling bashfully, with three, literally three, reeds on his back. The others had none.

"*Mucho trabajo*," one of them muttered, and was applauded by number two, who was drying his face with his pigtail while Chuchu carefully laid his three reed stalks in the boat. Caitano was already on board.

My three Mexican friends were bitterly disappointed and expressed their lack of appreciation of the results in no uncertain terms. Three stalks, after a whole day's hard walking on an island without food or drink. When we first came we had expected to find reeds on the mainland shore. My own disappointment was mingled with satisfaction. Three reeds did not make a boat. But they told me something more important. I had learned that the Sonora desert was not the original homeland of the reed boat.

In the village, Chuchu and his helpers were subjected to loud-voiced ridicule from the old people when he threw his three reed stalks down by the wall of the hut. One ancient crone was particularly irate and vociferous. In the end she stumped off, bent double, to her own hut and shouted through the opening. A moment later a wrinkled old Indian appeared and was dragged reluctantly out by his wife. He was almost blind and wore blue glasses. When he straightened up we could see that he had been an unusually fine figure of a man, tall and strong with distinguished features. The Seris Indians were different from all the other Indian tribes in Mexico. The Spaniards who saw them first described the natives of Shark Island as giants. The old man hobbled round the hut with his wife, we followed, and there on the garbage heap lay a reed boat. Its thin, bamboo-like reeds were gray and brittle with age and the ropes were rotten, but there was the boat in complete form. We helped to drag it in front of the hut door. Its wrinkled owner was intent on proving that a proper Seris Indian could build an *askam*.

The old giant turned out to have been the tribe's former chief. As dawn was breaking the next morning he took out a home-made coil of rope and a dagger-length wooden needle, polished smooth with use. Blind as he was, he groped his way and with his huge needle he sewed his crisp craft together, trying to strain the collapsed prow up into an elegant curve again. Luck was with us after all. The rubbish heap had given us exactly what we came for.

The last reed boat of the Seris Indians, and perhaps of all Mexico, was carried into the water. Caitano and son jumped on board. They settled themselves comfortably with a pair of old paddles and a long wooden spear with a running line. Paddling was something they could do, and soon we saw the brown backs with the black pigtails disappearing over the ripples on the long, slender reed boat. When they came back a huge turtle was waving its flippers on the reed floor between them. The half rotten reeds had absorbed a great deal of water but they were afloat.

This was Mexico. Where had the Seris Indians' tribal ancestors learned this? From one of the many neighboring tribes. Once there had been people on all sides using reed boats, from the Inca empire in the south to California in the north, and also on the inland lakes in Mexico itself. As late as the beginning of the last century, the French painter L. Choris painted three Indians paddling a reed boat along the wooded coast by San Francisco harbor. In Mexico itself reed boats similar to those of Peru had been observed on lakes in no fewer than eight different states, according to the noted Maya authority, Dr. Eric Thompson.[1]

I watched regretfully as Caitano's struggling captive was carried over to the turtle pen, while the lifeless hulk of the Seris people's last *askam* was thrown forever on the rubbish heap behind the old man's hut. There it lay, like a full stop to the last chapter of an unwritten book on the reed boat's story, forgotten for all time in the central regions of America.

[1] *Journal of the Royal Anthropological Institute*, London, 1951, Vol. 79.

Chapter Four

WITH BEDOUIN AND BUDUMA
IN THE HEART OF AFRICA

Africa. No continent has a more evocative name. Hear the word and the image appears before your eyes. A wall of green jungle, the huge tropical leaves pushed aside as lines of Negro porters with loads on their heads walk straight-backed into the camera lens. Giraffes and baboons loping slowly across the screen. Tom-toms. The roar of lions. I had never been in the African interior, only glimpsed it as if through a window, in the darkness of a movie or pressed between the pages of a book.

But there I was, in the African interior, in the heart of Central Africa itself. In a little hotel room in Fort Lamy, capital of the Chad Republic. I could not have been further from the sea. And that was a little paradoxical, because the visit was the first stage in preparing a voyage by primitive means across the Atlantic. The only water in the vicinity was a tranquil river. I could see it through the window: brown jungle water, red banks of clay, green landscape. Colors sparkled in the sun. A band of fishermen, their wet skins shining like licorice, stood up to their knees in water on a clay bank, pulling in a net. They had fixed a dense thicket of bamboo poles in the river bottom as a fish barrier. Yesterday I had seen seven hippopotami loafing on another bank farther up the river. Here in the capital they were protected. Crocodiles had been virtually exterminated because the skin was once an important part of the country's exports. The traffic at this season was limited to flat-bottomed canoes made of hollowed-out tree trunks: there had been no rainfall since the rainy season ended six months before, so the water was too shallow for motor boats.

The Shari River flowed smoothly and steadily northward, but the water it carried from the jungle never reached the distant ocean. From the vast jungle near the Congo border in the south it passes through savannah and semidesert on its way to the great inland Lake Chad on the southern borders of the Sahara. Here the heat is so intense that the water evaporates as quickly as it flows in. Lake Chad has many tributaries, but no outlets other than the blue sky, arching cloudlessly over the vast surface of the desert lake and insatiably absorbing the invisible vapor.

This was the lake I wanted to visit. But, easy as it might be to find on the map, it was extremely difficult to reach. On all the maps it stands out as the blue heart of Africa, but no two maps give the lake the same shape. Now it is drawn as round as a plate, now curved like a hook, and then again scalloped like an oak leaf. The honest maps show this inland sea with dotted outlines, for no one knows the shape of Lake Chad. It is variable. Thousands of floating islands drift about on the surface, sometimes sailing in one direction, then setting course for another part of the lake. They collide and amalgamate, they drift ashore and are transformed into coastal bogs and peninsulas. They are torn apart and sail off in different directions to new, unknown destinations. The lake, which sometimes covers an area of ten thousand square miles (the size of Lake Erie), often dries up to half that size, because the depth varies from three to fifteen feet. Nineteen feet is the greatest depth. In the north much of it is so shallow that papyrus reeds cover large areas, and papyrus also grows on most of the floating islands that sail around in an everlasting regatta.

The Republic of Chad gained independence from France in 1960. It has no railways. Nor are any roads open all the year round. It is a paradise for sportsmen and for those who want to see one spot in the world that does not simply reflect our own ubiquitous existence. The capital has first-class hotels, chemists, bars and ultramodern administrative offices full of black officials, most with parallel scars on chin or cheek signifying their tribal origin. The wide asphalt roads between the small gardens of French bungalows from the colonial period become more rugged and exotic as they run out into the sand between rows of Arab houses in the suburbs, and finally they disappear across the landscape as interminable caravan routes between isolated groups of round, native kraals. When the rains begin one must ride or fly to make a journey overland. But then the river is navigable for small boats, right down to the trading stores in the marshes where it runs into Lake Chad.

Three days earlier I had flown across the Mediterranean and the whole of the Sahara in a French plane that stops once a week at Fort Lamy on its way to more southerly parts of Africa. Anything destined for the Republic which is unsuitable for weeks of camel transport must be brought in by air: cars, bulldozers, refrigerators, gasoline. Yes, even lobsters and tender beef for the master chef at "La Tchadienne." They all come by air.

We left the plane, three men laden with film equipment and goods for barter with potential African boatbuilders. My companions were two cameramen: the Frenchman Michel and the Italian Gianfranco. We were going to study and film local boat construction. I had stumbled on a picture illustrating a travel article on Central Africa. It showed some ebony-colored natives standing by the water with a very remarkable and distinctive craft: the same type of reed boats I knew so well from South America and Easter Island. The picture had been taken on Lake Chad and the author himself was very emphatic about the striking similarity between this craft in the African interior and the type of boat which had been built since time immemorial by the Indians on Lake Titicaca in the Peruvian uplands. In Egypt this ancient African vessel had died out long ago, but here, isolated in the heart of the continent it still survived.

An old caravan route ran from the Upper Nile area through the mountains to Chad. In more recent times it was known as the trans-African slave route. I knew that the anthropologists had reason to believe that part of the Chad population had its ancient roots in the Nile Valley. This could explain why the Egyptian type of reed boat was paddled about side by side with dugout canoes carved from giant jungle trees. Chad was an African melting pot. Here the tropical sun burned down on a welter of human types and you would

have to be a specialist to distinguish between the different tribes
and languages. But one thing was clear to everyone. Just as Chad
represents a gradual transition from the Sahara Desert, whose sand
dunes roll in over the national frontiers in the north to the boundless
jungles of tropical Africa rolling in from the south, so is the northern
part of the country full of Bedouins and other Arabs, while the
southern part is inhabited by various Negroid people. They meet
on the central plains and in the capital, Fort Lamy, where they join
in a common effort to forge a nation from what chance once de-
marcated as a temporary French colony.

After a cold shower in our air-conditioned hotel we crawled
into a scorching hot taxi and drove to the official national tourist
bureau. The wide main road was seething with cars, bicycles and
pedestrians. Here and there among various shades of Africans we
saw a few white faces. These were French officials and colonists who
had chosen to stay on in the capital after the liberation. The tourist
chief was one of them.

We explained that we had come to ask the best way of reaching
Lake Chad, as we could find neither railway nor road marked on
the map. The tourist chief spread out a colorful chart and some illustrated literature on lions and al kinds of jungle game. We could go
and shoot them all for a reasonable fee, but we would have to travel
south, in the opposite direction from Lake Chad. We explained that
it was the lake we wanted to visit, that it was the only place where
we could see papyrus boats. The tourist chief folded the map and
said that if we did not want to go where he, the expert, recommended
he could not help us. He calmly aimed his paunch in the direction
of his inner office and left. I had to fish out of my passport an im-
pressively stamped letter of recommendation from the Norwegian
Foreign Minister and send a clerk in with it. The tourist chief's
paunch reappeared in the doorway. This time he explained kindly
that it was impossible to get to Lake Chad before the river reached
high water level. In any case, to find papyrus one had to go round
to the village of Bol on the northeastern shore and one could only
reach that by air. Did I wish to charter a plane?

If that was the only way, I did.

The tourist chief picked up the telephone. There were two single-
engine aircraft in the country. Both were in hangars, under repair.

A third taxi-plane had two engines, and therefore needed eight hundred yards to land in. The landing strip at Bol was only six hundred yards long. The tourist chief added that filming was forbidden in the country except with a government permit.

Moreover there was serious unrest in the Republic at the time. The Arab population in the area behind Bol was Mohammedan and had begun to rise against the Christian Africans in the south, which held power in the government. So it was very unsafe to venture into the northern part of the country just now. To prove his good intentions the chief placed the tourist office car and driver at our disposal. We could drive round and see anyone we liked in Fort Lamy and question people who knew conditions at the lake.

One address he gave us produced a smiling sturdy Frenchman with tattooed arms who was here to study the possibilities of improving the stocks of fish and developing modern fishery in Lake Chad. He explained that the only way of reaching the papyrus swamps near Bol was to drive by Jeep across the desert east of the lake. This was confirmed by a French doctor who was an animal trainer and the most enthusiastic traveler in the country. Both called attention to the present unrest in that quarter of the country, however, adding that there was in fact a large river boat on the lake, which made periodic round trips, buying up a sort of native corn. But it would be impossible to find it now.

Not many countries felt the need to keep an embassy in the Chad Republic, but France had one in its former colony. Michel presented us there, but the ambassador had only been there a month and none of his staff had ever been to the lake.

This was our third day in Fort Lamy and all we had done was to go from office to office, from bungalow to bungalow, calling on friendly people who offered us coffee, cold beer or whisky and gave us the address of someone else who might be able to offer a solution. Now we had come full circle, the last people we saw gave us the address of the tourist chief and people we had questioned the first day.

We decided to try to reach Bol on our own, by Jeep. We had the formal permission of the authorities. They had installed in Bol the only radio telephone in the whole lake area, and as a safety measure the Minister for Home Affairs would inform the sheriff in Bol of our arrival. I had only to go to the Minister of Information and get a document that would authorize us to use our movie cameras. Here, as usual, there were Negroes, not Arabs, in almost all the public posts. The Minister ran his fingers through his crinkly hair and roared with laughter as he proofread the document his secretary had transcribed from his dictation.

"The man is an archaeologist, ar-chae-o-log-ist," he told her, handing the paper back as he nodded toward me. "Change that to ar-chae-o-log-ist, otherwise the Mohammedans will chop off his head in the area he's got to cross."

I peeped cautiously over the frizzy-haired beauty's shoulder. French was the official language of the Republic, the only one that the many different ethnic groups had in common. On the paper I had been entered as "*archevêque*" instead of "*archéologue*," an archbishop instead of an archaeologist.

The mistake was rectified and the Minister reassured us that there was thus no question of becoming involved in religious controversy on the government's side.

With appropriate documents and two coal-black drivers, of whom one, Baba, said he had been in Bol before, we set out on the road from Fort Lamy long before sunrise next morning. We thought it safest to divide up into two Jeeps in case of accident in the desert, and this proved a very wise decision. In the lead car we had a yellow map without contours, on which the names Fort Lamy, Massakory, Alifari, Kairom, Ngouri, Isseirom and Bol were underlined in red. We had no difficulty in finding the first villages. They were efficiently signposted and the sand roads were firm enough for us to drive across the flat country at over sixty miles an hour, with no escape from the dust clouds which we ourselves sent whirling up toward the night sky. Along the first stretch to the north, bulldozers and labor camps showed that many road gangs were busy raising the road up above surrounding ground level so that it would become usable also in the rainy season. The first hundred miles were behind us when the sun rose over the plain. But then we branched off onto smaller and smaller side roads and soon the twentieth century had vanished over the horizon. Even just outside the capital, the buildings had given way to scattered groups of round, straw-roofed native kraals, mostly deserted. Gradually we found ourselves crossing large uninhabited tracts of desert, with scarce wheel tracks following the caravan route between villages where rows of low sun-baked clay houses harbored a medley of Arabs, and their goats, donkeys and camels. Then we were heading for sheer open space.

This was the desert. This was the southern border of the Sahara. The last thermometer we had seen registered nearly 50° C. (122° F.) in the shade. But where we were now there was neither thermometer nor shade. Behind us lay the savannah with fan palms and arid-looking trees, here and there enclosing stretches of genuine parkland, where gazelles, wild boars and troops of monkeys leaped clear of the track in company with gaudy tropical birds, while fat guinea hens scarcely bothered to hitch themselves out of the wheel tracks. The sand lay like snow on bare mountainsides, in drifts and dunes, over low, rolling crests and hollows in the landscape, where only sparse desert scrub broke the sun-drenched infinity of sand. Sun. It was directly above our heads, glittering on all the Jeep's metal, which was now so hot that we could not touch it. The brooding heat pinched our nostrils no matter where we tried to take in air—hot desert air, saturated with the dust that surged in from every side.

We frequently got stuck in deep sand dunes, and one Jeep had to tow the other out on a steel cable while long, scorching metal plates were thrust under the wheels to provide a solid surface. At intervals, first one Jeep and then the other would break down in the heat, its motor stone dead. Baba and his friend were brilliant mechanics and, armed with wrench and screw driver, they always managed. Where the sand was firm enough we traveled at dizzying speed. Time and again we lost sight of all wheel tracks and drove on a looping course until Baba thought we were on course again. And so we drove into a lonely village, unknown to Baba and not marked on our map. On a bend beside the first mud huts both Jeeps became firmly embedded in sand and we had to get out and dig again.

For the first time we felt slightly ill at ease. Desert sons swathed in gray rags and while burnooses, with expressionless faces and eyes fixed on us, came slowly—remarkably slowly—drifting toward us from all sides, never turning their gaze from our own. They showed no desire to greet us or to help dig out the Jeeps. Soon they were standing shoulder to shoulder, fixing us with eagle eyes, unresponsive to all our attempts at a smile or a greeting. No women. They were as dark-skinned as our two raven-black drivers, but the sharp features, hooked noses and narrow lips proclaimed them as Arabs. The harsh life of the desert had set brutal scars on their skins and minds alike. There was no charity here. No pity. And no telephone. The world beyond the sand dunes was represented only by our two Jeeps, which were stuck fast in the sand.

The metal plates were not in position under us and Baba and his friend sat helplessly behind their steering wheels, accelerating until the sand flew. The Arabs stood quite still, as if waiting for something, holding something back. There was tension in the air, the look in their eyes made one think of a wary pack of wolves, ready to leap or run at the first move of one male. It seemed imperative to act first. I tramped over to an apparent leader type among them and politely handed him our two spades, indicating that he should get two of the other men to dig. He hesitated in some surprise, then responded to the promotion. He took the spades and began passing the orders on, barking like an irascible sergeant. As I beckoned to the rest of the pack to come and help push, the powerful shoulder of the newly designated boss was suddenly at my side, while we were nearly trampled underfoot by the helpful mob who fought for elbow room to join in and shove. We shook hands and thanked them, then drove off with our swirling dust cloud, through the village and along a well-worn camel track, as fast as our wheels could whiz.

In midafternoon we passed through another sun-baked village, buried away between endless sand and sky. Here we felt equally unwelcome. The wheel tracks inevitably led to a market square in the midst of the adobe houses, and here we had to force our way through dense masses of people and closely packed flocks of resting camels, donkeys and goats. Angry, glaring Arabs pressed forward silently, without returning our greetings, as if by reading our thoughts they might find out if we were government representatives, come to impose Christianity or collect taxes. What else could strangers be doing out here in their desert realm? It was obvious that we were not welcome guests and again we bowled off at top speed into the desert.

It was nearly evening, but the heat still kept its choking stranglehold. Baba had a headache and the two men in the second Jeep, surfeited with dust, dropped further behind. The drinking water we had in a large can was sickeningly warm, with no power to refresh because it burned on our lips. In the villages we had not seen a single fruit, only clay jars and dried calabashes filled with mud-colored oasis water and dirty goats' milk. We had driven all day without seeing refuse of any kind near our wheel tracks. No scrap of paper, no plastic or empty can. Only once, on the road just outside the capital, had we noticed fragments from a broken bottle. Everything here was home-made: houses, clothes, harnesses. The traffic consisted of long caravans of small, heavily laden donkeys, Arabs swaying high up on their tall camels, and barefoot women trotting behind with jars and baskets on their heads. What you did not need for yourself was taken to market in the next village. It was a world set apart from ours, self-sufficient, unaltered, independent. The whole of our civilization could founder and they would get on just as well, as simply, as modestly, as safely, bound to tradition and to the earth.

Then the blue lake came into view. Shining like cold steel it lay behind a belt of sappy spring-green reeds—papyrus reeds. From the top of a sand dune we could see it, like a mirage, tempting us to leave the Jeeps and rush off, make our way through all that fresh green stuff and cast ourselves into the blue, blue water, drink, dive, cool off, get the dry yellow crust of sand out of our ears, nostrils and eye sockets, clean all the pores of our body, wash, drink again, drink, drink. We had been sitting in the Jeeps for thirteen hours and were just about to stagger, stiff and dazed, to the ground, when Baba stopped us: It was not safe to leave the Jeep here. Better to wait till we reached Bol. The village was on an open beach and if we kept going at full speed we would be there before nightfall. The desert was not safe at night.

We managed to control ourselves with difficulty. Water, so near, so divinely blue and beguilingly beautiful in its cool nakedness behind the curtain of reeds. But we took our seats again with dust in our mouths, and roasted and frizzled in the hot metal Jeep, while Baba turned the wheels in the opposite direction and tore down off the sand dune and into more sand, sand and desert.

We would be grateful to Baba later. When, just before sundown, the two Jeeps met the firm surface of the caravan route that runs to Bol from the desert villages in the east, we rushed straight through the empty market place and down to the beach below the houses. We were about to dive in with all our clothes on, when we heard a warning shout. There stood a serious, bearded young Frenchman who had been put ashore by the research team working in a boat on other parts of the lake. "Dive in and you'll be perforated with bilharzia in minutes," he said dryly. "The whole lake is full of them."

We looked at Baba. He shrugged his shoulders and sat down again, all dusty, in the Jeep.

That heavenly beautiful lake was home to some of Africa's most insidious creatures. Bilharzia, the little beast, is an almost invisible, millimeter-long worm, so thin that it can bore its way quickly right through a man's skin and lay eggs in his body, which is soon riddled with worms crawling about and eating him up from inside.

We thanked the Frenchman for his warning and asked him if there was a place where we could wash. He shook his head sadly. All the water here came from the lake and must be either boiled or left to stand for a day or two before it could be used.

The village seemed deserted until a giant black figure came striding out of a white-washed house with a small cortège, making straight for us. This huge man was the born chieftain type. He was acting sheriff in Bol, deputized to serve for another man who was on tour up-country. No one in Bol had received the promised advice of our arrival. Who were we, and where were our papers? Sheriff Adoum Ramadan had a toothache and was not in the best of spirits. Moreover he had Bol's total population of two thousand Arabs and Negroes to look after, of whom two hundred were village chiefs, so he had not much time to spare. Michel gave him a dose of aspirin and explained that we were looking for lodging, as we had driven continuously since leaving Fort Lamy the night before. "Then you have driven fast," said the sheriff tersely, affecting to miss the point. He inquired again why Fort Lamy had not advised him of our coming? The radio telephone was in order. What's more, we could thank the fates that we had got through, on the route we had taken. Five separate Jeeps had been burned by Arabs along the caravan route between Fort Lamy and Bol that month. The month before, sixty rebels had been shot in the area we had passed through. Two severed Negro heads had been found on the roadside and had recently been

displayed by the authorities for identification. We were bluntly told
to stay in Bol until there was a chance of leaving it other than
across the desert.

The sheriff with the gumboil sent one of his escort to show us the
way to a solitary cement hut down by the beach, while he himself
disappeared in the darkness toward the village with the rest of his
silent staff. The hut consisted of a passageway off which were
small rooms in the form of open cubicles. We had to step over men
and women already lying asleep. This was Bol's public guesthouse,
where any traveler could simply go in and lie down. The faces lifted
to peer at us as we stepped over them were hardly angelic. In one
corner there was a shower, but there was no water other than a dirty,
soapy puddle eight inches deep in a hollow on the earth floor. We
tried to pump, but gave up when we saw that the pipe led straight
from the lake full of worms. We had no choice but to sleep dry in our
desert dust.

Baba had just swept the floor where we were to unroll our sleeping bags when the sheriff dashed in, his big face now lit by a huge
smile. The toothache had gone. If he could have the rest of Michel's
medicine three beds would be brought down for us from the sheriff's
house. We slept with mosquito nets over our heads and pistols under
our pillows. All night long invisible strangers prowled about in the
pitch darkness, and several times I heard breathing close to my ear.

As the sun rose over the sea we were awakened by the muttering
of a row of Arabs kneeling along the wall, prostrated in prayer
toward Mecca. Others sat silently brewing tea on tiny open fires of
dry, broken papyrus reeds. We were taken to eat with the sheriff, who
was in radiant mood and refused to let us touch our own provisions.
We were to take all our meals as his guests as long as we were in the
Bol district. His cuisine was in fact quite excellent in its own way,
only one had to be careful not to close one's teeth completely because they would then inevitably crunch on desert sand.

That day I saw my first papyrus boat. It came drifting silently
past me over the glassy water on that enchanted lake, which had
completely changed its appearance from the day before. When we arrived, one large, low island had been lying in front of our hut; now
it had disappeared without trace and three other islands had loomed
up in different places in its stead. The smallest of them moved

slowly as I watched it, drifting off to the right, leaving a faint hint of a wake behind it on the left. It looked like a big, well-arranged flower basket, a thick bouquet of bristly golden papyrus flowers. Unruly, long-haired crowns, the tallest in the middle and the shortest leaning gracefuly out at the sides, reflected their yellow wigs and green stems in the sky-colored water. Small climbing plants and other flowers and leaves were dotted about among the reeds to make the composition aesthetically complete. With its turf floor of interwoven roots and plant fibers, the whole island floated majestically away without benefit of oars or engine, and yet the papyrus boat was traveling smoothly and surely past the floating flower basket. On board stood two tall Africans, dressed in white and erect as toy soldiers, punting the boat with long poles. The yellow boat and the straight black bodies were also mirrored in the lake and the reflection, sailing upside down, reminded me of those other reed boats which now actually were sailing upside down in relation to us, because they were on the other side of the globe, in South America. The boats on Lake Titicaca were so strikingly like the boat we saw now that they could easily have replaced the mirror image.

I was longing to try out one of these boats on the lake, but first of all I wanted to learn how they were built. The uninitiated could not hope to produce a boat in this particular shape by simply lashing papyrus reeds together on impulse.

The sheriff took us in a very solemn audience before Sultan M'Bodou M'Bami, the religious leader of the district and the most powerful man in the whole area. The sheriff himself and his deputy were Africans from the south, sent up from Forty Lamy to foster the political interests of the Christian government, while the sultan belonged to the local Buduma tribe and had the whole Mohammedan population of the area on his side.

The sheriff was broad and big-boned, like a good-natured gorilla, while the sultan was a beanpole of a man, a head taller then the average, with his skull and the lower part of his face swathed in a length of cloth over an ankle-length cloak, so that only the hooked nose and eagle eyes were visible. A large number of village headmen followed us, slipping off their sandals before stepping on the earth forecourt of the sultan's simple adobe house. Afterward we were installed around the wide sandy field in the middle of the town, the parade square where the sultan would appear on his rearing white thoroughbred in honor of his guests. While two men held the reins and constantly urged the stallion up on its hindquarters, the sultan sat immovable, surrounded by a flock of colorful brothel girls, who ran round and round him, brushing him with their airy veils.

When they had completed their turn, accompanied by drums and wooden trumpets, a dense line of horsemen appeared at the end of the square and thundered past us at a furious pace, swords drawn, yelling hoarsely. One of the riders was particularly aggressive. Time after time he raced past, his horse's hoofs close to our boot tips, while he leaned toward us, howling and grimacing savagely, his sword whirling appallingly close to our scalps. I tentatively asked the sheriff what this meant and was told that the rider was simply showing off. But Baba added that he was showing his contempt for us, who were not Moslem. The sultan, on the other hand, showed no antagonism. On the contrary, he evinced the greatest interest when he heard that we wanted to learn how to build papyrus boats. He sent us to his own kinsman, Omar M'Bulu a splendid representative of the Buduma tribe, who lived in a large beehive-shaped straw hut like all the other dwellings in the Buduma and Kanembu quarter of the district capital of Bol. Only the sheriff and deputy sheriff had their own white-chalked bungalows with red bougainvillaea growing on the walls, the rest of the town, belonging to the dominant Arab population, consisted of long, low huts of hand-formed clay bricks.

Omar was a stately man, tall, straight-backed, black as a stove pipe, with a completely smooth-shaven head and big, smiling eyes and teeth. He spoke both Buduma and Arabic in a low, friendly voice and ended every sentence with a hint of a smile. Omar was a fisherman, and did not hesitate for a moment when Baba asked him in Arabic to show us how to build a papyrus boat. He pulled out a long machete knife from the straw wall and barefoot he walked ahead of us to the lake with his blue cloak slung over one shoulder. The black sinews rippled as he bent and began to swing the knife at the root of the tall papyrus reeds, and long soft stems were thrown one after another in a heap at the edge of the marsh. His half brother, Mussa Bulumi, volunteered to help. He was older and smaller, equally shaven-headed, but without Omar's regal bearing. Mussa understood nothing unless it was said in Buduma, but made up for that by laughing at everything, whether Baba spoke to him in Arabic, Michel in French, Gianfranco in Italian or I in Norwegian. But Mussa was quicker than Omar at handling the reeds.

Large heaps of green papyrus were dragged up and dropped beyond the swampy ground. Two big reed boats, each of which could carry a dozen men, lay moored at the water's edge. We explained, by drawing in the sand, that we wanted a little one, about twelve feet long, which we could later transport on top of the Jeep. Two other Buduma tribesmen were summoned. They sat down in the sand under the only local tree and began scraping the pulp away from the leathery leaves of the doum palm until the rough white fibers emerged, split as thin as sewing thread. These the Africans rolled between palm and thigh until they had spun them into a sort of twine, and this in turn was plaited into solid rope. Now Omar and Mussa could begin on the boat while the others worked against time to keep them supplied with rope.

The papyrus reed was six to eight feet long and about two inches thick at the root, with a tricorne-shaped cross section. It was not jointed and hollow like bamboo but compact and spongy throughout its length, like a sort of stiff white foam rubber covered with a thin, smooth sheath. Omar began by taking a single reed and splitting it part way lengthwise into four strips, still joined at the thicker end. In the forks he stuck four whole stems, root first, and tied around them a loop so tight that the spongy ends were pressed together as compactly as possible. Between them again he inserted a steadily increasing number of reeds, which he lashed fast all the time with loops of rope so that the bundle gradually increased in thickness like the head of a projectile. Mussa joined him and the two boatbuilders each took an end of cord in their mouths and tightened the knots with all their combined strength, using black fingers and white teeth, arms and throat muscles swelling. The point was apparently to squeeze the cut end of the spongy reeds together until the pores closed. When the bundle increased to a thickness of about eighteen inches, it was continued lengthwise, keeping the same diameter, like a giant pencil. Finally the pointed end was lifted on to a sturdy tree stump and the boatbuilders began to jump and trample on the reed bundle until it curved like a huge elephant tusk. The shape of the upswept prow was now ready and, in a chain of loops, two shorter reed bundles were added outside the first, one on each side. By inserting one reed at a time the bundles fitted tightly together, the outer bundles assuming the cross sections of one waxing and one waning moon.

When the length of the boat reached the mark we had made on the ground the whole vessel was ready, in symmetrical detail, except for the stern, where the papyrus reeds still stuck out like the bristles on a broom. From here the boatbuilders could, if they wished, increase the boat's length indefinitely. The problem of shaping the stern was solved by Omar and Mussa in the simplest way. They took the longest machete knife and cut all the superfluous reed straight across as if slicing the end off a sausage. Then the papyrus boat was ready for launching, with pointed upswept prow and thick, flat, sawn-off stern. The work was completed in a day.

"*Kaday*," said Mussa, patting his finished product with a grin. That was the Buduma word for the reed boat on which the whole of their lakeside existence had depended since the morning of time, no one knows when. No one knows who were their teachers. Perhaps they developed the craft themselves. More probably the Buduma tribe had distant ancestors who had traveled the caravan route from the Nile Valley. This ancient boat had survived here, in any case, whenever reeds grew beside the lake, even on the opposite shores which belong to the Republics of Niger and Nigeria. Everywhere in this vast area the ingenious papyrus boats were built in the very same traditional way, except for variations in length and breadth. Nevertheless, four large wooden canoes, the hollowed trunks of mighty jungle trees which must have come down when the Shari River was in flood, also lay moored in a gap between the reeds where we carried our grass-green *kaday* into the water. We used the canoes as a bridge to go aboard dry-shod. Omar pointed scornfully at these cranky boats, which looked like elongated bathtubs half full of water. Those were the boats of the Kanembu. They did not know how to build *kadays* like the Buduma.

I was just about to jump aboard our brand-new *kaday*, which was floating on the water like a curved cucumber, when I saw a new face. That was my first meeting with Abdullah. He was just standing there when we needed him most, like a genie from Aladdin's lamp.

"*Bonjour monsieur,*" he said simply. "My name is Abdullah and I speak French and Arabic. Do you need an interpreter?"

That was just what I needed indeed. How else was I to learn anything from Omar and Mussa when the three of us were out on the lake in the little vegetable boat?

Abdullah behaved like a well-bred gentleman, swathed in an ankle-length white robe and with a bearing like a Caesar. His face was the blackest I had ever seen, his head completely smooth-shaven like Omar's and Mussa's, with a long scar running centrally down his forehead and over the bridge of his nose. Strangely enough, this tribal mark was more piquant than disturbing, and, with his intelligent eyes, lips that were always curling into a smile and teeth quick to part in laughter, Abdullah Djibrine was a true, full-blooded child of nature, an alert assistant, a really merry companion. He had already conjured up two roughly hewn paddles and he handed one to me.

As the four of us jumped aboard our narrow papyrus boat one after the other and the camera whirred to preserve the event for posterity, we witnessed a singular drama. It was market day in Bol and a colorful crowd of several thousand men and women had come in from the desert and from the islands on the lake. The market place was literally seething with life; scarcely an inch of the sandy ground could be seen for the men, women and children elbowing their way around, with jars, baskets and large trays on their heads, covered with fragrant vegetables, straw, skins, nuts, dried roots and African corn. Scarred faces, bare breasts, yelling children. Bright eyes, angry looks, laughing glances. The fragrance of spices mingled with the smell of donkey dung, dried fish, billy goat, sweat, and sour milk. The sun blazed down on them all; the buzzing of flies was completely drowned by babbling, screaming, muttering human voices crying their wares and haggling in three different desert languages. Hundreds of horned cattle bellowed and some thousands of donkeys, goats and camels brayed, bleated and trumpeted in vain against ringing metal, the rhythmic hammer blows of the weapon-smiths on dagger blades and spearheads. Now a picturesque group

of black figures was making its way out of the chaos toward the lake.
With shouts and blows they drove all their domestic animals before
them—mostly African cattle with huge, curving horns. Down on the
shore they took off their clothes and tied all their possessions in a
bundle. Then they drove the cattle into the lake and, with bundles
poised on their heads, set about swimming after them. In contrast
to Europeans, many of them seemed to be immune to bilharzia,
though the disease does play havoc with the lake dwellers and has
reduced many of them to complete wrecks.

The people swimming out there with their cattle had propped
themselves on tusklike floats, some of a balsa-like wood, others of
papyrus, exactly like the one-man floats I had seen in Peru and
on Easter Island. Soon all we could see were the black heads with
high loads balanced on the crown, the curved tusk tips projecting
from the water, and in front a welter of large-horned heads, representing animals making for a long island on the other side of the
sound. Abdullah explained that this was a Buduma family who had
been to market to buy cattle, which they were now taking home
to their own island. A white, sandy shore and scattered doum palms
proclaimed that the island was anchored to the bottom. Two other
islands covered with waving papyrus flowers, but sandless, were just
slowly bearing into the sound.

As we paddled out, we learned from Omar, with Abdullah
interpreting, that many Buduma families were living on the floating
islands too. Omar and Mussa had been born on such an island and
Mussa still lived on one. He had just come into Bol with some
fish. There were masses of fish in the lake, the largest bigger than a
man. There were crocodiles and hippopotami as well, but not many
were left. Cattle and other domestic animals sailed around with
their owners on many of the floating islands and it was often a
problem for the customs posts in Nigeria when a Buduma family
drifted into their Republic with herds and other worldly goods from
the Republic of Chad without passport as they had not left the
threshold of their own hut. When families moved their pasturage
from one island to another they would usually swim, but if they
wanted to go fishing or cross the great lake itself for distant shores,
they always used papyrus boats. In Bol we had heard that a few
papyrus boats were built large enough to carry forty tons or more,

and Mussa claimed that he had once helped to build a *kaday* big enough to transport eighty close-packed cattle across the open lake. Another had navigated with two hundred men on board. They could be built in any size.

Accounts of the *kaday's* loading capacity sounded incredible, but when Mussa, Omar, Abdullah and I had jumped on board our little rush-job of a boat, I began to believe in them. The boat was so narrow that if I wanted to sit I could ride astride it, yet there we were, all standing on it together and swaying, and the papyrus gave no hint of a bend or a wobble. The water, so blue at a distance, was far from limpid and I was not anxious to capsize into the worm-soup. Here in the sedge it was especially perilous, for the little worms come swimming out of a snail which lives on the reed itself. The two boatbuilders began to change places, swaying to and fro, squeezing past the rest of us, but hanging on to us at the same time, so that we would not topple overboard. Whatever they did, the little craft floated quite imperturbably, as high in the water as an inflated rubber dinghy. Out among the reeds on the biggest island we found an old, half-rotten papyrus boat drifting about almost level with the water line. Many of its ropes had rotted, but the wreck still bore me when I ventured cautiously aboard. How old was it? A year, suggested Omar, but of course he could not be sure. In any case the boat was far from newly built. And there it was, still floating on the lake.

We paddled about all day among the perfectly beautiful papyrus islands. The other men followed in one of the larger *kadays* that had been moored beyond the wooden canoes. Soon we were four papyrus boats out there together, playing out the lines of a fishnet while big *capitaine* fish splashed in the water about us. Evening came. Our first day on board a papyrus boat was over.

We three Europeans stood together outside the guesthouse, looking at the crowded stars. The other, more local wayfarers were already asleep on the floor, but we had just arrived home from a little hut where a solitary young man, Bill Hallisey of the American Peace Corps, had treated us to a shower from a home-made spray nozzle on a suspended petrol can. Bill was one of those extremely rare men who drove around in the desert alone, and his contribution had obvious results in the religious war. He sank wells and created water where conditions were most appalling, and in the villages where the water bubbled up, there were no Mohammedans who felt the urge to slaughter Christians. Now he was boring here, in Negro and Arab quarters alike.

We felt new-born after our washing ceremony and stood for a while enjoying the last breaths of fresh air before creeping into the stifling communal hut. We would have preferred to sleep outside in the sand, but it was not safe because of poisonous sand snakes on their nightly raids in the desert.

It was a hot, dark, moonless, tropical night and the stars blazed with adventure and romance. Only the cicadas and countless frogs whirred, hummed and croaked from near and far in the papyrus reeds. The desert was dead; both it and the village were silent, lost in the night. We took a last look at the stars and were just crouching to enter the doorway of the guesthouse and sleep, when I heard something and gripped the other two by the arms. We all listened. Suddenly from the desert came the distant, almost inaudible roll of drums and the sound of a tremulous wind instrument. The whole of the Orient was in this sound, which seemed to be made of the desert sand itself, played by the mild night air and carried by it through the darkness. There was not a light to be seen. I could not go to bed without seeing the strange sights which must be associated with this mysterious, barely audible concert. I wanted the other two to come with me in search of the sound. They were not tempted. They wanted to sleep. I took the smallest flashlight and put it in my pocket. It was no good using it except in emergency; the thing was to be inconspicuous if one wanted to look on undisturbingly and if one hoped to remain unnoticed. I did not feel entirely safe after all I had heard. The flashlight might be useful in a tight spot.

It was damnably dark. I took a bearing on the stars so that I could find my way back across the featureless ground to the guest-hut, which completely disappeared as soon as I had taken the first groping steps in the night. I had to lift my feet high and warily to avoid stumbling, and found that my footsteps were almost in-audible in the powdery sand. I walked for some minutes, but the sound of the drums seemed just as far away. Then I bumped into an adobe wall. The village. An Arab house. It was easy to feel my way along the wall to a corner and turn again in the direction of the sound. All went well until my groping fingers came upon a reed barrier. Not a single hut betrayed a glimmer of light. Here a wide sand road led between two reed barriers, directly toward the music, which seemed clearer now. I could even perceive the outlines of conical grass roofs against the stars, but below that everything was quite black. I tried to walk faster. The same moment I stumbled over something big, hairy, which seemed to grow into enormous proportions as it let go a devilish shriek and pitched me headlong on the sand. A recumbent camel had been startled awake. Its dry joints creaked as it rose and walked off, still invisible.

I stood still. Not a light. Still not a sound from the houses. Only the music, fully audible. Drums and wooden pipes, or perhaps some sort of trumpet. I groped my way on, right through the village, and the music was close. I could also see the glow of an oil lamp. When I had come out on the far side of the houses, I saw shadowy figures passing the lamplight in an unbroken stream, going in the same direction. There was an open space here, probably the beginning of the desert plain itself. I groped my way round the corner of the last barrier, a clay wall useful to lean against without making a noise. Now I began to see still more figures, many standing as well as some seated onlookers. I stepped over a couple of children squatting by the same wall and staring hypnotized at what was going on in the pool of light. No one reacted to my presence in the darkness. There were crowds of people here. Best to keep still and unnoticed by the wall. There were swathed shapes everywhere and all were staring at the endless procession passing the light.

But this was not a procession. It was a ring of people dancing round the light, masses of men, shuffling their feet, bending forward and back, reaching down to the earth and up to the sky, round and round in a big circle, while the imperative drums and the wind instrument sent their seductive oriental sounds outward into the dark night. I caught the barest glimpse of the musicians inside the circle. Something strange was happening in there too, which I could not really see. Two female figures came into view now and then inside the circle of dancers. Sometimes they seemed to be teetering on some sort of chair, sometimes someone seemed to be dragging them around backward by the hair. There was no way of getting a good view, but I was peering and concentrating in an effort to see better when a new move captured my whole attention. A dancer had left the circle and was dancing straight toward me in the same rhythm, holding in his hand a short sword which he swung in time to the dance.

It was a coincidence of course; of course he had not seen me in the darkness. Or yes, he was heading for me alone; there was no longer any doubt about it. In a moment the sword was whirling and flashing in front of my nose. I forced a smile at the dancing man to show that I could enjoy a good joke, but no white teeth gleamed back at me from that face. Somber and impervious, the dark Arab continued his dance and his defiant mock fencing in rhythm to the music. In the background I caught a glimpse of the ring of dancers carrying on unperturbed, all but this infernal fellow. After a few more attempts at a conciliatory smile it suddenly struck me that there really was nothing to smile about; the man was brazen and offensive, the situation was extremely humiliating, the skirmishing was now so aggressive that the tip of the sword was almost touching my nose and soon it was thrust past me into the wall terrifyingly close to either side of my head.

I thought desperately. If I seized the sword blade it would sever my fingers. I could not reach the man behind the sword. As he danced he seemed a little unsteady on his legs, almost as if he were in a trance. Was he drunk? I had seen no alcohol. Was he under the influence of drugs? I did not know. I did not know the answer to anything, but now I had to act or I would get the sword in my face.

So I began intuitively to do something that made me wonder if I had lost my reason. I was actually thinking that if the people at home were to see me now they would be certain I had gone raving mad. I began to dance myself. I began to dance in time with the sword-swinging bandit, marking time at first, in order not to run my nose onto the sword's tip. The Arab must have been taken by surprise if he reacted at all. I felt him lose the beat for a split second, but then he danced on, and the two of us danced, he backward, I forward in the same rhythm, out into the circle of light and into the ring round the light. They automatically made room for us and no one showed the slightest sign of surprise or change of rhythm. I was so blindly absorbed in following and

doing exactly as the others did that I took no further notice either
of the man with the sword who had summoned me to the dance,
or of the figures we were dancing round inside the wide circle.
When I had fully regained my powers of observation I saw only the
four musicians stamping around close to the lantern. I myself was
part of a great ring of dancing, coal-black men: Arab, Buduma
and Kanembu, as black by day as by night. The dance was relatively
simple; it came naturally if one followed the rhythm with a shuffle,
hop and bend.

It was a long time before I noticed that the ring was growing
smaller. People were stealing almost imperceptibly away. Soon we
were a tight circle of a dozen men revolving around the lamp and
the musicians. The trumpeter seemed to have been blowing from
his infancy because his cheeks were puffed out like a cherub's. As
he blew on the wooden trumpet it looked as if a doll's black rubber
cheeks were stretching until they turned brown. Perhaps the lamplight produced the effect. But one thing was evident. The sweat was
trickling down his forehead, and when I looked closer I could see
that it was streaming down the faces of all the others as well,
especially the dancers. Then I noticed something else. The other
dancers were holding a small coin in their fingers, which they raised
and lowered and slipped to the trumpeter when they fell out. I must
at all costs be equally generous if this were to end well, so I
danced with a Chad bank note between my fingertips. The trumpeter
immediately came tripping out with the drummers at his heels and
enthusiastically stuck his strident instrument in my face, the beat
quickened, the ring grew smaller.

There were only four of us left and the musicians were obviously
concentrating all their efforts on the one who had the most money.
The sweat dripped off the others and to my amazement they seemed
exhausted, as if they were taking part in an endurance test, although
it seemed no worse than a long "twist" or other fast dance at home.
Perhaps the desert horsemen were less used to personal exercise
and endurance than skiers in the north, because this was no more
than fun. But then the others might have been dancing for hours;
after all I had only just arrived. One could go on like this forever, just
dancing, shuffle-shuffle-hop-bend-and-stretch, although now it was
going faster, faster and faster, the musicians wanted to put a stop to

it, another man fell out, and yet another, it was frankly a contest, faster and faster, yes, now one really had to breathe hard, there was only one other dancer left, there he dropped out also, I was dancing alone, the trumpeter fell on my neck and secured the bank note. I stopped. People pressed in from all sides in the darkness. Staring white eyes and a medley of indefinable expressions; everyone wanted to have a good look.

I gulped in the night air, pleasantly tired and relieved to have escaped the man with the sword. I could no longer see him, but a heavily built man came up to me, pulling two hefty female figures out of the darkness. They were not particularly young and not particularly beautiful by comparison with many of the well-proportioned women one could see on the shore by day. Moreover, their skins were gleaming with sweat that was running from their foreheads. Perhaps these were the women who had been involved in something I could not see in the melee within the ring earlier. They were discreetly placed at my side like trophies. Hundreds of Arab and Negro faces thrust toward us in the dim lamplight. What now? How to slip away from this increasingly involved situation, away from the mob, back into the peaceful night from which I had come?

It was then that I felt a powerful hand slap me on the shoulder and there was Omar, his face shining like a sun in the lamplight. "*Monsieur, brave tamtam,*" said he, his teeth flashing approval. That exhausted his stock of French. Omar was my salvation. One familiar face. This was obviously a celebration for the masses, because neither sultan nor sheriff was present. Omar was respected, and when the onlookers saw that I was on friendly terms with the sultan's kinsman the ranks parted and we went off together through the empty village to the music of the cicadas.

Next day my standing in Bol had risen. Lively rumors were circulating about my prowess as a tom-tom dancer, as well as the large sum I had paid to the musicians. The sheriff, on the other hand, had received new reports of terrorist activities and Arab uprisings in the interior and insisted on our being his guests until we could leave safely by air. It was hopeless trying to contact Fort Lamy by radio telephone, but the African telegrapher could wire to say we wanted a taxi-plane whenever one was available.

We had a number of good friends in Bol by now and were enjoying the days spent in papyrus boats on the lake. A week passed. Then the sound of engines was heard over the floating islands and a little aircraft flew in low over the papyrus, skimmed the roofs of the village huts and landed on a leveled strip of sand, where we met the French pilot a moment later. He was ready to set off with the three of us at once, but the little plane could not carry our little reed boat nor the heavy film equipment, only essential clothing. The newly made papyrus boat was hoisted to the roof of one Jeep and all the equipment stowed inside the other with Baba, because both sheriff and sultan thought that no one would attack the two African drivers if they drove alone through the desert, with no strange white faces on board.

The last people to whom we said good-by were the two boat-builders, Omar and Mussa, and the interpreter, Abdullah. Both sheriff and sultan assented with obvious pleasure when I asked if the two Buduma brothers could join me later, in Egypt, if I needed expert reed boatbuilders. When Abdullah had translated my question from French into Arabic for Omar, and Omar from Arabic to Buduma for Mussa, the brothers were so delighted that they shook with laughter and nodded repeatedly, gripping my fist in both hands to confirm their enthusiasm.

"They say yes," Abdullah explained solemnly, "and I am coming along to interpret!"

We were already sitting in the aircraft, which would not start, so I did not pay much attention to my own reply, but time should show that Abdullah obviously did. Cables were coupled to the plane from Baba's Jeep and with their help we trundled forward and into the air over the Buduma huts, *kadays* and papyrus swamps. We had a perfect view of limitless golden sands behind us, which we had jolted over on our way to Bol, and below us lay Lake Chad, the world's most extraordinary island community. Beyond Bol it was a green-speckled jigsaw puzzle on a blue ground to which someone had given a casual shove. The floating islands were all the pieces, with their infinite variety of sinuous outlines, and an endless chaos of narrow blue channels wriggled round them like gaps in the disintegrated puzzle. On some of the green pieces there were tiny round grass huts and flocks of toy cattle moving about and grazing, and

here and there in the blue cracks the little yellow mustard seed
of a *kaday* appeared. Then we saw only blue and more blue until
we reached the mouth of the Shari River.

It took no more than an hour to fly straight across the lake, up
to Fort Lamy. And there we waited for our Jeeps, one day, two
days. Three days. Something serious had happened. The radio telephone to Bol was in operation and the friendly sheriff was able to
confirm that the Jeeps had left there long ago.

With the help of the garage owner in Fort Lamy we sent out
another Jeep which drove halfway back to Bol and returned without
finding anything but our own outgoing wheel tracks. Then we sent
the little aircraft to get a better view. It crisscrossed the desert
route for three hours without finding any Jeeps stuck in the sand.
The French scientists who had the research boat on the lake sent a
Jeep searching from Bol to Fort Lamy and back again. When it returned the driver had no news to report.

We informed the authorities. They could do nothing. The chief
of police explained that this was not robbery, it was civil war. We
missed the scheduled flight we were to have taken, which stopped at
Fort Lamy once a week. The two cameramen should have been on
another job in Ethiopia, but they missed out on their appointment
because they could not go without their expensive equipment.

Then we had an idea. With Michel as spokesman, we went
to the headquarters of the French military forces. Chad had become
an independent republic. The French had withdrawn discreetly from
the government offices, where there was not a white face to be
seen, but it was not difficult to find them when they were needed
and it proved a small problem for the French military chief to
locate the two lost Jeeps. Owing to the risings among the Arab tribes
in the north and east, the French had military patrols stationed at
strategic points in the desert. They had mobile radio stations and
were prepared to summon French parachute troops if terrorist action
took the form of organized rebellion. This happened some weeks
later. But it did not take the military chief many hours to report
that the two Jeeps had been found hidden in the shade of a big tree
in a remote desert village. Our two drivers had taken off on their own
with their valuable booty and tried to sell it to the Arabs. The
newly made papyrus boat, so important to us, meant nothing to

them so they had simply discarded it in the desert. To their disappointment they had found no one prepared to buy movie-making equipment, so all they had been able to sell was the gasoline, of which they had managed to tap the last drop from each tank. The patrol which caught the two fugitives reported on the air that if the Jeeps were wanted back in Fort Lamy we would have to send out another Jeep with fuel.

What happened to the faithless Baba and his fellow conspirator we never knew. They were not in the Jeep which a week later swerved in at the aircraft steps and delivered the stolen equipment as the big airliner stood ready and waiting to leave for Europe. On the other hand, our loyal interpreter Abdullah was later arrested and imprisoned by the local authorities, suspected of being my agent in Bol for the black slave trade to Egypt. But no one yet knew about that.

So the fascinating not yet amalgamated melting pot of Central Africa slipped away under our wings, with jungle and desert, Negroes and Arabs, blinding sun and our own giant aircraft casting the racing shadow of the twentieth century over the limitless Sahara as it passed, leaving no trace in the sand.

Farewell, Africa.

Chapter Five

AMONG BLACK MONKS
AT THE SOURCE OF THE NILE

To BUILD a reed boat you must have reeds. I needed papyrus reeds. Where would I find them? In Chad, the desert lake, to be sure. But no arteries led out from the heart of Africa to the surrounding world, no rivers, roads or railways. I needed more reeds than I could get out with a caravan of camels. Boatbuilders could be brought out by plane, of course, but not enough papyrus to build a ship. It was useless even to think of transport through the desert from the reed swamps at Bol to the airfield near the capital.

In Egypt? Indeed. Pharaoh lies in his tomb with reed boats painted on the stone walls. Stone and reeds. Stone in the desert and reeds in the Nile. Stone and papyrus reed were nature's gift to the ancient peoples of the Nile. And mud, which spilled over the riverbanks in its flight from the Ethiopian mountains. The peasant based his livelihood on the mud, the fisherman made his boat of the reeds, and Pharaoh cut up the rock itself while preparing for his next life. Of papyrus reeds Egyptian scholars made paper on which they wrote mankind's earliest history. Stone was transported on papyrus and papyrus boats were immortalized in stone. The papyrus flower appears again and again in the art of ancient Egypt. It was the national symbol of Upper Egypt, and in mythology the birdman

Horus, son of the sun-god Ra, tied it to the lotus flower of Lower Egypt when both countries became one kingdom.

To build a balsa raft one must do as the Incas did, penetrate the rain forests of Ecuador in search of fresh jungle trees full of sap to prevent water absorption. To build a papyrus boat one must do as Pharaoh did, send his men out into the great papyrus swamps along the shores of the Nile and cut fresh reeds. When a pharaoh wanted to build a boat he had no special problem. His skilled builders knew everything about papyrus and papyrus boats, after generations of experience. His labor force was unlimited and the building materials grew in boundless numbers just outside the palace gates. The papyrus swamps, on both banks of the Nile, stretched from the Mediterranean coast all the way in through his empire in the Egyptian desert.

But that was in former days.

"No papyrus grows in Egypt now," Georges Sourial assured me. Georges was an Egyptian frogman and knew the Nile like his own back yard. "There is plenty of stone, if you want to build a pyramid, but not enough papyrus for a toy dinghy," he added and steered the motorboat we were sitting in closer to the bank to give me a better view.

On the Nile was an endless traffic of sails and masts, gliding up and down between palm trees, sandbanks and cultivated fields, but not a single golden-haired papyrus reed bowed its bushy head over the bank. The papyrus had died out in Egypt some time in the previous century. No one knew why. The gods had taken back one of their oldest gifts, as if they had simply pulled it up by the roots. The stone was left, in mountains and in pyramids, but even the mud had almost gone, checked in its course by the country's new rulers, behind the huge concrete walls of the Aswan Dam. And when the papyrus disappeared from the banks of the Nile, so did the last Egyptian master of the art of building papyrus boats.

On camel and horseback, by car, train and boat, we traveled up and down the picturesque course of the Nile. We were guests on small weather-beaten fishing boats and freighters. We sat on gray, sun-baked decks, eating Arab bread and swallowing sour milk cheese scraped with our fingers from a lump on the deck, all in the hope of extracting information from the ragged river boatmen. They had

never worn shoes and seldom, if ever, spent a day on land, because
their wives, children, domestic animals and all their worldly goods
were on board. They had been born on board. The patched wooden
boat with a tent on top was the Nile fisherman's home, his village,
his world. We learned how people could be packed together and
manage all the usual activities of life on a deck area that scarcely
afforded elbow room; how to cook on an open fire in a clay oven
on an inflammable deck; how to keep provisions under a burning sun
on an open boat. We learned a lot. But if anyone learned anything
about papyrus it was the fishermen who learned it from us. They had
never seen a papyrus flower, not even the little bouquet which is
planted in honor of tourists in the fountain before the Cairo Museum. They had never seen the inside of a Pharaonic tomb. Never
the painting of a reed boat. Never heard from their forefathers
that any type of boat had even been used on the Nile other than
plank-built vessels like their own.

But the Nile was long. It stretched right across Egypt, across
the whole of the Sudan and on to its distant sources in Uganda
and Ethiopia. There, in the lakes at the source of the Nile, the
papyrus plant had survived and was said to thrive as well as on
distant Lake Chad.

Civilized peoples must have traveled far and wide during antiquity, because several of the old Pharaohs who ruled Egypt were
born in distant Ethiopia, where the Blue Nile has its source. But in
the dark Middle Ages the long course of the Nile had been completely forgotten. Its legendary sources were now assigned to the
mysterious and hidden "Mountains of the Moon." It was not until
about the days of Columbus that the people of Europe woke from
an enduring lethargy, and thus the upper reaches of the Nile were
rediscovered by Italian and Portuguese voyagers. Then, for the first
time, modern men learned that the Blue Nile flowed out of Lake
Tana, which lay high above sea level in Ethiopia's central massif.

By comparison with the Pharaohs we were handicapped. We
would have to travel right up to the source of the Nile for papyrus,
and the Nile is the world's second longest river. Papyrus grows in
Morocco and Sicily too, but not in sufficient quantities for boatbuilding. The Sudan was suffering from internal unrest and the
authorities were too suspicious of tourists to give a visa to someone

who claimed he had come simply to build a boat of papyrus. Ethiopia, on the other hand, was throwing open its gates to tourism. So we landed on a scheduled flight in the capital, Addis Ababa, ten thousand feet above sea level, in the heart of the proud old empire, on a green mountain plateau speckled with yellow wild flowers.

My companion on the trip, Tosi, was a freshly trained Italian cameraman, skinny, but head-and-shoulders taller than most people, so we had difficulty in folding him up in the little taxi-plane that was to carry us on to Lake Tana. His luggage consisted mainly of numerous bottles of anti-insect spray. Soon we were swooping like a swing-boat in the gusts of wind over Ethiopia's grass-covered hills. Below us lay the round grass huts of the country, scattered like beehives in picturesque groups on ridges and hilltops. The landscape itself was like an undulating golf course in every shade of green. Light green, dark green, reddish green. Green. Then it changed to mountain crags and deep, savage canyons with white torrents raging down them. Soon afterward we were swerving across the upper reaches of the Nile, reddish brown flood water forced between precipitous rock faces, describing wild loops in the depths of a winding gorge. The loops below us were nature's mighty hieroglyphs, recording the fact that since the morning of history this ancient river had been gouging its way down through the very mountain rocks, gnawing with the inexorable teeth of time, and spewing millions of tons of Ethiopia's mountain landscape, in the form of masticated mud and sludge, downhill onto the desert plains of the Sudan and Egypt. Since Pharaonic times the Nile had been feeding ceaselessly on Ethiopia's mountains and carrying their substance down to nourish the cornfields of Egypt. The deep scrolls of the Nile wrote history, from them came the fertile soil that gave rise to one of the most important shoots in early human culture.

Our meditations came to an abrupt end. Suddenly the plane plunged straight down for the cliffs, as the pilot pulled hard on the stick and a wing tip brushed the treetops on a ridge filling a loop of the gorge. The Nile disappeared; we could see only rocks and treetops. At the same moment we heard a deafening roar, thundering at us from every side and completely drowning the sound of the little engine. My stomach glued itself to my backbone and I gripped the seat and held my breath while the Nile gorge suddenly opened

before us in an infernal chaos. The whole huge river was torn
straight across and hung foaming like a mighty vertical wall before
our windshield. Turbulent masses of water surged over the cliffs in
front, to the sides, above, below; rushing vertically, horizontally,
seething white, thundering, smoking. The sun vanished behind precipices. Then the pilot pulled on his stick once again and we clutched
our seats while the elevators, helped by a powerful current of air,
thrust us upward and we flew into a glorious rainbow painted against
blue sky. We skimmed elegantly over the edge of the frothing witch's
caldron where smooth masses of water streamed toward us, collapsed
and fell vertically into the depths behind. As if at the touch of a
wand the Nile was horizontal under our wings again, but one floor
higher, and in a completely new version, sluggish, muddy and silent,
high up on an open plateau without a sign of a canyon or rock walls.
We were on the roof of the world, among rolling hills covered with
tropical evergreens, and between the greenery the sun twinkled in
calm water.

"Would you like another look?" asked the pilot and, without
waiting for an answer, he tipped the plane on its side and made
another circle back low over the same ridge, with the same exciting
sensation as we dived into the steaming gorge behind.

"Tissisat Falls," observed the pilot when our ears were function-
ing again. "The full breadth of the Nile drops off the high plateau
here. Local tribes call the Nile Abbay and the waterfalls Tis Abbay:
'The Smoking Nile.'"

Turning our heads, we could see the reason for the name. Where
the broad river suddenly ceased to exist a fine spray rose from the
nether regions, borne on an air current high into the cloudless sky
like the smoke from a giant campfire.

Shortly afterward we landed at Bahar Dar, and soon we were
filming the same roaring chasm from the ground. This was the
dividing line between two worlds, or a world on two levels. We knew
that up here people were still paddling about in papyrus boats as
in the Pharaoh's days. It was here that we hoped to find sufficient
supplies of papyrus, because it was only a day's march from the
Tissisat Falls to the source of the Blue Nile, where it flowed out of
great Lake Tana. We had landed in the legendary Moon Mountains
of the Middle Ages.

When we reached the source of the river, night was approaching. There was Lake Tana, serene in silver and black, reflecting late evening clouds and silhouettes of hills and treetops. And there was a movement out in the bay, long shadows as of swimming creatures with curly tails glided silently to and fro over the strip of silver. In the shadow of the woods they were invisible, but they stood out sharply in silhouette when they slid into the silvery light. Six of them—six papyrus boats gliding aimlessly about where Lake Tana ran between two jungle spurs and slowly began to move in the form of the Nile on its first noiseless passage toward Tissisat Falls. In each boat sat one, two or three figures, each holding his thin pole by the middle and dipping the ends alternately on either side of the narrow craft, as one paddles a slender kayak. Perhaps they were fishing in the river inlet, perhaps they were relaxing at the end of the day by playing in the peaceful eddies that marked the source of the Nile. A little further on, a single papyrus boat was racing down white rapids, perilously near to the great falls, but the black figure on board deftly maneuvered his small craft out of the white ruffles of foam and returned toward the lake, man and boat hidden in the shadow of a calm shore.

The Mountains of the Moon. Mountains towering toward the moon. This was how the landscape must have looked to the medieval explorers climbing up from the Red Sea far below, or from the plains of Egypt. Lake Tana itself lies about six thousand feet above sea level and the mountains encircling it reach to a height of twelve thousand to fourteen thousand feet. Yet the area of water was so great that you could not see the far shore. The lake itself was the home of the black monks. They lived on luxuriant, jungle islands a long way out, and for centuries the papyrus boats had been their only link with the outside world. Even at a distance at the late hour one interesting observation could be made. While the papyrus boats on Lake Chad were sliced straight across behind and only rose in front into an elegantly curved prow, this type, which had survived at the Nile's own source, had kept the ancient Egyptian form. Both prow and stern curved up above the waterline and the stern was bent in the peculiar ancient Egyptian curl over the boat itself. This sight in the still twilight at the source of the Nile was like a vision down the river, down through the ages, into the peaceful dawn of history.

The last of the tropical sun sank behind distant treetops and the light dimmed slowly as in a theater. With the passing of the light the dark mountains and the lake were left timeless. The mild night breeze carried pleasant whiffs of spice and a soft breath of mystery, a breath from those islands where the calendar stood still and the Middle Ages survived, protected and cherished by monks who for countless generations had perpetuated the traditional way of life, the robes, the ritual and the faith that their pious predecessors had brought to the islands when the Middle Ages were everybody's property. Although huge jungle trees grew on their islands, the monks had never taken to building canoes or plank boats. Their predecessors had paddled the papyrus boat from antiquity into the Middle Ages and now they were calmly paddling it on into the nuclear age. We had come to learn from the monks, we wanted to profit by their experience of papyrus boats, and no one knew better how to find papyrus in sufficient quantities to meet our needs.

Who had been the monks' teachers? Not only papyrus boats and pharaohs were shared long ago by Egypt and Ethiopia at the two extremities of the Nile. The dawning Christianity had also found its way from Egypt to Ethiopia a thousand years before the long hibernation of the Middle Ages interrupted man's contact between the lowlands at the mouth of the Nile and the highlands at its source. As early as the year 330, several centuries before Christianity traveled north to Europe, the Coptic Christian faith had spread from Egypt to Ethiopia. The early Christians settled then in the old kingdom of Axum, far up on the high mountains of Ethiopia north of Lake Tana. Later many of them fled southward and out to the hidden islands on the great lakes Tana and Zwai to escape persecution for their faith. The black monks who hid on Lake Tana have now been there for seven hundred years and have recruited new generations by paddling youths from the mainland out to the islands in their papyrus boats.

To meet the monks and investigate the papyrus supply at the lake we had hired a rugged old iron boat with motor and with a papyrus boat in tow. Two large iron boats had been brought up to Lake Tana by an enterprising Italian, who used them to compete with all the papyrus boats that ferried corn from small wharfs on the shore to the two big market places north and south of the lake.

On the first island we came to, huge jungle trees grew right down to the water's edge and their roots formed palisades and networks far out into the water. We wound our way through these stems in the light papyrus boat and jumped ashore under the foliage. Behind the first tree trunks was a small path and there two motionless monks waited for us, as if we had come at their command. They were wrapped in ankle-length cloaks with open cowls; ther feet were bare, their faces dark brown, with black beards. They fingered the diamond-shaped Coptic crosses that hung on their chests and bowed silently, indicating with a graceful gesture the way up the hill to the shrine at the top. Here small papyrus boats were propped against the sunny wall and loose reeds lay gathered in dry bundles. The church itself stood at the highest point, looking like a larger edition of the monks' simple dwellings which were dotted about the slopes. All were circular, with walls of upright stakes and thick, conical straw roofs. Someone beat on a flat stone slab suspended as a gong, which emitted a deep, melodious sound. Several monks came slowly strolling. Many were proud and handsome, like most Ethiopians, with dark skin, sharp features, hooked noses and black pointed beards, but quite a few looked undernourished and listless. There were very young boys, men in their prime, and bowed ancients with flowing white beards. All were poverty-stricken, shrouded in simple cloaks, with bare feet or open sandals. They ate what their small plots of earth produced, and fish from the lake. They prayed, sang and meditated.

We felt welcome. Here we would surely obtain valuable information. Two old men wearing turbans pulled out their barrel-shaped skin drums, beat on them with their palms and sang, in low, cracked voices completely alien, ancient church music, which must have been passed down from the oldest Christian community of Ethiopia. So must their ecclesiastical forebears have sung when they came paddling over the lake on their first exodus from the kingdom of Axum.

The island was called Covran Gabriel and the angel Gabriel with drawn sword was the first to meet us when the monks took us into their straw-roofed church. He was painted giant-size, surrounded by a colorful array of biblical subjects that decorated every façade of a central shrine, a sort of altar that filled the nucleus of the church from floor to ceiling, leaving room only for a circular

passage round it. Doors led out in all directions. All the Coptic
churches on Lake Tana were similar. Here one could see the whole
history of the Bible transformed into a color cartoon, and the monks
confirmed what the charming, naïve style suggested: that the paintings were two or three hundred years old, some perhaps older still.
We saw Pharaoh in the process of drowning with his Egyptian army
in the Red Sea, only bright steel helmets and the Pharaonic army's
rifle barrels protruding above the surface of the water!

We were courteously invited to enter in our stockinged feet,
and came out again with several hundred hungry fleas that had been
fasting on the old church carpets. I got off lightly, but the photographer's violent antics showed that the vanguard had already advanced from his socks to his armpits and into his hair. He was in
full retreat for the boat, where to the monks' horror he performed a
not entirely discreet striptease, under the insect spray. By then I
had alread pumped the monks of the little they had to say about
the floating quality of papyrus. Despite the fact that a papyrus
boat was to these islanders what a horse or camel was to the Bedouin,
none of them had tested its floating capacity for longer than one
day at a time. They had always pulled the boat ashore after use, and
raised it on end to dry; otherwise it would have gone on absorbing
water. Water-logged papyrus did not sink, said the monks, but it lost
all its carrying capacity. The bigger the boat, the longer it would
float, but it was not worth building big boats, because they were
difficult to haul up to dry. So we were not much the wiser.

The next island we came to was called Narga. It was flat and
papyrus grew in its shallow coves, but this was needed by the monks
to renew their own boats at intervals. "Papyrus rots," they said.
"We must build new boats at least once a year, even if we dry
them after each trip." In an open archway on top of a moss-grown
stone tower sat a solitary monk who said nothing at all. Nor did he
move. The tower had been built by the Empress Mentuab 250
years ago. The monk had sat himself down forever a few years ago.
He had vowed to serve God by sitting motionless up there for the
rest of his life. His brother monks fed him and regarded him as a
living saint, silhouetted against the drifting clouds.

We hurried over to the neighboring island, which rose high
above the water with its wooded hills. This is the holiest of all the

islands on Lake Tana, Daga Stefano. The island is so holy that no woman, not even an empress, may set foot on it. The last to try was Ethiopia's mighty Empress Mentuab, who was courteously turned away when she arrived with her court in a large papyrus boat and tried to land, two and a half centuries ago. She was obliged to move on to Narga, where she built the temple and the towers.

From the lake, this sacred island was lushly beautiful. We glimpsed a grass roof with a cross between the treetops on the ridge. A ragged monk with severe elephantiasis of the scrotum stood guard at the island's one landing place, and a line of small papyrus boats, set on end, leaned against the trees behind him. Full of curiosity and anticipation we jumped onto the rocks and stepped ashore on the holy island. The monk allowed us to study the boats and did not stop us when we started up the broad mud track to the ridge. Giant jungle trees, straw huts, monks. Silent bows, muttered prayers, fingering of small crosses. Papyrus? They all pointed in the same direction across the great inland sea. There. There it grew in unlimited quantities. That was where they gathered it themselves. Floating capacity? Eight days. A fortnight. If it did not sink under the load it would rot and break up in the waves in less than two weeks. Papyrus must be kept dry. Hauled ashore. They, too, knew no more.

We were not allowed into the temple itself. It looked ramshackle, with oval walls of stone, bamboo and straw. But beside it stood a cavelike cabin, full of sacred relics. Two smiling monks invited us into darkness, to a sort of chamber of horrors. Piles of white human skulls, old crosses and the holy personal effects of dead prelates. The largest treasures were long coffins of glass covered with cloth. When the cloth was folded to one side the half light revealed the shrunken, emaciated mummies of four old Ethiopian emperors. They lay with wrinkled arms and hands folded on their breasts, to spend eternity on the holy island. Their funeral corteges had crossed stormy Lake Tana with these royal mummies on papyrus boats, just as the Pharaoh's mummies had been ferried in silent procession down the calm Nile for interment.

Back in the sunshine we startled all the monks by playing their own voices back to them on a little tape recorder. Now everyone wanted to speak. Everyone wanted to sing. Soon they were all arrayed on some wide stone steps, peacefully singing ancient Coptic hymns in chorus. I squatted in front of them, recording. Behind me stood the tall cameraman doubled over his film equipment. He suddenly let go a roar and an oath so mighty that the needle on the tape recorder flipped right over before it fell back and stopped at zero. The monks sat petrified, their mouths shut and eyes wide. Behind me I saw my tall friend performing a wild war dance. He had kicked over his tripod and was frantically hauling his shirt over his head. Off it went, then he grabbed for his trouser belt.

"Stop," I hissed, appalled—and I was really furious—"have you gone crazy?"

No use. The trousers fell to the ground in a frenzy while the gesticulating photographer clutched his bare rump with both hands.

"Wasp," he yelled. "Wasp in my trousers!"

It was not altogether easy to forgive the cameraman for our embarrassing retreat from Daga Stefano, even if he was suffering tortures and could not sit down when we were back in the boat. Nor were there many monks left to say good-by to when I turned toward the singers on the steps, but those who had stayed thanked us kindly for a little contribution offered, in gratitude for their information on papyrus and in propitiation for the scandal on their beach.

The visits to the monks had given us the uneasy impression that the most important point about building a papyrus boat was to make it so small that it could easily be pulled up to dry after a day's use. That was hardly an appropriate plan for an Atlantic crossing. We never saw the monks leaving a reed boat in the water for a minute unless it was in actual use. To make them easier to pull ashore, all the larger reed boats on Lake Tana were built in two parts, which could be carried to dry land separately: a thin, boat-shaped basket with curved prow and stern, and inside this sort of hull a thick flat, papyrus mattress, shaped to fill the hollow space. The reed boats of the Buduma Negroes on Lake Chad were generally bigger and far more robust. There was in fact one noteworthy difference: the monks on Lake Tana laid great emphasis on making the papyrus vessels light without altering their age-old external lines, while the Buduma on Lake Chad concentrated far more on carrying capacity and strength.

On the way to the opposite shore of Lake Tana we passed

some low, scrubby islets where half a dozen hippos lumbered out, ducked and reappeared all round us. The boat crew assured us that these animals hated papyrus boats and would overturn them if they had the chance, because it was from such boats that hippos had been harpooned since time immemorial. We pushed our papyrus boat out empty, but the swimming hippos simply popped their heads up inquisitively all round it, snorted, blew and stared curiously.

To the far southwest the shore line of Lake Tana scarcely rose above the level of the water, and here we finally found the big papyrus marshes. The boat's crew told us that this area was unsafe because of bandits. "Some call them freedom fighters," said Ali, the skipper of the motorboat. "Actually they are just common robbers and they leave you in peace as long as you take care to pay tribute." One of the worst had just been shot by the authorities, the men told us. He had held sway along the lake for twenty-three years and killed forty-nine men. They had no problems themselves, because Ali paid the tribute.

We reached a spot in the endless marshes where a muddy current oozed its way between the papyrus stems and moved out over the lake like a broad stroke of red-brown paint. This could only be the outlet of some stream. In fact it was a little tributary, its mouth well hidden by the thick reeds. Because it drains into Lake Tana, source of the Blue Nile, it has been called the Little Nile. Many varieties of wading birds sat peacefully in or between the tall reeds. Only shallow papyrus boats can enter the Little Nile, which is so shallow that it is normally not navigable for more than a few hundred yards by motorboat. But now the water level was abnormally high and we ran over five miles up the narrow red river, to a village of round straw-roofed huts. This was the home of the Abaydar tribe, and men and women stood close-packed along the bank to stare at the metal boat. Ali explained that only two iron boats existed on Lake Tana. Both belonged to his Italian boss and neither had made the trip up the river before.

Several small papyrus boats were tilted down from the hut walls and part paddled, part punted out to us. The smallest were simply supports for swimmers, in the familiar elephant tusk shape, and we learned that they were called *koba*. They were made and used in exactly the same way as in Central Africa, in South America

15. *World expert* on ancient Egyptian boat illustrations, Björn Landström of Sweden, drawing an Egyptian papyrus ship for the boatbuilders Omar, Mussa and Abdullah from Chad, while the author explains the principle of the straddled mast to them. (Above)

16. *Papyrus reed* from the source of the Nile is examined by the papyrus boatbuilders from Chad. (Below)

17. *Behind the Giza pyramids* the Buduma Africans from Chad begin to build a papyrus boat, with Landström and the author looking on. (Above)

18. *The ancient Egyptian boatbuilder's art* comes home again. The boatbuilders from Chad train Egyptian helpers in an art their forefathers forgot when the papyrus reed died out in Egypt. (Below)

19 and 20. *Mussa and Omar* boatbuilding with fingers and teeth. (Above)

21. *Abdullah* helped us to persuade his compatriots to give the boat a curved stern in the Egyptian style. This added section was to prove the boat's weak point. (Below)

22. *A thick rope cable* was fixed in the ancient Egyptian manner right around the gunwale of the finished papyrus boat for fastening the mast stays.

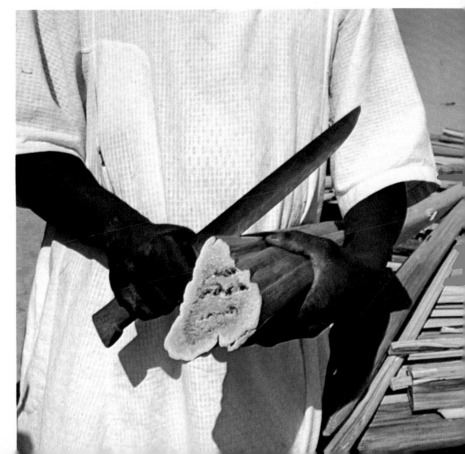

23. *Reluctant* inland Africans add more papyrus to the stern they did not want, while the author holds the fateful bowstring, which was later removed. (Above)

24. *The "paper boat"* on the desert sand was guarded night and day; one cigarette end could have sent the papyrus up in flames. (Below)

25 and 26. *Five hundred Egyptians* from the Cairo Institute of Gymnastics drag the papyrus ship from the buildingsite. (*Photo:* UPI, London) The building team, inset. Standing, from left to right, Muhamed, Mussa, the author, Abdullah, Omar, Corio; seated, second from left, Yuri; lying, Carlo.

27–33. *Seven men from seven nations.* From the top: Thor Heyerdahl, Norway, leader of the expedition. (*Photo:* Gösta Glase, Stockholm) (Left) Carlo Mauri, Italy, film photographer. (Right) Santiago Genoves, Mexico, quartermaster. (Left) Norman Baker, U.S.A., navigator. (Right) Georges Sourial, Egypt, underwater expert. (Left) Yuri Senkevitch, Russia, ship's doctor. (Right) Abdullah Djibrine, Chad, papyrus expert.

and on Easter Island. A slightly larger edition, on which a single person could sit, was called a *marotcha*, while the usual two-part boat, designed for two or more paddlers, was a *tanqua*. The largest *tanqua* we saw had nine men on board, but we heard that there were many which carried two or three tons of corn across Lake Tana. Occasionally a *tanqua* had been blown adrift and lain in the water for more than a week before the crew got it to shore again with the corn, which had then begun to sprout. The Abaydar people believed, as the monks did, that after two weeks a *tanqua* would be completely waterlogged and sink beneath the waves. The hollow hull of the *tanqua* was so thin that the reed raft undulated like a worm on the swell.

My suspicion was confirmed: Although the elegant shape with the up-curved stern of the Lake Tana *tanqua* came closest to the lines of the ancient Egyptian vessel, it lacked the rigidity and strength that characterized the *kaday* on Lake Chad.

Since papyrus and papyrus boatbuilders had vanished from modern Egypt, my best procedure would appear to be to bring papyrus from Lake Tana and boatbuilders from Lake Chad, while using the ancient Egyptian wall paintings as "blueprints" for the vessel I was to build.

Not too far from the village, I stepped ashore in an area that seemed totally devoid of people. Suddenly, a strangely majestic Ethiopian arose from the thicket of reeds along the riverbank. He was wearing a sleeveless cloak and carrying a long spear over his shoulder, like a fishing rod. With his proud bearing, pointed black beard, and sharp profile, he was not unlike Emperor Haile Selassie. His little son proved equally picturesque when he, too, emerged from the reeds, carrying a wicker fish basket on a pole over his shoulder. Ignorant of their language, I grabbed them in a friendly manner and maneuvered them into a suitable position as foreground for a series of papyrus pictures by the photographer. But, when I handed the man a small coin in thanks and prepared to jump back into the boat, he gave me a slyly condescending smile and politely indicated that he wanted to accompany us. And thus, our photo model and his son joined our little expedition down the river and out through the vast reed marshes to the lake. Once there, they both thanked us politely and were about to step ashore when Ali very anxiously got me to take out my wallet from my hip pocket. He thereupon brazenly withdrew an Ethiopian bank note equivalent to a week's wages and handed it to the bearded man, who smiled modestly and bowed elegantly before vanishing into the reeds with his son as abruptly as they had appeared.

"That was the biggest bandit along this shore," explained Ali, relieved. "I always give him something to keep him happy."

That night a cloudburst descended on us. We tied the boat to a tree on the bank and pulled our little papyrus *tanqua* over our heads as a roof. The thunder crashed as it can only crash when the clouds lie low over open water, and the deafening noise, accompanied by blinding flashes of lightning, showed that the storm was right over our heads. The lightning struck both lake and forest. A flash and a crash together, we felt the blast, and a great jungle tree splintered on the shore close to our mooring. The rain spurted in like jets from distant garden hoses. All our possessions were floating around in the boat with the day's catch of fish. The cameraman slept. In this weather there was no need for him to lie in wait with the insect spray.

In the deep south of Ethiopia the Rift Valley runs north and south between two mountain ranges in the direction of Kenya. The geologists have shown that this valley, parallel to the Red Sea, was produced by Africa's slow westward shift over many millions of years. A series of large lakes lies like a string of beads down this wide mountain valley. In one of them, Lake Zwai, papyrus boats are built. There is an excellent highway down the valley, and the other lakes are popular resorts for weekend tourists from the capital, Addis Ababa. They come here to hunt, fish and swim. But they do not come to Lake Zwai, the most beautiful of them all. For one thing, no road leads to this lake. But most important, papyrus grows there, and this plant harbors the snail that is host to the dreaded bilharzia worm. No swimmer, therefore, can set foot in this beautiful lake.

Two Swedes in Addis Ababa were able to tell us about this lake and its inhabited islands. One had read about the islanders because he was an ethnologist; the other had been on its shores himself because he made his living in Ethiopia as a birdcatcher. With provisions and camping equipment in a hired Jeep, we left our base

in the capital and raced off on first-class, good, less good and, ultimately, appalling roads. We found lodging for the night at a hos-
pitable Swedish mission-station high up in the hills east of Rift
Valley. With a resourceful Ethiopian teacher, Aseffa, as interpreter
and a young Galla Negro who "knew the way," we set off in the
Jeep next morning for Lake Zwai. A deep gully with a foaming
torrent barred all access to the vast plains leading to the lake, and
to get across this barrier we first had to struggle fifteen miles south
on a swampy mud road under construction. There we left the road,
crossed an incredible bridge of boulders and slabs and continued
thirty miles northwest, without road or wheel track. We followed
narrow bridle paths, animal trails and open glades between the
scattered trees, now this way, now that, and we constantly had to get
out and walk in front of the Jeep to find a passage. Our "guide" sat
stolidly without opening his mouth, and the few times when he did
point, he led us astray. There were no wild animals but many old
burial mounds, and often we saw Galla Negroes hunting in the
woods, spear on shoulder and dog at heel. One boy turned and raised
his spear in alarm when we drove the Jeep toward him to ask the
way, then ran off as fast as he could and disappeared among the
sparse acacia trees.

It was late afternoon when we reached a high rocky headland
projecting into Lake Zwai which afforded a splendid view of the
eastern shore and two of the distant islands. Up here were a tiny
wooden hut and a large tent, the Swedish mission clinic. The nurse
who ran the clinic alone was on holiday in Sweden, but a watchman
of the Galla tribe lived with his family in a grass hut nearby and
allowed us to use the tent. On either side we could see reed or
marshes stretching north and south from the foot of the escarpment,
and far below us the evening sun shone on a yellow dot that seemed
to be moving across the lake. It was a little papyrus boat slowly
making its way home to the nearest island.

Again the day dimmed as fast as on a stage, the way it always
does only eight degrees from the equator. Then the play began. Monkeys chattered in the trees round about. Hippos lumbered ashore and
went champing into the native maize fields. The howls and moans of
growing numbers of hyenas came nearer and nearer. Out on the
lake, far, far away we could hear drums. From the tent we could see

the light of campfires on the islands. Aseffa said the Copts were celebrating the prelude to their great Maskal feast. I was just stealing
out into the dark to watch the panorama when I ran straight into
two black and almost invisible figures with spears, standing right in
front of the tent door. It was the caretaker from the grass hut with a
relative who asked if we would like to see the hyenas. The men had
found their mule dead, and now the hyenas were busy eating their
fill. We stole into the thicket. From somewhere ahead of us came
heart-rending screams, yelps, snarls and barks. Around us in the
scrub on every side watchful hyena eyes shone like parking lights.
When we switched on the flashlight everything disappeared, inaudibly
and invisibly, as at the touch of a wand. Only the mule lay there,
bloody and torn. We switched off again and waited. Then all the
eyes lighted up again, pair by pair, on every side, and the beasts
howled, moaned and gnawed. After a while we heard crackling among
the bushes and boughs, and we switched the light on again. Only
half the mule was left; it had been divided into two and the whole
hindquarters had disappeared without trace. We hunted everywhere
in the bushes, which were covered with trails of blood, but half the
body and both back legs had vanished forever in the night.

Next morning we clambered down to the papyrus lake. Part of
the maize field at the foot of the cliff had been trampled by a single
hippo which had eaten hundreds of corncobs during the night. The
neighbor was busy chasing away monkeys intent on taking over the
leavings. Far out on the surface of the water we could see small
papyrus boats approaching from the islands. Where we were waiting,
a passage had been cleared through the reeds to a narrow landing place
on the quaking marshy bank, for here a narrow footpath led down
to the lake. We waited with ax and rope and two branches that
we had chopped off in readiness, each as thick as a man's arm and
twice his height. We had made a plan and now we were only waiting
for the papyrus boats to land.

Here they were. They were unlike those of the monks on Lake
Tana, and more like the boats of Lake Chad, with shorn-off stern and
just the prow curved up into a point. But they were small. There
was room for only one man on each.

The first two to arrive had come from the islands to barter with
the Gallas on land. One had grayish brown corn beer in a clay jar

and in the dried shell of a bottle gourd. The other had freshly caught fish. Soon the third came in too and began to drag his papyrus boat ashore. We stopped them. We offered to trade and soon we had hired the three small boats. We placed them side by side and lashed them together with our rope, reinforced by the two solid branches which we bound crosswise. This was our plan of campaign. We knew this was the only way of getting out to the islands. For out there lived the Laki people, the only people who had boats of any type on Lake Zwai, and by ancient custom they made them so small that no great number of invaders could use them to force an entry to their age-old retreat on the islands.

The Laki people were not related to the Negroid Galla, who lived all round the shores of the lake. The Galla were typical Africans who lived exclusively by agriculture and cattle farming. Their feet were solidly planted in the soil and they never attempted to build boats or rafts to venture out on the water. But the Laki people based their entire existence on papyrus boats. They cultivated the soil, but were also fishermen and traders. Despite their black skins, the Laki people were not at all Negroid. Like most Ethiopians, they had sharp, fine features, with profiles reminiscent of peoples in the Bible lands. Like the monks on Lake Tana in the north, they had migrated from the area near the source of the Nile. And like them they had also brought along the art of building papyrus boats when they fled into isolation on remote islands. As late as 1520–35 they had set out on their long journey to the Rift Valley, where they settled on the islands in Lake Zwai with all their religious treasures and ancient Coptic manuscripts. The manuscripts were said to be still out there, because, despite over four centuries of hostility with the Galla people on the shore, none of these landlubbers had ever succeeded in invading the islands. In recent years the enmity had died out, barter had gained the upper hand, and a few Laki families had moved to the mainland; but true to tradition not a single boat was built on the lake even now that could carry more than one passenger in addition to the oarsman. And there was so little room for the one poor passenger on the slender bundle of reeds that it would overturn unless he sat as still as a mouse, balancing either with his legs straight forward or straddling the bundles with water up to his knees.

So it was with pride that we regarded our own finished work, a stable raft of three Laki vessels lashed together. We collected the equipment and were about to board and set off for those alluring islands when we saw that one Laki tribesman was silently occupied in untying the knots and removing his own boat. He explained to Aseffa that he had come in from the island to collect wood for the Maskal fire, but now he had remembered that there was better wood somewhere else. A polite salutation and he hurried off with his vital third of our little raft.

It was late in the afternoon before we succeeded in hailing another Laki who was paddling along the shore and casting his net. There was a sparkle of leaping silver almost every time he hauled in the net. We bought the catch, twenty-one delicate *tulumu* fish, grilled one each over live embers and made the fisherman a present of the rest. The trade included hire of the boat and this time we made haste to shove off as soon as the raft was ready. It floated admirably with the two of us as well as the film equipment perched on a tripod; so Aseffa crept gingerly aboard to come with us as interpreter.

Around us the banks were covered with short rushes, but we could see no papyrus. The water was choppy and we paddled as fast we could until the mainland was far away and the green hills of the nearest island rose above us. We had come so close that we could clearly see picturesque round straw huts scattered among the foliage of large trees on the slopes. Then a tiny boat appeared from behind a headland and steered resolutely toward us. We were amazed to see a grave, dignified man in a sort of khaki uniform, paddling along astride the papyrus, with his legs deep in the water. He flipped the boat round and parked neatly straight in front of our prow. Through Aseffa we were given to understand that the man claimed to be some kind of sheriff or chief of this island, which was called Tadecha, and that he demanded to see our papers before allowing us to land. With the brisk official perched on a papyrus bundle, his behind wet and his uniform trousers up to the knees in water, the effect of the ceremony was undeniably comic. Aseffa asked if I had any papers; anything at all would do. I pulled out of my shirt pocket a letter from the Norwegian Foreign Minister, in French, one intended for use in the Chad Republic. Aseffa did not know a word of French, but standing on our raft he read aloud and with feeling a lengthy tirade in Galla of which I understood only the name of the Emperor Haile

Selassie, which recurred constantly. What Aseffa had concocted only
he and the sheriff knew, but the stern official raised his hand to his
head in a confused sort of salute, put his precarious craft into reverse
and disappeared again toward the headland from which he had come,
while we made for the nearest inlet in the grass-covered island.

It was a remarkably beautiful island, lush green, with rolling
meadows and neat fields of maize. Naked boys were fishing in the
inlet, women in home-woven garments made their way down to
the landing place with jars on their heads, a man was walking up the
slope with his slender papyrus boat on his shoulder, while chickens
and a medley of colorful wild birds were fluttering everywhere. At the
top of the ridge a cluster of sugar-loaf huts formed an open and
orderly little village. They were covered with high conical straw roofs
and the low walls were built in rings of stone and half-timber, daubed
with clay and painted in simple patterns. Against most of the huts at
least one, and often two or three snub-nosed reed boats had been
propped to dry in the sun. We were beckoned in by a handsome and
polite couple who offered us a bowl of freshly brewed *aidar,* or maize
beer. The man's name was Dagaga and the woman's Helu. The
hut had a trodden clay floor, neat and clean, with a standing loom
and enormous sealed ceramic jars, contents unknown. Bottle-gourd
vessels and a few home-made tools hung from the crooked beams on
the walls; the bed was of skins and the pillow the same little curved
wooden neck rest that was used in ancient Egypt. Dagaga and Helu
were carefree; they had a minimum of possessions but a maximum
of time in which to enjoy them. No refrigerator, but no bills either.
No car, but no rush either. What they lacked we would have missed,
but not they. What they had was what they needed and what we
strive to limit ourselves to when our vacations from the office let us.
When, sometime in the near future, the modern world reaches them
they will learn much from us and we nothing from them, but that is
tragedy for both sides, for both sides assume that we who have the
most are wisest, noblest, happiest. Are we?

I sat philosophizing in the shade inside the doorway while beautiful Helu of the intelligent eyes graciously served her unknown
guests. Dark-skinned, with sharp profile and narrow lips, there was
something noble about her bearing. Dagaga, with a baby goat in
his arms, was obviously delighted to be able to offer beer and hot

roasted maize. It tasted extraordinarily good. The view from the door, looking toward the green hills, was splendid. I would have like to lie there on the skins enjoying the play of colors on the lake as the sun went down and the last reed boats came home. Then I saw a flash on the horizon and heard a faint rumble. Black clouds were gathering. The film equipment! And all our things lying loose in the tent on the other side! If we were to reach the other shore before the storm broke we would have to hurry. The sun was low. Our wristwatches frightened us. There were no clocks in the house we were leaving; time was not in short supply and need not be measured there. We ran in long strides down the hill and shoved off in our three-part papyrus raft. Soon the island was slipping away behind us, its outlines blurred in the twilight. The last we glimpsed of it before the first drops obscured all vision were some subdued points of light high up on the ridge. Our Laki friends were sitting safe in their warm huts, calmly lighting the wicks in the bowls of their oil lamps.

The day after that was the Coptic Maskal feast, the most important day of the year, when all Christian Ethiopians celebrated what they called "the discovery of the True Cross." From our outcrop we could see great fires scattered over the islands. We had thought of going out again to ask the Laki people a few more questions about their experience of papyrus boats, but we were disappointed. Not a single Laki showed himself on the lake in a reed boat that day, and next day we saw only one or two fishing boats keeping their distance well out in the middle of the lake. Perhaps it was the sheriff who had hit on this method of avoiding a repeat visit.

We loaded the Jeep and set off for home. The return journey was simple. Even though it had been pouring rain, we could still see our own tracks. We had already left most of the plain behind us when we saw another Jeep through the trees. It was following our old track, but coming toward us. The Jeep was full of dark Ethiopians, with one sturdily built giant half a head taller than the others. We all climbed out and shook hands. The big man's elegant embroidered tunic was covered down to his chest by a bushy white beard and a large Coptic cross dangled against his stomach. Aseffa kissed the cross and explained that this amiable giant was the highest prelate of the Ethiopian church, Bishop Luke. Now he was on his way to Lake Zwai to

visit his fellow believers, the Coptic Laki people. He explained gen-
ially that he had a special mode of transport on the lake. He would
receive us on Devra Zion, the most important of the islands, if we returned the following week. We should approach the lake from the
very opposite side of the Rift Valley where there was a little leper
station with a small plastic boat.

Back to distant Addis Ababa. A few days later, the Jeep loaded
with new equipment, we were on the southbound tourist road that
runs along the west side of the Rift Valley. From here it was an easier
matter to reach Lake Zwai, but this was the wrong side, where there
was neither papyrus nor islands. The little leper station was closed,
the windows shuttered. Sitting on the steps was a Galla tribesman,
elephantiasis swelling one leg, who told us that the plastic boat was
in Addis Ababa for repair. There were no other boats on Lake Zwai,
he said, apart from small papyrus *yevella*, which only the Laki people
on the islands possessed.

We tried the Jeep northward along the shore. Impassable.
Southward we got a little way along a grass-grown path as far as a
small convent school. Also closed and deserted. Further passage was
blocked by a deep river, turning into fierce rapids. A sleepy monk sat
swaddled on the grassy bank, gazing at a hippopotamus that was
dozing with half its head above water in the shade of the hanging foliage of giant trees on the other side.

Boat? There was none. No one wanted to make boats on this
bank, where so many hippos had been wounded by hunters in reed
boats. A European and several Laki people had been drowned by
hippos the year before. Jeep track? There were none. Not on this
side of the lake.

Back to the main road. Further south along the tourist route.
Lake Langana appeared in an open landscape, stone and gravel, no
islands, no papyrus, no bilharzia—swimming pools, tourist hotels,
beer and pop. A sign boasted a plastic boat. We had come to hire it
and take it to Lake Zwai. So sorry. It, too, was in Addis Ababa for
repair. Back along the main road. Night and tropical cloudbursts. In
the village of Adamitullu we found lodgings. A Galla woman had a
boarded stall where she sold beer and Ethiopian pancakes filled with
peppery spices and meat stuffing. In the back yard were two small
bedrooms of planks and corrugated iron, a deep hole in the ground

for common use, and a barrel of water and an empty tin for anyone who also wanted to wash.

The cameraman opened his door a crack and inserted one arm and a large spray can of Flit. When he reopened the door he swept out a whole museum collection of lifeless insects. He slept on top of the bedclothes, Flit can in hand. For myself I found a Galla whom I supplied with a flashlight to guard the Jeep and, after clearing the room of everything except the bare iron posts of the metal bed, I lit a fire on the floor with our hostess's incense wood. It smoldered all night and sent sweet-smelling clouds of smoke and all six-legged creatures out of the window opening. Shortly after going to bed, I heard an oath and uproar from the next room. The cameraman rushed through the door and disappeared into the night. Next morning he was lying, curled up and completely consumed by bed bugs, on top of the load in the Jeep. Even there he had not slept a wink, he said, because a strange Negro had kept a light shining in his face all night. My guard reported proudly that it was he—he had taken good care that the tall fellow who had left his bed in the middle of the night had no chance to steal from the Jeep.

The guard was a find. His tribe happened to live near the southern end of the lake and he assured us that it was easy to get there, if he could come too. With guide and interpreter we lurched through groves of trees and crossed some sparsely grown wasteland, until we reached the southern continuation of the fierce stream that had stopped us the day before. Some crooked trunks, covered with stone and earth, had been laid as a cattle bridge over the torrent and here, inch by inch, we eased the Jeep across. Then we followed bridle paths, creek beds, clearings in the woods and clayey maize fields from one idyllic Galla village to another. For miles at a time we were followed by racing village children, who beamingly tore a passageway for us through all sorts of fences and filled the deepest gullies with stones and branches. The scenery was varied and beautiful, the bird life as exotic as in a zoo. The Galla tribes south of Zwai live their own lives in their own world, asking for nothing, getting nothing, and needing nothing. Their lives are completely undisturbed, untrammeled, unimproved and unspoiled. These were people who lived close to the earth and not one of them had been tempted to build a boat on the beach.

By the afternoon we had come so far that the largest Laki island was just opposite us. Its green hills were higher than any of the crests along the mainland coast. Soon only a broad sound separated us from Devra Zion, where Bishop Luke was supposed to be. We reached a Galla village on an open plateau. No one had a boat, but they all knew that Bishop Luke was out on the island now. He had been picked up in an extra large *obolu*, the Laki people's name for a papyrus boat which had been specially widened by lashing a shorter bundle of reeds on either side. What we had seen until now were simply common craft, so narrow that they overturned at the slightest careless move. In the Laki tongue they were called *shafat*, but the Galla people called them *yevella*.

We thanked them for the information and drove down a steep, twisting path to the shore, where we hooted until an inquisitive Laki came paddling across the sound in his little *shafat*. It was less than two miles from the spit of land to the island. We sent the man back to report that we had an invitation from Bishop Luke and must have an *obolu*. Not long afterward the cameraman and the interpreter were sitting with a Laki paddler on the bishop's wide papyrus boat. I myself rode pillion on an ordinary *shafat*, back to back with a Laki who kept the reed boat balanced with his paddle and taught me to sit with my knees straight out and my back pressed to his, in order not to overturn. The camera equipment was carried by a third Laki on his own *shafat*.

The papyrus on our *shafat* was carelessly bundled together with strips of bark that proved to be old and half rotten. About midway, I tried to support myself on the papyrus with my hands in order to raise my seat a little, since it seemed to have sunk uncomfortably low in the bilharzia-ridden water. Two of the bark lashings burst and at once the whole *shafat* was in the process of breaking up. The rowers on all three boats showed serious alarm, roaring incomprehensible orders to us and to each other in Laki and paddling in close formation in case we disintegrated altogether. We tried to keep our reeds together with arms and feet. It was easy to realize that if we sank it would be futile to try to board the other boats, which would overturn at once.

The island that had been so near suddenly seemed infinitely far away and I sat stock-still, hanging onto both sides of the papyrus bundle to prevent more of the bark strips from splitting. I could feel the seat of my trousers sinking steadily deeper into the lukewarm ripples, the happy hunting grounds of the insidious worms. Perhaps they were already on their way through the thin khaki trousers. Seldom have twenty minutes seemed so long.

The days of our *shafat* were over when we dragged the gaping papyrus wreck up on the grass on the far bank, but we were now ashore on Devra Zion and it was well worth the discomfort. From the reed belt, grassland stretched toward the hills like an open park, with great, ancient trees. Further in, weathered rocks rose like the carved pillars and terraces of a ruined castle, overgrown with flowering evergreens, creepers, cactus and strange trees. We trotted and walked at a brisk pace along the almost imperceptible rock path, seeing no signs of life other than monkeys and gaudy birds. We had circled a good deal of the south side of the island without seeing cultivated fields, huts or men, when we found ourselves standing on the edge of a cliff, looking down into a deep horseshoe-shaped valley. The whole area down there was grass-green marshland, covered with papyrus and other reeds, and teeming with tall wading birds and long-tailed monkeys.

On a dry sandbank by the lakeshore we saw Bishop Luke, leading a score of Lakis in the building of an extraordinary house. As we approached, it looked like a big two-story bird cage built of fresh-cut branches. The bishop, who greeted us with a mixture of heartiness and astonishment, explained that when the sticks and branches were covered with clay this would be a house where the Laki people could receive visitors from the mainland in the future. We stared at the marshland of this uninhabited and desolate valley. Steam rose from a hot spring that ran out into the lake a little farther off.

The bishop was obviously in a hurry to open his own food parcel, and to our embarrassment he insisted that we alone were to eat the best of the biscuits and fruit he had brought for himself. At the same time, he explained with ill-concealed anxiety that as soon as we had eaten we must start back again, because there was great danger from the hippos on the lake at night. We explained that we would have liked to sleep on the island. That was completely impossible, the bishop assured us, and now he became earnestly, though politely, intent on getting rid of us.

The parchment books? Could we see them?

The bishop hastily consulted a tall, thin man with intelligent eyes, a beak of a nose and a pointed beard. They nodded. But we would have to follow the tall man at the double, up to the temple and straight down again to the boats. Hasty but hearty good-bys were said. Our new long-legged guide was introduced as Bru Machinjo, chieftain of all the Laki people, who numbered some twenty-five hundred individuals on the five islands in Lake Zwai. With chieftain Bru in front and a train of Laki men behind, we trotted as long as we had breath up the hillside among boulders and cactus-like trees and arrived utterly exhausted, having staggered in single file for the last mile, at the island's highest peak. The landscape opened out into a magnificent view over the lake, the islands, the mainland shores and distant mountains. Below us, some one thousand feet above the level of the lake, we saw the round straw roofs of a village built in steps down the hillside. Above us lay a very small, square wooden hut, painted blue and green. Bru told us that this was the new monastery, where Bishop Luke lived during his visits. We were admitted by a monk and on a rough wooden shelf in the empty room lay a great heap of ancient manuscripts and books made of parchment, yellow with age, with and without bindings, helter-skelter, without order or system. Bru explained proudly that the Laki people's forefathers had carried them on their long migration from the north, many centuries ago. I rummaged at random in the heap and pulled out the largest book. The pages were nearly two feet tall, of treated goatskin, magnificently illuminated with pictures of the ancient fathers of the church, painted with colored cloaks and peculiar tiny feet. The text alone was a work of art: incomprehensible Ethiopian script, painted with delicate scrolls and decorations in black and red. Any library in the world would have locked such a work behind glass as an irreplaceable treasure.

The monk pulled out two big antique silver dishes with the Apostles engraved on the inside, which had also been carried on the migration. Here we were interrupted by exhortations to get down to the landing stage, for the sun was low on the horizon. We wanted to stay the night and delayed deliberately. We suggested sending a *shafat* over to the Jeep for food and sleeping bags. Impossible. No Laki would venture out again in the darkness. We must sleep on the mainland with the Galla people and come out again the next day.

Now I was really curious. What was going on out here, if no stranger except Bishop Luke was allowed to sleep on the island? It was twilight. I muttered something to the cameraman, and in the confusion as everyone scattered and ran down the hill I hid behind a stone slab. There I sat while the whole company ran on down the terraces and disappeared. Silence fell. Only the wind murmured in the treetops. I sat alone, feeling as if I were sitting on the roof of Africa. Far below I caught a glimpse of our two reed boats paddling away from the island while shadows spread over the distant lowlands. The huge lake swallowed the sun and the surface of the water glowed for a time like hot metal before it cooled, turning dark blue and then black, while darkness rolled on from the shore, up over the endless woods, over hill, over dale, in an unbroken wave to the world's end. Africa by night. I could no longer see the round straw roofs of the village below me. I could see nothing. I listened to an extraordinary warbling yodel mingled with the sounds of a religious choir some- where down in the village. It was too dark to move. I had to sit and absorb impressions with ears and nose. Bats. Rustling in the grass. Suddenly I felt a hand on my shoulder. It was Chief Bru, who silently took me by the arm and made a signal for me to follow him. He held me in a friendly grip and led me like a blind man down an in- visible path between boulders and rock terraces. We did not speak, for we had no common language. Since the interpreter had gone back across the sound there was no human being on the whole island with whom I could exchange a single word. The chieftain knew every step of the way and saw to it that I came down unscathed.

We passed the first beehive huts and continued down a few more terraces to an assembly hut that was larger than the others. Light shone from the low doorway, and it was from there that the peculiar singing had come. Bru drew me in among the elders of the tribe, who sat on low, carved stools and wood blocks near the door. An oil wick was burning in a bowl, throwing huge flickering shadows of many men on the round, clay-daubed walls. Farther in stood a row of young women in long white garments, bowing rhythmically and clapping their hands, while one yodeled and the others sang, monotonously and without accompaniment. In the half light behind the white-clad

nymphs I glimpsed some round jars, so large that each could easily
have held two grown men. A clay oven was smoldering, but there
was no smoke under the high roof, which was supported by a pole
with branches like the spokes of an umbrella. Together with the most
aged of them all, a real Moses with a long white beard, Bru and I
were placed inside the semicircle of men on elegantly carved stools,
and a little table covered with a cone-shaped wicker lid was brought to
us in the ancient Ethiopian manner. Under the cover lay enormous
wat, a staple food resembling pancakes as thick as foam rubber, in
two layers, spread with morsels of fried fish. A cocoa-colored powder,
which made pepper taste like candy, lay in a heap in the middle. In
this you were supposed to dip the pieces you had torn off. Everyone
was invited to wash their hands before we attacked the common
meal with our fingers, and Bru spent his time tearing off the best
pieces to place before his unknown guest. In a flash my hosts had
turned a mute stowaway into a guest of honor. While the chorus of
women swayed and kept up their strange incessant psalm-singing, a
silent man went round filling all the mugs with sweet maize beer and
finally with a very powerful sugar brandy. As the tongues of most of
the men were loosened they engaged one another in an exchange of
solemn monologues in Laki. I myself sat dumb as a post until I remembered the tape-recorder slung over my shoulder.

At first there was sheer consternation, because the women's choir
began to yodel full voice while the women themselves were enjoying
a break, and the men choked because they heard themselves speaking
while they were actually drinking. The evening was saved, the tape-
recorder was my ventriloquist, conversing with everyone in Laki and
bursting into shouts of laughter as if it understood all the jokes and
everything that was being sung and said in the meeting hut.

In the end it was the eldest who rose, and remained standing
when he felt the time had come to stop. All the women walked out
first in line, yodeling in chorus with a warbling note like a night owl's
as they left us, and from the darkness the owl sounds came back to
us individually until the women had all disappeared into their respec-
tive huts. The chief took me by the arm and led me to his own
house, which was exactly like the round assembly hut, but smaller.
By the faint light of the oil lamp I glimpsed the outline of someone
packing up bundles of clothes and carrying them out so that I could

make use of the hut's one bed. It was useless to refuse. Bru sat his guest down on the bed, which was of the same type as the ancient Egyptian Pharaoh's beds in Cairo Museum: a wooden frame on legs, holding an open net of interwoven strips of leather. Bru and his family moved out their own mats and headrests to lie on the floor in another hut, spreading clean skins and a home-woven cover on their own bed and signaling to me to lie down. I pulled off my long jungle boots while the chieftain sat at the bedside and directed his son to bring a basin and wash my feet. When they were thoroughly washed and dried, the boy bowed deeply and kissed my toes before he and the others were told to leave the hut. Here on Devra Zion the Bible story lived on in reality.

Fully clothed, but with clean, bare feet, I rolled up in the bed where I lay wondering why Bru and his wife were still muttering as its foot. They were consulting together irresolutely in hushed voices and kept looking at their guest in the bed, as though uncertain if I were all right or if there were anything else to be done. Then I saw that they were not alone. At the other side of the bed-end a vague figure was standing in the darkness. The oil wick was burning so low behind the roof pole that its outlines were barely visible. It was a young woman. She turned almost imperceptibly and as the soft light shone behind her profile I could see that she was beautiful. She must be one of Bru's own daughters. All three stood there for a long time, then the parents bowed and disappeared through the doorway. The lamp shed scarcely any light now and for a while I was uncertain whether the figure at the foot of the bed was still there or not. But then I saw her silhouette again. There she stood, almost without stirring. What now? Here I was in the chieftain's bed, his son had washed my feet and now his daughter was standing like a guardian angel at the bedside. It was then that I heard the cameraman's voice far away in the silence of the night. He was calling my name. I did not answer, in order not to break the spell. But the cameraman would not give up. The shouts came steadily closer, until he was standing in the doorway with Bru and his wife. He had grown anxious about me, he said, and he and the interpreter had paddled back alone to the island in the bishop's *obolu*. They, too, were served now with maize beer and fish-covered *wat*, and skins were laid on the floor for the newcomers.

Next day we were still the chieftain's guests and, with the interpreter to help, we found out everything we wanted to know. The papyrus in Lake Zwai grew along such an inaccessible coast that it would not be feasible to transport it from this lake in large quantities. The marshes round Lake Tana were thus the only answer. But we learned something else from the Laki people. Their *shafat* and *obolu* were more reminiscent of the reed boats in Chad, Mexico and Peru than of the *tanquas* on Lake Tana, which were built by their own Ethiopian kinsmen. The Laki people did not build reed boats because there was no timber on the lake; they did so despite the fact that wood was more readily available than reeds. The fact that nobody from the vast Galla area around the lake could transport us to the islands also proved that it was not given to everybody to build papyrus boats, even if they happened to live on the same lake. The art of building papyrus boats had been imported to Lake Zwai; it was not a local invention, but an inheritance from ancestors who came from near the source of the Nile, just as it had been with the monks of Lake Tana. Apparently, the papyrus boat had a peculiar way of following migratory people from the Nile Valley as part of their tradition.

But the Laki people had the same unfortunate experience as the monks on Lake Tana. The papyrus must be dried after daily use. If an *obolu* or *shafat* were left lying in the water it would be unusable after eight, ten or at most fourteen days.

I traveled back to Egypt with mixed feelings. Was it worth attempting the Atlantic?

Chapter Six

IN THE WORLD OF
THE PYRAMID-BUILDERS

"Y OU WANT to rope off a bit of desert behind the Cheops Pyramid to build a papyrus boat?"

The thickset Egyptian Minister adjusted his hornrimmed
glasses and looked at me with a questioning smile. He glanced half
dubiously at the Norwegian Ambassador who smiled politely back, as
he stood erect and white-haired beside his compatriot as a sort of
pledge that this stranger from the north was in his right mind.

"Papyrus sinks after two weeks even on a river—not my words.
They come from the president of the Egyptian Papyrus Institute,"
said the Minister. "And the archaeologists say that papyrus boats can
never have sailed beyond the mouth of the Nile because papyrus
dissolves in sea water and breaks up in the waves."

"That is exactly what we want to test in practice," I explained.

I had no better reasons to offer, faced with such a body of
papyrus specialists. The Minister of Culture and the Minister for
Tourism had left no stone unturned, following a request from the
Norwegian Ambassador. They had called in Egypt's foremost authorities as advisers and now we were seated round a large conference
table with museum directors, archaeologists, historians and papyrus
experts. The president of the Papyrus Institute, Hassan Ragab, had
given his verdict in advance. He repeated it. But he admitted, laugh-

ing, that since I was the only one of those present who had seen a papyrus boat in real life he would gladly support the idea if I were absolutely determined to make the experiment. He had only tested bits of papyrus reeds in his laboratory tanks, since no one in Egypt today could build him a boat. I thought for myself that he might as well have tested a piece of iron and he would have come to the conclusion that *Queen Mary* would sink. The building material is one thing, the boat itself quite another.

To the head of the Cairo Museum the idea of a papyrus boat on the ocean waves was absurd. Egypt had exported papyrus to Byblos for bookmaking in ancient times, he said, but of course the Phoenicians collected it themselves in their wooden ships, because only wooden vessels could cross this open corner of the inner Mediterranean. For a papyrus boat to cross the Atlantic was completely inconceivable, now as then. Any specialist could testify that a papyrus boat would not be able to go beyond the mouth of the Nile.

A long technical discussion ranged from the properties of papyrus to the differences between Old World and New World pyramids and hieroglyphs. Finally it was the director general for all Egyptian archaeological relics, Dr. Gamal Mehrez, who had the last word, "If anyone would reconstruct a papyrus boat from the wall paintings in our old burial chambers and try it out in practice, that would be a valuable experiment," he stated. And that was that.

The Minister of Culture authorized the controller of the Giza Pyramids to let us rope off the area we needed for the tent camp and building yard, in return for our promise not to dig into the sand, because we would be right in the middle of the ancient graveyard of the Pharaohs' families.

At the bottom of the steps of the government building was the brick barricade characteristic of wartime Cairo, and sandbags were stacked in front of all the windows. Here we parted from the Deputy Minister for Tourism, Adel Taher, who shook my hand with a broad grin before disappearing up the steps again.

"You must build that boat," he said. "We are all in favor of your experiment. It is a good thing to remind the world that Egypt does not only make war."

I was left with the smiling ambassador and thanked him sincerely for his invaluable support. Peter Ankar had been a good friend from the start. Many years of work in the Middle East, both as a UN delegate and as Norwegian Ambassador, with ancient history as a personal hobby, had made him a walking encyclopedia on all questions of trade relations and cultural contacts in these parts, from the most ancient times.

"That was fine," he declared. "You got the buildingsite, but no one shared your faith in the papyrus boat!"

"If there were no controversy there would be no need to try out the boat," I remarked.

In the hotel room I sat irresolutely on the edge of the bed. Certainly, I had the construction site. But I had not yet set all the wheels in motion. There was still time to withdraw. I had to decide now: full speed ahead on all fronts or drop the whole plan here and now. There was also the point that everything I owned was not nearly enough to carry out such a costly experiment. But publishers would probably be willing to gamble on the final outcome. What if there were no outcome? I sat fingering a small sheet of paper. The monks, the Laki people, the scientists and the papyrus experts all gave the papyrus boat a maximum of fourteen days in calm, fresh water and less in choppy salt water. I had personally sat for a few hours at a time on *kaday*, *tanqua* or *shafat*, and had the unpleasant experience of sitting in a papyrus boat while the reed bundle disintegrated. I knew that the totora reed in America was capable of long sea voyages and that it had a fibrous outer sheath and a spongy cellular center that resembled papyrus in every way, but perhaps papyrus absorbed water much faster than totora.

I unfolded the scrap of paper. The childish handwriting on it read:

Dear Thor in Italy,
Do you remember Abdullah in Chad? I am ready to come to you and build a big *kaday* with Omar and Mussa. We are waiting for orders and I am carpenter with Pastor Eyer in Fort Lamy.
Greetings, Abdoulaye Djibrine.

The laughing, coal-black face of Abdullah with the tribal scar over his brow and nose appeared before me and I had to smile at the touching letter. It was a marvelous thing that this illiterate in the heart of Central Africa had had the initiative to take my address to

a scribe in Fort Lamy and rouse me to action. Why did I hesitate?
Abdullah was ready and Omar and Mussa were prepared to come
with him. They built larger reed boats to freight their cattle on Lake
Chad than those used by the Christians to escape alone and take
refuge on Ethiopian islands, and they knew more about the floating
capacity of papyrus than all the scholars in the world put together.
They believed in their *kaday*. They were willing to build one big
enough to float for months and they were willing to come on board
themselves and sail to distant lands that I could only describe by
the number of days and moons it took to reach them because they
had not the faintest notion of geography.

It was Abdullah's letter that put an end to further hesitation. I
would rely on the men from Chad.

That evening a telegram went back to Addis Ababa, to the
Italian who owned the two big boats on Lake Tana. We had agreed
that as soon as he received a telegram from me he was to send Ali
with his people to the marshes along the western shores of Lake Tana
and cut 150 cubic meters, or about 5000 cubic feet of papyrus reeds
to be dried and collected in bundles at the northern shore of the lake.
Commendatore Mario Buschi was a middle-aged businessman, broad,
red-cheeked and bursting with initiative. He had personally organized
the transport of his two very heavy iron boats from the Red Sea up
to Lake Tana, and it was he who had arranged for the 180-ton
Axum monolith to be moved from the Ethiopian mountains to Rome
in 1937. He was now hoping to be asked to move it back again, since
the Emperor of Ethiopia was pressing the Italian government for the
return of the monument.

My first thought had been to float the papyrus down the Nile,
but this would have been too tricky, with all the waterfalls and the
restrictions of the Sudanese Republic in between. Buschi accepted as
a sporting challenge the task of transporting 500 papyrus bundles 450
miles across the Ethiopian mountains from Lake Tana down to the
Red Sea, because even if the stack of unpressed reeds bulked as big as
a small house, they would weigh only about twelve tons.

There was not a day to be lost. It was nearly Christmas. If we
were to cross the Atlantic before the hurricane season began on the
other side, we must set sail from Africa in May. I was afraid of having
the papyrus cut too soon, since old reed is not so strong, but unless it

were cut now we could not be ready to start in May. Cutting two or
three hundred thousand papyrus stems would take time, because it
was high water in Lake Tana at present and if the reeds were to measure about ten feet long the stem must be cut far below the surface of
the water. Afterward the reeds must be properly sun-dried or they
would rot in their bundles. Then would come the difficult journey
over the mountains and finally up the Red Sea. There was war in the
Suez area and all traffic was at a standstill. I would have to fight for
special permission to unload cargo in this area. In fact, the inflammable reed must be landed in Suez and transported along blocked
roads to rejoin the Nile near Cairo. Before the papyrus load reached
the pyramids, a camp with all conveniences including a cook and
provisions must be ready in the desert for the necessary guards and
labor force. The boatbuilding was to be headed by Buduma Negroes
from Chad, who were still living their simple ancestral lives on
floating islands in the most out-of-the-way desert corner of Central
Africa. When all was set for the building to begin it would be a
lengthy process to lash the hundreds of thousands of thin papyrus
stems into a compact seagoing vessel forty-five feet long and fifteen
feet broad. Also, plans and preparations had to be made in advance
for the transport of the finished boat to its launching place at some
African port on the Atlantic coast. Sail and rigging, ancient Egyptian
steering mechanism, wickerwork cabin, specially made earthenware
storage jars and ship's food prepared as in ancient times—there were a
thousand things to prepare. And less than six months to do it in.

So far I had only sent a telegram to Ethiopia. I sat down on the
bed again, counting on my fingers: December to May. I felt my heart
beating and began to pace the floor faster and faster. Paper and
pencil: I must start all the wheels rolling right now. All at the same
time. Most important of all, it would be necessary to find a crew who
wanted to take part in the experiment.

Naturally I thought first of my companions of a hundred and
one days on the balsa raft *Kon-Tiki*. We still met on every possible
occasion to revive old memories. But Knut Haughland, already busy
as head of the Kon-Tiki Museum in Oslo, had recently been appointed by the state to organize the immediate erection of a Norwegian Resistance Museum as well. Herman Watzinger, who had
long been the FAO fisheries expert in Peru, was just taking over

Captions for the following pages

34. *Expedition members.* Different languages, political background and religion. From the left: Abdullah, Yuri, Norman, Santiago, Thor, Georges and Carlo. In the background the expedition's Belgian adviser, Captain De Bock. (Above)

35. *United Nations flags* flank the row of those of participant nations, arranged in alphabetical order by Captain Hartmark from Norway. (Below)

36. *"I name you Ra* in honor of the sun-god," said the papyrus ship's Berber godmother, Aicha Amara, wife of the Pasha of Safi, who received a model reed boat as a christening present from the author and his wife, Yvonne. (Above)

37. *Baptized in goat's milk, Ra* was launched in the old port of Safi on the west coast of Morocco. Ra was the name of the sun in Egypt and in all the Polynesian islands. (Below)

38. *Yuri, the ship's doctor,* checking the provisions, which consisted of dried meat, fish, Egyptian biscuits and durable natural products. (Above)

39. *Fifteen wooden boxes* to provide floor and bunks for seven men in the basket cabin. They contained personal possessions, books, film equipment and a radio. (Below)

40. *Egyptian hardtack,* baked according to a recipe from Cairo Museum, was both tasty and easy to preserve. (Above)

41. *Some of the 160 ceramic jars* of ancient Egyptian design containing water, oil, honey, curdled butter and all kinds of dried fruit and nuts. (Below)

Captions for the preceding four pages

42. *Good-by* and good luck! The author's wife, Yvonne, waves as four rowing boats tow the raft-ship *Ra* and its crew out of Safi harbor, escorted by Moroccan fishing vessels.

43. *Bon voyage* was expressed with flares and sirens from all the boats in the harbor. (Above)

44. *The papyrus ship* was steered by three ordinary oars lashed forward and two long rudder-oars of the ancient Egyptian pattern aft. Abdullah, who still had not realized that the sea was salt, stood the first watch with the author. (Below)

45. *The open Atlantic* was waiting outside Safi harbor as the Egyptian rudder-oars had their first test in historical times. (Above)

46. *The sail is hoisted on the straddled mast* and the ancient Egyptian rigging is about to undergo its first trial. (Below)

47. *Under full sail*, with the solar symbol pointing our course westward and away from the threatening coastal cliffs of Africa.

responsibility for the department's head office in Rome. Bengt Danielsson, the lone Swede among five Norwegians, who since the trip had been based on Tahiti as a free-lance ethnologist, had just accepted the post of Director of the Ethnographical Museum in Stockholm. Erik Hesselberg was still the same chronic Bohemian, traveling the world with his guitar and his palette. He would say yes at once. But Torstein Raaby, who had once telegraphed "COMING" in answer to the invitation to join the *Kon-Tiki* crew, had ended his adventurous life in the icy wastes northwest of Greenland as radio operator on an expedition that had set out to cross the North Pole on skis.

On the *Kon-Tiki* we had been six Scandinavians. This time I felt tempted to assemble on the little reed boat as many nations as space would allow. If we crowded together we might manage seven men. Seven men from seven nations. Since I myself came from the northernmost country in Europe the southernmost part of Europe should provide a contrast, so Italy would be the obvious answer. Since we Europeans were "white" we ought to have a "colored" man with us, and the blackest Negroes I had ever seen were in Chad, so it would be logical to take one of the papyrus experts with us. Since the experiment was meant to demonstrate the possibility of contact between the ancient civilizations of Africa and America, it would be symbolic to take an Egyptian and a Mexican on the voyage. And, in order to have contrasting ideologies represented in this international group, it was an appealing idea to take one representative from the United States and one from the Soviet Union. All the other nations, excluded solely for want of space, could be symbolized by the flag of the United Nations, if we could get permission to fly it.

The times called for every sort of effort to try building bridges between nations. Military jets thundered over Sphinx and pyramids, and cannon boomed along the closed Suez Canal. Soldiers from the five continents of the world were at war in one foreign land or another. Where there was no war, men sat poised behind the atomic button, warheads primed, for fear of other nations. On a floating reed boat there was room only for people who could shake each other's hand. The voyage itself was intended as an experiment, a study trip into the dawn of civilization. But there was room for an experiment within the experiment. A study trip into crowded, over-populated tomorrow. With TV, jets, and astronauts, we were so busy shrinking the dimensions of our own globe that there was no elbow room left between the nations. The earth of our forefathers no longer existed. The once illimitable world can be circled in an hour and forty minutes. The nations are no longer divided by im-passable mountain ranges and infinite ocean gulfs. The races are no longer independent, isolated; they are connected and becoming crowded. While hundreds of thousands of technicians are working on atomic fission and Laser rays, our little globe is whirling at supersonic speed into a future where we are all fellow-passengers in the same vast technical experiment and where we must all work together if we are not to sink with our common burden.

A papyrus boat sailing along in the grip of the elements could be a micro-world, a practical attempt to prove that men can work together in peace regardless of country, religion, color or political background, if only they will see as a matter of self-interest the ne-cessity of fighting for a common cause.

I took up my pen and wrote to Abdullah. I confirmed that I needed Omar and Mussa and that he himself must come as interpre-ter. Was it necessary for me to come and fetch them, or could Abd-ullah make his way alone to Bol and bring the others as far as Fort Lamy, if I sent air tickets from there to Cairo and met them when the plane landed?

To my amazement a succinct reply arrived promptly from Abdullah via the scribe in Fort Lamy: Abdullah needed a certificate of employment to enable the three to leave the country; he needed three air tickets to Egypt; and he needed 150,000 Chad francs. If he had these he could arrange everything and I would be saved the jour-ney to Chad.

It was a sizable sum, even if the National Bank of Italy itself did not know the exact rate of exchange for Chad francs, and there were endless problems before the funds were safely in Abdullah's hands. Safely? I had put my trust in an alert and reliable expression, without knowing the first thing about Abdullah Djibrine, except that he was a man in a white tunic who had appeared from nowhere in Bol and disappeared again after acting as a voluntary interpreter. By his own account he was a carpenter. But if Abdullah was not deceiving me he would save me both time and money. If I did not have to pick up the Budumas in Bol, I would have time for an important last visit to the Indians in Peru, since I had to go to Mexico and the United States in any case to find companions for the experiment itself.

Two important collaborators had now been set in motion. Buschi in Ethiopia was to produce the reeds, Abdullah in Chad the builders. Reeds and boatbuilders should reach Egypt at the same time and by then the desert camp must be ready near Cairo. This was entrusted to the hands of a reliable friend, the Italian high school teacher Angelo Corio, to whom the Department of Education in Rome had granted six months' leave for language studies with our international team in Egypt. Corio arrived at the pyramids tourist-fashion, with suitcase and camera, and foundered under a ring of struggling dragomans who wanted to show him the Sphinx and teach him to ride a camel. To survive in this peculiar oriental environment he obviously needed a local contact man who knew the laws and customs of the land and could find the right doors to knock on. Ex-Colonel Attia Ossama was just such a man. Because of the war, his real activities, which were connected with the Sinai Peninsula occupied by Israel, were shrouded in mystery. But being courteous and blessed with a winning manner he had an entree everywhere and he undertook to act as middleman with the authorities and obtain permission to unload the papyrus in the Suez war zone.

The wheels were really turning now. Soon they were spinning in one country after the other. Telegrams and telephonic arrangements in foreign tongues, express letters with exotic stamps, and the whole project to be kept secret if work was to be completed undisturbed before the deadline set by the hurricane season. Participants from seven countries. I had found an Italian, had a possible Egyptian candidate and intended to choose the man from Chad from among the three boatbuilders, once they arrived. From Russia I was expecting a reply. I had to go to America. December had passed, January followed—three months were left. In Cairo, Corio was waiting for the papyrus load, which was now drying in the sun on the shores of Lake Tana, while Abdullah was out of reach, on his way to pick up the two others in Bol. In New York I met my American contact man,

Frank Taplin. Taplin was a hyper-energetic American businessman, campaigner for peace and active cog in the World Association of World Federalists, an organization working for increased co-operation between countries and expanded powers for the UN. The well-known New York editor Norman Cousins was president of the organization and a close personal friend of Secretary-General U Thant, who received all three of us on the top floor of the United Nations' imposing glass building.

Seven nationalities, black and white, from East and West, on a papyrus bundle, drifting across the Atlantic? We would be allowed to fly the United Nations flag as long as we kept to the rules: all flags on board must be of the same size and hang at the same height. We could have seven national flags in a row, with a UN flag at each side. U Thant's good wishes came from the heart. Where would we start?

"I had thought of Morocco."

"Then you must go and see my friend Ahmed Benhima, Moroccan Ambassador to the UN, fifteen floors down, on the twenty-third floor."

His Excellency on the twenty-third floor was a tall, distinguished diplomat, the last scion of one of Morocco's oldest and most active families. He received us with routine amiability and we sank into deep armchairs. He listened with complete composure.

"So you are going to set sail from my homeland on a papyrus boat," was all he said as he offered us cigarettes.

"Thank you, I don't smoke."

"What port will you leave from?"

"Safi."

"Safi! That's my own home town! Why Safi, in particular?"

Now his interest was suddenly aroused and he rose with an expression of great surprise and curiosity.

"Why Safi?" he repeated.

"Because Safi is one of the oldest African ports beyond Gibraltar. Casablanca is a modern port, but Safi has been known from ancient times. Safi lies just where a coastal sailor coming from the Mediterranean would be most likely to be swept out to sea by the elements. Just beyond Safi the ocean current and the trade wind seize anything that floats and send it to America."

"My parents live in Safi. The Pasha of Safi is a good friend of mine. I will write to him and I will write to my brother, who is Foreign Minister in Morocco."

This was an unbelievable bit of luck. We parted on the best of terms.

In New York I had a possible candidate for the trip and everything seemed to be going well until his better half was initiated into the secret plans. Then we all three hastily agreed that someone else must be found. There was barely time to have lunch with a new candidate before the plane took off for Lima in Peru.

A few days later I was sitting with a group of Uru Indians, frying fish on a floating island in Lake Titicaca. The whole island was a network of floating reeds, reeds piled on top of one another in thick stacks. As the bottom layers rotted and sank deeper, fresh totora reed was cut and stacked on top. All this part of the lake consisted of artificial reed islands lying side by side with narrow channels between them and living reed growing round them in all directions as far as the eye could see. Looking across this flat marsh-land where the Uru Indians passed their whole existence between fish and reed, one could see nothing but distant white peaks against the blue sky. House and bed were of reed. The boats were of reed, with a square sail of reed stems matted together. Dry reed was the only fuel for their cooking fires. Rotten reeds mixed with earth from the mainland were laid out in small beds on the floating islands and there the Indians grew their traditional sweet potatoes. There was no fixed point in their existence; the ground rocked under the Uru Indians' feet whether they were walking on the floor inside the hut or around the little potato field outside. I had come to have a supposition confirmed. The Uru Indians, like the Quechua and Aymara Indians on the shores of the same lake, and like the Buduma Negroes in Chad, did not drag up their boats to dry every day after use. Yet the boats did not sink in a fortnight. The reeds certainly did submerge gradually. One could see that by observing these floating reed islands, on which the Indians had to keep on building up the surface. But the elegant boats lay beside the islands and floated without fresh additions, just as on Lake Chad. The explanation for this was obvious. The reed boats here in South America, like those in Central Africa, were lashed together with strong hand-made rope, knotted so tightly that as many as possible of the cellular channels inside the reeds were closed. The small boats in Ethiopia, on the other hand, were simply held loosely together with strips of bark of papyrus fiber and the porous reed was not sufficiently compressed to prevent the absorption of water.

There were still twelve days left before Abdullah and the boat-builders were due to arrive in Cairo. He had been sent air tickets for February 20, calculated to coincide approximately with the arrival of the papyrus in Suez. Quite a lot could be done in the twelve days I had left. And with my friend Thorlief Schjelderup, a noted Norwegian philosopher, athlete and cameraman, I left the bobbing islands of the Uru Indians to visit the desert area on the north coast of Peru. Here we were to see South America's most beautiful pyramid, an enormous symmetrical construction of adobe bricks. The colossus lay hidden and forgotten behind weathered sandstone mountains on the desert plain in the Chicama Valley, so far unexplored by science but thoroughly plundered by grave-robbers, who had opened a crater right to the bottom and transformed the stepped pyramid into a sort of square volcano. This gigantic edifice towers so high above the desert that the people of the valley simply call the ancient monument *Cerro Colorado*, "Red Mountain." But for the symmetrical stepped sides, and the walled enclosure in front of the pyramid, one would, in fact, have to look closely to see that this was not a mountain but a man-made composition of millions of sun-baked bricks. For someone who had been in Egypt the week before, there was an almost baffling similarity in architectural form, astronomical orientation, dimensions and building materials to the oldest of the pyramids on the Nile. *Cerro Colorado* had been erected by an unknown priest-king of antiquity when mighty civilizations began to flourish in Peru, long before the Inca culture succeeded the Chimu culture, itself a successor to those first unknown preceptors whom science, for want of a name, has called the "Mochica" people. It was they who built these very first and very largest of pyramids on the coast. Who were the Mochica people? Science has become more and more aware that some form of contact existed between the culture-bringers on the north coast of Peru and the pyramid-builders in old Mexico. Beyond this little or nothing is known of their origins. Among their realistic self-portraits in ceramic

are bearded men and individuals with strongly Mediterranean features; some could have been portraits of typical Berber types in
Morocco today.

There was even time for a flying visit to Mexico, where my
companion on the visit to the Seris Indians, Olympic swimmer
Ramon Bravo, could think of nothing he would rather do than
embark on a reed boat. He had been having some stomach trouble,
but was sure he would be in top form before it was time to set out
from Morocco in two and a half months.

A small plane, a short drive, a few steps on foot, and we were
standing in the Mexican jungle, observing a pyramid in the rain.
A pyramid in the rain. This was just what we had been hoping for,
and down it came. Thorleif was soaked to the skin, standing in his
shirt, wind jacket tucked round camera and film, while the tropical
rain poured down, dripping and streaming from block to block
down the mighty Palenque pyramid. The clouds hung low over
the treetops in the dense jungle that rolled in from the ridge behind us, its gigantic trees thrusting forward on all sides to the very
foot of the pyramid. In clearings around the pyramid lay moss-
grown ruins of stately buildings, tumbled and derelict, with something
for every taste. Having come to the site for no other reason than
to sense in one's blood-stream a little of what had passed in America
before Columbus, one had to overcome the first sentimental wave
of enthusiasm and admiration, and then sit down and try to understand what lay behind this impressive complex of ruins. There was
a curious aura of mystery here, something unwritten and unsaid that
compelled attention, conjecture. This was not the time to be content
with preconceived ideas. This was not the time to get absorbed by
one fascinating detail, or fall into ecstasies over dimensions, beauty
or ingenious technique. This was simply the time to absorb the fact
that rain was pouring on the pyramid, and that the enormous
complex ruin, with its pyramids, temples and palaces, was the relic
of human beings like ourselves, neither superior nor inferior. They
had arrived here as pioneers a thousand years before Columbus and
cleared a space for themselves in the jungle for house and home,
farms and religious buildings. The spectacular pyramids and temples
had been designed and calculated by skilled architects—remarkably
skilled, if one thinks of most Indians who were living and still live

in the same jungle, building huts of branches and leaves with no thought of making a single rectangular block out of what nature has given them in the form of boulders or solid rock. I had once tried to square off a round stone. I had not succeeded, although I had steel to carve with and the Indians had only stone tools. Only an expert would be able to cut smoothly polished blocks from the hard rock—not I, not one of my friends, be he town or country-dweller, and no Indian that I had ever met. It can be done, but not by just anyone. What was the truth about the jungle ruins of Palenque?

A mad idea occurred to me that archaeologists, in reconstructing the unknown, might benefit from consultation with police detectives, those specialists who need not know archaeological terminology or excavation technique, but who are endowed with a basic all-round suspiciousness, practical insight and flair, and some experience in the calculation of probabilities. For what is criminal detection if not the logical reconstruction of unwitnessed events of the past? Here was a large pyramid in the deep forest. Had ordinary Indians put it there? Or had people other than primitive hunters from Siberia mixed with the aboriginal population in Mexico's primeval forests?

It was natural, said those who believed that only barefooted savages and no civilized peoples were able to travel before Columbus' day: it was natural that human beings in similar environmental circumstances should create things that looked alike. It was natural that people in both Egypt and Mexico should have laid stones on stones until they became a pyramid.

It began raining immoderately now, and we tried to find shelter under some outsize leaves.

Similar environmental circumstances! Was there a greater contrast than Egyptian desert and Mexican jungle? Moist plant life made the hot air we were breathing as humid as in a greenhouse. Nothing but dripping foliage, lianas, trunks, rich humus. Not a stone to be seen, except for the big chiseled blocks once brought by man and now lying heaped in overgrown ruins. Was it *natural* to lay stone on stone in the Mexican jungle? Then why not in the African jungle, in the North American prairies or in the meadows and pine forests of Europe?

Where had the architects of the Palenque pyramid found their materials? Perhaps they had dug deep into the mold beneath the roots of the jungle giants; perhaps they had gone to some faroff ridge and hacked away at a solid mountain wall. Here in Palenque, in any case, the idea had come first and the right building materials had been found subsequently, after an expert search.

And in Peru? Was it natural to lay stone on stone until pyramids arose in Peru? Along the thousand miles of desert coast where Peru's pyramids lie scattered in the sands there is no usable stone at all! One must go far up into the Andes to find the closest stone quarries. In the Mochica Valley where we had just been, stone was of such poor quality that the pyramid-builders had been obliged to manufacture some six million large, brick-shaped adobe blocks before they had sufficient materials to build their pyramid, which covered an area of some four thousand square yards and was one hundred feet high. And there were other adobe pyramids in Peru larger than *Cerro Colorado*.

It was thought-provoking to sit, cold and wet, under the big leaves and look at the streaming pyramid, with memories of Peru and Egypt fresh in one's mind. In Egypt it was natural to build with stone, to take tools to the rock itself, because naked cliffs rising from the desert sand were the only natural building material apart from reeds. But where in Mexico was pyramid-building natural? It was known that the Aztecs on Mexico's open plateaus and the Mayas in the dense jungles of Yucatan had learned pyramid-building from their predecessors. Archaeology had disclosed that the earliest civilization in Mexico, the one which had given the impulse to all the rest, had begun on the tropical coast of the Mexican Gulf, where the ocean current reaches land after its passage of the Atlantic. Was it more natural to build pyramids there? On the contrary. There the unknown originators of Mexico's earliest culture had made their way beyond the far horizon to find an accessible stone quarry. In some cases gigantic blocks of twenty and thirty tons had been transported from quarries as far as fifty miles from the buildingsite. Today no one knows the identity of those dynamic masons and architects, who built in the lush jungle and yet knew more about selecting stone than wood. For convenience they have been given a name, "Olmecs." If the many extremely lifelike sculptures on their abandoned stone monuments are self-portraits, then some of the Olmecs had round faces with flat, broad noses and thick lips and looked completely Negroid, while others had sharp features, hooked noses, mustaches and flowing beards and looked remarkably Semitic. The Olmecs were the clue to the whole riddle. What was their real name, who were they, why did the Olmecs suddenly begin to quarry stones and build pyramids? The Olmecs also manufactured artificial building bricks in the jungle. Why? One of their hundred-foot-high pyramids was built of sun-baked adobe bricks, like those in the deserts of Peru, like those of ancient Mesopotamia, and like some of the oldest pyramids in the Nile Valley. Adobe is not a natural building material in the jungle.

The dripping edifice we were looking at confused the whole issue. A few years ago, in 1952, a discovery in this jungle pyramid had shaken the scientific world and immediately upset rigidly held dogma. Quite unexpectedly, a secret entrance had been found to a narrow passage with a stone stairway winding down through the center of the pyramid. It led to a heavy stone door. This opened into a magnificent tomb with a colossal stone coffin where the body of a mighty priest-king lay buried—just as in ancient Egypt. There should not be burial chambers in Mexican pyramids. This was one of the two most cogent reasons for rejecting the idea of transoceanic contact. The similarity between the pyramids was superficial, they said. The pyramids on the two sides of the Atlantic not only had different functions but were also built in different shapes. In Mexico and Peru the pyramids had stepped sides, in Egypt the sides sloped smoothly.

This question of shape had always been a truth with modifications. Anyone who had traveled in the Nile Valley knew that there were stepped pyramids in Egypt too and that they were the oldest, the original form, not only in Egypt but in Mesopotamia. Egypt's civilized neighbors in the Old World, the Babylonians, built their pyramids in step form and placed a temple on top, just as in ancient Mexico. And now, in addition, suddenly here was a priest-king, laid out in a coffin at the heart of a Mexican pyramid. His family also claimed descent from the sun and placed a gun-god of jade in the tomb, while his architect arranged the ground plan of the pyramid with astronomical accuracy according to the passage of the sun, as in Egypt. He, too, had been placed in a huge stone sarcophagus. He, too, had been given a splendid mummy mask over his face, as was customary in Peru and in Egypt. The mask was not of gold but of jade mosaic, with eyes of shell and pupils of obsidian. He had also believed in a life after death and was therefore equipped with jars and dishes for food and drink and adorned with crown, earplugs, neck chain, bracelets and rings of mother-of-pearl and jade. The coffin was painted inside with red cinnabar, and remnants of red cloth still adhered to bones and jewels. In the Egyptian manner the sarcophagus was closed with a lid made from a single carved slab that weighed many tons, wider than a kingsize bed and twice as long. The lid and the walls of the tomb were decorated with reliefs of priests or priest-kings, all in profile, some wearing false beards as a badge of rank, just as was the custom among the hierarcy in ancient Egypt. When everything was ready, half a score of young men were killed and laid outside the door of the tomb to serve as slaves in the next world. Then the opening to the sun-king's burial chamber was sealed with a gigantic stone door and from it a secret staircase was built up through the interior of the pyramid, which was finally filled in with stone and rubble and sealed. Inside and outside the sun-king in Palenque had followed the ancient Egyptian formula for pyramid burial. The only innovation was the erection of a little stone temple on top of the pyramid, in the true Mexican style—that is, in the Mesopotamian manner.

We went down the winding staircase and looked at the grave. It was built before the rest of the pyramid as part of the master architect's original plan, with gigantic slabs in walls and roof, cut, fitted together with hair's-breadth accuracy, and polished to a high sheen. The rest of the pyramid was constructed above when the tomb was complete. White stalactites hung like rows of calcified icicles from cornices on the walls and gave the carved priests in their luxurious ceremonial garb an air of deep-frozen antiquity. The air was fresh and cool. As in Egypt, the architect of this pyramid had provided the necessary air-conditioning. A narrow air duct curved from the coffin all the way up the side of the stairway and two large ventilation channels ran right through the walls of the huge pyramid into the fresh air on either side.

When we climbed the long stone staircase between narrow walls I had another look at the construction. The shaft of the staircase had a hexagonal cross section with angular walls, so that the flat ceiling was narrower than the width of the stair. Only in one place in the world had I groped my way up steps with precisely the same extraordinary design: in the pyramids of Egypt.

Was all this so completely natural? It was indeed impossible to explain as the result of someone merely stacking stones in a heap. We emerged between the big carved stone blocks and found ourselves engulfed once more in green jungle which would have overwhelmed the whole complex of ruins had the Mexican Institute of Archaeology not fought continuously to keep these national treasures out of the clutches of the vegetation. The jungle strives hard to reconquer the fertile terrain once wrought from it by the stonemasons who settled among the trees.

Beside this royal tomb was still another burial pyramid, built above a natural cave, with stone stairs and a long shaft leading up through the interior of the structure, and containing a confusion of human bones. If this pyramid, like its neighbor, had been built for a single priest-king, it was certainly plundered before historic times, the bones of less prominent individuals being tossed down into the empty vault.

Here was more food for thought under the trees in the pouring rain. Skeptics insisted that the tradition of building tomb pyramids was utterly different from that of building temple pyramids—and, on this basis, they rejected the possibility of trans-Atlantic contact. But if their claims are valid, it means that two entirely separate civilizations flourished side-by-side in the jungles of Mexico—a ridiculous conclusion that no one would draw. It would make the problem more involved than ever.

Back in Mexico City we called upon Dr. Ignacio Bernal, head of the institute in charge of all these Mexican antiquities as well as the National Museum of Archaeology, one of the largest and most modern in the world. Mexican archaeologists had gained a reputation for being in the forefront of the isolationists; the older generation in particular maintained rigidly that all the ideas underlying the Mexican ruins had been born inside the borders of the country by barbarians moving down from the north. Now we were about to challenge this opinion by sailing westward in an African reed boat. How would the Mexican specialists take that? I decided to call upon their foremost representative, Dr. Bernal, who obligingly told the museum custodians to let us in with cameras and tape-recorders. As I dragged him into position in front of a large stone stele bearing a realistic relief of an Olmec with a long beard, he looked a bit skeptically over his shoulder at this symbol of the enigma behind Mexico's earliest exponents of culture. Bearded Olmecs introduced pyramid-building to beardless Indians.

"Dr. Bernal," I said, "do you think that the ancient cultures of Mexico developed without outside influence, or do you think that some ideas may have been brought across the sea in primitive vessels?"

"That's the most difficult question you could ask anybody," replied the man.

Surprised, I pushed the microphone closer to Dr. Bernal. "Why?"

"Because I see certain things that tend to prove contact, others that tend to disprove it. So at this stage I really don't see how I can say yes or no in any way."

"Then perhaps we can agree that the problem is still unsolved?"

He hesitated barely a second.

"Yes," he said with conviction. "That's exactly what I think."

We recorded the same interview twice, to ensure against technical failure.

Just at that time the expedition's secret plans had leaked out in the daily press via Cairo. The news had reached Mexico too.

"You want to try out a reed boat at sea, do you?" asked Dr. Santiago Genoves, smiling. He had come to see his colleague, Dr. Bernal, just as we were about to leave the museum.

"Right," I said. "Would you like to come too?"

"Yes, and I mean it."

I looked at Dr. Bernal's Mexican colleague in astonishment. Dr. Genoves was a well-known expert on the aboriginal population of America. I had met him at international anthropologists' congresses in Latin America, Russia and Spain. Small, but incredibly resilient and robust, he gazed calmly back at me.

"Sorry, but the place has already been taken by another Mexican. It will have to be next time," I joked.

"Put me on the waiting list, then. If necessary I can come at a week's notice!"

"Agreed!"

Little did I suspect that these words were to prove prophetic, when the little scientist smilingly took my hand in a firm clasp and said good-by.

New York next morning. A hotel room crowded with journalists. The expedition was no longer a secret here either. The papyrus had reached Cairo. The building was about to begin. The three men from Chad would be sitting in the plane at that moment, Corio was waiting with camp and labor force ready, and tomorrow we would all assemble and begin. My own plane would leave that night, so I had one day left for the last hectic preparations in New York. Then a telegram arrived. I had to sit down as I read it:

ABDULLAH ARRESTED. BOATBUILDERS STILL IN BOL. TELEPHONE
IMMEDIATELY.

The telegram was signed by my wife.

A hasty call to our home in Italy confirmed that this was no joke. The post had brought an envelope from Chad with a little note from Abdullah. It said simply that he could not go and collect Omar and Mussa because he had been arrested. He would write again in a month. Greetings, Abdullah.

Abdullah in prison. What had he done? Where was he? No one knew any more than Abdullah's note told us. Mussa and Omar were still living on their floating islands south of the Sahara, east of the sun and west of the moon. Without them, no boat. In eleven weeks we must put to sea from Morocco if we were to avoid the hurricane season. Behind the pyramids in Egypt a whole staff was waiting in a camp for the visitors from Chad, with beds made and table laid. Someone would have to go to Chad on the spot and bring the papyrus people to the buildingsite. It would have to be me. There was a plane to Chad from France every Wednesday morning. So I would have to be in Paris on Tuesday, with a visa for the Chad Republic. Today was Friday, George Washington's Birthday, and everything in the United States was closed. Tomorrow Saturday, no public offices open. Then Sunday. I had one day, Monday, to arrange the visa and new traveling plans, as well as the financing of another trip to Central Africa, which had not been included in the project.

Three days wandering among the New York skyscrapers followed without taking one practical step. Everything was closed. On

Monday morning the New Yorkers poured back to their offices. Telephones were answered. People from every nation in the world met in the UN building. But no one from the Republic of Chad. The Chad representative was in Washington for the day, a friendly voice explained, and I would have to go there to get my visa for Chad. My wallet was flat. My publisher, a possible source of a loan, was in Chicago. The tickets to Paris that evening were in order, but the long extension, the flight to Chad, called for both visa and money. The telephone at the Chad Embassy in Washington was silent. The Norwegian Embassy, on the other hand, promised to seek out the ambassador for Chad if I would wait patiently at my hotel. From Chicago, however, came a request to rush immediately to a bank at the other end of New York. Abdullah's obscure fate in distant Chad complicated the situation further. U Thant's office stated that the Secretary-General was prepared to write a helpful letter of introduction if I could come to his office at once. Before I was out of the door a man came rushing in—Mr. Pipal, chief of an international press agency, offering an advance against contract for news of the voyage. The telephone interrupted us. The visa was promised that day if I could get on the next shuttle plane to Washington. The press agency director helped to fling winter clothes into one suitcase and summer clothes into another, attended to the bill and would take the baggage to the Paris plane that evening. Thorleif in the next room dropped his rolls of film and made for U Thant's office. I rushed to the airport. Traffic jams in New York, in Washington, in the air, but brilliant co-operation between Norway and Chad in the capital. Two men welcomed me back at Kennedy Airport in New York that evening as I came rushing out of one plane and into another with the Chad visa in my passport. One had the envelope from U Thant, the other, two packed suitcases.

"Thank you. Good-by. Good-night America. Good-morning Paris." A glimpse of my wife at a stopover in Nice on the way due south in the next plane. Dictation pad, telegram forms: Hold everything till we arrive with the boatbuilders from Bol.

The Sahara was under our wings. The heat surged in when the door opened. We were in Chad. The low buildings of Fort Lamy seemed to stretch out endlessly now that I was searching for Abdullah. Abdullah's only address was a post office box. The key to the box belonged to a missionary. He had no idea where Abdullah was, because he had finished his stint as a carpenter. But friendly Pastor Eyer clambered into his car to drive round the Arab quarter and search.

The receptionist at my little hotel in the center told me that the next outgoing plane left for the Sudan in a week, but my tickets for Egypt were invalid because no one in Chad could provide an Egyptian visa. Israel had an Embassy here, but not Egypt. Nor did Norway, Italy or England either.

The room contained a bed, two pegs on the wall and a fan that sounded like a prop plane starting up. I sat on the edge of the bed for a long time, trying to solve the tangle with a pocket atlas. Someone knocked. There stood a tall man in an ankle-length white tunic and with a minute rainbow-colored cap on the crown of his head. He flung out his arms and laughed aloud, teeth and eyes flashing in competition on his happy face.

"Oh boss, oh boss, Abdullah has had a hard time, but now everything is all right!"

Abdullah! He was literally dancing with joy at the reunion.

"Abdullah, what happened?"

"Abdullah went to Bol; four days I paddled on the lake in *kaday* looking for Omar and Mussa, who were fishing a long way out. I found them. I paid their debts. I was going to take them to Fort Lamy. Then the sheriff came. He said I was a bad man, who would do anything for money. He said today I sold two men to Egypt. Tomorrow perhaps to France or Russia. I was arrested. I was sent under guard to prison in Fort Lamy. I was alone. I used the rest of the money to get out."

What a story. Abdullah arrested in Bol on suspicion of slave-trading. The old slave route passed Chad, and the memories obviously lived on. Now Abdullah could not return to Bol. In fact, Mussa and Omar could not leave Bol unless I collected them myself with a formal labor contract stamped by the authorities in Fort Lamy.

For five days Abdullah and I toured all the imposing government buildings in the capital and tried to get a legal labor contract drawn up for the two men I was to fetch from Bol. Intelligent, alert faces everywhere. Friendliness ready to burst out from behind the official masks. Ultramodern offices. Particularly elegant was the towering colossus of the Foreign Ministry ornamented by four-teen empty fountain pools lined up in front of the steps. But when Sunday came I sat down hopelessly on the edge of my bed and turned off the deafening propeller. Let flies and heat have their way. I was fed up. Five days and not one stamp, not one signature on one single document. We had succeeded in tracking down a mission-ary with a single-engined plane who could land on the lake with pon-toons, but if I tried to carry off the two Buduma without stamped papers I would suffer the same fate as Abdullah.

We had begun by going to the Director-General for Home Affairs, who knew about Abdullah's problems, but he could only see a foreigner via the Foreign Minister, who could only be seen through the Chef de Cabinet, who could only be reached through the Head of Protocol. Three days had passed before we got to the Foreign Minister, because everyone had to hear all the details and study U Thant's letter. The Foreign Minister, sitting behind padded doors, was a veritable giant, friendly and informal, with a wisp of black beard on his chin, bushy hair and parallel scars over forehead and cheeks. Before passing us on to the Home Office he took the matter up personally in two meetings with the President of the Republic, Tombalbaye. President Tombalbaye thought the whole case was so unusual that his Council of Minister would first have to decide whether a citizen of Chad could be allowed to travel the high seas in a papyrus *kaday*.

To gain time I assured him that the only urgent problem was to get permission to take three Chad citizens to the calm shores of the Nile in order to build a *kaday* on land. We were then sent on to the Ministry for Home Affairs, which sent us to the Ministry of Labor, which sent us to the printers as they were short of forms. Twelve double-page contract forms were completed for the three men; then we had to go to the head of the Ministry of Works for stamps and signature. As fate would have it, he discovered two paragraphs in the printed contract forms that put a final stop to all further progress.

The contracts could not be stamped until they were signed by the two men waiting in Bol. Still worse, it was stated in print on the form itself that it was invalid without a medical certificate. How were we to get one? There was no doctor in Bol and the sheriff refused to let them leave there without a stamped labor contract. The head of the Ministry of Works summoned a representative of the Ministry of Labor, who stared gloomily at our fine contracts. The position was clear. Both were kindness personified, but they pointed at the words; I could see for myself. Labor contract invalid without medical certificate, medical certificate impossible without departure, and departure illegal without labor contract. *Ergo* impossible.

Dog-tired, I slammed the hotel door behind me and switched on the fan at full blast. Tomorrow was Sunday. I was seething with fury and sat on the edge of the bed, writing in my diary: "Hopeless lunacy. But this parody of a system is not the fault of the people of Chad, who are basically friendly, intelligent and wonderfully uncomplicated people; it is a distorted image of *us*. African culture was not like this, it is *we* who have taught them this new way of life."

One thought was buzzing round in my head: black shadows from white clouds. I turned off the fan and slept to the sound of distant military trumpets from President Tombalbaye's palace. Sunday. I went to see the flying missionary. He had petrol. Early on Monday morning he started the propeller on his plane and then he and I were skimming over the roofs of the government offices, over savannah, desert and floating islands. We landed outside Bol, sending up sheets of spray. We had twenty-four pages of printed contracts and an empty suitcase on the plane, so we would sink or swim by the fact that the documents bore no stamps or signatures but our own. The masses of printed words impressed both sheriff and sultan, who let Omar and Mussa step forward from the crowd.

That same evening two terrified Budumas were sitting behind us in the little plane when we took off again from the waves beyond their grass huts. The shore was black with friends and relations, the sultan and the sheriff at their head, gazing up at their two fellow tribesmen, courageous adventurers, who sat gripping their seats and staring down like vultures at the little world they had grown up in. Their expressions gave nothing away, for was there not a row of burn marks on their arms to prove that they could voluntarily bear red-hot iron without complaint? The two long-

distance travelers had come with what they stood up in; tattered
tunics and home-made sandals. The suitcase we had brought for
them was as empty as before; they had nothing to put in it.

In Fort Lamy they embraced and rejoiced hugely over finding
Abdullah a free man again. In the market place Omar was fitted
out in light blue from neck to sandals and Mussa entirely in yellow.
In the fluttering new robes the blue and yellow figures strode ahead
of us to the police station, wide-eyed with wonder at their new
passport photographs.

"Names?" asked a helpful police sergeant.

"Omar M'Bulu."

"Mussa Bulumi."

"Age?" asked the minion of the law.

Silence.

"When was Omar born?"

"Four years before Mussa."

"1927? 1928? 1929?"

"I think so," said Omar diffidently.

"Born ca. 1929," wrote the sergeant. "And Mussa?"

"1929," said Mussa quickly.

"Impossible," declared the sergeant. "You are four years older."

"Right," agreed Mussa. "But we were both born in 1929."

"Born ca. 1929," the sergeant wrote for Mussa as well.

The passports had to be signed. Omar regretted that he could
only sign in Arabic. He took the pen, sat down and made some
elegant flourishes in the air over the paper, upon which he decided
to hand the pen back to the sergeant who wrote his name for him.
Mussa suggested that the sergeant should sign for him at the same
time. But their passports could not be issued without labor contracts,
so we went off to the Catholic Hospital for a medical certificate.
There was a lively scene when a nun told Mussa to undress as far
as the waist and he innocently pulled the long robe up to his navel.
When Omar was to be X-rayed he was invisible on the screen until
the baffled nun turned the light on again and found he had climbed
up and was hanging over the top of the X-ray apparatus on his
stomach. The Sudan required a smallpox certificate and the men
were given the vaccine but no certificate, because the hospital had
run out of forms. With Abdullah we rushed to the printers, who

refused to print new forms until the hospital had paid off their old debt. At Sudan Airlines the clerk found three old smallpox forms in a drawer, but just as the hospital was about to fill them in a French doctor appeared with Omar's X-ray photograph, which showed a large growth on the liver. Big Omar was seriously ill and strictly forbidden to travel. Mussa would not travel without his brother, who knew Arabic. The papyrus project was crumbling in ruins.

What could be done for Omar? We all trooped in to the French senior physician, a smiling colonel.

"*You,* here?"

The meeting was warm and we were both equally surprised. The last time I had met Colonel Lalouel he had been an army doctor in Tahiti. We worked out a solution together. If Omar were forced to return to Bol he would be without medical care. So I guaranteed that he would see a doctor in Cairo and took a prescription for injections and tablets, assuming responsibility for Omar's cure.

Then the Sudan flight left. At the last moment Mussa and Omar were pushed up the steps, finding it difficult to see because they had found yellow and blue glasses to match their clothes. Loud cries from Abdullah when he put his head inside and saw the aircraft fittings, while the other two were lost in admiration of the cabin, which was larger than the sultan's house in Bol. Soon we were above the cloud ceiling and while Abdullah and Omar examined in detail the mechanism of the seat belt and the adjustable seat, Mussa with stoical calm drew out a yellow handkerchief and sat polishing his naked skull and his sandals alternately. When the stewardess passed with the candy tray, each took handfuls and sat holding his booty until he saw other people putting their candy wrappers into the ash trays. Then they pushed all their candies in and spent the rest of the journey trying to coax them up again through the narrow opening. I was concerned for Omar's liver when I saw him begin on the lunch tray, with butter on his fruit salad. Soon we crossed the desolate and arid frontiers of the Sudan and landed in the late afternoon at the capital, Khartoum.

Now there was no holding my companions. No one in Bol had seen a house with two floors, but here in Khartoum the houses lay on top of one another in layers and even Abdullah went into transports when he saw a four-story building. There would be trouble if my companions were let out of sight for one minute in this teeming

Arab city where we had to spend the night, and since my friends would not yet merge inconspicuously into their surroundings if they came with me to a big modern hotel, I decided to go with them to a small fourth-class boarding house in the poorest Arab quarter. Reception and rooms were up on the third floor of an antiquated building, with kitchen and dining area out on the roof. All three were overwhelmed at this fairy-tale house. The two brothers behaved oddly on the stairs. Advancing with great circumspection they lifted their feet as deliberately and warily as if they were climbing a rugged mountainside. I realized that this was the first time they had climbed a staircase. Both in Bol and on their floating islands all their huts were built on the ground, with only earthen floors. The hotel rooms faced inward and were windowless, with bare light bulbs hanging from the ceiling and several iron beds in a row. The two men from Bol had never seen a bed and, when Abdullah explained that it was for sleeping, Mussa and Omar lay down on their stomachs and crawled underneath to try it. There they turned over and lay outstretched with their noses in the bedsprings, while Abdullah doubled up with silent laughter and beckoned them out again for the benefit of the astonished proprietress, who peeped beneath the mattress and wanted to know what they were looking for. On the roof we were given a little table with a fork and plate each, already laden with large pieces of meat, tomatoes, potatoes, leeks and beans. The function of the fork was quickly appreciated. I was just about to stick mine into a tasty piece of meat on my plate when another fork forestalled me and quickly popped my morsel in Omar's mouth. I prepared to secure another, but—oops!—Abdullah's fork was there and I had to steer for a potato to avoid a collision. I surveyed the situation and saw the forks dueling to and fro across the table, each man eating from the plate where he had spotted something tempting at that moment. My table fellows were used to eating with their fingers from a common dish in the middle and found the fork an excellent extension of their range at a meal where the food had not been placed in the middle, accessible to everyone.

I went to bed slightly hungry. The only bathroom in the hotel resounded with amazed and admiring exclamations. Abdullah wanted Sudanese currency in case a lady should happen to visit his room. Next morning he woke me before dawn. He had heard that time was not the same all over the world and now he wanted to be certain that the pilot and I had agreed on a common time for the flight to Egypt to avoid his leaving Sudan before us.

At the airfield there was a catastrophe. No one noticed that my companions from Chad lacked Egyptian visas, but the Health Department, checking all papers, discovered that their fresh vaccination against yellow fever would not be valid for another week. They had slipped into the Sudan through the Health Department's oversight; now at least they would not be allowed to slip out again until the vaccination was valid. My three companions were stopped and all bargaining was quite useless. In the meantime I had passed through to the airfield, where I discovered a wide gap in the fence. The watchful Abdullah saw my beckoning finger. He and the others left the line, where the Health official formed a barrier. The three of them filed round the building in their white, blue and yellow robes and the plane left with all four of us on board. The two men from Bol sat down politely and fastened their seat belts like experienced globe-trotters, smiling at the pretty black stewardess and each taking a single piece of candy from her tray.

Cairo. Reception committee at the foot of the aircraft steps, with the smiling Norwegian Ambassador, Peter Anker, at its head. The Tourist Ministry's representative waved us through without a word about visas or yellow fever, and the ambassador's chauffeur, in elegant uniform, bowed to Mussa, Omar and Abdullah as they gathered their skirts about their legs and maneuvered themselves into the ambassador's big car. There were shouts of delight and devout murmurs from each of the men in the back seat at the sight of the first bridges, underpasses, and apartment buildings. A mosque, another one, the whole town was full of mosques; it must be Paradise. But when the buildings in the center began to cover whole blocks and rose so high that the three of them could not see the roof-tops without rolling down the window, they grew more and more silent. This could not be real. Mussa grew drowsy. Omar sat stiffly and the whites of his eyes showed when he stole a nervous glance to the side. Abdullah, on the other hand, sat with his clean-shaven scalp thrust forward, drinking in with wide-open eyes and mouth every last detail, from trainlines and makes of cars, to neon signs and human types.

"What's that?" said Abdullah.

We had left the modern city and were crossing the Giza plain. I was prepared for the question, but wanted to watch Abdullah's reaction. The others sat upright, dozing, but Abdullah had been staring ahead for a long time, eyes and mouth growing larger and larger in the dusk.

"That is a pyramid, Abdullah," I explained.

"Is it a mountain or did men make it?"

"Men made it in the old days."

"Those Egyptians! They are further advanced than us. How many people live in there?"

"Just one man, and he is dead."

Abdullah burst into admiring laughter.

"Those Egyptians, those Egyptians!"

Two more pyramids appeared. Now Abdullah, too, was quite silent. The whites of his eyes gleamed. The three men from Chad were guided by flashlight on a long walk from the car through sand dunes to Corio's tent camp, which showed ghostly white in the moonlight, down in the shallow depression behind the pyramids and the Sphinx. Little did the three men walking over the moonlit sand suspect that they were the first papyrus boatbuilders to pass the Sphinx's paws for perhaps thousands of years. Nor that the sand they were treading covered ancient tombs where the Pharaohs' own boat-builders lay, lost and forgotten with a skill that was now returning to the foot of the pyramids again, by a long, a very long and round-about route.

"Goodnight, Abdullah. You have a tent to yourself. Mussa and Omar will be in the one next to yours."

Dazed with incredible impressions and new knowledge, all three stole a last glance at Pharaohs' skyscraper mountains that towered over us like shadows thrown by our tents against the multitude of stars. "One man in each, and he is dead," Abdullah muttered to Omar in Arabic. Omar did not bother to translate into Buduma, for his brother was already lying on his back and snoring, sated with experience, in his camp bed.

As the morning sun shot its first red arrows of light over the tent roofs from its cover behind the sand dunes on the horizon, the tips of the three pyramids glowed like hot lava on a chain of volcanos.

It was still dark and cold when the three men in their long garments crawled out and squatted to watch the glow of the pyramid tops. They were waiting for the sun to reach down to ordinary human beings shivering on the cold sand, waiting for sunrise before prostrating themselves in prayer to Allah. When the sun rose the three black men knelt in a row and bowed, their foreheads to the sand. Their shaven skulls gleaming like polished shoes and pointed directly at the waking sun-god Ra, because Abdullah had figured out that Mecca must lie approximately in that direction. The sun rose and lit up the dunes. Then we all caught sight of something unusual, something from the living world amid all that dead sand and stone. The papyrus! There it lay waiting for us in huge stacks, some yellow-green and some golden as the sun itself. Abdullah took a long knife and we all gathered in tense expectation to hear the expert's verdict. This was the first critical encounter between boatbuilders from Central Africa and raw materials from the source of the Nile. Abdullah sliced off a reed with a simple stroke and the other two squeezed the severed end and felt down the long stalk.

"*Kirta*," murmured Mussa.

"*Ganagin*," Omar translated to Abdullah in Chad Arabic and his teeth flashed delightedly.

"Papyrus, they say this is real papyrus," explained Abdullah in French, and everyone felt relieved and happy. The papyrus was of the finest quality.

Together we chose a flat stretch of desert beside the tents and here we measured out a boat fifty feet long and fifteen broad, outlining the contours with a stick in the sand.

"The *kaday* must be this big."

"But where is the water?"

It was Mussa who asked, and Omar nodded.

"Water?" said the rest of us. I said: "Didn't you find a barrel of drinking water outside the cookhouse tent?"

"Where is the lake? We can't build a boat without leaving the papyrus to soak," said Mussa, gazing suspiciously around him at the endless sand dunes.

"But you told us that we must dry the papyrus in the sun for three weeks before it could be used," I exclaimed.

"Yes, of course. Fresh papyrus is no good, it has to be dried to strengthen it. Afterward it has to be soaked before we bend it, otherwise it snaps like kindling," said the three black men.

There we were. In the desert sand. The camels had water in their humps, we had some in a barrel with a tap. Far down in the valley ran the Nile. Far away. All the sewers emptied out there. Modern Nile water would certainly rot the papyrus twice as fast as the river water of the Pharaoh's days. The two men from Bol had not warned us. In the lake-side world they knew there was water everywhere, nothing but water and floating islands; their concept of our planet was a huge lake with a desert along one horizon.

"Where is the lake?"

Mussa looked distrustfully at us and Omar became uneasy. We had to find a solution on the spot.

"We will fetch it!"

There was no choice. It was too late to move the camp and the huge stack of papyrus. The Nile was filthy anyhow and we dared not soak the papyrus in the sea before it was really necessary, since experts claimed that sea water dissolved the cell tissues in the reed. We had chosen this particular buildingsite because of the surroundings: the pyramids, which symbolized ancient civilization, and the tombs, which would give us the opportunity to check up on individual details in the old paintings as work proceeded on our own craft. And in this desert climate we were certain of keeping the papyrus dry, as the boatbuilders had said it must be, both in Chad and in Ethiopia.

"Abdullah, explain that we are going to fetch the water."

In the Jeep, Corio and I bounced over the sand ridge and down into the nearest Arab quarter. Here we bought bricks and cement, found a mason to build a reservoir, and a truck driver who undertook to drive twelve old gasoline drums full of tap water out to us in the desert every other day. Our friends from Chad were taken shopping for clothes in Cairo; as far north as Egypt it was cold for them, with nothing under their robes. And Omar began his medical treatment. Next day the first bundles of papyrus reed were put to soak in a rectangular brick basin built in the sand in front of the tents. Now we could really see how well papyrus floated. Three men had to jump and dance about to submerge a single bundle, and we had had five hundred bundles shipped from Ethiopia. If we thrust a single papyrus stem, thick end down, into a barrel of water, it would shoot up into air by itself like an arrow as soon as we let go of it.

Two learned men with friendly faces and full, flowing beards, watched closely as we began on the papyrus boat. Both shook their heads, uncertain what to believe. One was Egypt's chief curator of antiquities, who paid us frequent visits from his nearby worksite. He was piecing together the huge cedar boat of Pharaoh Cheops, which had recently been discovered beneath the sand at the foot of the largest pyramid. The other was the Swedish historian, Björn Landström, the world's leading authority on ancient Egyptian boat design. He had come on one of his frequent visits to the country to catalogue and draw every single vessel depicted in the numerous tombs of the Nile Valley. The week before, Landström had informed the press of his lack of faith in the seaworthiness of any kind of papyrus boat. But his first meeting with our real papyrus reeds and the confidence of our experienced boatbuilders from Chad undermined his skepticism and he offered to stay in Egypt and place all his theoretical knowledge at our disposal.

So the teamwork began. Landström knew nothing of papyrus reeds, nor of the technique involved in the chains of ropes which were to lash the bundles together into a boat, but he knew what the final shape of the ship was to be, and many details that were outside the Buduma Negroes' experience. He knew how the stern of a Pharaonic vessel should curve gracefully into the sky as high as the bow, and also the shape and placement of bipod mast with rigging, sail, cabin and steering mechanism. He sat down on a bundle of reeds and sketched a complete papyrus ship for us, and his drawing was to serve as our construction plan, showing the shape and all the proportions.

Mussa and Omar shook with laughter, because at Chad they had never seen what they termed a boat with a prow fore and aft. But they started building straight away. With four stalks bound together with twine at one end they began to build the boat we proposed to test at sea. Into these they pushed in more papyrus reeds and the bundle and rope grew thicker and thicker, just as they had in Chad. When the cone-shaped bundle was about two feet thick and the ropes as thick as a man's little finger, the bundle was lengthened into a cylinder, with rope rings of constant thickness placed two to three feet apart. Now there was room for Abdullah as well, and the work was in full swing. We had to go down to the Arab quarter and recruit more assistants. Abdullah interpreted to the best of his ability, in his Chad Arabic.

"Bot," cried all the Egyptians. That was their word for reed. And then everything went like a conveyor belt. Two men hung onto the end of long wooden levers, pushing the rebellious papyrus bundles under the surface of the water in the brick basin. Two others sliced off all the rotten root ends and carried the fully soaked reed bundles up to assistants who were waiting to pass the stalks one by one to the three men from Chad. They forced them with all their strength into the bristling bundle of what was to become our boat, until the rope rings were stuffed as taut as barrel hoops. Abdullah was self-appointed foreman and worked and gave orders at breakneck speed. At first the Egyptian assistants looked down a little on the three raven-black men from Central Africa. They had seen nothing blacker even in their own baker's ovens. But Abdullah put them all in their places with his sharp tongue and brilliant mind, and soon the other two had also won general admiration for their stoic calm, sense of humor and practical intelligence. Two rascally watchmen with turbans and old muskets, an excellent cook and a laughing child of the sun as messboy all helped to make up an agreeable camp, framed by a symbolic rope barrier that encircled tents, papyrus heap and buildingsite. Already English, Arabic, Italian, Buduma, Norwegian, Swedish and French were in daily use around the same long table in the mess tent, and yet, even now, the international crew for the expedition was not present.

On the third day the clash between tradition and scholarship began. By now the reed roll was so long that it was time to narrow it off into a point behind, but this the Buduma brothers flatly refused to do. They wanted to extend it without altering the diameter and then slice it off like a sausage, as they had always done on their own lake. No kaday could have a bow at both ends! With Abdullah as interpreter, Landström, Corio and I tried to explain that this was to be a papyrus boat of the special design that the ancient Egyptians used, and their boats were pointed at both ends. But the generally cheerful Mussa turned and went off to bed. Omar tried to make us understand that although it was right to begin a papyrus roll with

four reeds and make it thicker and thicker, it was not possible to make
the thick end thinner and thinner and finish with only four reeds.
With that he, too, trudged off across the sand and we were left
disconsolate with all our Egyptian helpers.

Before the sun rose next morning the two brothers had slipped
down to the buildingsite and by the time the rest of us were up they
had already done what they wanted to do. We ran down in the desperate hope of stopping them. Then we stood staring at the boat and
at each other. Landström had made a construction drawing that
showed seven separate rolls curved to a point front and back and then
lashed side by side to give the boat width. But the two brothers had
already begun the second roll by weaving it directly into and together with the first in a compact, firm whole. Not only were the
ropes woven together in parallel chains across the boat, but a handful
of papyrus reed from one roll was regularly woven diagonally into
the rope rings of the neighboring roll, so that they formed an inseparable whole. The technique was so superior to anything a non-
initiate could have thought out that the scholars could only capitu-
late. A thousand years of practice swept away the theories of a single
lifetime and the result was a compact amalgam of papyrus pontoons,
of which only the very first had a full moon cross section, while the
rolls on either side had the graduated cross sections of waxing and
waning moons.

On the seventh day a sandstorm came ripping across the Sahara.
The sand stabbed against the tents like petrified rain and the pyramids slowly disappeared from view. With stinging eyes and crunching
teeth we had to hammer the long tent pegs deeper into the sand and
stretched a tarpaulin over the papyrus heaps because the dry, light
reeds were beginning to fly through the air toward the pyramids.
The reeds, bristling like hedgehog quills from the unfinished stern
section of the two rolls, snapped like straw in the storm, while the
finished section was as compact and robust as a tree trunk. The storm
grew more violent and the sand dashed itself against the camp like
hot hail for three days. On the fourth day the wind died down and we
went to work as drizzle began to fall over the desert. Jars of water
were collected from the basin and poured over the pointed bow of the
boat, which now consisted of three interwoven cylinders, and when
the bow was sufficiently pliable all the men were set to work bend-

ing it up into the high and elegant curve of the Pharaohs' ships. But
at the other end the bundles were still as straight and bristling as
giant shaving brushes. Mussa and Omar would not yield. Then we
took the three men from Chad on the adventure of their lives, to a
big store in Cairo, where they traveled up and down the escalators
and were allowed to choose a gift each. They gleefully chose wristwatches, and Abdullah promised to teach them to tell the time. That
same afternoon an extravagantly happy Mussa discovered that it was
possible after all to cut off enough papyrus to create a sharp point
at the stern, bend it upward and then patch on more reeds in a makeshift way so as to get the general Egyptian shape we wanted. We
were all relieved. As the improvised stern curved into the air the construction assumed the form of a real ancient Egyptian vessel and
when the picturesque boat began to look like a crescent moon against
the pyramids of the sun, it aroused enthusiasm among scholars and
laymen alike. None of us imagined that this improvised afterthought
of a stern was later to prove an Achilles' heel.

Four rolls were gradually assembled on both sides of the longest
central roll and then a second, similar layer of nine rolls was secured
on top of the first. In addition an extra roll was placed along each
side of the deck as a bulwark. The three central rolls were thicker, so
that they projected eight inches below the rest, like a sort of broad
keel.

In April the sun began to blaze down on the Sahara with an
intensity that could be recorded in terms of work rate and water
consumption. The boatbuilding in the sheltered valley behind the
pyramids began to figure in the local press and television. The papyrus
boat was constantly being confused with Pharaoh Cheops' cedar
ship which Ahmed Joseph was reconstructing a few hundred yards
away. Dragomans and tourist guides who were out of work because
of the crisis in the Middle East, hit on the idea of conducting such
tourists as they could find to look at a genuine Egyptian papyrus
ship. Tourists from every continent, and photographers and journalists
who had poured into the country to report the Suez hostilities found
their way by camel and on horseback, or trudging on foot, to the
papyrus boat. It had now become the latest local attraction. While
rope barriers were trampled down and disappeared, the guards struggled to hold back the mass of people from the fragile boat, over which

the keenest onlookers scrambled in their eagerness to pose for photographs and without thought for the bone-dry reeds that snapped under their boot heels. The camels actually ate of the boat. Papyrus scraps and whole reeds as souvenirs, with or without autographs, disappeared in all directions and Abdullah was so busy being nice to everyone who wanted his autograph that he forgot to oversee the work. Mussa and Omar stood with rolls of rope in their hands, flirting with beauties from Nigeria, Russia and Japan. We tried to work at night with lamps and flares, but the danger of fire from sparks and kerosene was so overwhelming that we had to stop. We really had built ourselves a paper boat. One match, and the whole thing would go up in a sea of flame and collapse a few seconds later in a little pile of ashes on the sand. We were panic-stricken over all the tourists who smoked and leaned with their cigarettes close to the side of the vessel. We hung up large signs in English and Arabic, "Smoking forbidden," and told the day-watchman that he must point out the placard to everyone who came. Soon afterward we found the old man himself sitting with his ancient rifle right under the papyrus bow, peacefully puffing at a home-rolled cigarette. I pointed furiously to the placard over his head, but he smiled back, unimpressed, and explained that he could not read.

The cabin was woven by an old basketmaker down in Cairo. It was of flexible wickerwork, with floor, walls and roof all one piece. This basket cabin where we were to live was twelve feet long and eight and one half feet wide, with a curved roof under which we could stand with bent head at the highest point, and a door opening three feet square in the middle of one long wall. Ceiling and long walls were continued three feet beyond one of the short walls, as an open storage alcove for the baskets of provisions.

During the work we had to make repeated trips to the old tombs to study details of the fresco paintings. The pictures of long wooden ships always showed a thick cable running from bow to stern high above the deck. It was kept up by two forked posts located fore and aft. The purpose of this arrangement was to keep both boat ends tensioned and thereby prevent the vessel from collapsing fore or aft and thus breaking amidships. Evidently the papyrus boats could be allowed more flexibility lengthwise, because they lacked this tension cable. On the other hand, they had a short cable running diagonally from the in-curled tip of the stern down to the afterdeck, making the stern look like a harp with a single string. I spent hours pondering the function of that string, convinced that it must have a practical purpose, though all the scholars and even the practical men from Chad said that its only function was to preserve the in-curved shape of the stern. Of course. But why, why this in-turned whorl? Just a matter of beauty, everyone said. None of us could work out a better reason, but this was reason enough for us to copy the old pictures on this point as well. The bowstring stayed there for many days, but one fine morning it had gone. Our friends from Chad had removed it; it hampered them in their work and was not needed any more because the curl on the stern now stayed immovably in place by itself. We asked them to tie the rope on again at once, but yielded to the logical argument that if the curl began to straighten out we could simply tie the bowstring on again ourselves whenever it was needed. It was not needed now.

Whereas the wooden boats had their giant cable strung between two forked posts, the paintings and reliefs showed that papyrus boats had a thick twisted cable made fast round the edge of the whole deck to hold the vessel together lengthwise, increase rigidity and give a grip to all the mast stays, which, of course, could not be lashed directly to the thin reeds.

As we wandered through subterranean chambers, corridors and colonnades, wall paintings three to four thousand years old helped us to relive the life of those days on the water, with the help of the artists' lifelike reproduction of every detail, often in low relief, covered with durable colors. We had to try to gain an insight into the forgotten life of former mariners through the ancient series of drawings, for no living man had experienced what we were now attempting. Often it was difficult to distinguish between pictures of wooden boats and papyrus boats, because the wooden boats generally followed the papyrus boat in shape. But the tomb paintings sometimes showed workers actually collecting reeds in the papyrus marshes and carrying the bundles on their backs to boatbuilders, who tied the reeds into a watercraft with coils of rope fed to them by small apprentices.

On board various papyrus boats were depicted baskets filled with fruit, bread and other pastries, jars, sacks, cases, bird coops,

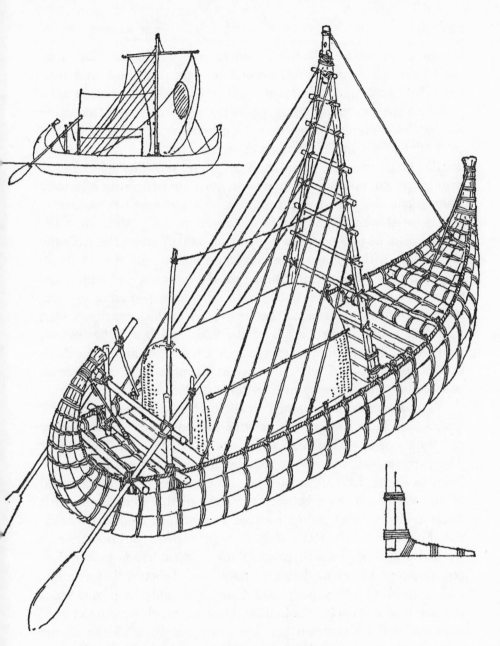

This is how Björn Landström imagined Ra.
Right, detail of the mast foot.

monkeys, live calves, fishermen, hunters, traders, warriors, and cruis-
ing royalty. Here were whole funeral corteges, with gods and birdmen. Here were naked fishermen working with nets, fish traps or hook
and line. Here were flotillas of embattled papyrus boats. Here were
warriors harpooning hippos from the papyrus deck and bird hunters
catching feathered species among the reeds. Here were women sitting
on the cargo, nursing their children. Here was Pharaoh himself,
with his queen, on a ship's throne at a groaning table, with a steward
ready to fill his cup. Some paintings depict Pharaoh symbolically,
as a giant straddling the length of the boat; others show in detail
twenty pairs of oarsmen in a papyrus or papyriform vessel with the
bipod mast, with rigging so big that half a dozen seamen were climbing yardarms and stays and hauling on the halyards, and with a sail
system so advanced that it testifies to a fully developed art of seamanship five thousand years ago. The finest papyrus ships are represented
with ornamental animal heads at the ends and beautifully carved,
painted and gilded cabin poles, sun roof, rudder-oars and other ship's
fittings, all on a level with the ancient Egyptian skill and taste in
architecture and everyday articles on dry land.

The Pharaohs had enough stone to build pyramids as large as
mountains. They had enough papyrus too, so there was nothing to
prevent them from building reed boats as large as floating islands.
The papyrus boat we were to make was only a modest fifth of the
Sphinx's length. We felt small when we came out of the underworld
of mummies and stood between the paws of this stone monster. It
made us realize what giant structures ancient men could have made
out of light reeds. The teeth of time devour papyrus, but not stone. If
we had only had the wall paintings of that subterranean world to
go by, no one in our modern age would have believed that a sphinx
and pyramids of such superhuman dimensions could have been made
thousands of years before Columbus. However much we like to regard
ourselves as the generation that has finally sloughed off the animal
skin, the pyramids are there to remind us to tread warily. It is no
proof of intelligence to underestimate the level of others because
they came into this world before we did. We are harvesting the
fruits of their labors. They roamed about the world equipped with the
same senses and inclinations. Their relics proclaim that intelligence,
inventiveness, organization, dynamism, curiosity, taste, aspiration, and

all the other impulses behind men's actions, good and bad, place ancient man and modern man side by side. It is only the calendar and the technology we have built up together that reveal the passage of five thousand years.

When the last bulwark of papyrus began to take shape on each side of the deck I had to fly off for a visit to Morocco. It was necessary to prepare for the arrival of our boat and our ultimate departure from the ancient port of Safi, which none of us had seen. Soon after my return to Egypt the last papyrus stems were put in place. Two hundred and eighty thousand reeds had been used. The building was finished. Six reeds were left lying on the ground.

On April 28, the anniversary of the start of the *Kon-Tiki* expedition twenty-two years before, the papyrus boat was ready to be towed away. The area behind the pyramids was swarming with people. The Tourist Ministry had set up chairs beneath a canvas canopy, and the governor of Giza took his place with Ministers and foreign ambassadors. Today others were doing the work and Abdullah, Mussa and Omar had put on their finest garb and taken their places among the audience. Broad-chested and squat, with raised neck and curved tail, the papyrus boat looked like a big, golden hen brooding on round logs in the sand in front of the pyramids. We had built it lying free on top of a large wooden sledge, and four long cables were stretched out in the sand in front of this support. Busy men were laying out a slipway of telephone poles on which the sledge could be towed over the sand dunes. For assistance in this task the president of the Papyrus Institute in Cairo took me to the Egyptian Institute of Gymnastics, where we convinced the director that we had set up a splendid training program for rope-hauling out in the Giza sands. We would provide transport, how many men could the school supply?

The school could supply five hundred physical training students, and here they were, arrayed in white shorts, with their gymnastics instructor organizing them in long rows along the ropes. Two men stood on the boat issuing directions, and one stood in front on the sledge, giving start and stop signals with a conductor's baton. There was something biblical about the scene. Perhaps it was because the old-fashioned boat, lying there, solid and home-made, with the basket cabin on its deck and the pyramids in the background, made one think of Noah's ark lying abandoned in a desolated world after all the animals had left it. Or perhaps it was because Moses had come here to the pyramids, he who began his days drifting alone in a papyrus basket by the banks of the Nile. But what is certain is that when the man on the sledge raised his stick five hundred young Egyptians threw themselves into the traces until the desert resounded with rhythmic roars; the timber began to creak and the big papyrus ship moved slowly forward against the background of the pyramids fixed in their ancient places. Not a few of the onlookers shivered, suddenly aware of ghosts walking under the broiling sun.

Ola ho-o-o-op! came the rhythmic shouts from the Egyptian throats, while timber squeaked and whimpered and stone grated, while the sun blazed down on the pyramids as it had always done, and played on the muscles of a thousand arms and a thousand legs conducted by the same baton, proving that men can move mountains without machines—if only they pull together.

The little desert valley seemed forlorn and strange when the tents were left alone with the pyramids and the papyrus boat no longer provided a focal point, having moved out of the picture toward the asphalt road to Sahara City. There the wooden sledge with our Noah's ark was hoisted onto a large trailer used in the building of the Aswan Dam. And while cheering gymnasts were thanked for their hard work, the oldest and youngest means of transport in Egypt rolled together along the asphalt road by the palm-covered shores of the Nile, to its mouth in the port of Alexandria.

Here we felt at once that the dry and brittle desert ship was beginning to absorb vitality and toughness from the moist sea air. The papyrus became as resilient as rubber. The mummy-ship awoke to new life on its first meeting with the ocean.

Chapter Seven

OUT IN THE ATLANTIC

SAFI. The fresh scent of the salt Atlantic. The rollers broke against the steep coast, sending high white cascades up toward the old fortifications that Vasco da Gama's brother-in-law erected when the Portuguese took over the defense of the port in 1508 by agreement with the Berber chief Yahia ben Tafouft. Between medieval fortress walls and 450-year-old Portuguese castles an energetic community of Arabs and Berbers now work peacefully together in the world's largest sardine fishery, and the port teems with colorful fishing boats, while large ocean-going vessels glide in and out to collect sulphate or trade goods with Morocco's most important inland town, Marrakesh.

We were sitting up in the Pasha's palm garden at the top of the town, looking down on the endless open sea stretching from harbor to horizon. Safi's harbor had been used by the Berbers for a thousand years before the Portuguese came, and by the Phoenicians for at least a thousand years before that, for they used to trade along this open coast farther down than the present Kingdom Morocco. Just below Safi they had an important outpost on the little island off Mogador where the archaeologists are constantly excavating Phoenician relics. So long before Christian times there were already seafarers and traders, as well as colonists, trafficking between the innermost Mediterranean coasts and these old ports on the western-

most outpost of Africa's Atlantic coast, where the ocean current
sweeps everything it can get hold of to the other side of the Atlantic.

All those who passed through the Strait of Gibraltar, the
ancient Pillars of Hercules, had found shelter here if they, like the
Phoenicians, ventured down along these low Moroccan cliffs and
open sandy beaches. A reed boat could also have made its way
down here to Safi, by progressing in short hops along the curved
coast of Africa, for no one doubted that such a vessel would float as
long as it stayed close enough inshore to be dragged up at any
time and dried when necessary. The question was: how long would
it float if it left the coast and began to sail the open sea?

We know that the reed boat was used on the Atlantic coast
beyond Gibraltar. It survived tenaciously on both sides of the Strait
of Gibraltar. It is still in use among fishermen living in the shadows
of the mysterious Nuraghi ruins on the west coast of Sardinia. Nor
would our own version be the first the people of Morocco had seen.
At the mouth of the Lucus River on the Atlantic coast between
Gibraltar and Safi the reed boat survived as a fishing vessel and
means of transport until it was finally replaced by Portuguese plank
boats at the beginning of this century. In 1913 members of a
Spanish scientific expedition found that the ancient El Jolot tribe
in this area was still building reed boats that could carry five or
six fishermen and were navigated by both oars and sail. They expressly pointed out that it was the same type of vessel as the
ancient Egyptians had used and they also emphasized that this
design had not only survived in Morocco but was still in use on
the Upper Nile, in Chad, and on Lake Titicaca in South America.
They invited ethnologists to find out what connection could have
existed between boatbuilders in such widely separate places, and
stressed that as far as these so-called *madi* on the Atlantic coast
in Morocco was concerned, they seemed to be the most robust
and sturdy of all known reed boats.[1]

"You want to see a reed boat?" asked the head of the local
coastal district, slightly offended when I proposed to visit the Lucus
River. "Then you have come to Morocco a generation too late.
Here we can show you boats of plastic!"

[1] A. Cabrera: "Balsa de juncos en el Bajo Lucus," *Revista del Istituto de
Antropología de la Universidad Nacional de Tucumán*. Vol. 1, No. 2. Tucumán, 1938.

Colorful mobs of many racial types had gathered to watch as the reed boat built by our friends from Chad came rolling along the streets of Safi on wheels. Now it was ready for launching in the midst of the beached fishing boats in the harbor. Abdullah tried hard to explain our project to Berbers and Arabs in his own dialect. Mussa and Omar had said good-by. They had flown back from Cairo to Fort Lamy via Khartoum with heavy suitcases and the means to buy both wives and cattle at home in Bol. On parting Mussa whispered that he had found a secret place in his fine new suit where he had hidden all his money so that no one could find it. Proudly he raised the lapel of his jacket and showed me an ordinary inside pocket. Omar had finished his treatment and was envious of Abdullah, who with his knowledge of French and perfect health had been chosen to sail with us on the *kaday*.

Abdullah had no intention of returning to Chad until the guerrilla war was over. He was coming to sea with us at all costs, even without the consent of President Tombalbaye and his Council of Ministers. With our Italian camp organizer Corio, he accompanied the papyrus boat as a passenger on a Swedish cargo vessel supposed to sail directly from Egypt to Tangier in Morocco. No sooner had we waved good-by to Abdullah in Alexandria when the captain received orders to change course and call at Port Said on the Suez Canal for a cargo of onions. Here Abdullah had a chance to observe how the white man lives up to his own teaching. He was awakened by cannon thundering along the Suez Canal, while missiles exploded at random on ramshackle Arab houses ashore. He stood on the ship's deck beside the inflammable papyrus boat and looked up, startled but unafraid, as something came sailing over the ship and exploded in the harbor area. The dock-workers disappeared and the ship was delayed for several days before it got away from Egypt. But now the papyrus boat had come safely through to the starting point in Morocco and Abdullah was busy tidying it up. It had shaken down a little on the journey overland from Cairo to Alexandria and from Tangier to Safi. It seemed slightly broader and flatter and the horntips, fore and aft, were a little battered and scorched after butting everything from bridges to high tension cables en route. But day by day the golden reeds grew steadily more supple and firm as they absorbed the damp sea air.

Today the reed boat was to be launched. It happened to be
May 17 and Norway's National Day. The Pasha had personally
organized the launching from the same slipway that was used to
launch the fishing smacks of Safi. As the King's representative he
had great authority, and he used it for the benefit of the expedition.
From the day I arrived with the letter from his Moroccan friend,
UN Ambassador Benhima, all doors in the Pasha's home were open
and a spontaneous friendship arose between us. Pashsa Taieb Amara
and his wife Aicha were exceptional people. Both were equally
active, equally alert and interested in social problems. He had used
his power to establish modern schools, youth centers, workers' hous-
ing, seamen's homes and libraries and had brought activity in place
of idleness to the old seaport. Madame Aicha was one of the twenty
ladies chosen for membership in King Hassan's council.

She arrived in her long Berber robe with a brightly colored
ceramic pitcher in her hand and we rose from our camel-skin pouffes
to go down to the port.

"Since I, a Berber, am to baptize the boat, I think goat's milk
would be most suitable," she said, showing my wife, Yvonne, the
white contents of the pitcher. "Goat's milk is Morocco's ancient
symbol of hospitality and good wishes!"

The harbor was packed with colorful throngs of people. Our
golden boat was decked out festively, with the flags of all the
participant countries fluttering in the wind. Aicha smashed the fine
pitcher into a thousand fragments against the wooden cradle, so
that goat's milk and potsherds sprayed over papyrus and distinguished
guests alike.

"I name you *Ra* in honor of the sun-god."

Chains and cogwheels began to screech at once. The crowd
pressed back. As the papyrus boat began to glide down the slipway
toward the water I exchanged looks with the loyal friend of the
expedition, Ambassador Anker, who stood straight and smiling, with
milk-spots on the lapels of his dark suit. He and his wife had come
from Cairo to see us off. We must have been thinking the same
thing: Let's hope the worst obstacles are behind us now. But others
were thinking the opposite. Just as the bows touched the surface
of the water a wide-eyed photographer leaned toward me and said:

"What will you say if it goes straight to the bottom now?"

There was no time to answer. *Ra* floated out. The wooden cradle sank slowly to the bottom with the iron truck to which it was secured, but *Ra* detached herself and lay on the water like a fat goose, while scraps of papyrus and wooden props from the sledge bobbed up round her and followed her out like a flock of goslings. A sigh of relief and admiration rose from the crowd on shore. Some had expected her to capsize. Most had thought that she was certain to list, because she had never been on trial and was not very symmetrical on either side of the center line. This was handwork, and measured along the railing, Mussa's side proved to be sixteen inches longer than Omar's. But the balance was perfect, no matter how many people jumped on board. The only part below water was the eight-inch depth of the three central rolls, which, as noted, formed a kind of keel almost six feet wide. The rest of the wide boat lay right on the surface, like a life buoy.

A tugboat was ready to tow *Ra* over to a big barge, where we made fast, so that the papyrus would not be shredded to ribbons against the stone pier in the tidal water. We lay here for a week, allowing the reed below the water line to absorb its fill, while we fitted our vessel out for sea. In this week the various members of the *Ra* expedition met one another for the first time. I had planned it this way. There would be time enough to catch up on each other's life stories in the tiny bamboo basket that was to be our common home at sea in the weeks ahead.

There was Norman Baker, from the United States. As the only real sailor on board he had been appointed the expedition's navigator and radio operator. Thorough and reliable, he sat in the cabin entrance examining his equipment, allowing no detail to pass without an expert check. My own previous acquaintance with Norman was rather fleeting. He had come aboard my ship once, in his modest, calm way, when I was in Tahiti with a Greenland trawler I had chartered for an expedition to Easter Island. Norman had just reached Tahiti then, as navigator of a tiny ketch that he and an American biologist had sailed a good two thousand sea miles from Hawaii. He could navigate. He was also a commander in the American Navy Reserve and an instructor in oceanography at the Navy School in New York, though in civilian life he was a building contractor in the skyscraper world of that vast city.

"Have you really no experience of the sea?" asked Norman skeptically, turning to Yuri who sat, round and cheerful, beside him in the cabin opening, fingering a breathing apparatus.

Yuri Alexandrovich Senkevich was Russian and the expedition's doctor. He grinned broadly.

"I have been in a Soviet ship to the Antarctic and back," replied Yuri, and began to talk about luscious girls in Manila. But Norman was more eager to hear if Yuri had really spent a full year in the coldest place in the world. Yuri had. For a year he had been doctor to the Russian research station at Vostok, about ten thousand feet above sea level, right on the South Polar icecap, where the temperature can drop to −100° Fahrenheit. Yuri was the only one of the men I had never met before. We were both on tenterhooks when his plane landed in Cairo. I had taken a chance by writing to the head of the Russian Academy of Sciences, President Keldysh, an intelligent and unassuming scholar who is in charge of all science in the Soviet Union, from sputniks to archaeology. I reminded him that he had once asked why I never took Russians on my expeditions. This was the opportunity. I needed a Russian and I needed a doctor; perhaps President Keldysh could recommend someone. My conditions were that the doctor must be able to speak another language besides Russian, and that he must have a sense of humor. The Russians had taken the last point very seriously. When Yuri emerged from the Aeroflot plane, loaded with gifts and medical supplies, he had taken a vodka for fear of not being funny enough. And Yuri fitted straight into the picture at once. His knowledge of English was minimal, but enough to ensure that the point of a joke was never lost. Son of a doctor and born in Mongolia, Yuri was something of an Asiatic. He had been chosen from among the younger scientists at the Soviet Department of Health, where he specialized in the problems of astronauts under acceleration and weightlessness. After inspecting the airy wickerwork cabin that was to be our living capsule at sea, he had a number of humorous comments to make in the astronauts' favor.

The Italian Carlo Mauri was also quite a new acquaintance. He was to be the expedition's cameraman. A friend from Rome was to have come, a film producer who was one of Italy's best frogmen and had just been down filming the *Andrea Doria* at the bottom of

the Atlantic. But when Abdullah landed in prison and I disappeared
unexpectedly into the African interior, he had lost faith in the
whole project and proposed Carlo Mauri as a substitute. Mauri, red-
bearded and blue-eyed as a Viking, was also without the slightest
experience as a sailor. He was a professional mountain guide and
Italy's most noted alpinist. He had either led or participated in
fourteen international mountain-climbing expeditions which had
taken him to every continent. Many of the worst precipices in the
Himalayas and the Andes were as familiar to him as some of the
stiffest peaks in Africa, New Guinea or Greenland. One leg had
been seriously fractured by a bad fall in the Alps, which finished
his ski-teaching, but as a mountaineer he was more active than ever.
Carlo happened to be down on the South Polar icecap when he
heard about the papyrus boat project; and as he had gone there
after filming polar bears in the ice channels of the North Polar
icecap, he liked the idea of a spot of warm, ice-free bath water on
the Equator.

At the eleventh hour we had almost lost our Mexican member.
My friend Ramon of the trip to the Seris Indians was rushed to
the hospital for an extremely serious operation just as the papyrus boat
left Alexandria en route to Morocco. The tragic message arrived in
the middle of a press conference and was withheld until a journalist
asked for the names of the participants. Our otherwise smiling
ambassador sat serious-faced in the front row, fingering the paper.

"From Mexico—" I began, when nervous fingers passed me the
telegram. It stung like a whiplash. If only Ramon pulled through
nothing else would matter. It was difficult to finish the sentence.
The press grew restless.

"From Mexico—Dr. Santiago Genoves!"

The meeting adjourned. Two telegrams went off to Mexico at
once. One to Ramon in the hospital and one to Dr. Genoves, the
Mexican anthropologist who had said half in jest that he would
come if he had a week's notice. Now he had a week's notice. And
he came. That energetic man had even managed to stop over in
Barcelona to receive Pope John XXIII's Peace Prize for 1969 as a
reward for his campaign against war and aggression in the book *Pax?*
which he was now in the process of filming. From Spain he had
reached Morocco just in time to supervise the transport of the reed

boat overland from Tangier to Safi. Now he was already in action as the expedition's quartermaster, busy stacking pear-shaped Egyptian jars on the uneven reed deck, where they toppled over unless propped against one another, padded with reed fragments and made fast with rope. Coconuts in the husk served excellently as fillers. We had had 160 of these amphorae made on the pattern of the ancient Egyptian jars in the Cairo Museum, and Santiago handled them with the same solicitous care as he handled the ancient Indian skulls at Mexico University. He numbered and listed jars, baskets and goatskin containers, writing it all down with a scientific thoroughness that reflected his long work as editor of the International Yearbook of Physical Anthropology. I had caught glimpses of Santiago at scientific congresses in many countries. He had escaped from Spain during the Civil War, but since then I had met him there too, and now most recently in Mexico, where he was research professor at Mexico University, specializing in the problem of the mixed origins of the American Indian tribes. He, too, had absolutely no experience as a sailor. In one particular this muscular little scientist differed from all other scholars I knew. He had been a professional soccer player.

If anyone could have had less knowledge of seamanship than Yuri, Carlo, and Santiago, it must have been Abdullah Djibrine, the desert dweller from Chad, who had grown up in the heart of Africa and did not even know that the sea was salt. Now he was to join the expedition as papyrus expert. Perhaps it was this exotic character whom I knew best, after two journeys to Chad and seven weeks spent together behind the pyramids. Resourceful and quick-witted, but wary as a gazelle with everyone and everything, perhaps Abdullah did not even know himself too well. All I knew about him, after discarding his own tall tales about trips to Paris and Canada, was that he had been born in a little village near the papyrus marshes of Lake Chad, where the men of the tribe had taken him from his mother by force in order to cut the distinguishing mark down his forehead and nose when he was so young that he could barely remember it. Apart from that, he had grown up to become a carpenter and a lady's man. As a good Mohammedan it was his right to have several wives, and my duty to provide for them. One Chadian wife with three children, and a second whom he had married at the last minute, created complicated monthly currency transactions with the Republic of Chad, and he had seized his chance to marry a third in Cairo during the one week when I was away on a quick trip to Morocco. A wedding feast in style had been postponed until I returned and could play host. It had taken place, with belly-dancing and Egyptian musicians, on the roof of his father-in-law's Arab house, and Mussa and Omar were so taken with the beautiful, shy bride that they stuffed most of their week's wages down her already well-filled brassière. So now I had monthly foreign exchange problems in Egypt too, and vowed that in Morocco Abdullah would not be allowed out of our sight.

The youngest of the party was the Egyptian, Georges Sourial, a gifted chemical engineer, professional frogman, incorrigible playboy, six time judo champion of Egypt and once of Africa. He stood six foot five in his stockinged feet and, with a body like Tarzan's, Georges had not done a stroke of work since his college days, but frolicked in the clubs of Cairo and the waves of the Red Sea. He horrified friends by breaking six bricks with one blow of his hand, he bore the scars of a shark bite on his leg and was the only man I knew who dared to dive down to deadly moray eels and feed them with fish held in his own mouth while patting the hideous beasts as if they were domestic pets. Georges was no sailor either; he knew the sea only from below, and when he asked to join us after reading the verdict of the papyrus experts he gave a charming reason for coming along. He said it was because he was happier under water than above it. Like other old Coptic families in Egypt, the Sourials also traced their origins back to the days before the Arabs arrived bringing the teachings of Mohammed to the land of the Nile. From the day he first glimpsed the ghosts of a chance of coming with us, Georges, who usually slept like a mummy for fourteen hours of the twenty-four, suddenly began to rise at dawn and make himself useful in the camp behind the pyramids. His odd acquaintances in the most obscure corners of Cairo brought us into contact with an old sailmaker who still sewed with needle and thread, the basketmaker who wove the cabin by hand, a baker who could bake an Egyptian bread according to the recipe from the Cairo Museum, and a whole community of potters who lived on an isolated hillside in the suburbs. There they would stand waist-deep in clay slip, stirring it with their

bodies and limbs before they began to turn the potter's wheel with
their bare feet. Thus our 160 amphorae were made according to the
five-thousand-year-old example in the Cairo Museum.

Day by day the papyrus bundles absorbed more and more sea
water as they lay bobbing on the waves, while on board there was
hectic, almost feverish, activity. The weight of papyrus and rope
had previously been about twelve tons, but ton after ton was
absorbed below the water line without sinking the boat. At the
same time tons of cargo and superstructure were being loaded on
deck without the vessel heeling visibly. She lay steady as an island.
The heaviest burdens were the great bipod mast, which was erected in
front of the wickerwork cabin, and the bridge, built of lashed poles
placed behind the same cabin so that we could see over its roof. With
this weight added to that of the cabin, the heavy rudder and the
spare timber for repairs that lay on deck, the papyrus rolls were
carrying a good two tons of wood cargo in addition to over a ton of
water in heavy jars and at least two tons of food supplies, containers and equipment.

Activity during the last week was frenetic. Each day the papyrus
spent in sea water represented a day of its life lost, according to the
experts, and that was reason enough to hurry. A no less compelling
reason was that, with every day that passed, the hurricane season on
the other side of the Atlantic drew nearer. As if by a miracle our
schedule had held, with a failure margin of only one week, including
the detour to Chad and all other obstacles. But now the bustle was
reaching a real crescendo. We no longer had a day to lose. We
packed and carried and rolled cargo on the dock side. We climbed and
hauled and knotted on masts and stays. We cut and whittled and
lashed with ropes and leather on steering bridge and oars. The
deck seethed with willing helpers. Captain De Bock, veteran of the
Franco-Belgian expedition to Easter Island and an experienced sailor,
had calculated the probable line of drift of the papyrus boat before
taking leave from his post as Harbor Pilot guiding 50–100,000 tonners
in and out of Antwerp harbor. Now he stood, stout and reliable, on
the papyrus deck supervising stowing and lashing according to the
best nautical traditions. His Norwegian colleague, Captain Arne
Hartmark, had previously captained my own expedition vessel to
Easter Island. Here he was again, clinging to the masthead of *Ra*,

securing the rigging in a seamanlike manner with mountaineer Carlo Mauri. Herman Watzinger from the *Kon-Tiki* expedition had come from Peru, on his way to Rome, to give us a helping hand at the start, and Frank Taplin had come from New York with renewed good wishes from U Thant.

Our wives and the Pasha's wife, Aicha, squatted round the jars in the warehouse on land, packing sheep's cheese in olive oil, fresh eggs in lime solution, dried fish, nuts and mutton sausages in baskets and sacks. Aicha mixed ground almonds and honey, butter, flour, and dates, into *sello*, a sort of powdered substance that represented Morocco's oldest and most easily preserved traveling food. The last days, when the Pasha of Safi had to provide us with a police barrier so that the work on the dock would not be brought to a complete standstill press, photographers, and public jostled shoulder to shoulder in a spirit of amiable curiosity. One man fell over the edge of the wharf, jars were smashed, and a kerosene lamp was trodden flat.

Then the great day dawned. The *Ra* had now been lying in the harbor absorbing sea water for eight full days and had consequently lived out more than half its lifetime, according to the experts. The day dawned with a mild offshore breeze that increased in strength. By eight o'clock on the morning of May 25 the fluttering flags on both *Ra* and the old Portuguese citadel up on land were pointing straight out toward the open Atlantic. Rais Fatah, the sardine fishermen's spokesman and the expedition's local adviser, a black-skinned giant of an Arab, came rowing across the harbor with sixteen of his men, divided among four open rowboats which were to tow *Ra* out of the harbor.

There was hectic activity down on the long stone pier. The mass of people was jammed together in an impenetrable wall, and photographers were sitting in all the boats and on top of the cargo cranes. Aicha needed police help to get through to the dock side and present a parting gift: a lively little baby monkey, which the Pasha's people had recently caught for us in the Atlas Mountains and named Safi. It clung desperately to the ship's godmother until it noticed that one or two of the men on board had fur on their faces. Then it jumped happily over to the boat and played a vigorous part in a melee of farewell embraces and good wishes in many languages,

Captions for the following four pages

48. *Alone on the ocean.* Beyond the Moroccan coast, wind and current began to tug the papyrus ship away from the mainland of the Old World.

49. *Experimenting* with unknown rigging and steering gear. Before we learned the trick we had broken both rudder-oars and the yard that supported the sail.

50. *Streaming two sea anchors,* we drifted southward along the African coast without sail or steering oar. (Above)

51. *The broken rudder-oars* spliced with rope and hardwood by Abdullah the carpenter. (Below)

Captions for the preceding four pages

52. *Norman* emerged from the wicker cabin with his sextant after a bout of influenza, and announced that we were drifting toward the reefs of Cape Juby. (Above)

53. *Safi the baby monkey,* a happy farewell gift from the Pasha of Safi, enjoying herself on the mast and swinging ropes. (Below)

54. *Salt meat* being sliced for soaking in sea water by Georges. (Above)

55. *A broken jar* of nuts solves the rationing problem for Safi. (Middle)

56. *Fresh eggs* having preservative lime paste rinsed off by *chef de cuisine* Carlo. (Below)

57. *Galley* under the bottom step of the mast, presided over by Georges and Santiago while the cook takes photographs. (Above)

58. *Quartermaster Santiago* found that the papyrus deck buckled so much that the jars had to be well padded in order not to chafe holes in each other. (Below)

59 and 60. *Flying fish* landed on board in large numbers and were either fried for breakfast or used as bait. (Above)

61. *A dorado* caught by the author using flying fish as bait. (Below)

while the fishermen, unmoved by all the uproar, attached a rope
from each of the four dinghies to the thick rope we had secured right
round the reed boat at the water line. Now they were waiting for
orders to row us away from the seething mass of people. One after the
other we tore ourselves away and jumped down from the high stone
wharf to the soft, vegetable deck of the papyrus boat. Abdullah,
Georges and Santiago blew kisses, and handed autographs up to the
dock side; Carlo gave his blond Italian wife a last farewell kiss; Norman, who was struggling with a sore throat, escaped from the good
wishes and admonitions of the American ambassador; while the
Russian ambassador gave Yuri a touching hug on this, his first
departure from Soviet guidance and organization. I myself found a
microphone stuck into my hand and paid a last debt of gratitude to
all the expedition's friends and collaborators who were now suddenly
left behind on the dock, although we felt that their place was on
board with us; Ambassador Anker from Cairo, Pasha Amara and
his Moroccan helpers, Captains De Bock and Hartmark, Corio the
camp master, Herman Watzinger, Frank Taplin, Bruno Vailati. Then
I jumped on board with the rest. It was almost like walking on a
mattress. I signaled to Rais Fatah, the men on land cast off, and
the fishermen leaned to their oars and began to row. The time was
eight-thirty. Slowly our broad reed bundle began to move away
from the quay.

Then began a shrill chorus of wails, so unexpected that at first
everyone jumped and then every one of us was left with a lump in
his throat. All the fishing boats in the harbor had started up their
rending sirens, accompanied by deep blasts from factory and warehouse whistles on land. Ships' bells were rung, the crowd cheered
and a cargo ship lying at anchor outside the harbor began to send up
crackling signal rockets which burst in a shower of stars and slowly
settled on the water ahead of us in a blood-red carpet of smoke. I
was a royal farewell that almost scared us. Time had not allowed us
to test our vessel before departure. And now we stood on our strange
boat, tugging experimentally as the curious rigging and fiddling about
with two parallel, oarlike rudders, set aslant, of a type no man had
tried since the last Egyptians recorded the system for posterity on
their tomb walls, before the artists and their boats vanished from
the surface of the earth. What if we could not make the mechanism

work? What if we came swimming back to the wharf from papyrus bundles scattered to the four winds by the waves outside the harbor wall? The whole harbor began moving behind us. An escort of fishing smacks, yachts and motorboats followed us past the farthest break-water, while all the sirens and bells continued to sound as if for the New Year celebrations. Above us circled an Embassy plane and a helicopter that had come down from the capital, Rabat. Outside the breakwater the uproar died away, the ocean seas began their swell, the smallest escort vessels turned around and put back to calm waters and we were alone with the Atlantic and the big fishing boats accompanying us. Our four rowboats cast off, and with good wishes in Arabic the oarsmen headed back with the smaller motorboats toward the high pier.

For the first time we hoisted Ra's sail. Large and heavy, made of strong Egyptian sailcloth, it was a good twenty-six feet high and twenty-three feet wide along the yardarm at the top, narrowing down-ward in the ancient Egyptian manner to a mere fifteen feet, the breadth of the papyrus boat itself, at the lower end near the deck. A couple of light puffs of wind barely pushed the heavy yard clear of the straddled mast, showing that the good offshore wind was already dy-ing away. And then the big, wine-colored sail hung almost motion-less, displaying its rust-red sun disk, the bright, freshly painted sym-bol of Ra. The whole row of flags arrayed in alphabetical order hung idly like a colorful clothesline over the cabin roof: Chad, Egypt, Italy, Mexico, Morocco, Norway, U.S.A. and U.S.S.R., flanked at either end by the United Nations' optimistic flag, with its white globe on a light-blue field.

Abdullah and I stood, each holding the tiller of a big rudder-oar, on the bridge behind the basket cabin, looking anxiously from the slack sail to the white breakers washing against the stone breakwater only a few hundred yards away. Were they coming closer? Yes. A sighting from the tip of the jetty up to a tower on the fortress wall showed that we were drifting slowly back toward land. Perhaps the long, mountainous point, which projected to the north and sheltered Safi, prevented the offshore wind from filling the sail. We tossed a rope end to the nearest fishing smack and soon we were moving at full speed in a straight line out to sea, with an escort of fishing smacks putt-putting all round us. At this speed we were not obeying

the laws of nature. The first thing to happen was that a line with a
net full of live lobsters that we were towing spun into our wake and
wound itself round one rudder-oar, which bent in an ominous arc
and threatened to break. A slash with a sharp knife, and the oar blade
was saved, but several days' banquets vanished in the waves behind us

The next thing to happen was that one of the three thick row
ing oars we had bound to the side of *Ra* as a leeboard was snapped
across by the speed alone. It was to this very oar blade that Norman
had nailed our future life line to family and friends ashore: the
copper plate that was to act as ground to our little portable radio
Metal obviously had no place on a springy papyrus boat; the oar blade
had broken at the exact spot where the copper plate ended and was
barely saved by being trailed along by the grounding wire.

This was no good. Wind or no wind, we would have to manage
on our own. We stopped the escort, hauled all our ropes on board
and hoisted our sail again. We noticed how violently the big fishing
smacks round us were rolling by comparison with our own raftlike
vessel which, like its predecessor, the balsa raft *Kon-Tiki*, simply
rocked gently up and down on the long rollers. The wind blew first in
light puffs, then with steadily increasing strength. But it was no
longer an offshore wind. The northeasterly typical of the time of
year had veered to the northwest and was blowing straight toward
the low cliffs that stretched southward from the safe harbor of Safi
We were still so close inshore that we could make out all the houses
We could even see the treacherous surf creeping silently up and down
the mustard-brown cliffs where the green lowlands of Morocco washed
their sun-heated façade in their eternal confrontation with the sea
That was where the wind would send us, unless we succeeded in
maneuvering the papyrus bundles.

All seven of us on board were equally in suspense about one
thing—how the steering mechanism would function. This was the
greatest lurking factor of uncertainty, for we had no teacher. Our
hope was that, beyond the Moroccan coast, wind and current would
carry us directly away from land so that we would have a week or two
for experiment without risk of being washed up against the cliffs. It
was the coast we were afraid of, not the open sea. We had avoided the
sea outside the estuary of the Nile for our experiment, for fear of be
ing washed up on the coast before we had discovered how the Egyp

tian steering system worked. Out in the open Atlantic, off Morocco, we assumed there would be room for trial and error, because the elements there usually carried flotsam straight out to sea.

We had constructed the *Ra*'s steering device according to the numerous models and wall paintings from the earliest Egyptian era. We had tried in vain to procure the cedar from Lebanon that the Egyptians had used for these huge rudder-oars, but the few surviving cedars in the ancient Phoenician kingdom were now protected in a national park. So we had to make do with a heavy Egyptian wood *cenebar*, for the bipod mast, and we had carved two twenty-five-foot steering oars, with blades as large and wide as the average writing desk, from an African jungle tree the Moroccans call *iroco*. These were now made fast slantwise aft on either side of *Ra*'s peaked stem. The lower part of the shaft, close to the blade, rested on a solid log lashed on across the boat aft. About twelve feet farther up and forward, the oar rested on a thinner cross log, which also served as the stern guardrail on the bridge. Where each of the two oar shafts met these crossbeams they lay in a rounded groove lined with leather and were rigidly lashed with thick ropes so that the oars could not jump out or swing sideways, but could only rotate round their own longitudinal axis. This made them useless as steering oars in the ordinary sense of the word. They could not be used like the long, free-swinging oars in the stern of *Kon-Tiki*, because they were tightly strapped top and bottom. Instead, each of them had a tiller of hardwood lashed fast at right angles across the shaft near the top, and a long thin rod hung horizontally from the end of one tiller to the other, secured with freely moving rope hinges, so that if a single person stood in the middle and pushed this horizontal rod from one side of the bridge to the other, both oars turned together round their own central axis, like two parallel, slanting rudders. The system was so ingenious and apparently different from the steering devices used by living peoples today that we all cheered with relief when for the first time I tentatively pushed the suspended crossbar to port and *Ra* slowly, but co-operatively as an amiable horse, obeyed the signal by turning her bows to starboard. I promptly pushed the bar over the starboard side and *Ra* swung slowly to port.

There was no doubt about it. We were using a steering mechanism which in historical perspective represented the forerunner of the rudder, the missing link between a primitive steering oar and a modern tiller. At some point in antiquity the Egyptians had discovered that pushing a long steering oar sideways to make a sailing boat turn was unnecessarily laborious. All you had to do was to twist the shaft so that the blade was not perpendicular in the water and the vessel would swing just as well. So they put a crossbar on the shaft and had invented the steering device we were now testing. The thin rod suspended crosswise between the two tillers was simply an improvement to enable a single helmsman to control an oar on each side of the boat at the same time. All that was needed then was for the sailors of old gradually to discover that if they placed the oar blade with the shaft vertical instead of slanting, and continued to twist the little crosswise handle, they had invented what we know today as the rudder.

Abdullah of the desert, standing with gleaming eyes on the bridge at my side, now also grasped the long, thin horizontal rod. Four hands made steering easier still, and down on the deck the others scurried about, organized by Norman, hauling on ropes that set the mainsail in the position where it could best catch the changing wind. Our first hesitant steps were being followed by excited journalists and experienced old salts on board the chugging vessels that circled about us, and everyone seemed as relieved as we were to find that the reed boat really could be navigated. The northwesterly was blowing us straight toward land, but we managed to beat almost 90° up into the wind so that we took it on the starboard beam and traveled southwest, parallel to the land. The combers were rolling steadily and strongly here beyond the open coast where Cape Badusa gave no lee and the fishing smacks, crowded for the occasion with more or less seaworthy passengers, began to turn back. One after another they blew their horns and waved good-by. The last I saw was my wife, Yvonne, who was trying, seasick as she was, to regain her sea legs long enough to wave both arms at once. The helicopter disappeared and the airplane made its last farewell pass just over our heads.

Then we were alone with the sea. Seven men, a monkey gamboling gleefully in the stays, and a wooden cage full of cackling fowl and a single duck. It was suddenly so strange and quiet, with only the sea swelling and frothing round our peaceful Noah's ark.

As soon as Norman had managed to hoist the big sail and see to it that the sheets and tacks were secure, he came stumbling aft along the papyrus deck and confided to me that he was now feeling really ill. He was white-faced and red-eyed. Yuri wobbled over on unsteady legs and confirmed to our general consternation that Norman's temperature was 102°. Influenza. The sea wind was flinging itself at us in colder and colder gusts, and our Russian doctor ordered our American navigator to bed immediately in his sleeping bag inside the wickerwork cabin. With that our only sailor was temporarily out of action.

The onshore wind strengthened and the sea began to pile up in foaming breakers. When the largest waves came surging toward us *Ra* simply lifted one side and amiably let them pass under the rolls of reed. But now and then they smashed so vigorously against the oar blades that both shafts bent visibly and I had to roar at the powerful Abdullah to slacken his iron grip and yield a little to the pressure so that the oars would not snap.

Everything was going well and we were in high spirits—even the unfortunate patient, who lay bemoaning his uselessness. Carlo had quickly revealed himself as the vessel's supreme knot expert, quite used to both sleeping and eating suspended on a rope. Now he enthusiastically served hot coffee and the cold chicken legs we had brought with us and informed me gleefully that life at sea was just like life on the mountaintops: the same fellowship with nature, the same challenging duel with the elements, the same *joie de vivre* and necessity for quick solutions to unexpected problems.

We held our course steadily across the wind at a speed of about three knots, and the coast did not seem to be coming any nearer. It was three-fifteen in the afternoon and I felt that everything was going so well that Abdullah and I could be relieved by the two men on the next watch. Carlo and the judo champion Georges took over, fresh and vigorous, and Abdullah crawled into the cabin for a well-earned rest while I picked my way forward along the papyrus rolls to take a look at the foredeck, which was so stacked with jars, goatskins and baskets of vegetables that all further passage forward was barred for the time being, unless one balanced on the outermost round reed bulwark. Just forward of the wind-filled sail Santiago sat with a broad smile on his face, leaning against the chicken coop and enjoying the view of the distant coast. Stiff after nearly seven hours at the rudder-oar, I dropped down beside him and relaxed for the first time in many hectic weeks. There we both sat and reveled in the papyrus boat's superb ability to ride out all the waves that lifted and flung themselves against us on the starboard beam without disturbing our trim, without even giving us a harmless drenching. I stretched out and was enjoying the glow of happiness pervading my whole weary body when I was suddenly jolted out of my blissful state by an appeal from three panic-stricken voices:

"Thor! Thor!"

It was barely five minutes since I had been standing on the bridge. I sprang up and grasped the edge of the suddenly flapping sail in order not to lose my foothold on the reeds. Hanging on to it, I clambered around it over the water and made my way toward the stern with a thousand fearful misgivings buzzing in my head Yuri came wobbling toward me like a drunken tightrope walker, so overwrought that he could only speak Russian and gesticulate toward the stern where the two men on the bridge were leaning forward, shouting to me in helpless desperation. So everyone was still on board. As long as we could manage to stay on board we would be all right. Georges waved his arms and Carlo yelled in Italian that the rudder-oars were broken. Both of them! One look was enough to reveal the extent of the damage. Both oar shafts had snapped at the throat, just above the shoulders of the blade, and the two big, yellow-brown blades had come to the surface and were being towed behind like surfboards. *Iroco* could not possibly be the robust wood we had been told it was. Fortunately we had tied a rope to each blade in the Egyptian manner, so that the oar itself could not slip away aft, and we hurried to pull in the vital broad wooden blades before the ropes were chafed away. Carlo and Georges were left with two empty shafts projecting into the water aft, with no flat surface to control our course, no matter how they twisted the handles.

It was like a punch in the solar plexus.

"Do we have to give up?" Carlo asked in a low voice. The three men aft fixed me with looks of miserable inquiry.

Before there was time to answer, I realized that *Ra* was coming slowly about. With sail filled again and bow pointing in exactly the right direction the reed boat continued serenely on the very course we had been trying to hold by force. In that second I understood what had happened and felt a surge of relief. Two perpendicular oars, which were still made fast as a lee-board forward, had truly come into their own now that there was no longer a rudder projecting aft as a keel. The onshore wind was thus pushing the stern sideways to leeward and the bow away from the coast. The whole vessel now obediently turned along a course that automatically pointed away from land.

"Wonderful!" I shouted in English, putting the most obvious joy into my voice in order to instill my own new confidence into these men who, with good cause, were about to abandon all hope of continuing the voyage across the Atlantic.

All the uproar brought the feverish Norman crawling out of the cabin just in time to receive his share of my jubilant shout. Delightedly, he asked what the good news was.

"Wonderful!" I repeated enthusiastically. "Both rudder-oars are broken! So for the rest of the voyage we can use the ancient *guara* method of the Incas!"

Norman stared blankly at me with bloodshot eyes, uncertain whether to laugh or cry. The others scrutinized me closely, all obviously wondering if I had gone out of my mind as a result of the accident or if I was conversant with some Indian witchcraft they knew nothing about. For, sure enough, *Ra* was holding her course more steadily than ever, as we could see both from the compass and from the line of the bow in relation to the coast. Carlo considered me for some time. Then the unhappy expression disappeared from his blue eyes and he gradually began to roar with laughter, until his red beard shook. Then Abdullah in the basket cabin woke up too, and soon we were all laughing uproariously with relief and delight at this vessel that steered herself. All we had to do was go and sit on the cargo. Up on the bridge the compass needle was left alone in its well-secured binnacle, pointing due southwest. It was there we wanted to go, and it was there the *Ra* was obediently heading under full sail in briskly foaming seas, while we all enjoyed life as passengers.

"Now we really are castaways," I admitted to my still slightly bewildered companions, but I hastened to add that for the experiment this was the best thing that could have happened. Something just like this might have befallen ancient vessels of this type that sailed past Gibraltar and tried to steer farther along the Moroccan coast. Now we would really see where they would have landed.

Carlo was beaming like the rising sun. He just went on shaking his head and laughing. One only had to let nature have its way, he agreed, and the elements took care of transportation. We had one spare rudder-oar on deck but we did not put it out for fear of breaking it as well before we had seriously begun to cross the great Atlantic Ocean. In any case the *iroco* wood had proved so brittle and insubstantial that we would have to reinforce the reserve oar before risking it in the waves.

Toward evening Yuri came crawling out of the cabin with an anxious expression.

"Now we have two patients who absolutely must stay in bed," he explained.

For the past two days Santiago had been tormented by a sort of eczema below the belt. The sea air seemed to have made the disease break out in full vigor. His skin had peeled away in several places and he himself feared that he might have caught the dangerous *tiña* sickness he had seen on the Canary Islands, for which we were now heading. Yuri was afraid Santiago might be right; *tiña* was a dreaded disease, widespread in North Africa.

When night fell we saw the lights of several ships passing us in both directions, some at disturbingly close quarters, and Carlo clambered up and made a little kerosene lantern fast to the swaying masthead, since there was an obvious danger of our haystack being rammed and sunk. The night watches on deck were divided between Italy, Egypt and Norway. Russia had more than enough to do caring for U.S.A. and Mexico, and we preferred to let the carpenter from Chad have his sleep out so that he could attack the problem of repairing the rudder-oars next day. The wind alarmed us by blowing in treacherous gusts toward land from both northwest and westnorthwest and I spent most of the night keeping my eye on a lighthouse blinking away on shore, until it, too, disappeared. As long as it was pitch dark I dared not succumb to the temptation to take a nap. With the navigator struggling with waves of fever, our only hope of judging the distance from the land was to gaze into the darkness for a light. Each new ship that appeared ahead or to port made my heart thump with excitement; was it a light from the coast, were we drifting toward buildings, or was it simply other seafarers? Not until we saw the red or green running lights could we relax, especially when we had assured ourselves that they would pass out of range of a collision. As long as there was enough water round us we had no serious problems.

When day dawned in the east and there was no land in sight we turned a smiling Yuri out into the morning chill, equipped as if for the Antarctic. It was his watch now, but he could do nothing on the steering bridge. So he simply sat down, solid and confident, in the cabin opening and filled his pipe while the rest of us crawled into our warm sleeping bags and let the papyrus bundles sail the sea for themselves. I was not the only one to be dog-tired after twenty-four hours of hectic vigilance. Sleep came before I had time to become really familiar with the highly personal character of the basket cabin and its energetic efforts to outdo the papyrus bundles in peculiar creaks, snorts, cracks and whines.

Our first day on board the *Ra* was over.

Chapter Eight

DOWN THE AFRICAN COAST TO CAPE JUBY

A cock crowed. There was a scent of fresh hay. I was on a farm. No, I was certainly not on a farm, because I was being carried helpless on a swaying stretcher. I woke up in a sleeping bag and heard water gurgling beneath me and waves foaming against my ear. Of course: I was on a boat. I half-opened my eyes and saw blue-gray waves through the chinks in the wicker wall before my nose. I was on the *Ra!* The scent of hay came from the mattresses which were filled with freshly dried Moroccan grass.

Cock-a-doodle-doo! I heard it again, now that I was awake, and shot on all fours to the opening in the bamboo wall to look ahead. We must be really close to the coast, about to run aground. Outside I could see nothing but breaking wavetops as far as the eye could reach, but straight ahead the view was blocked by the burgundy-red sail, taut as a drawn bow shooting us over the surface of the sea. Through the rushing of the waves in front of the sail I could hear a furious cackling and again a clear cock crow. Of course, it was our own poultry in the big chicken coop forward. Relieved, I crawled out, clad only in my underpants. Outside the air was icy and Yuri was sitting on the deck of the bridge, wrapped up like an Eskimo, writing notes.

We must be far out at sea by now, because there was a biting north wind with chaotic wave crests leaping ten to twelve feet above the troughs, and even from the masthead the horizon showed only an undulating transition between sky and sea at all points of the compass.

"Where are we?" asked Yuri.

"Here," I replied jokingly, and fell into the cabin over the navigator, who lay sprawled as if unconscious, while pills and germs raced round inside him. Only he knew how to use a sextant. I only knew how to drift about on a log raft. Heaven knew where we were. What I needed was a sweater and a windbreaker. A very cheerful whistle cut through the orchestra of creaks and the roar of the waves, from the narrow passage between sail and cabin. Carlo's ruddy, bearded face appeared behind the bamboo wall.

"Come and get it! Hot *karkadé* tea à la Nefertete, and mummy-bread-and-honey Tutankhamen!"

Abdullah woke up in the cabin and shook his African neighbor Georges awake. Ravenously we swarmed round Carlo, who had served breakfast on the lid of the chicken coop, and every man found himself a big jar, a potato sack or a water-filled goatskin to sit on. We would get the deck tidy and make life comfortable gradually, as soon as we had mastered the steering gear.

"Where are we?" asked Georges, echoing Yuri's earlier question.

"Here," Yuri repeated on his way to the patients with two hot cups of *karkadé*.

"Africa is still *there*," I added, waving a hand over to port. "Is there anything else you want to know?"

"Yes," said Georges. "How did the old boys in the past find their position at sea without sextant or compass?"

"They could work out east and west by looking at the sun," explained Carlo, "and north and south from the Pole Star and the Southern Cross."

"And they could get the latitude by measuring the angle from the horizon to the Pole Star," I added. "It's always 90° seen from the North Pole and the same star is right down touching the horizon when seen from the Equator. If you are at 60° north, the Pole Star is 60° above the horizon and if you are at 32° it is 32°. If you can see the Pole Star, you can read your latitude directly from it. The Phoenicians, Polynesians and Vikings knew this, but longitude they could only guess roughly by calculating the distance according to their speed. For ancient navigators, however, the invisible ocean current was always an uncertain factor once they lost sight of land."

In the Egyptian museum back home in Cairo Georges had seen his countrymen's instruments, many thousands of years old, for measuring the angles of the celestial bodies, and he knew how important the sun and the Pole Star were in all their calculations, both astrological and architectural. On *Ra*, we could always tell direction by the sun, moon, and major constellations. And I decided to put together some sort of home-made device that would show us our latitude without our needing any special skills or modern instruments.

The red Egyptian *karkadé* tasted like hot cherry juice and was both refreshing and stimulating. The Egyptian bread biscuits looked like flattened buns. They were crisp and so tasty that, with or without honey, none of us had eaten better expedition rations. In good heart for a new day, we all went in and exchanged good wishes with the two brave patients in the cabin. Norman was really ill, but both his and Santiago's morale was first class. Santiago's problem was that the degree of humidity on the *Ra*, barely two hands' breadths above sea level, made all our clothes, sleeping bags and blankets sticky with salt sea air and his skin was being constantly chafed, so that the slightest movement hurt him. Yuri had his hands full with the two of them. Ill as they were, it must have been something of a strain for them to lie idle and listen to the heart-stopping, deafening bangs, squeals, creaks, and snorts that every single big wave forced out of the papyrus bundles, as they bent, buckled and stretched again in their many ropes. From time to time it sounded as if a hundred thousand Sunday editions of the New York *Times* were being torn to shreds under the heaving boxes on which Norman was sleeping. Sixteen wooden boxes were stacked on the wickerwork floor of the cabin, two under each man, with straw mattresses on top, and two spare boxes were reserved for Norman's radio and navigating equipment. As the papyrus undulated like a banana peel on the waves, the flexible cabin floor followed the movement, and with it, too, the boxes and straw mattresses, and the vertebrae and back of the man on top. Or the shoulder and hip, depending on whether he chose to lie on his back or on his side. It was like sleeping on the back of a live sea serpent.

Out on deck this sinuous action of the *Ra* was no less obvious. If one stood aft looking along the deck one saw the yellow railing billowing companionably with the masses of water below, and if one leaned outboard to catch a glimpse of the high, pointed bow forward of the sail, both it and the foredeck could be seen to rise with rhythmic restraint, as if to take a look over the wave crests. In the next breath the bow plunged down so steeply that its tip was barely visible above the chicken coop. The whole of the *Ra* was like a great, puffing sea monster, swimming with long undulations and snarling, snorting and bellowing to scare any reefs or obstacles out of its way. The oddest thing was the straddled mast with the big sail. It was like a huge distended dorsal fin, moving back and forth in time with the movement of *Ra*'s big round bundles of muscle. One moment there was a good three feet between the mast and the cabin wall where Carlo had stacked the cooking boxes, the next the distance had closed so much that one had to watch out in order not to get his toes caught under the cabin floor or the foot of the mast. Mast, cabin and steering bridge were all simply lashed to the flexible deck with rope and were therefore allowed considerable play. Had this not been so, we would not have survived even the first day. Had we not followed all the ancient rules, had we hammered the bridge together with nails, made the cabin of rigid planks or secured the mast to the papyrus with steel cable instead of rope, we would have been splintered, sawn and ripped to shreds by the very first seas. It was the suppleness and flexibility of every part which ensured that the sea practically never had a chance to snap the yielding papyrus fibers. All the same, it was quite a shock on the first day when carpenter Abdullah took out his measure and showed us that the elevated deck of the steering bridge periodically gaped a full eight inches from the back wall of the cabin, only to return a moment later and squeeze so tightly against the cabin wall that to have a finger caught between would have been disastrous. It was vital to keep really alert and have an eye on every finger until we were thoroughly at home on board. We looked forward with some anxiety to the probable behavior of our paper boat in a few weeks' time since it was already so elastic and loose-jointed on the second day at sea.

From experience with the *Kon-Tiki* I already knew before we set out that the most dangerous threat to raft voyagers was to have a man overboard. We could not go about and sail into the wind, at least not with our present lack of experience. A good swimmer could not catch up with us at the speed we were moving. We had a huge crate containing a six-man life raft of foam rubber lashed fast between the legs of the steering platform aft, but that was only for use in extreme emergency and could not be launched without cutting away the whole bridge. An ax hung ready for that purpose. But even the rectangular life raft, if launched, would have no chance of overtaking the *Ra* and we would drift separately. Carlo Mauri had made each of us a six-feet life line with a mountaineer's hook on it, and we always had this rope tied round our bodies, with the hook ready to be slipped over lashings, stays or woodwork as soon as we moved outside the cabin. Therefore, rule number one was: stay on board. Never move from one place to another without your own rope's end ready for immediate attachment.

I stuck to this rule to the point of absurdity, regardless of the weather, and told my companions about Herman Watzinger, who had only just been saved by Knut Haugland when he fell overboard from *Kon-Tiki*. Georges the diving champion and Abdullah the Central African had difficulty in understanding that it was not enough for them to be roped up only when alone on nightwatch, or hanging over the crossbar aft, answering the call of nature. Georges finally took the order to heart when he realized it was important to me. But every other day I continued to find Abdullah singing happily on the very edge of the papyrus roll, with his life line hanging down like the tail of a monkey. Finally I went for him.

"Abdullah," I said. "This water is bigger than the whole of Africa and a thousand times as deep as Lake Chad where Georges can dive to the bottom."

"*Ah, oui,*" said Abdullah, impressed.

"And it is full of fish which eat men. They are bigger than crocodiles and swim twice as fast."

"*Ah, oui,*" repeated the receptive Abdullah, always grateful for new knowledge.

"But don't you understand that if you fall overboard you will drown, you will be eaten, you will not see America?"

A broad and fatherly smile spread over Abdullah's face and he placed a huge hand kindly on my shoulder.

"You don't understand," he said. "Look here!"

He pulled up his thick pullover and revealed a well-filled black stomach. Round it was tied a thick piece of twine, and from the twine four small leather pouches hung against the small of his back.

"With these, nothing can happen to me," he assured me. He had been given the pouches by his father and they had been filled by a medicine man at home in Chad. Judging by others I had seen on sale in the market place in Bol they contained leopard claws, dyed pebbles, seeds and dry scraps of plant. Abdullah pulled the jersey down again conspiratorially and nodded in triumph. Was my mind at rest now? Nothing *could* happen to Abdullah. But to please me he, too, agreed to rope himself up.

Abdullah's first shock came when early in the morning he rushed to tell me that salt had got into the water. Into all of it. How had it happened? I, too, was seriously alarmed and asked him which jars he had tried.

"Not a jar, there!" said Abdullah, shaken, and pointed out to sea. This was the first time we realized he did not know the ocean was salt. When I explained that it was salt all the way from Africa to America he asked wide-eyed where all that costly salt had come from. After the geological explanation he was in despair. Santiago had said we must be economical with our drinking water on board; we could only have one liter, or slightly more than one quart per man per day. Abdullah said he would need at least five times as much, because as a Moslem he had to wash arms and legs, head and face every single time he prayed. He prayed five times a day.

"You can use sea water for your prayers," I assured him. But Abdullah could not. According to his religion, pure water must be used for the washing ceremony. There was salt in this.

The problem of the salt was still under discussion when Abdullah had another fright. Georges had pulled the sleepy baby monkey, Safi, out of her bed in a perforated cardboard suitcase where she had spent the night, and in her excitement the little lady had made a tiny pool on Abdullah's mattress. Now Abdullah was really beside himself. Had the monkey done this? If a dog or monkey did his business on a believer's clothes he could not pray to Allah for forty days! Abdullah began to roll his eyes in utter desperation. Forty days without Allah!

Georges settled Abdullah's moral scruples with a white lie. It was not the monkey, it was sea spray. Practical wishful thinking made

Abdullah accept the explanation without poking his nose further into the slightly odorous problem. I decreed that in any case the monkey must begin to wear trousers and in addition must never again be allowed to sit on Abdullah's mattress.

"Abdullah," I added, "you who need pure water for your prayers, have you ever thought how many monkeys and dogs live round all the wells in Chad? Out here there isn't a dog for miles around and the little that Safi produces we leave behind us. There is nowhere in the world where you can find purer water than at sea."

Abdullah listened and thought. A moment later he was subjecting a canvas bucket of sea water to lengthy scrutiny. Then the ceremonial washing began, at breakneck speed and with the graceful dexterity of a conjuror. After that Abdullah went up to the compass, where Yuri helped him to find the approximate direction of Mecca. With the sincerity of a convinced monk he knelt on his own mattress in the cabin opening and bowed repeatedly toward the east with his forehead to the mattress cover. Then he took out his long string of beads and began to reel off prayers. The prayers ran along the string of beads like peas out of a sack, but Abdullah's spirit was so genuine that all of us, whether Catholic or Protestant, Copt, nature philosopher, or atheist, had to respect his pious conviction.

The wind was increasing in strength. It became almost violent. Without rudder-oars we had absolutely no control of the craft, but *Ra* still chased along in a seemingly perfect direction. Abdullah, now feeling clean inside and out, joined me on the bridge with knife and drill. We had to find some way of lashing the broken oar blades back to their shafts. Abdullah was in high spirits, humming Central African jungle tunes while struggling to keep on his feet with his long white tunic catching the gusts of wind. Carlo joined us with his alpine knot-craft and we had almost repaired the first oar when the wind became really bad. A couple of powerful gusts from different directions suddenly took the sail aback and it twisted before we had a chance to readjust the sheets and tacks.

A head wind flung itself with all its strength against the big sail. While the heavy yard, twenty-three feet long, from which the sail hung, crashed so violently against the top of the straddled mast that the wood at the top threatened to break, the whole of the big mainsail flapped in savage jerks, threatening to split itself against the mast.

The thrashing sail overturned fruit baskets and caught on the chicken coop, making the poultry cackle and squawk to rival our shouted orders. A square provision basket was suddenly bobbing about in our wake. No one knew what was in it, because quartermaster Santiago was lying in bed with his list of inventory. Yuri almost had to hold him and Norman down in their bunks by force while I clambered onto the bridge and tried to lead the battle against the giant sail. A man's voice was faint in the stormy gusts that flung his words out over the foaming wavetops, together with the flaps, bangs and screeches from sail and papyrus bundles.

It was no good trying to lower the sail now; it would fly out to sea like a kite. We must get the vessel back on course, partly by turning the sail and partly by turning the hull. Big Georges, with an ordinary oar braced against the raised papyrus tail, was set to row *Ra*'s stern section up into the wind. An umbrella-shaped canvas sea anchor was slung overboard on a long rope; nothing is more effective in reducing speed and keeping stern to the wind. On the bridge I saw the compass needle turning slowly while I fought desperately to hang on without being pulled overboard by a sheet that jerked and lashed like a whip. I tried to secure it to the side of the bridge, making sure at the same time that the incomplete crew was hauling on the right ropes and yet properly secured by life lines. In the gusts of wind I bawled orders in Italian to Carlo, in English to Yuri, in French to Abdullah and in English, French or Italian, just as it came, to Georges, but the truth was that I did not even know the names in my own mother tongue of the ropes I was asking them to haul on. So my admiration for the powers of comprehension of this international team of landlubbers reached a peak as the day went on.

When we had salvaged the precious sail, fastened the sheets, bound all our ordinary rowing oars like Indian *guara* to the side of the ship fore and aft and hauled the sea anchor in again, everything proceeded peacefully, as before. We had a little breathing space in which I tried to invent some short words that everyone could understand when it was vital to save seconds, should anything of the sort happen again. Between the powerful gusts of wind, weak-voiced fragments of good advice emerged through the wickerwork walls from the feverish Norman. He had done his utmost in advance to teach all the rest of us the English expressions for pulling in, slacking off, or letting go the halyard which hoisted the sail, the tack controlling each end of the long yardarm from which the sail hung, and the sheets attached to the sail's two loose bottom corners, to port and starboard. But practice had now shown us that, since three of the men fit for duty understood either little English or none, the result was always a gamble if I shouted to Yuri or to Carlo: "Pull in starboard tack!" or to Abdullah: "Let go port side sheet!"

No sooner were the five of us sitting, panting but triumphant, on the bridge trying to work out a few short practical expressions, Esperanto style, than warning poundings started up again in the mast. Although this time everyone was at his post in a flash, sail and craft succeeded in turning round again. This happened time after time, time after time. We drifted farther on the same course, but sidewise or sometimes even stern foremost, with sail and yard struggling at chaotic angles. We had to make sure the sail was always filled to save the yard from breaking, but sometimes we only succeeded by turning the sail to the wrong side. By turning it round outside the port leg instead of outside the starboard leg of the straddling mast, the sail would willingly fill, but then we automatically sailed almost at right angles to the course we needed in order to keep clear of land. For painfully long periods at a time we headed under full sail straight for the African coast while we rowed, hauled on ropes, wrestled with the sea anchor and tried to lash the rowing oars in different positions, *guara* style, in our efforts to return to the proper course. But without the big rudder-oars the boat absolutely refused to accept any compromise. The sail sent the boat either directly southeast or directly southwest; nothing in between. Every time an unruly gust turned us about, so that we were stuck with *Ra*'s nose pointing southeast, the coast of Africa came nearer and nearer. Carlo spent his time up at the wildly swinging masthead, but fortunately saw no sign of land. Nevertheless we knew that the coast, which swerved inward south of Safi, bulged out again toward us further down. No sooner had we got control of the sail one way than it twisted the other way and flapped about with such violence that every one of us had to grab it and use all his weight and strength in order not to be swept out to sea. One piece of headgear after another flew overboard; the most regretted was Abdullah's rainbow-colored Moslem cap, which was practically part of Abdullah himself. But now each man was automatically making himself fast every time we changed places. The monkey had her own private little rope and performed rapturous gymnastics upside down on the mast stays. The poultry were safe in their cage, which by now had been covered over and made fast out of range of the sail.

As the day passed the changing wind blew in such mighty gusts that there was constant danger of losing the whole rigging before we regained control of the steering. The sail would have to come down. We had no alternative but to try to lower it in the squalls.

No sooner had two men loosed the halyard, while the other three of us stood ready with the sheets to guide the yard with sail down to the deck, than a mighty blast came and swept the heavy mainsail out like a flag over the sea. Yuri and Abdullah fought desperately to recapture the loose sheet that fluttered over the wave-tops to port. The other three of us hooked feet and knees round anything we could in order not to be lifted overboard with the starboard sheet—our last chance of preventing the sail from disappearing forever beneath the waves. There was a frightful creaking from the mast and all the ropes which held it, and the papyrus bundles shrieked and heeled over so that for the first time we had an uneasy feeling that our miracle boat might actually be capable of capsizing. One thing was certain: no other fifty-foot sailing boat in the world could have withstood this gigantic pressure without immediately capsizing, unless the mast broke first.

Inch by inch we managed to recapture the yard and most of the sail, but large sections of the sail still lay overboard on the combers in folds containing many bathtubfuls of water, and in our struggles to drag this heavy weight free of the sea's grasp we knocked off yet another of our precious rowing oars, which disappeared under a wave and bobbed up tantalizingly in our wake.

"See you in America!" Carlo shouted at the oar. "But we're going faster than you!"

Soaked with sea water and laden with the weight of a yard six feet wider than the whole deck, the jumbled sail had to be turned and stowed lengthwise along *Ra*'s port side. Triumphant, but as exhausted as if we had lasted twenty rounds in the ring, the five of us sat on top of the soggy mess of canvas, trying to restrain this rebellious burgundy-red flying dragon which was still jerking convulsively as its folds were inflated by the wild gusts of wind. Finally the brute was securely bound.

It was suddenly strangely quiet on board. There was only a rhythmic, peaceful creaking, which made us feel that mother sea had adopted the reed boat Ra as a marine cradle full of unruly fellows who now had to be rocked to sleep before they hurt themselves by overturning the whole cradle. Ra, stripped to the bare mast, once again set her course as she wished, parallel to land, no longer threatening to run us ashore.

I looked at Carlo. He began to smile. He chuckled. Then he began to laugh without restraint. We all stared at him.

"Now we have neither sail nor rudder-oars. There is nothing left on this craft to obey human orders any more. Nature is in command now. As soon as we stop fighting her, we can just relax and enjoy ourselves."

We began to look about us. Nothing but peace and order everywhere. No yard, no sail, no engine, no worries: here we were, rocking in a communal papyrus hammock, while the mighty ocean current took us where it liked, and that was just where we wanted to go. Abdullah crawled into the cabin and lay down with his tiny pocket radio against his ear. Georges wanted to fish. Yuri ate an orange and went off with the skin to make a glass of liqueur by adding surgical spirit, while Carlo began to poke about in sacks and baskets to find the raw material for a better meal. Santiago lay motionless in the cabin with his little book of inventory and called out the numbers on the jars that contained water, dates, eggs, olives or grain for the chickens. I took the hunting knife to whittle that instrument I had been planning to make, which could give us our latitude. Then Norman could not restrain himself any longer.

"This is all very fine, fellows," he groaned. "But not for the people at home. We promised to go on the air yesterday. They have to know that everything is OK, otherwise they will think we have gone down."

Yuri agreed and helped the feverish Norman to roll the mattress away so that they could open the locked case under his legs and pull out the little emergency transmitter with the built-in, hand-operated generator. A little later Safi radio replied clearly to Norman's call and was told that we had broken both rudders, but were continuing across the Atlantic Ocean with no problems. He also warned them that there would be no regular contact in the future, because the oar carrying the grounding plate was broken and lying on the deck. If we dropped it overboard in the seething waves the dancing copper plate would cut through both rope and papyrus. Norman was so weak that he sank back in his sleeping bag while Yuri packed up the radio. Carlo crawled in with a hot drink.

Georges caught no fish but came into the cabin with an idea. Why not hoist the sail reefed? Even a tiny spread of sail in this wind would help us to travel faster. The sail was deliberately sewn in such a way that we could reef and lash either one or two-thirds of it, so that we could hoist only the top strip of sail if the wind was too strong. I thought this a good idea and Norman nodded feebly. The five of us crawled out on deck again, heartened by a mighty Stone Age lunch based on salt sausage and fresh vegetables. After a desperate struggle we managed to turn the yard with the water-filled bundle of sail from the port side so that it lay spread out across the vessel, projecting three feet into the waves on either side. It was difficult to reef the sail in a wind that varied in strength between stiff breeze and light storm, but with our combined efforts all went well. We lay on top of it as we inched it out over the chicken coop and the rest of the cargo, and then rolled it up until only a third of the surface was left unfurled. Great was our triumph when this narrow strip of sail filled with wind at the masthead. With the sea anchor hauled aboard and the small rowing oars bound in place, we skimmed southwestward over the wave crests, rejoicing in this fresh victory over the elements.

Fifteen minutes passed. It was early afternoon and only our second day at sea. Abruptly a squall struck the sail again. We leaped to the tacks and sheets as one man when we heard the first thud of the heavy, wet roll of sail, which now hung bunched together at the masthead, and hammered the rigid yard against the mast. The next blow sounded like a scream for help from the masthead, and our hearts contracted as we heard the blow extend into a terrifying crash and a crack that jarred bone and marrow. We looked up and saw the whole, indispensable yard that held the sail outstretched slowly sagging on either side of the central point, while the sail shrank inward

Captions for the following four pages

62. *Lunch round the chicken coop*. When Norman and Thor took too long, Safi the monkey and Sinbad the duck came to book seats for the next sitting. (Above)

63. *The author's "nosometer,"* notched with a knife, measured the angle of the Pole Star and thus showed *Ra's* precise latitude. (Below)

64. *LI2B calling*. Norman operating the little transmitter that kept in touch with radio hams, while the author reads a report. Yuri sits outside the cabin door with the monkey. (Above)

65. *Change of watch* every two hours through the night. Georges struggles to wake up when Santiago and Yuri go off duty. (Below)

66. *Basket cabin interior*. Norman calculating the day's position, which is logged by the author. (Above)

67. *The weeks pass* and hair and beards grow. Georges trims Santiago. (Below)

68. *The steering oar* breaks again and the blade is salvaged by Yuri, Thor and Abdullah. (Above)

69. *The logs snapped* and the steering oars were in constant need of repair, while the papyrus rolls bent like rubber. (Below)

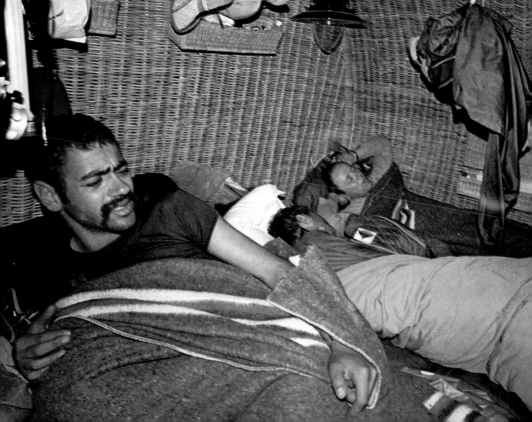

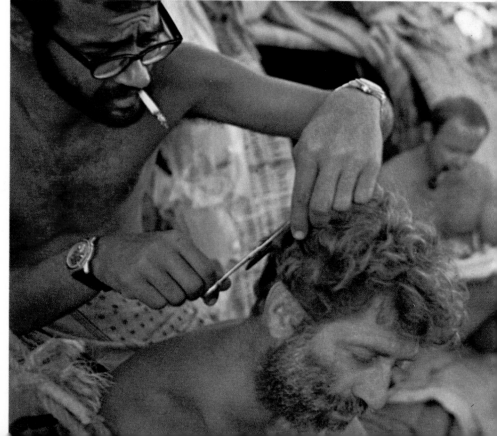

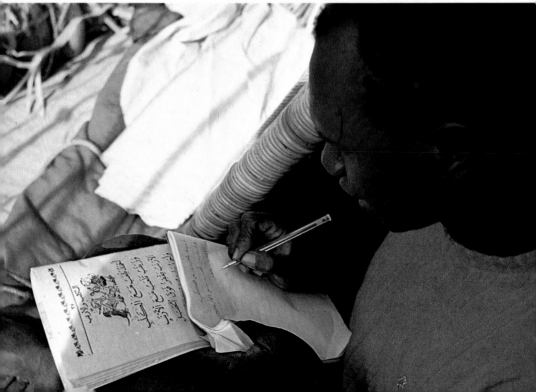

Captions for the preceding four pages

70. *At the masthead.* Norman was the expedition's only professional sailor. (Above)

71. *"No more beard,* after a year on the South Pole icecap," said Yuri, rigging a shaving mirror on the broken rudder-oar. (Below)

72 and 73. *Atlantic pollution. Ra* lay so low in the water that the expedition could see asphalt-like clumps of oil in countless numbers all over the ocean. The photo below was taken by Georges, swimming on a life line.

74. *Papyrus life belt.* Egyptian Georges reviving the art of his ancestors (see photo 12). (Above)

75. *Leisure pursuits.* Georges teaching Abdullah to write in Arabic. (Below)

like a bat folding its wings. Sharp splinters of broken wood stuck out
of the yard like angry claws. We had to lower the whole mess to
prevent the canvas from being ripped to shreds by the broken wood.
And we were only two days out of port. Two days.

No sooner was the wreckage of the broken yard and sail lying in
a heap on deck than *Ra* became as docile as before and our magic
reed rolls continued to undulate in the desired direction like a tame
sea serpent with us on its back.

"There you are, you see," said Carlo, and crawled into bed,
gratified.

Abdullah scurried aft and washed himself up to the knees and
elbows for his next prayer to Allah. Yuri sat down chuckling with
his pipe and diary in the door opening and I sat down beside him
with my whittling.

"Everything under control?" asked Santiago, cautiously sticking
his nose out of his sleeping bag.

"Everything," we chorused. "Everything. Now we have broken
everything that can be broken. Now there is only the papyrus left."

The rest of the afternoon passed peacefully inside the cabin
while the storm howled outside. We had not seen a ship, but shared
the night watch between us, because we were lying right on the
coastal shipping lane round Africa. We were constantly climbing
up to the masthead on the lookout for a light from land. Collisions
with ships and the perilous cliffs on shore were the only things we
feared.

Half an hour after midnight I was shaken awake by Carlo, who
was leaning over me, holding a kerosene lantern. With wide, anxious
eyes he whispered that there were lights all along the horizon on the
port bow. We were being driven sidelong by a strong northwester,
straight toward them. I had gone to bed fully dressed and had only to
tie on my life line before crawling out on deck. A bitingly cold wind
of moderate strength, and an overcast sky. Through the pitch-black
night I saw all the lights spread out along the horizon. As Carlo said,
they lay ahead of us in our line of drift. Four were very large and
another faint. It had to be the Moroccan coast. Carlo was up at the
swaying masthead. We seemed to be approaching fast. The other
three fit men were turned out. Now we would have to try to row
our reed bundles to save ourselves from a tragic fate on the rocks.

Then both Carlo and I thought we glimpsed a green light. Another, and a red one too. It was not land! A scattered fleet of big fishing smacks was sailing straight toward us! Blue with cold, the crew crawled back to bed. Soon afterward three big, rolling vessels rumbled close past our bows. A fourth lay broadside to us after stopping its engine so that *Ra* was heading straight for the pitching ship's side. I shone my flashlight on cabin wall and papyrus rolls and blinked "*Ra* OK, *Ra* OK." The big sea-fishing boat started up again and glided away, so slowly that we barely avoided a collision. It sent some incomprehensible flashes from the masthead and gradually disappeared in the darkness. Georges stood watch, wrapped like an Egyptian mummy in wind jacket and blankets, and I crawled into bed. Even hoarse shrieks from a hundred thousand tethered papyrus reeds were not enough to drown the uninhibited, rapturous humming of the son of the Nile, which the stern wind blew in through the thin wickerwork wall, all that separated our cozy den from the ferocious universe outside.

It was still cloudy when day dawned, our third day on board. The wind was less fierce, but the seas were more agitated than ever. We observed with satisfaction that the waves leaping madly round us simply lifted us into the air. The sea carried us forward gingerly like a ball and not even the most treacherous breakers managed to pour water on deck. The whole cargo was dry. With neither sail nor rudder, with neither sextant nor position, with no land in sight, the third day was a day of peace, during which we managed to finish splicing one rudder-oar and reinforced the middle section of a long reserve spar that was to replace the broken yard.

Abdullah was busy washing his smooth-shaven head for prayer when he stopped and uttered a hoarse cry of protest. The sea certainly was not pure! Someone had done his business out there and he had smeared it on his head. In the bottom of Abdullah's canvas bucket large and small black lumps were circulating. We looked overboard. Hundreds of similar clots were floating past us on both sides. Soft, asphalt-like lumps. An hour later they were still floating just as thickly round us. It must be the waste from a tanker. From the masthead, we looked for the culprit, but there was no ship in sight, and the sea continued to be covered with black lumps all day.

Toward afternoon we drifted past a big moonfish that lay idly on the surface, and later we were visited by nearly a hundred porpoises which suddenly surged up round us, leaped vertically out of the waves in a cheerful reel, and gave Abdullah indescribable pleasure before disappearing as suddenly as they had arrived.

The fourth day was noticeably warmer and calmer and the sun appeared through rifts in the clouds. For a long time we could clearly see the distant blue silhouette of the mainland rising in a couple of hump-shaped mountains. Santiago was really sick but Norman was much better, with no fever, and Yuri allowed him to crawl out and take the sun's meridian. But since we had no chronometer on board and the emergency radio could no longer pick up Safi radio, we lacked the to-the-second time accuracy required to fix a reliable position. This worried the two men in the cabin, because Norman thought that since we could still see the mainland we would not be able to pass outside the Canary Islands. We were drifting into the dangerous passage between the island Fuerte Ventura and Cape Juby on the African mainland. Santiago, who had lived in the Canary Islands as a boy, could confirm what Norman's reference books showed, that Cape Juby was the terror of all sailors because from the rocks a treacherously low sandbank juts out like a tongue into the most dangerous ocean current, just where the African coast turns south.

We were sitting forward on the heap of sail having a meal when we heard an eager yell from the ever-observant Abdullah, who had already finished eating.

"Horses! Horses!" He corrected himself: "Hippos!"

We looked where he was pointing and in a moment they came surging up again, two great whales that squinted at us with small indolent eyes and puffed through their blowholes, spouting up a mixture of air and spray. Abdullah had never seen such big hippos in Chad and it made his day. That a mammal could have a fish's tail seemed to him utterly preposterous, and yet one of the whales raised its tail politely to wave good-by and Abdullah was dumfounded at the inventiveness of Allah.

On the fifth day we awoke to a biting north wind and a violently restless sea. We put on all the clothing we owned. Abdullah's teeth chattered. For five days breaking seas had been flinging themselves constantly against *Ra*'s starboard beam just as we had calculated, because the whole of our journey would lie in the belt of the north-east trade winds. For this reason we had built the cabin's door opening on the opposite, that is the left or port side, which would be in the lee. We had also displaced the entire cabin and the heavier part of the cargo toward the starboard side so that the wind that filled the big sail from that side would not succeed in capsizing the whole boat. Both we and our advisers were well aware that sailing boats must be loaded with the main weight on the windward side in order not to capsize. By the fifth day bitter experience was beginning to show us that in this respect a papyrus boat turns counter to every other boat in the world. It is the only sailing boat that must be loaded more heavily on the lee side. The reason is that on the windward side the papyrus absorbs many tons of sea water above the water line, because waves and spray are always washing up over the whole side of the boat, whereas everything above the water line on the lee side remains dry and light. The weight of water on the exposed windward side gradually becomes so enormous that the vessel heels over *against* the wind instead of *with* it in the normal way.

It was too late to move the cabin amidships. It was lashed fast with stout rope running crosswise right through the bottom of the papyrus boat. We moved all loose cargo from starboard to port but that did not seem to be enough. The papyrus above the water line on the starboard side must have absorbed several tons of sea water, which now accompanied us on our voyage as an invisible cargo, weighing more than the few hundred pounds of food and drinking water that we had managed to transfer to the other side. We were actually sailing in a vessel that listed chronically to windward.

Norman was at last completely restored and while the rest of us restowed the cargo he tried to secure the unruly copper plate under the water so that he could make radio contact and thus get an accurate time. He had good reason to suspect that we were nearer the coast than he had estimated without chronometer time yesterday, and that we were actually drifting straight toward land at Cape Juby.

During the night a full gale blew up. The wind howled through all the mast stays and *Ra* seemed to grow more and more dislocated. The stormy seas flung themselves on us more savagely than before.

We kept double watch all night in order not to be caught unaware
by the sandbanks of Cape Juby, and we kept a close eye on all our
ropes. Not a line had snapped. Not a papyrus reed had worked loose.
But the timber of the bridge ground so violently against the wicker
corner of the cabin that everything within that corner was covered
with an even powdering of fine sawdust. Santiago was suffering from
insomnia, for at night it was almost impossible to get a wink of sleep
unless one was dead tired, as the cases heaved about beneath us, while
cabin, bridge and masts swayed out of step, making a racket like a
thousand cats with their tails stuck between the ropes. The whole
cabin was also leaning so severely to starboard that no one could lie
on his side without rolling over. The others lay four in a row, but we,
lying feet-to-feet with them, were only three because the radio and
navigation corner were on our side. Abdullah was always rolling down
on Georges who rolled down on Santiago, until Yuri, who was at
the bottom of the slope, received the others with knees and arms
because the wall would not allow him to roll farther. I had bundled
all my extra clothing under the starboard edge of the mattress and
Carlo had done the same, so that we would not roll down onto
Norman and the radio corner.

The storm continued to rage all night, with waves twelve to
fifteen feet high. The gusts sent a fine salt spray over the boat. During
the morning of the seventh day Ra seemed, oddly enough, to become
a little less disjointed; the ropes seemed to be tauter. The crest of an
enormous, towering sea, which quite inexplicably broke over us aft
and buried Norman to the waist, had difficulty in running out through
the papyrus. The sea spray on the deck and the moisture from below
had apparently made the papyrus reeds swell until they filled all the
ropes and all the interstices. So the vessel seemed more rigid and
robust than before; it was just unfortunate that she listed so badly to
starboard.

We were all filled with admiration at the splendid way in which
Ra rode out the storm; then Norman informed us that we were
heading for the rocks. We had a choice between trying to hoist the
sail in the powerful north wind or drifting straight toward land. We
agreed unanimously to try to hoist the sail, two-thirds spread, on the
newly reinforced yard. Even Santiago came staggering out, and with
the whole crew in action we got the sail up and the one spliced rudder-

oar out into the water astern. We skimmed like a flying fish over the crests, away from land. Soon afterward we heard another crack, the thick shaft of the spliced rudder-oar snapped like a matchstick and we could haul only the blade on board again. But the landlubbers had been gradually turning into a team of seamen. In one tiger-spring Abdullah was there, grasping the port side corner of the flapping sail, and Santiago crawled out and hooked himself fast beside him. Carlo and Yuri vanished without a word behind the cabin on the starboard side and slackened the sheets. Georges, clad only in his underpants, grasped one oar and rowed the stern up into the wind while Norman and I adjusted the small vertical oars until Ra, with no helmsman, pitched again over the wave crests like a weighty fish. So we held our course for the rest of the day, without a single reed being damaged by the storm. It was the thick wooden structures, not the thin reeds of the hull, which presented us with problems.

Next night the storm died down, but not the seas, which were running up to eighteen or twenty feet high. The cabin, no longer symmetrical, was leaning to windward like a tipped hat. I crawled out on deck in the darkness before my own night watch to survey the vessel. When I crawled under the sail to get a clear view ahead, my heart almost stopped beating. On the starboard bow was a tall broad lighthouse, illuminated with colored lamps and surrounded with a multitude of other lights. We were headed to the left of the whole immobile complex and accordingly bound straight for land. This lighthouse, which lay so far out, could only be Cape Juby.

With feverish haste we began turning the sail to alter course as best we could without rudder-oars. This was not enough; we just began to lose leeway and simply continued to approach land to the left of all the lights. With hearts beating we quickly realized that we could not pass outside, that we were racing blindly toward the invisible rocks. It struck us in the last minute that the lights were rocking slightly as if tower and houses were built on a floating pier rather than on sandbanks. Then we rushed past on the inside: the complex was detached from land. It proved to be a huge oil-drilling platform anchored off the African coast, lighted to the top with colored lamps to prevent collision with ships and aircraft. We just stood and stared. Then I yelled brusquely to Georges, who stood shivering, holding the little oar. Why the devil did he not pull on some clothes or get back into his sleeping bag before we had another man sick in bed!

On the seventh day we still had two-thirds of the reefed mainsail hoisted and seemed to be sailing in competition with high, surging swells traveling the same way as ourselves. Heavy banks of cloud were rolling up from both sides of *Ra*, but straight ahead there was a rift of blue sky between the two fronts. It all indicated that the Canary Islands and the African continent each lay hidden beneath one of the dense cloudbanks, and the blue strip of sky arched above the open stretch of sea between them. *Ra* willingly allowed herself to be steered toward the blue. Yuri's medical skill had got both Norman and Santiago on their feet again, but Georges was temporarily sent to bed with severe back pains after straining himself with the oar, half naked in the ice-cold night wind.

About noon Carlo was busy hauling on ropes which might succeed in bending the basket cabin to a more even keel. Standing on the bridge, I thought to my horror that I could see low green grassland through the binoculars every time we were lifted particularly high on a wave crest. A moment later Carlo was at the masthead with Norman at his heels. They called down that there was an uninhabited green slope running parallel to our own course, six sea miles away, at most, and perhaps even closer. We altered course as much as we possibly could. Soon the grassland disappeared from view. It must have been the low banks surrounding Cape Juby, where the coast swung southward. It must have been the last corner of Africa that we had put behind us, for there was no more land to be seen.

Carlo set about to prepare our first big feast, so Abdullah slaughtered three chickens over the rudder bar. Yuri's liqueur was ready. There was a lot to celebrate. First we would drink a funeral toast to the *iroco* tree. It was much too brittle for steering oars. Then we would drain a beaker to the papyrus reed. What a phenomenal boatbuilding material! It was now May 31 and the papyrus had been in the water for two weeks without rotting and without disintegrating. On the contrary, it was stronger and more pliant than ever. Not a single reed had been lost. We had been sailing for a week from Safi to Cape Juby, farther than from the Nile estuary to Byblos in the Phoenician kingdom. As far as from Egypt to Turkey. So we had already proved that the Egyptians could have delivered their own papyrus wherever they liked on the coast of Asia Minor without the help of foreign wooden ships.

Skol, Norman. *Skol,* Yuri. *Skol,* you fellows. *Skol* to Neptune and to all Abdullah's hippos. Safi sat between us on the chicken coop, drinking from a freshly opened coconut.

Then I heard someone babbling about "white houses" and leaped to my feet to look. Georges was lying on his stomach in the cabin opening, pointing inland to where we had seen the low banks disappearing. They had reappeared, this time rows of small white houses. A typical North African Arab village. To the right of all the houses lay a picturesque old fort. Here it was, Cape Juby, which we were sure we had already passed. We had been celebrating while in the greatest danger. We were gliding past the treacherous spit of land that had haunted our thoughts for a whole week and had claimed so many wrecks over the centuries. For a week we had been struggling to steer away from land, and here we were, passing on the current within gunshot of Cape Juby.

The white houses sank into the sea as quickly as they had appeared. We were drifting fast. Good-by, Africa. Good-by, Old World. We have no rudder. We don't need one on this voyage.

A big gull came out and landed on the upright papyrus bundle in the bows. It was chased off by the duck, which was taking an airing outside the chicken coop. The gull took off. Soon afterward we were surrounded by a whole flock of screaming sea birds, while the chickens cackled in their cage, which served as our dining table.

"I know what that first gull flew off to tell the others," said Carlo. "It said it had found a floating bird's nest off Cape Juby."

Chapter Nine

IN THE CLUTCHES OF THE SEA

THE CANARY ISLANDS were behind us. In eight days we had sailed the same distance as across the North Sea from Norway to England. A vessel that does not lose its battle with the seas on such a long voyage is usually considered a "seagoing" watercraft. Despite broken rudder-oars and yard, despite the mal-treatment of inexperienced, non-Egyptian landlubbers, and despite storm and waves, Ra was as buoyant as ever. The whole cargo still lay safely out of reach of the ocean. We sailed on in high seas that had little in common with the serene waters of the Nile.

We had passed the Canary Islands in a drizzle without catching sight of land. Now that the sky arched blue over our heads we could see the flat, low carpet of cloud, lying along the African Gold Coast, which marked the position of the continent to port. The position of the Canary Islands off the starboard quarter was clearly marked by the invisible volcanic cone of Teide on Tenerife, twelve thousand feet high, which sent passing humidity up into cooler altitudes where it condensed into a succession of little puffs of clouds which the wind carried out over the sea like the ribbon of smoke from a big steamer.

Abdullah, who knew no islands other than the flat ones floating on Lake Chad, was alarmed when he heard that there were islands out here in the fierce seas, with men living on them. He wanted to know if they were black like himself, or white like us. Santiago, who had lived on the Canary Islands and was also an anthropologist, told us about the mysterious *Guanches* who were living on these distant islands when the Europeans "discovered" them some generations before they sailed farther and "discovered" America. Some of these original tribes on the Canary Islands were dark and rather short of stature, while others were tall and fair, with blue eyes, blond hair and aquiline noses. A pastel drawing from the Canary Islands in 1590 shows a group of such *Guanches* with full golden beards, all fair, with long, yellow hair hanging in soft waves down their backs. Santiago could also tell us about a full-blooded, fair-haired *Guanche* whom he had known personally when he was up at Cambridge. This *Guanche* was a mummy brought from the Canary Islands. The original population of the Canaries had practiced both mummification and cranial trepanning, just as had been done in ancient Egypt and Peru. The fact that the fair *Guanches* resembled Vikings rather than the races generally associated with Africa has led to endless speculation about prehistoric Scandinavian colonization, and even to theories that the Canary Islands are the remains of the lost Atlantis. But mummification was never practiced in ancient Europe, and skull trepanning was extremely rare. These and many other cultural features clearly link the *Guanches* with the ancient cultures of the North African coast. The indigenous population of Morocco, collectively referred to as the Berbers, many of whom the Arabs displaced southward into the Atlas Mountains over a thousand years ago, was just such a mixed race as the *Guanches:* some short and dark-skinned, others tall, fair, and blond, with blue eyes. Fairly pure descendants of both these Berber types are common in Moroccan villages to this very day.

We looked at the puffs of clouds from the skyscraping but extinct volcanic cone on the Canary Islands. In clear weather the peak itself could be seen from the Moroccan coast. There was no need to go to Scandinavia or dive to the Atlantic sea bed to find the homeland of the *Guanches*. They could quite simply have originated in the indigenous population of the very nearest continent, who in ancient times had succeeded in crossing the same stretch of sea which we ourselves had now cut across in our reed boat.

The real mystery of the *Guanches* on the Canary Islands was not so much who they were as how they got there. When the Europeans found them, some generations before Columbus, they owned no boats of any sort: not even a log raft or canoe. And there were large trees growing on the Canary Islands, so they were not short of timber. Both the dark and the fair *Guanches* were exclusively farmers, who bred sheep. They had managed to bring live sheep with them from Africa to the islands. To leave the African coast with women and live sheep on board, you must also be either a sailor or a fisherman, at all events not just a herdsman. Why had the *Guanches* then forgotten the boats of their seafaring forefathers? Could it be because their forefathers knew no boats other than the sail-carrying reed boats, *madia*, which have survived on the north coast of Morocco to the present day? A boatbuilder who only knew how to build reed ships and had never learned the principle of joining flat planks together to form a hollow, watertight hull, would be left helpless and shipless on the beach when his own reed boat decayed with age and no papyrus or other floating reeds grew on the island where he had landed.

Ra suddenly began to pitch and complain so violently that we had to forget the *Guanches* and rush to the sail, which was beginning to flap. The wind had not changed, but a series of waves had caught up with us, growing more and more tempestuous, with deeper and deeper troughs into which we sank, and higher and higher crests which threw themselves after us from on high, but never broke over us because our golden paper swan simply raised her tall tail daintily and let the seas slip under us as quickly as they came. Abdullah had a headache and could not keep his food down. Yuri suspected seasickness, although Abdullah had shown no symptoms until now. He sent Abdullah to bed with dry Egyptian "mummy" biscuits, while Santiago was allowed to come out on deck with the rest of us, for Yuri had now succeeded in healing his skin. Norman was in tremendous form, and we were sitting round the chicken coop, enjoying Carlo's hot risotto with almonds and dried fruit, when someone shouted, "Look up!" Startled, we all looked up, and almost ran for our lives as a gigantic comber came reeling toward us, high above the cabin roof. Then it dwindled into a little drift of foam that trickled, sputtering, under our reed bundles while we stared down into a deep wave valley. More waves of the same type followed. When the sea behaves in this way for no apparent reason, it is usually off an estuary, where the waves are forced higher and higher by a strong current. We must have entered an area where the strong ocean current from Portugal had been intensified by compression as it passed the narrow straits between the largest of the Canary Islands. So we traveled still more briskly on our chosen course. This was the Canary Current itself, running toward the Gulf of Mexico.

Up, up, up, and down into the depths. Abdullah was asleep and missed the five great cachalot whales that surged up right alongside the papyrus and sank before Carlo could reach for his camera. Up, and deep, deep, deep down. Then some piece of timber creaked and cracked again. Another of our small rowing oars had been reduced to matchwood, for only a stump of shaft was left hanging outside the papyrus rolls. Even the small oars were beginning to be in short supply. Something had to be done. Should we try to steer in to the Cape Verde Islands and get some stronger wood? A unanimous "No." But we carried with us as cargo a strong square spare mast of Egyptian *cenebar* wood. So far the masts had not broken; they had even weathered the storm. Therefore, we would probably never need the spare mast, so we bound it instead as reinforcement to the thick, round *iroco* shaft of the hitherto unbroken spare rudder-oar, which we had been keeping in reserve. The result was a rudder-oar so thick and heavy that all seven of us had to lend a hand in order to lift it when it was ready to be lowered into the waves late at night. There was a full moon and the stars were glittering. Running seas came chasing after us, shimmering, high, fierce and black, but they did not frighten us, for they never got the upper hand with the papyrus. It was only timber which the seas hated and destroyed as quickly as we pushed it over the side. As long as it lay unused on deck the wood remained undamaged, together with 160 fragile ceramic jars and all the rest of the cargo. But now the giant oar had to go out and do battle with the sea.

Santiago and I took our places on the steering bridge, where we held onto the end of the twenty-five-foot-long oar shaft which had to be made fast up at our level. At the same time, down on the papyrus deck, all the others stood hanging onto the long heavy oar blade. This had to be pushed out into the waves and then fastened with its neck section resting on the port side end of the thick crossbeam that projected for this purpose on either side of the afterdeck.

Sea and papyrus were tossing wildly when the order was given and the giant oar pushed out. A mighty wave rose at once and lifted the blade out of the hands of the five who were trying with every ounce of strength in their bodies to secure the thick ropes which were to hold it in place. On the bridge Santiago and I barely managed to cling to the upper, narrow part of the shaft that was to be bound to the solid guardrail of the bridge. But as the wave hissed beneath us and passed amidships, a gap opened under Ra's stern and the runaway blade of the rudder-oar slammed down with all its weight against the crossbeam. It was like a colossal sledge hammer whirling down on an anvil. The next wave lifted it again for a second blow; the five men below fought desperately to recapture the rogue hammer with rope loops and bare hands, while Santiago and I were tossed up and down like weightless puppets, unable to do anything but guide the thin end into position every time the oar floated, enabling us to lift its upper end. When the wave troughs allowed the full weight of the oar blade to fall, the two of us on the bridge were flicked into the air, while the five men on deck slung all their ropes round the throat of the blade in unsuccessful attempts to fasten it to the crossbeam before the next wave tore it out of their hands sending the oar up, and us, on the other end of the seesaw, plummeting down again. We came down so hard and fast that our fingers and feet would have been crushed had they been in the way when the heavy oar shaft smashed into the guardrail round which we had to hook our legs. This was the only way in which we could prevent ourselves and the oar from being catapulted overboard. So frenzied were the undisciplined antics of the leaden rudder-oar that we all soon realized we might have to let it go before it hammered the crossbar aft to pieces, and with it all the ropes that held the papyrus together.

But the thought of being reduced to a haystack drifting helplessly sideways to America gave us the extra reserves of strength of wild animals and before we knew what had happened the oar had fallen into a lucky position enabling all seven of us to catch it in the ropes at the same instant. We got the monster tethered to Ra top and bottom with rope cables so thick that the seas could not budge them. This meant that once again we had one of ancient Egypt's two rudder-oars in position astern. The shaft was shapelessly thick and awkward and rotated badly because it had been spliced to the square reserve mast, but it was so strong that when the waves tried to snap it off the whole papyrus boat would twist before the shaft broke.

Santiago declared that it had been the most harrowing experience of his life. Yuri treated a couple of us for minor finger injuries, but that great hefty rudder-oar kept us on such a steady course that we were able to crawl exhausted to bed and divide comfortable night watches among ourselves. The watch had only to look out for ships that might run us down. The moon, the constellations and for once the constant direction of the straight lines of frothing wavetops showed the night watch that the course was steady. He sat enjoying himself in the shelter of the cabin opening on the lee side and only when the watch changed did we crawl up to the bridge to take a look at the compass. The little man-made compass. But we soon learned that the starry sky above our heads was itself a giant luminous compass with its scintillating disc facing downward. We were heading due west. We did not care much where we were going; in any case it was now away from land.

For three days we sailed with no problems, while we repaired the other rudder-oar with patched-up bits of two different broken shafts. No spikes or nails were used. All the joints were made of rope, otherwise the wood would have splintered at once. The powerful running seas continued, drenching the windward side of *Ra* so that the papyrus rolls became still wetter, right up to the railing, and weighing that exposed beam deeper and deeper into the water. As long as the seas were running so high we were not going to risk putting out the other repaired rudder-oar, but we kept it ready in case the one strengthened with the spare mast should break, for now and then it bent ominously in its worst encounters with the sea. On the other hand, we did risk setting the full sail, and that went well. The wind was from the north and bitterly cold, although we could still glimpse the low sky ceiling along the coast of the Spanish Sahara. As far as possible we restowed the cargo on the port, or lee side, which was as high above the water as when we set out. Under full sail our heavy, broad reed bundle picked up speed again and moved westward at a steady rate of about sixty nautical miles in twenty-four hours, or 2.5. knots, and we could clearly see our own wake behind us. After eleven days' sailing we had covered 557 nautical miles as the crow flies, and we had to put our watches back an hour.

For two days ships had been constantly appearing round us. Once we could see three big ocean-travelers at the same time. We must be on the Great Circle route round Africa. The brightest of our kerosene lanterns had to be hung at the mast head to avoid collisions at night. But soon the sea was empty of human voyagers and only schools of porpoises danced about us, some so near that we could have patted them. One or two lethargic moonfish drifted past, and the first flying fish began to shoot up under our bows. The sky was empty of living things. Only the occasional lost insect blew aboard and a pair of small petrels flew in rapid darts between the wave troughs. This little sea bird sleeps on the water, because it floats over the highest seas as lightly as papyrus. In the last few days masses of small brown beetles had begun to creep out of holes in the papyrus and we only hoped that the sea water would kill off eggs and larvae so that we would not be eaten away from within. The skeptics who had seen the camels trying to eat the side of our boat had prophesied that the reed might well be fodder for hungry marine creatures. Up to now neither whale nor fish had tried to feed off our floating sheaf, but we were not at all happy about these emerging swarms of beetles.

Sun and moon rolled westward in turn to show us the way. The lonely night watches gave us in full measure that timeless perception of eternity that I had experienced on *Kon-Tiki*. Starry sky and night-black water. The immutable constellations sparkled above us, and just as brightly beneath us the shining phosphorescence glittered: the living plankton glowed like sparks of neon on the soft dark carpet on which we were floating. With the sparkling plankton beneath we often seemed to be riding under the night sky on a billowing mirror; or perhaps the sea was crystal clear and bottomless, so that we could see right through it to a myriad of stars on the other side of the universe. The only thing that was firm and close in these omnipresent stellar heavens was the supple bundle of golden reeds we rode on and the big, square sail that stood like a shadow against the stars, broader above, by the yard-arm, than across the bottom, near the deck. This ancient Egyptian outline of the trapezoid mainsail in the night was enough in itself to turn the calendar back thousands of years. Silhouettes of sails like this are not seen against the sky of today. Strange squeaks and snorts from papyrus, wicker, wood and rope did the rest. We were not living in the age of the atom bomb and the rocket. We were living at a time when the earth was still large and flat and full of unknown seas and continents, when time was the common prerogative and no one was short of it.

Stiff but fitter from the struggle that now lay behind us, we changed night watch by the meager light of kerosene lanterns swaying above our undulating vegetable deck. It was unspeakably good to crawl to rest inside a warm sleeping bag. You woke up with such an infernally good appetite. You felt an extraordinary physical well-being. Small pleasures grew big; big problems felt small. The Stone Age life was certainly not to be despised. There was no reason to believe that people who lived before us, using their bodies strenuously, merely endured hardship and never received their share of life's joys.

Over sixty miles' progress westward could be plotted on the chart every day, even though the horizon never changed. It remained the same every day and at all hours; it moved with us keeping us always in its center. But the masses of water also moved invisibly with us. The Canary Current was a fast-moving, salt-water river flowing toward the setting sun, keeping eternal company with the trade wind, westward; air and water and all that floats and blows, westward. Westward with sun and moon.

Norman and I stood together on the bridge, he with a regular sextant, I with a "nosometer." "Nosometer" was Yuri's approved denomination for a home-made instrument I had carved from two flat pieces of wood, to measure the latitude. They were joined to a little wooden block, cut in a curve so that it fitted against the nose, hence the name. With the block exactly at eye level, the idea was to look along the upper surface of one piece of wood with the left eye and hold it so that it pointed at the horizon. The other flat piece was attached to the same block with a leather hinge and was supposed to be tipped up under the right eye so that it pointed exactly to the Pole Star. The angle between the two pieces could be read directly off a disc placed on edge between them, and this angle represented our latitude without any further calculation. This extremely primitive "nosometer" appealed to everyone's sense of humor because it was so incredibly simple and quick to use, and moreover seldom resulted in an error of more than one degree. This was accurate enough to enable us to make a chart of our daily position and it was amazingly close to the correct version marked off on another chart by Norman.

We gradually began to learn interesting lessons from our testing of the papyrus boat. The slanted rudder-oars had been first to disclose their secrets, and shown themselves to be a missing link in the evolution of man's earliest steering mechanism from oar to rudder. Next the wash-through bundle body of the raft-ship itself began to expose its true qualities: in addition to an almost unbelievable loading capacity the papyrus reeds possessed both a toughness in rough seas and an enduring buoyancy that was out of all proportion to the preconceived verdict of modern man. Yet it was the rigging that revealed the most significant secrets about this ancient vessel's forgotten history, showing that it had been originally developed as something more than a river craft. In the design we followed, Landström had copied all details of mast and rigging from the ancient Egyptian wall paintings. A strong rope ran from the mast-head to the bow of the boat. But no corresponding rope ran from masthead to stern, although one rope forward and one aft would have been all that was needed to hold the straddled mast erect on a river boat in calm waters. The architects of the ancient Egyptian ships, however, had, for some unknown reason, carefully avoided running any rope from the masthead all the way aft. Instead, they had secured five of six ropes at different heights on each leg of the straddled mast. These ropes were stretched diagonally down in parallel lines to either side of the vessel a little aft of midships. In this way the whole sternmost part of the boat was free of mast stays and could rise and fall on the waves with no attachment to the mast. No sooner had Ra begun to pitch on high seas than we realized how vital this special system was. The stern hung behind the rest of the boat like a trailer that was allowed to ride up and down freely over all the bumps. Had it also been secured by a stay to the masthead the mast would have broken as the first big ocean rollers surged beneath us. In our dance over the high wave crests the middle section of Ra was rhythmically thrust upward while the full weight of bow and stern sagged simultaneously in the wave troughs on either side. Had both ends of the hull been attached to the mast, it would have snapped under the burden. As things were, the mast supported the curved bow and held the central part of the soft deck suspended in a straight line. The aft third of the boat was allowed to follow the motion of the sea.

Daily, all praised this ingenious arrangement and special function of the rigging. Norman, the naval expert, immediately realized what this special design indicated. There was no mistake about it. The creators of the old Egyptian rigging had prepared their flexible reed boats for the meeting with ocean swells. After the third day at sea I was already writing in my diary: "This rigging is the result of long experience in navigation on the open sea; it was not born on the calm Nile."

But there was another detail of the special Egyptian ship design that we took a longer time to understand, and for that we were to pay dearly. Every day we looked admiringly at the broad, in-turned curl on the high peaked stern. What purpose did it serve? We placed no reliance on the general conviction that this curl was simply intended to beautify the shape of a river boat. Yet as the days passed we ourselves were as unable as the Egyptologists to detect any practical function for it whatever. We did constantly make sure, however, that the curl was not beginning to straighten out. It remained in perfect shape, so our friends from Chad seemed to have been right in thinking that they had done their work so thoroughly that it would keep its curve without having to be tethered to the deck by rope. The only mistake we were aware of having made so far was in stowing the cargo as in an ordinary sailing boat in those first days. No living man, only our own costly experience after sailing in the trade-wind belt, could have taught us that a papyrus boat should have its heaviest cargo concentrated on the lee side. Now we were already so waterlogged on the windward side that the starboard gunwale was inexorably approaching the water level. This was most conspicuous far back on the starboard quarter, where as time passed we were able to do our washing over the side without hanging head downward with our legs in the air as we would have had to do anywhere else on the boat. Eventually, we did all our washing there, and, in fact, everyone found it extremely handy.

On June 4 the rough seas began to calm down, and next morning we awoke to a new world. It had turned nice and hot, and the sea was a procession of long, shining rollers. We received another quick visit from five big whales: a majestic assembly. Perhaps they were the same ones which had called on us before. They were beautiful and friendly in their own element and we thought with horror of the day when mankind would have succeeded in launching its harpoons into the last of the sea's warm-blooded giants, so that in the end only the cold steel hulls of submarines would be frolicking in the ocean depths where the Almighty—and most men—would rather have seen the whale suckling its young.

It was so nice and hot that Georges tore off his clothes and dived overboard with his life line on. He disappeared under the *Ra* in his diving mask and came up again with a shout of delight which made Yuri and Santiago dive after him, each on his life line, while the rest of us watched and waited our turn. Only Abdullah still sat in the cabin opening watching the calm seas, sulking. Unless the wind came back we would be becalmed here and never get to America. Norman consoled him with an explanation of the invisible ocean current. Perhaps we would not cover over sixty miles a day as we had before, but we would certainly manage thirty.

Soon everybody had been under *Ra*'s belly except Abdullah. He washed himself in the canvas bucket on board and knelt facing Mecca for lengthy prayers. Perhaps he was praying for a wind.

The exhilarating salt-water bath made everyone feel new-born again. And to see the *Ra* from below was among the greatest of all thrills. We felt like little pilot fish swimming under the curving belly of a gigantic yellow whale. The sunbeams were reflected like searchlights from the depths and played up against the papyrus bundles over our heads. Sea and cloudless sky together created the bluest blue round the big, shining yellow whale that glowed above us. It was swimming so fast that we were dragged along behind it on our ropes unless we ourselves swam as fast as we could in the same direction. For the first time we were able to see that we had zebra-striped pilot fish faithfully swimming in wedge formation in front of the reed prow, just as I had seen them swimming in front of the logs of the *Kon-Tiki*. We sailed past the stump of a big African tree that lay wallowing heavily in the rollers. A fat little pampano fish peeped out from under the trunk and waggled its tail as hard as it could to get across to the *Ra*, where it found one or two smaller relatives already darting to and fro round the big oar blade. Now and then they darted off and took a playful nip at Yuri's white skin.

Here and there on the underside of the papyrus hull, small long-necked barnacles were beginning to grow, waving from their blue-black shells with orange gills like soft ostrich feathers. But there was no sign of seaweed or other plant growth to be seen anywhere. The papyrus reeds, which in the Sahara sand had been grayish-yellow, shrunken and dry, had swollen under the water into smooth, shining stalks of gold and when we pressed them they were no longer brittle and fragile as before, but hard and resilient as automobile tires. Not a single reed had worked loose or broken. The papyrus had now been in the water for three weeks. Instead of dissolving by decomposition after two weeks it had become stronger than ever, and there was no sign of the reeds losing buoyancy. The list to windward was due to water absorbtion *above* the water line, adding an extra weight of useless cargo.

Overjoyed at what we had seen, we scrambled back onto the papyrus deck and soon afterward chicken feathers were floating in our wake again as Carlo cooked us a banquet.

Emboldened by our observations we now decided to lower the other repaired rudder-oar into the sea as well. We would never know more peaceful seas than these. But this second oar with its spliced double shaft was so long and heavy that darkness had fallen before we managed to maneuver it clear of all the stays and over the cabin roof to windward, where it was to be pushed out. The rollers were peaceful, but still high enough to guarantee problems if we attempted to put the oar out. The blade would begin to jump before we could get it down in the right groove and lash it on. Having learned by experience, we decided to postpone the launching until daylight, so we left the mighty rudder-oar safely lashed with the long shaft in the air and the blade on deck, farthest aft on the windward side.

Next morning the weather was still wonderful and I clambered aft over the jars for a morning bath. There sat the morning watch, Yuri, happily enjoying himself washing his underclothes, but on board, without the canvas bucket. Every roller sent a little ripple over the papyrus gunwale at our lowest point, starboard aft, where the tremendously heavy unlaunched rudder-oar was now also weighing us down. The rhythmic trickle was just enough to keep a little pool at the deepest point aft.

"This yacht is getting more and more and more practical," observed Yuri happily. "Now we have a washstand with running water."

We hastened to launch the heavy rudder-oar so that the waves would support most of its weight, but our lowest corner continued to let in the ripples and as long as it simply provided us with a washbasin this was generally popular. We checked the curl on the stern. It was just as before and showed no signs of straightening. For safety's sake Georges swam underneath Ra and discovered for the first time that the bottom was beginning to sag just aft of the basket cabin. But the papyrus bundles were whole and strong and when he squeezed the reeds air bubbled out. The reed was just as buoyant as before. We must simply have been carrying too much weight aft.

Now we moved all the cargo from the afterdeck so that the only weight left behind the cabin was the heavy crossbeam on which the two rudder-oars rested and the steering bridge itself, which stood on poles and sheltered the crate containing the life raft.

The ripples continued to wash in over the starboard quarter. We made another thorough inspection both above and below water. It was obvious that the Ra had preserved her original shape perfectly, from the bows back to the point where the last pair of stays ran down from the masthead and were secured to either side of the boat. Aft of this point there was a visible kink where the whole afterpart of Ra began to tilt gently downward.

We began to ponder again. It was the freely trailing aft section of the boat that had taken a downward turn, while everything which was attached to the stays held up by the mast was still as it should be. The bow was as high as ever. Our proud golden swan still stretched her neck; only her tail was beginning to droop. If the mast could only have supported the strain of a stay to hold up the stern as well, this would not have happened. But if we tried to hoist the stern up with such a rope, the mast would break when

the first roller passed under us. The stern must be allowed to undulate. But it must not be allowed to sag at a permanent angle
in this way. We tried to pull it up with ropes stretched diagonally
to either side of the cabin. We tried to fasten a thick stretcher
from the stern, over the guardrail on the bridge and on across the
cabin roof to a pole erected on the foredeck. This was the ancient
Egyptian method of lending rigidity to wooden ships, but there
was no such horizontal hawser shown on paintings of papyrus
boats. And however much we strained and hauled on all these ropes
we did not succeed in heaving the afterdeck up again. Carlo tied
all sorts of ingenious knots and hauled harder than anyone on wet
ropes, until the palms of his hands began to swell up like white
macaroni.

The days passed. More water washed in over the stern every
day. The fine curl at the upper end of the stern arched as elegantly
inward as ever, showing no sign of losing its decorative shape, while
its bottom extension slowly gave way beneath it. But the curl was
serving no purpose and was beginning to overload the weak afterdeck
which supported it. All the storm waves that had washed over the
peaked stern had caused it to absorb quantities of sea water above
the water line. Since the stern was broad and thick and stood taller
than the cabin roof, it must now, in its soaked state, weigh at
least a ton. Should we cut it off? That might bring the underlying
stern section up again. But it would be like cutting the tail off
a swan. We did not have the heart to disfigure our proud craft.

But how, how, how the devil had the creators of this extraordinarily ingenious vessel succeeded in keeping the showy tail in
the air without a rope to hold it up? On the contrary, they had
used a rope that seemed to tether it down to the deck. The boatbuilders from Chad had fortunately dispensed with that. We had
not missed it up to now. Or? Or! I threw down the coconut I
was scraping out and began to draw frantically. Well, blow me
down! I shouted for Norman, Santiago, Yuri, Carlo, the whole
crew. I had found the mistake. We had not known how to put
the curly tail to its intended use. This, too, was something that
only bitter experience could have taught us, because all those who
had learned the purpose of the curly tail from its inventors had
been in their graves for thousands of years. The peculiar arch over

the afterdeck was not built for beauty. The rope, which everyone thought would serve only to hold the cocked tail in tension, had a completely different function. The arch of the tail stood by itself. The rope was not intended to pull the curved tip down, but the afterdeck up. The high, harp-shaped stern was meant to act as a powerful spring, supporting the free-swinging afterdeck while the stays to the masthead supported the rest of the papyrus boat. To enable the papyrus ship to sail the open sea without breaking, its brilliant architects had divided it into two linked components. The forward part was kept up by the straddled mast with its parallel stays; the afterpart was allowed to move independently, but always returned to its place, thanks to the bowstring attached to the big spring arching above it.

We tied the bowstring in position, but it was too late now. After three weeks the afterdeck had developed a kink, lowering the curved sternpost so much that we would have needed a crane or something to lift it from above. As things now stood, no rope could correct our situation. We had to suffer because we, like everybody else, had assumed the peculiar arch of the tail to be the ancient boat designers' decorative end, whereas it had been their ingenious means.

Yuri and Norman stood in the pool of water astern, staring at the slowly sinking golden tail. Suddenly they began to sing with one voice:

"We don't want a yellow submarine, a yellow submarine, a yellow sumarine . . ."

Neither did we, so soon all seven of us were standing in the stern, singing Yuri's refrain in chorus. No one took it more seriously than that. Indeed, the rest of the boat was bobbing like a champagne cork, so Yuri and Norman set about washing socks and trying to find a rhyme for "submarine."

To my mind our main problem was not so much how the papyrus reed would ultimately survive its interplay with the sea, but how we seven passengers on board would ultimately survive our interaction with each other. In the basket cabin, which measured eight and one half by twelve feet, there was not even elbow room between us when we lay down, and the papyrus deck was so full of jars and baskets that there was no room to put a foot down. This meant that, outside of our sleeping bags, we lived either on the narrow papyrus roll in the shelter of the port cabin wall, or up on the little steering bridge which could be spanned with both arms, lengthwise and crosswise. Everyone was within speaking and touching distance of everyone else day and night. We were stuck together like seven-headed Siamese septuplets, with seven mouths speaking seven languages. We were not only black and white, from communist and capitalist countries, we also represented the extremes of educational level and living standards. When I visited the one of our two Africans in his home in Fort Lamy, he was sitting on a fiber mat on the earth floor with no other furnishings than a kerosene lamp that stood in the middle of the mat, while his passport and travel tickets lay on the floor in one corner. With the other African, in Cairo, I was ushered in by bowing oriental servants between the pillars of a rich man's home, with massive French furniture, tapestries and antique heirlooms. One crew member could not read or write; another was a university professor. One was an active pacifist; another a naval officer. Abdullah's favorite occupation was listening to his little pocket radio and dispensing news about the fighting between the Israelis and the Egyptians on the Suez Canal, of which he himself had caught a glimpse. His own African government in Fort Lamy supported Israel against Egypt and the other Arab countries, and now they had asked France to drop parachutists to suppress the Arab rising in the desert beyond Bol, where we had met. Abdullah was a fanatical Mohammedan and therefore supported the Arabs. Norman was a Jew. Georges was Egyptian. Their distant relatives were shooting at each other from opposite sides of the Suez Canal, while they themselves lay side by side in a wickerwork cabin, afloat on the Atlantic. Abdullah dispensed news with equal enthusiasm about the war in Vietnam. He was completely bewildered because Yuri and Norman, who were both white, represented two countries which were hostile but wanted peace and therefore helped the yellow-skinned men in Vietnam to kill each other. He wanted Norman and Yuri to agree on an explanation of this anomaly. There was ample fuel on board for a serious conflagration. Our paper boat was loaded with psychological gasoline and the heat generated by friction in the little basket capsule could only be extinguished by the ubiquitous waves.

The most insidious danger on any expedition where men have

to rub elbows for weeks is a mental sickness that might be called "expedition fever"—a psychological condition that makes even the most peaceful person irritable, angry, furious, absolutely desperate, because his perceptive capacity gradually shrinks until he sees only his companions' faults while their good qualities are no longer recorded by his gray matter. The first duty of an expedition leader at any time is to be on guard against this lurking menace. In the days before departure this had been thoroughly impressed on the whole crew.

I was therefore not a little alarmed when on our third day out I had already heard the peaceable Carlo roaring in Italian at Georges that he might be a judo champion but he was so disorderly and messy that he needed a nanny. Georges hit back, but after a quick and heated verbal duel both of them shut up and only the papyrus could be heard creaking and whining as usual. The next day there was another explosion between the same two. Carlo was tightening a mast stay when Georges angrily threw down his fishing rod and ostentatiously went to bed. On the bridge Carlo confided to me that playboy Georges was beginning to get on his nerves. Carlo himself had gone to work, carrying heavy rice sacks, when he was twelve years old. He had made his own way with his bare hands without benefit of schooling. This lazy rich man's son from Cairo was a spoiled brat who simply dropped everything and expected the rest of us to tidy up for him. I promised to speak to Georges, and agreed with Carlo that Georges did not yet quite understand the spirit of expedition teamwork; to him this was all a new sort of game, a contest of endurance and muscle power. But Carlo must also try to understand that up to now Georges had only lived in a home where he simply threw everything down without a thought and yet always found it in its right place, because the house servants or his wife or his mother picked it up and kept everything tidy. Carlo had learned in the school of life, Georges had not. We would have to teach him.

Soon afterward I found a moment alone on the bridge with Georges. He was unhappy because he had answered Carlo rudely, but he had done so because Carlo was always interfering in Georges' own affairs. It was easy to explain to the attentive Georges that there was no room for one's "own affairs" on board, except inside each man's private box. No one was obliged to clear up after anyone else and no one was entitled to strew the deck, inside or out, with hand-harpoons, flippers, reading matter, wet towels, soap or tooth-brushes. Everyone on board was equal and no one had to clean up after anyone but himself.

A moment later Georges' fishing tackle, tape-recorder and dirty clothes had been picked off the deck and cabin roof and Carlo and Georges were suddenly hauling together on the same rope.

The next serious threat to peace did not come until we had everything so well organized on board that we introduced galley duty. Carlo had voluntarily offered himself as permanent cook, a generous gesture that assured him great prestige and popularity. Now the rest of us were to take turns in being orderlies and cleaning up the galley boxes, pots and pans for one day at a time. The orderly list was chalked on a blackboard on the bridge and no one had remembered that Abdullah could not read. He did not realize that two of the others had taken this turn before him, and when Santiago showed him the dirty pots and the scrubber Abdullah got a headache and flung himself on his bed growling:

"I get it. You are white, Santiago, and I am black. That's why you want me to be a servant to the rest of you."

Santiago was an apostle of peace but this hurt him worse than a dagger wound. He flared up.

"And you say that to me, Abdullah!" he snarled in pure rage, "when I have spent six years fighting for Negro equality. The most important thing about this whole voyage for me is the very fact that—"

Abdullah heard no more. He pulled his sleeping bag over his head. When he looked out next time he happened to catch a glimpse of me staggering aft with the dirty stack of pots. His eyes widened.

"You and I have simply traded days," I explained.

Next day Abdullah was standing happily in the stern humming and singing his rhythmic African songs while he scoured the pans.

The next day brought a shock for all of us. Georges came and asked me quietly if he alone could be responsible for order in the galley for the remainder of the voyage. It was such a tedious business rotating the job and there were others who had more impor-tant duties to perform.

So it was Georges—yes, Georges—who became permanent orderly, and after that the kitchen on the *Ra* was spick and span and no one else had to think about washing the pots.

Then there was a time when Norman and Carlo began to react ominously against Yuri and Georges, who did nothing without express orders, while they themselves were always on the lookout for work from morning till night, quite apart from their own duties. They could accept the fact that Abdullah took no personal initiative, but the other two, who both had university backgrounds, should not simply wait for orders. At the same time Yuri, Georges and Abdullah were beginning to be irritated by Norman and Carlo. They were too military, they gave orders instead of speaking pleasantly, as one does among friends, and they did not know how to relax and enjoy the mere fact of being alive. Moreover Santiago was an artful dodger. If there was something heavy to be moved he would stoop down himself and take hold, then call the others to help, and the next moment he would be standing smiling and pointing while the musclemen, Georges, Yuri and Abdullah, did the lifting and carrying. And then there were those who felt hurt because I as leader would not chase a man out of his sleeping bag if he was taking a nap while others worked on their own initiative. The other group thought I ought to have more control over those who barked military orders instead of calling in a friendly way. This was neither a naval vessel nor a company of Alpine troops: we were seven companions on an equal footing.

But the miracle happened. Instead of all these small frictions growing into expedition fever, each man tried to understand why the others behaved as they did, and here Santiago's philosophy and research on peace versus aggression benefited all of us. Yuri and Georges began to admire Norman and Carlo because their initiative and energetic efforts improved conditions for all of us, and Norman and Carlo changed their view of Yuri and Georges, for no one on board tackled stiffer tasks or was more willing to help as soon as he was asked, or realized that help was needed. Santiago was the diplomat and psychologist who helped Dr. Yuri to bandage invisible wounds. Yuri, our doctor, was hard-working, responsible and tireless. Abdullah was admired by everyone for his lightning intelligence and eagerness to learn, and for his ability to adapt to cultural modes completely different from his own. Abdullah himself liked everyone, because he could see that he was one of the family although the rest of us were white. He would coax Yuri to produce a medicine that would give him, too, a beard like all the rest of us, and simply could not understand why the well-groomed Yuri would sit in the pool aft shaving every morning, when all the rest of us were beginning to grow red or black mustaches and beards. Unable to grow hair on his face, Abdullah started growing hair on his head. He stopped shaving his black scalp, which until now had shone like patent leather. Soon he had crinkly hair growing so thick that he carried his big carpenter's pencil stuck in it like a red hairpin.

Georges had a few peculiarities. During the day he slept easily. But at night he could not sleep unless he had pillow on his chest and music by his ear. For this purpose he had brought a tape-recorder with a limited number of his favorite pop tunes. The noise from the papyrus and ropes drowned the music for those of us who lay farthest away, but that same noise meant that Yuri had to give sleeping pills both to Georges himself and to Santiago. Georges' tape-recorder played Georges' tunes day and night. One day the tape-recorder disappeared. I had seen it half a minute before. At that time it was lying on the bridge and playing alone at Abdullah's feet as I passed, while Abdullah stood with his back to it, steering. Norman was hanging half overboard, making an oar fast. Carlo, Santiago and I were passing to and fro in the stern, moving the cargo, while Yuri and Georges worked on the other side of the cabin. Suddenly the music stopped. A minute or two passed before Georges clambered back over the cargo to start it up again. The tape-recorder was gone. Georges searched everywhere. In the stern, in the bows, under the mattress, on the cabin roof. Gone. Gone forever. Who was the culprit? The African judo champion swelled like an angry gorilla. Who, who had thrown his tape-recorder into the sea? Now the voyage was finished for him, done for: without his tunes he could not fall asleep. Who—who—who had done it? The air vibrated. No more sleep! Little Safi clambered as far up the mast as the rope reached; she did not intend to take the blame.

Abdullah could have kicked the tape-recorder overboard, but he was much too fond of music to do that. Norman could not reach it, and Georges had Yuri in sight the whole time. It could only have been one of us three who had been passing to and fro in the stern. Carlo was the only one who went on moving jars imperturbably, as if nothing had happened. Carlo! There was no doubt in my mind. He must still be mad at Georges, so he had done it. Crazy. Unlike Carlo. Now we were all sitting on a powder keg while the fuse burned.

"Georges," I said. "You really have turned into an orderly man, but how could you have managed to leave your tape-recorder so far out that it fell into the sea?"

"It may have been near the edge," said Georges, "but at worst it would have fallen on deck, not overboard."

Inwardly I agreed, but I had to save Carlo.

"It was right out on the starboard corner," I said firmly. "If anyone brushed against it while we were heeling sharply to starboard it would have fallen into the sea."

Georges continued to search in the most absurd places, then dropped off into his sleeping bag. He slept like a log instantly, and we did not waken him until next morning, when Carlo whistled his cheerful mealtime signal and served us a delicious breakfast of fried ham and eggs. With meals like this, who could be angry with Carlo? The tape-recorder was never referred to again on the voyage. Not until we had landed on the other side did Santiago lay his hand on Georges' broad shoulder one day and say calmly:

"Georges, how much do I owe you for the tape-recorder?"

We were all equally astounded. Georges turned slowly, terribly slowly, until he was broadside to the smiling little Mexican.

Then he himself beamed from ear to ear and said:

"What tape-recorder?"

That was the end of the discussion.

"How could you take such a risk?" we asked Santiago later. He admitted that he had been very doubtful whether he was doing right or wrong when he flipped the recorder into the sea, but he was quite convinced that if it had been allowed to go on playing the same tunes much longer one of us would have gone insane and hit the owner over the head with it.

While the weeks passed with the seven of us in the cramped cabin crowded together as if we were at a non-stop party, *Ra* rolled on in the center of an unchanging horizon that accompanied us like a magic circle. From June 4 to 9 the sea ran in high but gentle swells, the wind was light, and some of the men felt the urge to sleep at all hours of the day. The papyrus had stopped whining and growling and had begun to purr like a cat enjoying the sunshine. Norman disclosed that he was worried. We were drifting slowly southwestward and unless the wind returned there was a risk of our being caught in the eddying currents off the coast of Mauritania and Senegal. We had come into one of the trans-Atlantic shipping lanes, constantly sighting passenger steamers and cargo vessels far and near, and on the night of June 6 a big, lighted ocean liner headed straight for us. It was steering so directly toward us that the officers on the bridge could not possibly have spotted the glow from our little kerosene lantern at the masthead, so we gesticulated violently with our flashlights. The light wind gave us very little chance of escaping with the help of the rudder-oars. The monster rumbled along, lights blazing, and was beginning to loom threateningly over us when it abruptly turned toward our starboard beam and silenced its mechanical thunder. Some angry reprimand was flashed at us from the bridge, so fast that we could only catch the word "please" before the giant glided silently past under its own impetus, a few hundred feet from the papyrus bundles. Then its propellers were churning the water again and the steel giant rumbled on its brightly lit way to Europe.

Next day we were sailing in slack winds through an ocean where the clear water on the surface was full of drifting black lumps of asphalt, seemingly never-ending. Three days later we awoke to find the sea about us so filthy that we could not put our toothbrushes in it and Abdullah had to have an extra ration of fresh water for his ritual washing. The Atlantic was no longer blue but gray-green and opaque, covered with clots of oil ranging from pin-head size to the dimensions of the average sandwich. Plastic bottles floated among the waste. We might have been in a squalid city port. I had seen nothing like this when I spent 101 days with my nose at water level on board the *Kon-Tiki*. It became clear to all of us that mankind really was in the process of polluting his most vital wellspring, our planet's indispensable filtration plant, the ocean. The danger to ourselves and to future generations was revealed to us in all its horror. Shipowners, industrial leaders, authorities, they would have seen the sea gliding past at a fair speed from an ordinary ship's deck and would never have dipped their toothbrushes and noses in it week after week, as we had. We must make an outcry about this to everyone who would listen. What was the good of East and West fighting over social reforms on land, as long as every nation allowed our common artery, the ocean, to become a sewer for oil slush and chemical waste? Did we still cling to the medieval idea that the sea was infinite?

The strange thing is that when you are bobbing over the wave crests on a few papyrus bundles, aware at the same time that whole continents are gliding past, you realize that the sea is not so limitless after all; the water that rounds the African coast in May passes along the American coast some weeks later with all the floating muck that will neither sink nor be eaten by the inhabitants of the sea.

On June 10 the wind strengthened. That same day Abdullah slaughtered our last chicken and then there was only a duck left in the poultry coop. The heavy coop was thrown into the sea, where it would gradually absorb water and sink. But no one had the heart to slaughter the duck. It was spared and christened Sinbad, and after that it waddled about the deck, to the real indignation of Safi. With a line tied to its foot and a basket as its one-room residence, it became master of the foredeck, while Safi kept to the cabin area. If one of the two wandered by an oversight into the other's territory it ended either with Safi screaming with fury because she had been nipped on her tailless behind by Sinbad, or with Safi leaping triumphantly home with a duck's feather in her hand.

During the night the seas piled up and became really fierce. Often it was quite uncanny to stand on the creaking, swaying steering bridge and see nothing in the world but a lighted patch of sail and the lamp at the masthead, which swung like an unruly moon among the stars when one glimpsed their light between racing storm clouds. Now and then a venomous snake seemed to be hissing right at one's back and a foaming wave crest would come rushing along at the height of one's head, invisible in its blackness apart from the white foam on top that seemed to be sailing alone through the air, whispering to itself. The pursuing creature reached us and lifted us in the air with its huge watery muscles, only to let us go again and drop us so deep that the next white phantom following behind hovered over us at a still greater height. We were worn out, dead tired, after two hours' intensive night watch at the two rudder-oars, even though we were generally using only one of them, allowing the other to work in a fixed position.

Daylight found *Ra* more loose-jointed than ever before. In the Egyptian style, each leg of the straddled masts had simply been planted in a shallow groove in a wooden block lying like a shoe on top of the papyrus base. A short, naturally knee-shaped section of a tree was fixed with its horizontal part tied to the wooden shoe and its vertical end to the mast leg. These rope lashings round the foot pieces were now so slack that the rocking mast feet threatened to jump out of their slots. At roof height the mast was swaying as much as two feet toward and away from the cabin wall. The thirty-foot high masthead was swinging about so violently that Carlo only just managed to hang on through the wild antics up at the top. All the stays that ran like parallel harpstrings from each side of the *Ra* to the masthead were also slack, so slack at one moment that they hung in loops, giving the masts no support, while at the next they all tautened together with a jerk so violent that we were afraid the mast would break, or the papyrus bundles would be torn to shreds, for all the stays were fastened to a single thick rope cable tied right round the edge of the *Ra*. We hammered wooden wedges round the mast foot and tautened the boisterous shrouds one by one, at the risk of the first taut stays being jerked away while the rest were still slack. At last we had the dancing mast captive again.

The sea was full of life today. Flying fish rained about us. Another moonfish drifted by, large and round and inert. Something invisible engulfed the hook on Georges' fixed fishing rod and made off with the whole line. Before he could pull it in, a hulking great fish swallowed the first, so Georges' catch was a severed fishhead. Meanwhile *Ra* was skimming over the wave ridges at record speed and we were all disappointed when Norman announced a moderate day's run after taking our noon position. We were being pulled south by a lateral current. In the last twenty-four hours the starboard corner of *Ra*'s stern had sunk so far that the lower crossbeam of the steering gear was always dipping into the waves and acting as a brake. The water was permanently ankle-deep aft, and wavetops were constantly

washing right up to the crate containing the life raft under the
bridge. The crate shifted every time and chafed at the ropes holding
the papyrus together.

The sea was equally agitated and unpredictable next day and an
increasingly strong north wind brought the cold back with it. While
Yuri was trying to adjust the ropes on the steering spar splashing
in the waves, he caught sight of a blue bubble that he grasped and
tried to pull off the end of the spar. Yuri had never seen a Portuguese
man-of-war and had no idea what was happening when in the
next moment he was entangled in the long, stinging tentacles of
one of the Atlantic's smallest but most lethal monsters. That wily
bubble is not a single animal but a whole colony of minute creatures
that live in an extremely complicated symbiosis in which each and
every one has its special properties and tasks. The largest creature,
which constitutes the bubble itself, has no purpose other than to keep
the extraordinary community afloat and sailing. It tows a bundle of
filaments several yards long, made up of all the bubble's little fellow
citizens. Some are hunters that provide food for the rest of the colony,
others are responsible for reproduction, while yet others are soldiers
that literally shoot caustic acid into victims and enemies of the bubble colony. Very large Portuguese men-of-war have paralyzed and
killed human beings.

The violent burning pain spread through Yuri's skin into his
nervous system, paralyzed the muscles of his right hand and began to
affect his heart. It took our unfortunate ship's doctor a good four
hours draining the medicine chest for anything from ointments to
nerve and heart pills before he allayed his own pain and got the
movement back into his right hand.

On June 13 an icy north-northeast wind was howling through
the stays and whining in the wickerwork cabin walls, while the seas
rose higher and boiled more savagely than anything we had seen up
to then. There were howls, creaks and groans from every section of
the heaving vessel, and breakers running across each other and over
each other's backs crashed aboard aft. Some of the wave peaks sent
tons of water at a time surging over us and we could actually see the
stern section sinking gradually deeper under the pressure of the heaviest cascades. There was nothing we could do but wait until the
masses of water had rushed out again on both sides of *Ra*, leaving

us with our once popular bathing pool now sunk knee-deep in water. Abdullah was in high spirits and assured us that this misfortune aft was unimportant. We would not sink as long as the ropes held. Blue with cold, but humming, he ambled about in oilskins with his transistor to his ear. He had tuned in to a French-speaking Arab station that was reporting on the revolution in Chad, where the Mohammedans currently had the upper hand.

A splendid blue-green dolphin played round the papyrus bundles most of the day, but after breaking Georges fishing line, it would not allow itself to be either hooked again or speared. Carlo was going to prepare dried fish for lunch when a wet fish crashed in full flight onto the back of his neck while others thudded against the cabin wall around him. Eleven flying fish lay floundering on the deck ready for the pan.

From June 14 to 17 the sea was constantly seething and inexplicably high waves crossed from two or three directions at once, an interplay of currents and countercurrents from unseen coasts. Georges had pains in the back and had to be helped to bed. Abdullah was sick, but cured himself with a concoction of twelve boiled garlic cloves. The bridge began to creak and sway and had to be hastily reinforced with fresh ropes and stays. Yuri had the bright idea of moving Sinbad the duck aft where she swam about happily in the inboard pool. Safi was so cross at this that she got diarrhea, but kept to the outer edge of the papyrus rolls as always on such occasions. She had become incredibly clean. Suddenly a school of tuna fish, about six feet long, shot out of the water, frightening Safi into hysterics; she hid in a basket and no one could coax her out of it until Georges put her in her special sleeping box inside the cabin after dusk.

Once again the masts were jumping in their flat wooden shoes, while *Ra* writhed about in the wildest gymnastics to follow the chaotic dance of the waves. She was making a new, hoarse sound we had not heard before—like a mighty wind roaring to and fro as ten thousand bundled reeds bent in the water. The floor, walls and ceiling of the basket hut were also twisting and heaving with a new sound. The boxes beneath us jammed askew, so that the lids stuck, and we could lie, sit or stand on nothing that did not twist us with it. The stays were holding the masts in ominous tension, but we dared not slacken or tauten them in these powerful seas. It was bitterly cold, but Georges, Yuri and Norman all took a swim under the reed bundles for safety's sake. They came up and assured us with chattering teeth that the papyrus below us was in perfect condition, but now the sagging stern section was now exerting a severe braking action. Something had to be done.

Then the starboard rudder-oar tore itself loose from the steering bar and danced madly in its efforts to wrench itself free of the bridge as well. There was a fierce battle in the deluges of water before we captured it and bound it in place with our thickest rope. There were fish everywhere and Georges managed to spear a dolphin in the chaos. Something must be done to check the water, which by now was breaking in with insane fury aft. How long would the stern section continue to support these tremendous periodic loads? A wooden boat would have broken in two.

We had to try to stem the flood of water. We collected all the spare papyrus we had and Abdullah, assisted by Santiago and Carlo, stood thigh-deep in water aft, tying on papyrus rolls as a bulwark against the seas. The water rose to their chests when the worst seas sent their crests surging on board. Abdullah was washed overboard several times, but was saved by his life line and only laughed as he scrambled on board again. After all, he was wearing his magic belt. When the work was finished he gave thanks to Allah.

What I had feared happened. The higher we built the dam, the more water found room on board the tail, because the papyrus bottom had swollen tight and held the water in. Since there was no free outlet, the stern section was being pressed still lower by the enormous weight of water. So we tried to remove Abdullah's bulwark again. But as the original railing had now been pushed farther under water than before, so many tons of sea water surged in that the box containing the life raft began to float between the poles of the bridge. We could only tie the reed bulwark hastily on again. We even took a knife and cut away the ropes of two small papyrus boats we had on board for an emergency and used all this liberated papyrus to raise Abdullah's reed gunwales. Finally we undid our Egyptian life belts, made according to the paintings in the ancient tombs. When at last we had not a single papyrus reed left to fall back on, the sides were higher, and the pool aft therefore even deeper than before. It now filled the whole afterdeck, but there was much less force in the water cascading in over the papyrus barrier. Midships and foredeck were dry as before.

On June 17 the storm reached its height, the wind turned westward and the high seas became more regular. We found flying fish everywhere; there was even a little one floating in the coffeepot. We must have returned to the main current, for, thanks to a momentary gap in the heavy cloud ceiling, Norman was able to report that we had sailed 80 nautical miles, or 148 kilometers in the last twenty-four hours, even with a broad, sagging stern slowing us down like a lobster tail. That amounted to something, even on a world map.

During the worst of the storm we were about five hundred nautical miles off the West African coast, heading straight for the Cape Verde Islands west of Dakar. Both the north wind and the current were carrying us straight toward this large group of islands that might loom up around us at any moment, and this gave us an uncomfortable feeling of insecurity as we drifted and struggled in the storm with an intractable stern section behaving like a yellow submarine. Late one evening when the thought of the islands out in the darkness was haunting us badly, Norman took out the U.S. sailing directions for the area we were in and read aloud to us by the light of the kerosene lantern. It swung from the heaving ceiling, making our shadows dance about us, distorted and elastic, in time to Ra's deafening spectral orchestra.

We learned that cloudbanks and haze could lie so thickly round the mountainous Cape Verde Islands that the white surf against the rocky coast often became visible before land itself had been sighted, although the highest peaks reached nine thousand feet. In addition there were powerful currents near the islands, so treacherous that they had caused innumerable shipwrecks. The heavy rollers round the island group were most active during the full moon and the new moon. "Great caution is therefore necessary when navigating in the vicinity of these islands," Norman read aloud in conclusion. It happened to be a new moon.

"You heard what he said, boys: great caution," remarked Yuri sardonically, pulling his sleeping bag up and his leather cap down until they met at his nose.

There was not much we could do. The moon was new. The night

was as pitch black as the day was misty gray. For the last four days the islands had lain straight ahead in our line of drift and now they must be somewhere just in front of us. They could appear that night or next morning if we were caught by a strong southerly crosscurrent. Rain was falling from low clouds and neither sextant nor "nosometer" could tell us where we were.

June 18 was a dramatic day. The Cape Verde Islands had to be somewhere just ahead or off the port bow, swathed and hidden in fog and rain clouds. Just two weeks before we had passed the Canary Islands at close range without seeing them through the cloudbanks. But today more serious problems were brewing than the ones lurking beyond our decks. We had been together in tolerance on the papyrus bundles for twenty-five days and the reed had been floating in sea water for at least a month. Despite all our adversities the *Ra* had sailed well over a thousand miles round the whole northwest coast of Africa. Now the voyage across the Atlantic from continent to continent was to begin. If the Egyptians had sailed as far from the mouth of the Nile as we had now sailed from Safi harbor, they would have reached far up the Don in Russia, or else passed through the Strait of Gibraltar into the Atlantic. The Mediterranean was obviously not big enough to exhaust the range of a papyrus boat.

But damn that stern section! If only the ancient scribes had left directions, we would have understood the principles of the papyrus boat in advance; then we could have looked forward to the trans-Atlantic crossing without problems. Now the waves were not slipping under us and lifting us up any more. They were creeping over our stern and pushing us down. The night before a big sea had lunged right over the cabin wall and I was awakened by a bucket of cold water in my face. Salt water was running down inside my sleeping bag.

"We are starting with a handicap," I admitted to the others.

It was then that Santiago threw a match into the powder keg.

"Let's cut up the life raft," he said suddenly.

"Of course," I said. "Now we have broken up the two little papyrus life boats, so just let's cut up the rubber life raft as well."

"I mean it," said Santiago. "We must try to raise the stern. We have no papyrus left, but the life raft is made of foam rubber. We

can cut it in strips and use it in the same way as the Egyptians would
have used spare papyrus."

"He's crazy," came mutters in several languages.

But Santiago was obdurate and refused to give in.

"You brought a life raft that only takes six men and there are
seven of us," he challenged me. "You explicitly said you would never
get into it yourself."

"The next size up was a twelve-man raft," I explained. "That
was too big. But it's true that I shall stay on our nice big bale of
reeds if you six decide to move to that little rubber thing there."

"Me too," said Abdullah. "Let's cut it up. Its wooden crate just
keeps gnawing our ropes away."

"No," I said. "The rubber raft is meant to give everyone a feeling of security. This is nothing but a scientific experiment. Without
the rubber raft no one would be able to leave the papyrus boat if
he wanted to."

"Come on, where's the saw? What's the good of something we
will never use?" Santiago insisted provocatively.

The rest of the crew were indignant, but everyone went aft to
have a look, at least, at the heavy packing crate that Abdullah wanted
to get rid of.

There was no ship behind the back wall of the cabin any more.
The only thing that projected out of the water there was the curved
tailpiece which rose in lonely majesty, separated from the rest of *Ra*
by the rippling waves that swept in from one side of the boat and
out at the other. The crate with the life raft was sloshing about in
green water between the legs of the bridge.

Abdullah seized the ax that hung ready, but Yuri protested
furiously. It was absolutely crazy! We must think of the people at
home. Norman agreed with Yuri: our families would despair if we
had no lifeboat. George took the ax from Abdullah. Carlo began to
waver. He wanted me to make the decision. For the first time on the
voyage a serious breach was opening. On a vital decision opinions
were sharply opposed and both parties grew steadily more bitter in
their uncompromising demands.

We all went and sat together on the foredeck on our goatskin
containers, sacks and jars, while Carlo served salt meat, onion ome-

lette and Moroccan *sello*. But this was the calm before the storm. The dry reeds in the papyrus deck at our feet bent and straightened like strips of paper, keeping time with the seas that were still high and choppy. The reed was stronger under water where it was wet. With her two spliced rudder-oars lashed fast and her lobster tail hanging down and acting as a brake, *Ra* steered herself before the wind. Yuri, Norman and Georges reflected the murky thunder clouds hanging over us on all sides, as they grimly cracked almonds in their fists, prepared to defend their position. It was essential to lance the boil.

"Many things can happen," I said, trying to keep my voice cheerful. "Let's think about all the situations where the life raft might be useful. I'm most scared of someone falling overboard."

"I'm most scared of being rammed by a ship," interjected Norman, "and then of fire on board."

"The bows are floating splendidly, but not the stern," said Yuri. "No one knows if the reeds will still be afloat in another month's time."

"True enough," I admitted. "And it's still theoretically possible that the skeptics are right and the papyrus will gradually rot and disintegrate in the sea water."

"What I'm scared of," came quietly from Georges, who was never afraid of anything, "is a hurricane."

No one could think of more than these six good reasons for keeping the life raft in reserve. But six reasons were enough. We therefore agreed to find out what each man would do in each of these six eventualities. We counted on our fingers.

First possibility: man overboard. Everyone felt safe because we were all roped up like mountaineers. We also had a life belt trailing on a long rope astern. If a lonely night wanderer stumbled over the jars and fell overboard, launching the life raft would not help him. (For one thing, the raft was intended for an extreme emergency and could not be launched without our cutting down the entire bridge. Furthermore, it was deep and rectangular, with two inflatable tents that opened both below and above deck, no matter which side came uppermost. It was thus not intended for fast sailing and would be left far behind the *Ra* even if we lowered the sail. Accordingly, the

life raft would be of little avail if a man fell overboard. No argument
about that one.

Second possibility: collision. Everyone agreed that if *Ra* were
split in two we would not have time to launch the raft, and if it
was already afloat we would still all prefer to clamber back on the
much larger remaining portions of the *Ra*.

Third possibility: fire. In the Sahara, *Ra* would have burned like
tissue paper, but here it would be difficult to set fire to her. In any
case we had a fire extinguisher. Smoking was only allowed on the lee
side, where sparks blew overboard, and the windward side was so
soaked with water that it would float, fire or no fire elsewhere on
board. No one would prefer the little life raft to the large, wet,
unburned portion of *Ra*.

Fourth possibility: the papyrus might sink under us. One
month's experience showed that even if the papyrus absorbed water
it sank so slowly that there would be plenty of time to send out an
SOS. But we would also have to send out an SOS if we transferrred
to the crowded lifeboat. We would all rather be able to stretch out in
our comparatively spacious basket cabin than sit squashed together
in that little lifeboat tent, waiting for rescue.

Fifth possibility: the papyrus might rot and disintegrate. We
already knew from sight and touch that the papyrus experts had mis-
calculated on this point. Their laboratory experiments had certainly
been made in still sea water. We all agreed wholeheartedly that both
the papyrus reeds and the lashings were stronger than ever, so we
were absolutely unanimous in ruling out that emergency.

Sixth possibility: hurricane. We could run into one at any time
as we neared the West Indies. A hurricane might carry away masts and
oars and steering bridge, might even rip off the sunken stern. But
we had lived through more than one storm on the *Ra* now and were
certain that the tough wicker cabin would continue to cling to *Ra's*
central reed bundles, leaving us a raft with more room, water and
food on board than the little foam rubber raft could possibly provide.
Nobody would move to the rubber raft in a hurricane.

Before we had finished we were all in high spirits. No one had
preferred the life raft to *Ra's* reed bundles in any conceivable situation. Yuri was visibly relieved. He grinned and shook his head, marvel-

ing. Carlo laughed. Norman drew a deep breath and was the first on his feet.

"OK. Let's get the saw!"

Everyone wanted to make for the stern, but such heavy seas were breaking over the submerged deck aft that three men made quite enough extra load there. Norman, Abdullah and I waded into the stern. With ax, knife and saw we attacked the heavy packing crate and then threw planks and plastic inner container overboard. These sorts of things were out of place on *Ra*. The green foam rubber raft came into view. Under it Abdullah was appalled to see that several of the ropes holding together the *Ra* herself had been chafed through by the movement of the crate in the cascades of water. Rope ends bristled from the papyrus like ghastly skeletal claws. Only the swelling of the reed had prevented the ropes from slithering through and allowing the whole stern to break apart. Abdullah fell on the loose ends and tied them together with extra rope. We stood knee-deep in foaming water and Abdullah showed us how the skin on his legs was peeling in wet white flakes, after all the work in sea water over the last few days. Then I felt one of the mightiest of the towering waves crashing against the *Ra*, lifting us up and twisting us abruptly sideways. I was staggering in an attempt to regain balance when I heard the deafening roar of tons of falling water and breaking timber. The sea surged in up to my waist from behind, while wood and rope yielded to the power of the ocean and slowly collapsed. I was swept to port by the torrent of water and bent to grab a rope before I could be washed overboard when I felt a great weight of broken timber thumping over my back. I heard Norman's voice bellowing: "Look out, Thor!" and was sure that this deafening sound of cracking wood came from the entire bridge subsiding in its lashings and breaking over our heads. As our foundations rocked and broken timber held me down in the surge of water, I expected at any moment to find the three of us being towed along behind *Ra* by our life lines with bridge and stern torn off and left floating in our wake. Then the floods subsided and I found myself left knee-deep as before with broken timber pressing me down.

"It was the double-shaft rudder-oar that went," shouted Norman, helping to free me.

Above us bobbed the splintered ends of two big logs lashed

together. The thick, round original shaft and the square balk of the spare mast bound to it as reinforcement, had broken off side by side. The big oar blade was left hanging on the ropes, lashing like the tail of an angry whale, but in a flash Norman was there with Carlo and Santiago to haul it in, while Abdullah wrestled alone with the rubber raft, now floating freely onboard, and I struggled with a two-hundred-pound keg of salt meat, which had suddenly broken loose among the bridge poles and threatened to cause disaster unless prevented from crashing about in the cascades of water.

That night Abdullah assured me, when I came out for the change of watch, that we were now surrounded by kind big swells with no nasty little waves on their backs. *Ra* rode smoothly and rhythmically; two small rowing oars were temporarily tied on where the big port rudder-oar had been. When we switched our flashlights on we could see a squid swimming as though behind the glass of an aquarium when the water rose like a wall beside us. The Egyptian sail occasionally stood out clearly against twinkling gaps in the cloud ceiling, but the horizon was invisible in the darkness. What sometimes seemed to be stars low on the horizon often proved to be florescent plankton twinkling brightly at eye level, carried up on an invisible wave crest.

It certainly felt very odd next day to begin attacking our un-damaged life raft with a saw. Norman and I looked at each other and I paused uncertainly for an instant before sending the saw rasping through the green canvas cover and into the foam rubber. Then we all set about dismembering our only means of getting away from the boat we were standing on knee-deep in water.

"People will think we are crazy. No one will understand," said Yuri, grinning.

But the decision was unanimous and well-weighed. The life raft was reduced to narrow strips, the shape of papyrus bundles, then pushed under water and lashed fast to the surface of the sunken deck. The miracle happened. The stern began to rise. It lifted enough to give us better steering control over the boat, and once again the waves slid under us without filling our swimming pool with such floods of water. The event was appropriately celebrated. However, the sea gradually stole on board and plucked the sawn-up foam rubber away bit by bit, until only the natural papyrus stems were left. Neptune might have been telling us: "No cheating. Pharaoh's men had no foam rubber." So our delight was short-lived, but with the disappearance of the heavy crate with the life raft we had removed a dangerous load from the afterdeck.

On June 19 we found ourselves dancing in heavy swells augmented by waves reflecting from cliffs on shore that stirred the sea into indescribable turmoil. The deck of *Ra* billowed like a carpet and in some places dry papyrus crinkled itself into little curls on top of the bundles. Between mast and cabin, where two men could usually walk side by side, one man had to watch out before slipping through alone, and the little gap between bridge and cabin wall opened and closed like a nutcracker. If we sat on the narrow crack between two of our sixteen boxes in the cabin, we were nipped in the bottom. For the first time a clay jar was crushed to pieces and the nuts spilled out, to Safi's delight. We discovered that another was empty of water because friction with the neighboring jar had worn a round hole in its side. The starboard rudder-oar was spliced and launched, while water gushed round our bodies, but soon afterward there was another crack and the blade was floating astern again, while the sail swung round and imprisoned Carlo and Santiago, who were busy tapping water from a goatskin. They were bowled over toward the open railing and would have finished up in the sea had they not been roped up. A big flying fish sailed on board and swam happily for a time in the pool aft while Abdullah floundered about vainly trying to catch it.

In the struggle with rope and sail and broken rudder-oars I got my hand pinched and it was hurting even more that night when I came on deck to relieve Santiago. He pointed silently. A light to port. We clung to the guardrail, legs braced, so as not to tumble over while we stared. Cape Verde? No, a boat. It was heading for us. It was signaling. The flashes were too fast for us to read, but it was asking about something.

"*Ra* OK, *Ra* OK," we flashed back in Morse. The boat was close to us now and we guessed that it was a patrol boat from Cape Verde. It was rolling violently, while we were calmly undulating with the waves.

"*Ra, bon voyage,*" it finally flashed slowly. Have a good trip.

Then it turned away and the comforting lights vanished in the darkness.

"Have a good trip," I said to Santiago as he went to bed.

Two hours later I had already begun to whistle carefully through the wicker wall to waken Yuri in all the noise. He was to relieve me, but the others must be left to sleep. Then I felt as if Neptune himself had taken hold of the oar blade out there in the blackness of the sea. Vast forces wrenched the oar from me and the whole vessel heeled, while white furies thundered out of the darkness and buried everything under my legs. The bridge vibrated and the crack of breaking wood was loud in my ears again. Was it the bridge collapsing this time? No. It was the other rudder-oar. Now we had nothing to steer with. I had to yell through the wickerwork and rouse everyone. The sail thrashed. The water seethed. Ropes and timber screamed louder than shouted orders. It began to rain. We threw out both our sea anchors. Then all was well.

"They wished us a good trip," said Santiago, staring out into the night. We felt alone as never before. There was no light to be seen now from land or ship. At last the whole Atlantic lay open ahead of us.

"Good watch, Yuri. You have no problems—nothing to steer with."

Chapter Ten

INTO AMERICAN WATERS

W E WERE having a party on board the
Ra. Sky and sea smiled. The tropical sun burned down on the
dry foredeck and the Atlantic washed quietly to and fro across the
afterdeck. Inside the basketwork cabin it was cool and shady. A
blue Atlantic chart was tied with twine to the yellow wicker wall.
On it was drawn a line of small penciled circles. The last was quite
new and showed that today we had crossed longitude 40° W. and
were therefore in the American half of the Atlantic. For several
days Brazil had been our nearest fixed point, because we were now
much closer to the South American mainland than to Africa, but
as we were sailing almost directly westward we would be crossing
the widest part of the ocean, and then the West Indies would
be the nearest landing place ahead.

This was an occasion for celebration. Our Italian chef, Carlo,
had extra help in the galley from gourmet Georges, who produced
the choicest dishes out of the contents of our ceramic jars. After
an hors d'oeuvre of Moroccan olives, sliced salt sausage and sun-
dried Egyptian fish roe, we were each served an enormous omelette
of fresh eggs filled with artichoke hearts, onions, whole tomatoes,
scraps of smoked mutton and peppered sheep's cheese, and with
a choice seasoning of all sorts of special spices, from Egyptian
kamon to Moroccan desert herbs and red pepper. For dessert we

had raisins, prunes, almonds and best of all, triple rations of Madame Aicha's honey-sweet Moroccan *sello* crumbs.

Who missed refrigerators and can openers? None of the representatives of seven countries who sat stuffing themselves with this variation of a Pharaonic feast, while our papyrus ship marked the occasion by heading under full sail in the right direction, with no watch on the steering bridge.

We had a floating grocery store on board. Santiago, our Mexican quartermaster, kept order in the store and Carlo was the only legal customer. Only Safi was caught shoplifting. Unable to read Santiago's numbers, she had a peculiar talent for removing the cork from precisely those jars that contained nuts. From Santiago's little book the rest of us knew that jars 1 to 6, for instance, contained fresh eggs in lime solution, 15 to 17 were full of whole cooked tomatoes immersed in olive oil, 33 and 34 contained peppered sheep's cheese cut in cubes and likewise immersed in olive oil. Into jars 51 and 52 Aicha had pressed Moroccan butter, boiled and kneaded with salt, in the Berber manner. Jars 70 to 160 contained only clear spring water from a rural well outside Safi, but as they do in the desert, we had slipped small lumps of pitch into the water with which the goatskin bags were filled. Otherwise it would go bad. In the other jars and in baskets and sacks we had honey, salt, peas, beans, rice, various types of grain and flour, dried vegetables, *karkadé*, coconuts, *karubu* beans, nuts, dates, almonds, figs, prunes and raisins. Our baskets of fresh root crops, green vegetables and fruit had come to an end in two or three weeks. From the roof of the wicker alcove projecting forward beyond the cabin roof we had hung salted and smoked meat and sausages, bunches of onions, dried fish and nets of pressed Egyptian fish roe. Under this hanging delicatessen stood wickerwork baskets containing dried bread of various types, made from ancient Egyptian, Russian and Norwegian recipes. We wanted to find out if a papyrus boat could really be used at sea, not if we were capable of eating authentic Egyptian dishes. On the other hand, we also wanted to find out if jars and baskets could last the journey, and whether raft voyagers could live without cans and frozen food if their fisherman's luck gave out. Obviously there were no problems in filling a papyrus boat with any food that could be stored on any ocean-going vessel.

Captions for the following four pages

76. *African Neptune* crossed our bow in mid-Atlantic while Sinbad the duck acted as *Ra*'s figurehead. (Above)

77. A *sack* fastened to a life belt was thrown overboard from the American ship and Georges swam after it while Santiago and Yuri held him on the life line. (Below)

78 and 79. *The catch* was some weekly magazines and a pile of fresh fruit.

80 and 81. *Ra in mid-Atlantic* photographed from *African Neptune* en route from New York to Cape Town. The sail had faded but the hull was sound.

82. *Shipboard feast* at halfway point. From the left: the author, Yuri, Santiago, Georges and Norman. Special refreshments for the occasion. (Above)

83. *The author's chart* after a full month's voyage. We passed the fortieth meridian and were then in the American half of the Atlantic. (Below)

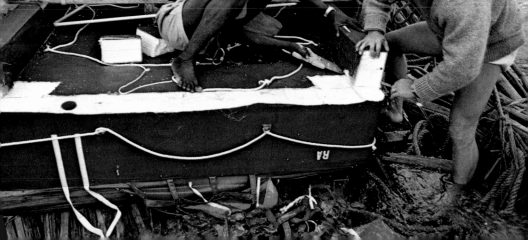

84. *Listing to windward* as opposed to the leeward list of ordinary sailboats. Only bitter experience could teach us that a reed boat has to carry its ballast on the opposite side from other sailboats because the reed bundles absorb more water on the windward side where the waves splash higher. (Above)

85. *Problems were beginning aft,* but at first Santiago found it practical to be able to wash clothes on board. (Below)

86. *The afterdeck sagged* still further and it was difficult for Norman and Georges to work aft when the rudder-oars broke in the darkness of the night. (Above)

87. *Abdullah praying on night watch* with a string of beads on the steering deck. (Below)

88. *There was no boat left* aft of the steering deck but Yuri held the course steadily as long as the rest of the vessel was riding high. (Above)

89. *Our only life raft* is cut into strips by unanimous decision. The foam rubber was tied to the afterdeck to lift it but everything was washed away by heavy seas. (Below)

90. *In the grip of the sea.* Alpinist Carlo, knot and rope expert, helps sailor Norman to secure a sea anchor when both rudder-oars break again.

Crossing the fortieth longitude inspired Georges to break with ancient tradition. He opened one of *Ra*'s two champagne bottles, while Yuri served his own hair-raising home brew in hand-painted wooden Russian beakers. Abdullah refused. He patted the visibly taut skin of his stomach and disappeared beyond the cargo of jars to wash in our inland sea before giving thanks to Allah.

When he returned to his earthly friends he wanted an explanation of the pencil line on the chart to which he owed such a splendid meal. That we were constantly adjusting the clock, because the earth was round and the sun did not shine at the same time on all sides of a sphere, he could understand. And that Carlo had a watch with an automatic winder that went just as well after lying unwound in a box on board for five weeks he could also understand, because the *Ra*'s wickerwork cabin was more mobile than any walking person. But what he did not understand was that every day we marked our route on a chart where the sea was divided by straight lines running down and across. Today we had passed the fortieth longitude and up to now he had not set eyes on a single one of them. Norman explained. Land and sea were divided into imaginary squares with numbers on them, so that people could tell by the numbers where they were.

"Aha," said Abdullah. "On land the squares keep still, but at sea they move west with the current even if there is no wind."

"We have to imagine the lines on the ocean bed," interrupted Norman. And then he explained that we had begun our journey in Safi, which lay on longitude 9° W., and today we were passing longitude 40° W. At the same time we had also been traveling south, all the way from latitude 32° N. down to 15° N., so now we were just as far south as Abdullah when he was at home in Chad.

Then Abdullah himself pointed out that the westernmost point of Africa, Dakar, lay 18° W. and the easternmost point of Brazil, Recife, lay 36° W., so now that we were on 40° W. we had passed the nearest corner of Brazil and had good reason to celebrate the fact that we were now in the American half of the Atlantic.

Out on deck the feast went on. Yuri had climbed on the lid of the galley chest and stamped and leaped in the Russian manner as vigorously as the pitching boat would allow, while he sang Russian folk songs. When he came to "Song of the Volga Boatman" we all joined in. Then Norman jumped onto the box with his harmonica and led the whole chorus in "Down in the Valley" and other cowboy songs. Italy followed with heroic Alpine marches, Mexico with catchy revolutionary tunes, Norway with gay sea shanties and Egypt with an exotic whimpering accompaniment to his belly-dancing. But Chad took first prize partly because Abdullah was so absorbed in his own performance and partly because there was such an absurd contrast between the ubiquitous backdrop of sea and the Central African standing on a box drumming on the bottom of a pot while singing his pulsating jungle tunes.

The watch disappeared aft at intervals to look at the compass. We were sailing due west with the wind at our backs, still at an average speed of fifty to sixty nautical miles a day. For six days after passing the Cape Verde Islands off the coast of Africa we had had an infernal time keeping control of our sagging stern section with the help of our clumsy stumps of botched-up rudder-oars. But out here in the middle of the ocean the waves had become much more co-operative and we had achieved a sort of *modus vivendi* with the sea around us. As long as we let the waves tag along free of charge as far up the boat as the cabin wall, the ocean let its current send both waves and men speeding westward at a good pace. Carlo was one of those who suffered in silence at the sight of *Ra*'s tall sternpost emerging in solitary splendor from the sea astern. It was humiliating to see our once proud golden bird swimming with the neck of a swan and the rump of a toad. But on a day of celebration like this we just had to keep to the swan's big neck and torso and forget that aft of the cabin we were a toad.

By sundown we had created an orchestra from Carlo's kitchen tools. *Ra* was creaking so softly that we drowned the mewing of the papyrus with our chosen instruments. Carlo could not get at the galley box, so he simply served Russian dried bread and honey. The bread tasted better to us than the finest cake, but it was handed out in big black lumps as hard as coal. I had eaten a good many pieces when there was a snap and my only crowned tooth flew off across the papyrus and I sat there feeling foolish and exploring the revolting little hole with the tip of my tongue.

"Lousy communist bread!" remarked Norman with a sidelong glance specially aimed at our Russian ship's doctor.

Yuri bent and picked up the little chip, which he examined closely.

"Lousy capitalist dentist!" he parried.

With shouts of laughter, song and music the party went on until the sun-god Ra sank into the sea, right in front of the nose of his marine namesake. The shining celestial sphere seemed to be enticing our own swan-necked *Ra* westward, ever westward. Such eternal movements westward must have offered immense entice-ment to genuine sun-worshipers. Resplendent lancets which no royal crown could match radiated like a diadem from the sea's edge into the sky. A tropical sea's attempt to emulate the northern lights: first in dazzling gold, then red as blood, orange, green and violet, turning gradually to black, while the twinkling stars emerged equally slowly from their invisibility as the sun-king disappeared. His majesty had gone. His little people of the sky flocked out to join the procession to the west.

We lay on our backs on full or empty goatskins, philosophizing. Outside the cabin there was no limit to our view, nothing to hinder or confuse our thoughts. It had been a fine day, we were full, we had feasted and laughed, now we simply wanted to look at the stars and let our thoughts linger or wander where they would.

"You're a good guy, Yuri," said Norman. "Are there any more like you over there in Russia?"

"Two more," said Yuri. "The rest are better on the whole. But are there any decent capitalists left in your country, now that you have come with us?"

"Thanks for the compliment," said Norman. "If you think I'm decent, you'll have something to look forward to on the other side."

There was a peaceful discussion on communism and capitalism, on anti-communism and anti-capitalism, on autocracy and dicta-torship of the masses, on whether to prefer food or freedom, on why the people's representatives hate each other when common citi-zens everywhere get along so well as soon as they are able to meet. Whether the hippie movement in East and West was created by youth or by its parents, whether it would die out or increase with the advance of civilization, whether it could be thought of as a sort of warning barometer, showing that the civilization that we and our fathers had believed in and feverishly built up night and day was not going to be accepted by future generations. Egyptians and Sumerians, Mayans and Incas built pyramids, embalmed mummies and thought they were on the right track. They defended their ideas with slings and bows and arrows. We think they were wrong about the purpose of life. So we build nuclear missiles and go to the moon. We defend our policies with atom bombs and anti-missile missiles. Now our children are beginning to sit down in protest. They hang Indian ornaments round their necks, let their hair grow and play guitars on the floor. They retreat by artificial means into themselves, a longer journey than to sun or moon.

One grows philosophical when stars and plankton are twinkling in a world that is as it was before human beings saw it, before they got going on it with their thousands of millions of busy fingers. It is easier to be tolerant of each other's views when you are sitting together in the starlight and know that you will sink or swim together, than when you sit on opposite sides of national frontiers with your nose in a newspaper or the TV screen. There was never any heated verbal duel of a political or religious nature on board the *Ra*. To each his own opinion. We were supposed to represent the most extreme contrasts, and so we did, but we found that the lowest common denominator was not so low after all. It was easy to find. Perhaps it was because we seven on board saw ourselves as a unit in relation to our only common neighbors, who happened to breathe through gills and had quite different interests and ambitions from our own. In spite of everything, human beings were confoundedly similar, even if some had beaky noses and others flat.

There was a splash in the darkness, a heavy fish flailed against papyrus deck and wicker wall. A jubilant shout from Georges announced that he had speared a two-foot-long dolphin. By the light of the fishing lamp we saw squid keeping pace with us by swimming backward in jerks with all their arms stretched over their heads. They filled themselves with water and forced it out in powerful squirts that shot them backward through the water. The jet system. They had acquired it as a means of escape from their pursuers. They acquired it before we did. The cachalot whale that had visited us could dive to a depth of three thousand feet, where the tremendous pressure was a hundred times that of the atmosphere, and yet it would not bang its head against the bottom in the absolute darkness, because it had a built-in radar. It had acquired it before we did.

"Yuri, as an atheist, do you think there may be an intelligent system in all that, twinkling up there among the constellations, when no human beings have been up there to put things in order yet?"

"I'm not a real atheist, it's just that I don't believe in all that nonsense that goes on in church."

"In any case, Darwin and the church agree that sun and moon, fish, birds and monkeys were created first. When man got his chance at last, everything was ready and waiting. In fact, now we are simply trying to find out how our own brains and intestines as well as the entire universe is composed and made to function."

It was pleasant to lie completely relaxed in friendly comradeship with a peaceful sea and to gaze up at exactly the same view that seafarers and desert wanderers had gazed up at for thousands of years before us. Modern city dwellers, dazzled by street lights, have lost the starry sky. The astronauts are trying to find it again. I dozed. We decided we would all go to bed except for the watch. We had hard days behind us and did not know what was to come. Another storm would be no joke. The afterdeck was not there to protect us. We had spread canvas over the short back wall and long starboard side of the cabin after torrents of water from the stern had poured down the necks of those of us sleeping with heads against the back wall. I thought with mixed feelings of my chief impressions of the last few days, before we had come out here into calmer seas.

The first night, after being robbed of both our rudder-oars off the Cape Verde Islands, Yuri and Georges had worked out a temporary method by which two men at a time could steer tolerably well by simply hauling on the sheets of the sail. After all, the important thing was to keep the stern into the wind, so that the sail was filled and did not flap and slap against the mast. All we had to do was to ride with the weather. The first night after the Cape Verde Islands, we had been beset by huge waves that thundered the back wall of the cabin, high up, before pouring overboard on both sides of the boat. This incessant slamming against our bedhead had made it difficult enough to fall asleep, and if we did sleep we were soon roused to crawl out into the night and do battle with the vast canvas sail. Breaking waves and slashing canvas. We were tossed around like dolls, thrown headlong across the cargo of jars and tumbled about from cabin wall and ropes to the outermost edge of the boat. Salt water ran off our backs and faces. Back into our sleeping bags. Out again. Fourteen flying fish on deck for breakfast. Seven dolphins caught in a row. Crazy Georges. Abdullah cannot eat them all. Let them swim with us, then we will have them fresh when we need them. Two disappeared in the pool aft, one swam about under the bridge and one hid under the steering spar. There was an underwater battle between fish and man before they were caught in bare hands. The fish was one powerful slippery bundle of muscle. One hand round the narrow tail root and one through the gills prevented the floundering fish from following the water as it poured overboard from the rolling vessel. The crossbeam on which the bridge poles were supported slid away. A crack, and the whole bridge gave way. Rope, rope! Water over our heads. Splendid job. Now it's holding. Enjoying yourself, Carlo? It's just like in the Alps. Don't go to sleep here, Georges. We'll carry you to bed. Damn, how my arms ache! Was I asleep? Not quite. Are we still on the *Ra*? Yes, the papyrus is creaking. There are stars outside; we are far away from the misty coast.

It was difficult to keep the first days after Cape Verde distinct in one's mind. Time flowed together. But in the logbook is a note that June 20 was the hardest day up to then. On June 21 the entry reads that the night was the worst we had seen, and the day no better. But even without sail or rudder-oars, and with sea anchors trailing to slow us down, we were still able to log a day's progress of thirty-one nautical miles toward America. This was the lowest recorded on the voyage. On June 22 the submerged end of the steering spar had such an unsteadying effect on our course that Georges had to dive down in diving mask and saw the thick spar off under water. While three of us hung completely or partly overboard in the twilight a dozen black-and-white spotted porpoises came up from below and played along the papyrus roll we were hanging on, so close that we could touch them. The small whales gamboled up to the reed bundles and rolled about without a splash in graceful play, more like soap bubbles than hundreds of pounds of solid muscle. With Georges overboard and Abdullah and me sitting on the submerged edge, the waves rhythmically rising to our chests, we were meeting the whale in the whale's own habitat. These mammals did not disturb us and we let them play in peace in our common bath water. That day we discovered for the first time that the waves which struck the cabin wall were forcing their way further in, over the wickerwork cabin floor, between the wooden boxes we slept on. The bottom of the case where Norman kept his radio was soaking wet. The cabin was beginning to tilt so sharply to starboard that several of the men tried to turn their mattresses crosswise.

On June 25 atmospheric conditions were strange. The temperature vacillated between cold and tropical heat. Once or twice there was a wave of heat carrying a distinct scent of dry sand, just as I had known it in the Sahara. Had I not had confidence in our approximate position, I would have thought that we were navigating just off a desert coast. Only later did I learn that sand from the Sahara regularly rains down on Central America. That night the seas were worse than ever. We had to move everything we could even farther toward the foredeck. All the boxes we had been sleeping on in the cabin were awash, although the pliant Ra was hurling herself over the chaos of waves as never before. She rode like a magic carpet.

So it was that we eventually emerged into quiet weather, with a fresh breeze, rolling seas and sunshine. The trade wind blew steadily from the northeast and the elements behaved more or less as one is entitled to expect in these latitudes. As the weather changed, the first shark came patrolling toward us and suddenly skimmed so close by Georges' legs that he had to draw them in. But it simply glided on and disappeared in our wake.

June 28 was one of the most splendid days we spent on Ra and everyone busied himself peacefully with his own affairs. Georges sat in the door opening with Abdullah, teaching him to read and write in Arabic. Others sat with laundry, fishing rods or diaries. Then we heard a heart-rending wail—from the equable Norman! For a while he had been overside near the port bow, securing the broken oar blade that held his grounding plate, but now he was hanging as if paralyzed, his face contorted, unable to pull his body on board. Everyone thought the worst: shark. We ran to pull him up. There were no limbs missing, but the culprit was hanging on. The lower part of Norman's body was entwined in the glistening pink filaments of a big Portuguese man-of-war. Norman was in a coma when he was dragged into the cabin and given cardiac stimulants.

"Ammonia," said Yuri tensely. "We have no ammonia. It's the only thing that helps to neutralize the caustic acid which is permeating his body. Urine is full of ammonia, all of you. This is serious."

For two hours Yuri sat massaging Norman with a rag dipped in a coconut shell full of urine while the patient writhed in pain and convulsions until he became inert and slept. His legs and the lower part of his body were covered with red sting marks like welts. When Norman awoke and looked from his own leg to all the innocent bubbles of foam that were floating as usual on the shining waves, he shouted like a drunken man, "Look, baby men-of-war! Now the whole sea is full of them." He subsided with a bowl of hot dried-fruit soup. Next day he was still out of sorts and raged at Georges, who had suddenly got under his skin. But by evening the two of them had shaken hands and were sitting together singing cowboy songs.

On June 30 we drifted once again into a part of the ocean covered with oil clots. We were traveling in the same direction, but with our big sail we moved much faster. Still we seemed unable to get away from them; we passed untold numbers of the black floating lumps from morning till night. Then a splendid full moon rose behind us in our wake. An unforgettable night, with moonlight on yellow papyrus and burgundy-colored sail. The stars were beginning to fade on the eastern horizon. It was no longer May, nor even June; it was the beginning of July and we were still afloat with tons of useful cargo left.

On July 1 a ship bristling with masts and derricks appeared on the horizon to the northwest and passed us at close range, heading southeast. We were just crossing the shipping route between the U.S.A. and South Africa. We all stood on the bridge, the cabin roof and the steps of the mast to watch almost with nostalgic feelings this pleasant fragment of our own twentieth century until the last masthead disappeared over the horizon. Then we were alone again with the sea. More alone than before. Georges stayed up on the bridge, humming in a rather melancholy manner. Then he gave a roar.

"They're coming back!"

It was true. Over the horizon where it had just completely disappeared the same ship hove into view again and now it was heading straight for us. The crew must have been discussing the extraordinary contraption they had passed and now the skipper had decided to come back and take a closer look. The ship came steaming straight toward the Ra. *African Neptune*, New York, was the name on the bow. It swung in alongside Ra, with all the decks filled with waving people.

"Can we do anything for you?" Norman yelled to his countrymen, bubbling with exhilaration.

"No thanks, but perhaps there's something we can do for you," came the shout from the bridge.

"Fruit!" the crew of the Ra called back in many languages.

But the Ra herself continued to forge ahead and was just about to run her papyrus nose straight into the iron hull when our frantic shouts and gestures startled the skipper into starting up the propeller and hastily getting out of our way. Having something delivered to such an uncontrollable wanton as Ra was not easy. The sea-god's namesake made a wide detour round the sun-god's little namesake and as she crossed our line of drift a bag attached to an orange life belt was thrown into the sea. It whirled away far out of reach in the boil of the big ship's propeller. Georges had already put on his rubber suit for protection against Portuguese men-of-war and dived out with a long line tied round his body. When we pulled him in he brought an unforgettable catch: thirty-nine oranges, thirty-seven apples, three lemons, four grapefruit and a wet roll of American magazines. We waved and yelled our thanks. The foredeck had suddenly turned into a rainbow banquet. Fresh fruit and fruit salad in a world of salt. Cores for Safi and seeds for Sinbad.

Here, in mid-Atlantic, we enjoyed some of our best days on board the Ra. Abdullah's papyrus bulwark and Carlo's jungle of guy ropes on all sides of the cabin and stern seemed to be holding us up a little more or less by the hair. Seen from the rolling ocean vessel we must have looked quite presentable. We on board the reed boat were all equally impressed by the incredible strength and loading capacity of the papyrus. Paper boat? Perhaps. But it was only the wooden parts that broke. Papyrus had proved to be a first-class building material. Its strength in sea water had been completely misjudged by the theorists, whether anthropologists or papyrus experts. It was equally wrong to believe, as we ourselves had believed, that the ancient papyrus boats, as painted on the walls in Egypt, were primitive vessels. The only thing an Egyptian papyrus ship had in common with a raft was that both floated equally well even if their bottoms were holed. Both the *Ra* and the *Kon-Tiki* were raft-ships, because they had no hull. But otherwise, to compare the reed boat *Ra* with the log raft *Kon-Tiki* was like comparing an automobile with a cart. Even a horse can make a cart go, but to drive a car you need instruction and a license. We had neither. We had set off on a sophisticated Egyptian vehicle, never dreaming that it was so specialized and unlike a simple raft in that one had to know the ingenious controls to make it work. It was made of first-class materials, but, like a car, if one was not instructed in the purpose and use of all the parts one could easily ruin something important before discovering by experiment how to make it all function. We were learning constantly, both from our failures and from our successes.

On July 4 Georges shook me awake. I could see he had an anxious expression. He thought he could see water spouts in several places on the horizon. Black ribbons between sea and sky looked menacing as the sun rose, but they were simply scattered showers. Soon rain was pouring down on reed deck and wicker roof. The unaccustomed rumble of thunder woke the crew and everyone came out into the dawn to wash the salt off his hair and body. We had so much water in the jars that we did not need to collect rain. Scattered showers continued all that day, and the next, and the next. The waves flattened out as the rain subdued them, but the reed boat became completely drenched. After three days of showers it was heavy and sodden. The trade wind turned fitful and shifted here and there, playing idly with draperies of rain squalls. The *Ra* seemed to be stealing along on tiptoe, with barely a creak. Was it the calm before the storm?

There was plenty of opportunity to swim and enjoy a fish's-eye view of the swollen strength and toughness of the papyrus bundles. One fly in the ointment was that once again, for two days running, we sailed through hundreds of thousands of small black clots traveling, as we were, to America. Out in the middle of Columbus' ocean we floated among them, and our hands turned black when we fingered them. Some were covered with small shells.

Hundreds of long-necked barnacles and a terrified little crab had made themselves at home on *Ra*'s belly. Now and then we saw big shoals of flying fish swimming ahead of us like herring. They were timid, but our little pilot fish and pampano, the first striped, the second spotted, became so bold that they took nips at us and bit holes in the sacks of dried fish when Carlo hung them overboard to soak.

On July 5, Egyptian Georges saw a rainbow for the first time in his life. The sunset on the same day was at least equally vivid. Enough paint for a hundred rainbows was smeared by invisible paintbrushes across the arch of sky toward which we were sailing. Norman sat doubled up in the cabin, working with chart and ruler on a board hung on the wickerwork wall. The rest of us lay on dry straw mattresses, waiting for the calculations to be done. Through the chinks in the front wall we could see the riot of color fading while Carlo lighted the kerosene lantern, which then disappeared with him up the steps of the mast.

"We have now sailed 2150 nautical miles," said Norman at last. "That means we are now much more than halfway. The distance from here to the West Indies is 1300 miles, that is much less than the distance back to Safi."

"The tail is holding us back, otherwise we would have sailed even faster," said Yuri. "Yesterday we were down to about forty miles."

"The tail slows us down, but the worst thing is that it makes us yaw too," Norman said. "Today we oscillated between 30° north and 30° south of the main course the whole time, although we all took turns at the rudder-oars. Sixty degrees of error, that's a lot of extra miles. I am simply measuring the shortest distance between each midday position. If the tail had not sent us on such a zigzag course we would have been there by now."

"The people who knew all the tricks of the papyrus boat could have been across long ago without problems," said Georges.

The papyrus creaked peacefully and there was a gentle splashing behind our bedhead, as if someone were using a bathtub behind a screen.

"I thought the sea got worse the farther out one came but it's the other way round," murmured Santiago. "Among anthropologists we often speak about how primitive sailors might have traveled to this or that place, as long as they could keep close inshore, but that's the worst place of all!"

"Along coasts and round islands the seas and currents are squeezed into all sorts of extraordinary eddies and backwashes," I confirmed. "In fact, close to land the sea runs amok much more easily than in the open, where swells have more room and do not bunch up into steep waves and breakers as readily. Even a storm is more dangerous on the coast."

"The mistake," said Santiago, "is the anthropologists and other scientists are always arguing about whether reed boats and rafts can cross an ocean or not, and they never reach any agreement. But if anyone tries to find out in practice he provokes wrathful indignation, because the answer comes in an unacademic way."

This was a problem with which both Santiago and I were intimately acquainted. I was independent and could laugh it off, but Santiago had had a hard time getting permission from his university to join in anything as "unscientific" as a voyage by reed boat. Papyrus could be tested in a bathtub. Scientists work in libraries, museums, laboratories—they do not play savage on the Atlantic.

The only thing was that here we were, at sea, with our beards and sunburned noses, getting an answer quite different from the answers in the textbooks. A result quite different from that of the specialist who had put his papyrus stalk in a water container. If you test a bit of balsa wood in the laboratory it sinks in a week or two. But if you do as the Indians did, fell standing timber and leave it in the sea with the sap in, the unexpected happens and you can stay afloat on balsa wood for 101 days and land in Polynesia. Now, the papyrus experts had put bits of papyrus stalks in a tank of still water, and besides quickly losing buoyancy, the plant tissue began to develop bubbles and decay. Two weeks, maximum, the textbooks said. Seven weeks had now passed. We and tons of cargo were being carried by exactly the same type of reed that sank in the laboratory. Why? Because the specialist experimented with loose reeds in a bathtub, while we sailed a completed reed boat on the salt sea. Experience had shown reed boatbuilders from Egypt to Peru that reed absorbs water through the shorn-off, porous end, not through the tight fibrous sheath that covers the stalk. So they used special techniques to build their reed boats, compressing the ends of the reeds so that they let in almost no water. *Papyrus* and papyrus *boats* proved to be two quite different things. Just as *iron* and iron *ships*.

"As long as the ropes hold," Abdullah said daily, "we shall float. If the ropes get slack the papyrus will absorb water. If the ropes break, we shall fall through."

Before two months had passed we had become so familiar with our environment that we often really felt as if we were contemporary with the men who had created the papyrus boat and loaded it as we had with jars and baskets, skin containers and coils of rope, salted and dried food, nuts and honey. Ancient and medieval seamen must have experienced our many moods before us. Nothing we were doing was new, nothing we were doing seemed strange. We felt a strong kinship with our ancient predecessors. Common problems, common joys, the same yellow reed craft floating between sky and sea. On our reed bundles we were outside time; none of us was a scientist now, we were all statistics in a scientific experiment that had been started up and ran by itself. Gradually time had begun to lose its dimensions. As our ancestors seemed to crowd in on us, past centuries shrank, the image of time became distorted. The Vikings were just over the horizon up there in the North Atlantic, Columbus was bobbing along in our wake. Soon the pyramid-builders had become Georges' grandparents, or at least he was beginning to feel prouder and prouder of his Egyptian forebears, whom he had previously regarded as something unreal and irrelevant in a tedious school curriculum.

"If the stern holds I would gladly go on through the Panama Canal and across the Pacific," Georges would daydream. "If we don't make it this time I shall build a new one and sail across again. It's obvious that my ancestors were the first to cross the Atlantic, at least in one direction."

"It's not so obvious," Santiago and I would argue, to Georges' bewilderment. "What is obvious is that if they had tried, they would have made it. The reed boat is much more suitable for sea travel than anyone thought. But it was not only the Egyptians who had reed boats; they were used in ancient times from one end of the Mediterranean to the other, from Mesopotamia to the Atlantic coast of Morocco."

"Then why did we copy Egyptian tomb paintings if we did not want to copy the Egyptian sailors?"

"Because only Egypt has contemporary illustrations that show all the construction details. It is thanks to the Pharaoh's religion and the preservative desert climate that we know so much about everyday life in Egypt four or five thousand years ago."

One of the sixteen wooden boxes we used to lie on in the cabin was full of books about the world's earliest civilizations. In a work on ancient Mesopotamia there was a picture of a stone slab from Nineveh, showing a splendid relief of reed boats at sea in war and peace. The ruins of Nineveh lie far inland, nearly five hundred miles from the mouth of the Tigris and over one hundred miles closer to the Phoenician port of Byblos on the Mediterranean. Mesopotamian stonemasons, soldiers and merchants had contacts with both the Mediterranean Sea and the Persian Gulf. The stone slab from Nineveh, which is now preserved in the British Museum, shows that their sailors used two types of reed boat. Seven of the boats on the slab are depicted as reed bundles lashed together in the Egyptian manner, with both bow and stern curving upward. They are full of men, and the waves round them represent the ocean itself, since a most realistic giant crab dominates the center of the picture, surrounded by swimming fish. Double ranks of armed warriors have boarded some of the larger reed boats and are busy driving their crews into the sea. Some crewmen are diving overboard, others are swimming, and several reed boats are fleeing from the naval battle, their bearded sailors humbly praying to the sun. A straight coast and two small islands covered with tall reeds encircle the seascape, and three more reed boats are hidden among the reeds. On board the boat by the farthest island, archers kneel side by side ready for battle,

but by the mainland and the nearest island the scene is peacefully idyllic: groups and rows of men and women sit in reed boats,
chatting and gesturing amicably.

This relief told us a great deal. For instance, we noticed the difference between the boats on the open sea and those among the
reeds by the shore. In the former both bow and stern were peaked and
curved up as in the ancient ships of Egypt and Peru, while the sterns
of the coastal boats in the reed marshes were sheered off broad
and straight. They offered no protection against waves from behind
but were ideally suited to being beached and up-ended for their daily
drying, as small reed boats were, and still are, in both the Old and
New Worlds.

Thanks to this realistic temple relief from ancient Nineveh, and
the funerary art of ancient Egypt and Peru, we know that fully
measured manned reed boats of the same design, as well as small
tusk-shaped ones, were once important cultural factors common to
the earliest civilizations in Asia Minor, North Africa and South
America. After the collapse of the mighty civilizations of old, reed
boats disappeared entirely from the Nile Valley, yet small versions
of the two types depicted in the Nineveh relief have survived to the
present century: in Mesopotamia, Ethiopia, the Sahara region, the
islands of Corfu and Sardinia, and Morocco on one side of the
Atlantic and in Mexico and Peru—with Easter Island as an off-shoot
—on the other. Two clearly defined geographical areas: the one dominated by ancient Mediterranean civilization and the other by ancient
American civilization. And now, here we sat, the seven of us plus a
monkey and a duck, far over on the American side, on reeds grown
and lashed together in Africa. We were beginning to ask ourselves
where the Old World left off and the New began. Where could the
dividing line between the two reed boat areas be drawn? Land vehicles
are kept apart by oceans; watercraft are united. Dividing lines can
be drawn on the stationary sea bed, but not on the mobile surface
where boats belong. Because, in a matter of weeks African waters
become American waters, just as surely as, in a matter of hours, the
African sun becomes the American sun.

In the thousands of years since man developed navigation, were
we the first to lose steering control on a primitive craft caught by
the eternal current south of Gibraltar?

The Egyptian Georges, who had previously been interested only in judo and frogman techniques, had suddenly developed a passionate interest in the amazing world of antiquity. Was there no written evidence to show that the ancient Egyptians had established colonies beyond Gibraltar?

No, there was not. But the Phoenicians, who for thousands of years were their nearest neighbors in the eastern Mediterranean, had plied regularly beyond Gibraltar and down the whole open coast of Morocco, far beyond Safi and Cape Juby. Potsherds with Phoenician inscriptions and other relics from organized Phoenician colonization are now constantly appearing along the west coast of Africa, farther south than we ourselves had followed it. Only a few years ago science had no idea that these earliest known seafarers from the easternmost corner of the Mediterranean had had an important trading colony on the flat island off Mogador, south of Safi. Phoenician relics, including factories for the production of dye from the purple mollusk, are now being dug up both there and down on the Rio de Oro coast, south of Morocco. Modern archaeologists have discovered that the Phoenicians had a solid foothold among the *Guanches* out on the Canary Islands and that they used these oceanic islands as a staging post in order to pass Cape Juby and Cape Bajador in safety. Because of their advanced trading posts they had to sail beyond these dangerous points, which we ourselves now had barely managed to clear in our reed boat.

There is a written record by the historian Herodotus, after his visit to Egypt, stating that in the time of Pharaoh Necho, who ruled about 600 B.C., the Egyptians had dispatched a Phoenician fleet to sail around Africa. Being responsible for the expedition, some of the Pharaoh's own men obviously participated, although it is expressly recorded that ships and sailors were Phoenician. They sailed down the Red Sea and returned through Gibraltar three years later, having twice encamped to grow crops. They could report that the sun had moved to the north as they sailed around Africa. More than a century later one of the greatest Phoenician voyages put on record was led by Hanno, with the aim of establishing colonies for trade outside Gibraltar. Sixty galleys, each equipped with sails as well as fifty oars and packed with a total of thirty thousand prospective settlers of all trades, navigated into the unsheltered Atlantic. The vast fleet passed the ancient colony of Lixus, the Eternal City of the Sun, and anchored six times along the Moroccan coast to disembark colonists. They followed the dangerous shores farther than us, rounded Cape Juby and passed the Cape Verde Islands off Senegal, to reach as far down as the jungle rivers of tropical West Africa.

It is known that the Phoenicians even had overland trade relations with jungle tribes of West Africa. They made use of Numidian caravans that crossed the continent to bring back ivory and gold as well as lions and other wild animals wanted for the many ancient circuses entertaining spectators in all important cities westward from Syria and Egypt to the Mediterranean islands and the Atlantic coast of Morocco. Centuries before Christ, all of North Africa was thus entangled in a cobweb of explorations and trade routes. The intrepid Phoenicians were deeply involved. Again, who were these Phoenicians about whom we know so very little; from whom did they descend and who taught them to sail? Thanks to the Romans we have simply inherited the word "Phoenician" as a convenient sack into which we put anything sailing from the inner Mediterranean before Roman times.

On a desolate beach just south of our starting place in Safi, an angled breakwater made of tens of thousands of megalithic stone blocks still projects toward the reefs and provides a magnificent harbor. Fantastic quantities of gigantic quarried stones have been dragged out into the sea by experienced marine architects, who built such a lasting bulwark that the Atlantic waves have not succeeded in washing it away after thousands of years. Who needed such a big harbor on that desolate sandy point before the Arabs and Portuguese had yet to sail down the Atlantic coast of Africa?

On a rounded hill surrounded by sandbars through which the broad Lucus River meanders into the Atlantic, on the northwest coast of Morocco, stand the gigantic ruins of one of the mightiest towns of antiquity. Its past vanishes into the darkness preceding written history. Huge blocks weighing many tons were transported up the slopes and lifted on top of one another in giant walls that can be seen from the sea. The megalithic blocks are cut and polished, the joints accurate to a millimeter, with the specialized technique characteristic of megalithic walls in Egypt, Sardinia, Mexico, Peru, Easter Island—the very areas where reed boats were in use. And it is also here, near the sea at the foot of the ancient ruins, and only here, that Moroccan reed boats, *madia*, have survived to our own times. The oldest known name of the megalithic town is *Maquom Semes*, "City of the Sun." The hill now surrounded by sandbars was an island in the Lucus estuary when the Romans found it. They wrote that fantastic legends were associated with its earliest history. They called the town Lixus, the Eternal City, and built their own temples on top of the ancient ruins. Their buildings and colonnades seem pitifully small compared with the colossal blocks in the walls on which they rest. Roman historians placed the grave of the hero Hercules himself on this island in the river. With the open Atlantic for background Roman artists made a giant mosaic portrait of the ocean-god Neptune, with crab's claws bristling from his hair and beard. Then the Romans disappeared, and the Arabs who followed and merged with the original population on the surrounding plain call the ruined town *Shimish*, "Sun." In their stories the last queen who ruled there was called *Shimisa*, "Little Sun."

The extremely few archaeologists who have embarked on small test digs there have found that the Phoenicians used "Sun City" long before the Romans. But who founded it? Perhaps the Phoenicians. If so, Phoenician megalithic stone masonry was equal to the best on both sides of the Atlantic. The Phoenicians' home was in the distant eastern Mediterranean, present Lebanon. Yet, "Sun City" was no Mediterranean port, but a true Atlantic harbor established where the powerful current swings westward through the Canary Islands to end in Mexico. How old are the walls? No one knows. They are covered to a depth of fifteen feet by the detritus of at least Phoenicians, Romans, Berbers and Arabs. The Romans believed in Hercules and Neptune, but not in the sun-god, and the Roman ruins lying uppermost are therefore not solar-oriented. But recent test digs down to the very bottom have shown that the lowest and largest of the giant blocks, those which were already covered with detritus when the Romans came, and which the Romans therefore failed to demolish or rebuild into their temples, provide the foundations for extensive buildings carefully oriented to the sun. The Phoenicians, like their Egyptian neighbors, and in most of the earliest Mediterranean civilizations, were sun-worshipers.

Sun City, the Eternal City, Hercules' last resting place, older,

according to the Romans, than Carthage. . . . Why all this tribute
to a remote megalithic Atlantic port? Why should it lie beyond
Gibraltar? The founders of this Eternal City lived as many sea miles
from the Phoenicians in Asia Minor as from the Indians in America.
To keep in touch with Asia Minor they must have been real masters
in navigation, maneuvering off the dangerous coast of North Africa,
where no regular current and wind could help them there or back.
It would have been infinitely easier for the residents of this Atlantic
port to cross the ocean and take their stonemasonry techniques
to the Indians of America. They would only have had to pull in their
oars and let themselves drift like us. If Phoenicians founded Sun
City, their sailors must have taken priests, architects and other representatives of the nation's élite with them on their voyages of
colonization outside the Mediterranean. In fact, the maritime Phoenicians are known first and foremost as traders and intermediaries
of civilization in the ancient world. If it was the Phoenicians who
lived in this Atlantic city, they knew all about the ancient pyramids
of the Old World. They knew both the stepped and the smooth-sided
types. We know Phoenician expeditions sailed on Egyptian request.
There was Phoenician timber in the ships buried round the Egyptian
pyramids, Egyptian papyrus in the books of Phoenicia, and Pharaoh
Rameses II had his own portrait, with inscriptions, carved in three
places on the Phoenician coastal cliffs. In peace and war there were
intimate contacts between the two countries. In fact, since modern
scholars did not believe in the seaworthiness of Egyptian papyrus
ships, it has been assumed that Egyptians used Phoenician ships—
even to collect their own tribute from the Mediterranean islands and
the Syrian coast. They knew both those built of stone blocks and
those built of sun-dried adobe bricks. Those perhaps best known to
them were the terraced adobe pyramids of Asia Minor, which differed from the Egyptian in having a narrow staircase or ramp leading
up the middle of one or more of the pyramid's terraced sides to a
little temple on top, just as in the earliest pyramids built on the
American side of the Atlantic. Yet their contact with Egypt was also
intensive.

"But we Egyptians sailed the sea too," Georges would argue,
and as a good Christian Copt he quoted the Bible, where Isaiah
(18:2) reports that his homeland was visited by Egyptian messengers

who came across the sea in boats made of reeds. In the new edition of the King James Bible it was even specified that these reed boats were of papyrus. Georges also reminded us that Moses himself (Exodus 2:3) was set adrift on the Nile by his mother in a papyrus ark daubed with pitch and bitumen. In Egypt, Georges had shown me the walls of Queen Hatshepsut's temple at Luxor in the Nile Valley, covered with paintings showing that she had sent an expedition of several large wooden ships right down the Red Sea to Punt in Somaliland, to return with all sorts of merchandise, including whole exotic trees for replanting in the queen's garden.

What Georges did not know was that modest merchants with ordinary papyrus boats had sailed even farther than the queen's famous fleet of wooden luxury ships. Eratosthenes, chief librarian of the huge Egyptian papyrus library in Alexandria on the Nile estuary before the tens of thousands of irreplaceable papyrus manuscripts went up in flames, reported that "papyrus ships, with the same sails and rigging as on the Nile" sailed as far as Ceylon and the mouth of the Ganges in distant India. The Roman historian Pliny (*Historia Naturalis*, Book VI, XXII, 82) later quoted that learned librarian in his geographical description of Ceylon, saying that while the papyrus ships took a full twenty days to sail from the Ganges to the island of Ceylon, the "modern" Roman ships made the journey in seven days. This casual but most important written reference enables us to work out that the ancient papyrus ships made the same speed through the ocean as *Ra* did before we allowed the stern to sink and become a brake. In fact, measuring the distance between the Ganges River and Ceylon, we can calculate from the information preserved through Eratosthenes that the papyrus ship, with Egyptian rigging like ours, must have averaged about seventy-five nautical miles in twenty-four hours, which is slightly more than three knots.

But the Indian Ocean was not the Atlantic. Perhaps the Egyptians had also sailed out through Gibraltar, but no evidence has been preserved to prove it. The Phoenicians, however, knew the rocks and beaches along the coast where we had begun our voyage. They had gradually learned the secrets of local currents.

The mystery surrounding the earliest traffic on the very ocean that washed up over our afterdeck, sent flying fish on board and drove us ceaselessly forward, became still more challenging when we lay with

our beards stuck in learned books, feeling like ancient seafarers reading about ourselves and our own times. Looking up I saw the Mexican
tapping water from a goatskin bag into an amphora; the Egyptian
swayed past with a papyrus life belt over his shoulders; while the
monkey poked its funny little face in and stole my "nosometer,"
which I used to determine the angle of the Pole Star.

"Bearded men drifting westward across the Atlantic," I wrote
in a message to the head of the Archaeological Institute of Mexico,
with a joking reference to ourselves and the bearded Olmecs who
founded the earliest Mexican civilization. It was only when Norman
took our little radio set out of the case beneath his sleeping bag
that antiquity disappeared in a flash and for some minutes we were
living in our own, modern world. Dick Ehrhorn, a ham radio operator
in Florida, had built the little set, and soon after we lost contact
with Morocco we suddenly heard a voice over the microphone saying,
"LI2B LI2B, this is LA5KG Chris Bockelie in Oslo." After that,
Chris traveled with us in the magic box right across the ocean. Beside him there was room for his compatriot, Just, LA7RF in Alesund,
Frank I1KFB in Genoa, Herb WB2BEE in New York, Alex
UA1KBW in Leningrad, the builder of the set himself, Dick W4ETO
in Florida, and other voices that for the men of antiquity, would
have been genies from Aladdin's lamp flying invisibly across the sea
and landing in our little box among the goatskin bags and jars.
Through the radio amateurs our families knew we were alive. Like
us they had the chart of the Atlantic on the wall and marked our
position at intervals. Halfway across we exchanged greetings with
U Thant and the heads of state of our seven countries of origin. The
Presidents of the two super powers in East and West sent us friendly
greetings that arrived on the same day. When Norman closed his
"Pandora's box" again we went straight back to antiquity, just as we
had been wrenched into the present when he opened it and filled
the cabin with a chorus of cackling metallic voices: radio hams in
every conceivable country trying to help us with contacts. When
they had gone the water gurgled and splashed and the ropes moaned
desolately as before. In our world there were only sea and flying fish,
and then a green back gliding past the bottomless depths.

Bearded men: that turned out to be one of our last humorous
reports. Fate held us in the hollow of its hand. Our tail was under

water, helping the waves to surge freely up to the back wall of the cabin, like breakers on a beach. Little fish were living on board on the afterdeck. If we escaped a storm we would drift ashore in America this way in a week or two, with cabin and foredeck chock full of food and other cargo. But if we met one more storm we would come out of it a wreck. Since leaving Morocco, only *African Neptune* had photographed *Ra* at sea under full sail. To see the whole *Ra* in perspective we had to swim out on a life line. For us, who for weeks had seen only each other with some limited section of the vessel as background, it was really thrilling to grasp all in one view. Georges swam out with an underwater camera, stretched up from the crest of a wave, and snapped *Ra* struggling along as others would have seen us.

On July 7 the papyrus ship was still looking beautiful, with its golden bow high and the burgundy-red sail tauter than ever, because we now had the east wind at our backs. But if a storm came the *Ra* would never emerge looking as she looked now, and the film of the expedition would have no long shots of the papyrus ship sailing on the open sea. All the film Carlo had already taken might be damaged too. So in the next radio contact with Italy I gave my wife, Yvonne, the job of finding a motion-picture photographer who could meet us with a small vessel at sea off the West Indies. Even if I did not hint at it by so much as a word to my own friends on board, I felt at the bottom of my heart that this might also be a safety measure. If lives were at stake the responsibility ultimately devolved on me.

What was the photographer to bring with him? Everyone wanted a little fruit, Santiago a box of chocolates. Nothing else. We had more water and provisions than we could use. Salted meat, ham and sausages, jars and baskets full of honey, eggs, butter, dried fruit, nuts and Egyptian bread biscuits. The deck forward and to port of the cabin was still so covered with food that it was hopeless trying to find room to put a foot down.

Bearded men. Only Yuri stood up to his knees in the bath water aft and shaved. Red beards and black beards. Abdullah now had hair on the top of his head. Black hands and white pulled on the same ropes. It had been so in ancient times as well. Nothing new. The wall paintings of ancient Egypt show men with yellow hair and men with black hair building the same papyrus boat. Under the sand where we had built *Ra*, at the foot of his own pyramid, the Pharaoh Chephren,

Captions for the following four pages

91. *Central African Abdullah* did not fear the sea because he had three leather pouches of magic amulets tied to his back. (Above)

92. *Two Africans* bind reeds as a bulwark against the sea, Georges under the water and Abdullah above. (Below)

93. *"The sea is salt!"* exclaimed Abdullah, and asked for extra rations of fresh water to wash himself before saying his prayers to Allah.

94. *New bunk sites* had to be found every time the sea smashed the boxes we were sleeping on in the basket cabin. Norman chose to sleep on the food baskets. (Above)

95. *Sharks* began to gather round the raft-ship as we approached the West Indies. (Below)

96. *The last storm* carried the galley overboard and smashed all the boxes, but the padded jars were still full of drinking water. (Above)

97. *Radio hams* on both sides of the Atlantic were following the *Ra* experiment through reports on the amateur wave length. Norman and the author with the expedition's transceiver. (Below)

Captions for the preceding four pages

98. A *small American yacht* came out from the West Indies to film the last leg of the expedition. (Above)

99. *Ra was devastated* after the last storm, but the little yacht found the crew of seven men, one monkey and one duck alive and the cargo safe. From the left, Norman, Georges, Yuri, Abdullah, Thor, Carlo and Santiago. (Below)

100. *The mast is cut away* by Santiago and Norman. With the ropes chafed through on the windward side, so much papyrus was lost that the heavy bipod mast could no longer support the sail.

101. *Everything of value* is transferred to the yacht. Georges swims with the mast, the author passes equipment to Santiago in the yacht's rubber dinghy.

son of Cheops, buried his queen and had her portrayed for all time
with yellow hair and blue eyes. In a glass case in Cairo Museum,
among the mummies of his kinsmen with their straight, black hair,
lies Rameses II himself, with soft, yellow, silky hair topping his
hook-nosed mummy skull. The north has no monopoly on blond,
fair-skinned peoples. This racial type was present in Mediterranean
areas, including Asia Minor and North Africa, long before the pro-
genitors of the Vikings existed in Scandanavia. If there is any physical connection, it must have been from south to north, because the
Viking period began three thousand years after the Pharaoh Chephren buried his blue-eyed, blond wife besides his father's mighty cedar
ship in Egypt.

Blond men with beards. They were as common among the original population of the Atlas Mountains as among the Berbers on the
plains round the City of the Sun on the Atlantic coast, where their
descendants can still be seen. They had sailed from the African
coast with their women and sheep into the Atlantic and settled as
Guanches on the Canary Islands.

Blond men with beards, who were not Vikings, because they
built pyramids and worshiped the sun, ran through all the legends
associated with the ancient American cultures, from Mexico to Peru.
Throughout tropical America, wherever pyramids and carved stone
colossi lie—as abandoned ruins from bygone days—the Spaniards
learned that they were not the first bearded white men to come
sailing across the Atlantic. The legends told in detail of teachers,
similar in appearance to the Spaniards, who had once mingled with
the aboriginal Indians and taught them how to build adobe houses
and live in towns, erect pyramids and write on paper and stone. In
other words, white, bearded travelers were credited everywhere with
having merged with the original local inhabitants and laid together
with them the first foundations of local cultures. The Indians themselves had no beards. The Spaniards exploited the legends in order
to conquer both Mexico and Peru, but the legends were not created
by the Spaniards. A thousand years before the Spaniards came, American artists from Mexico to Peru were making ceramic figures and
stone statues of bearded men. Before the Vikings began to sail the
Atlantic the Mayas had painted white men with long golden hair in
a legendary sea battle taking place somewhere on the Atlantic coast

of Mexico. Some decades ago, when American archaeologists opened
a brightly painted pillared chamber inside one of the largest pyramids
at Chichén Itzá, they found splendid mural paintings, which they
copied in minute detail before the humid tropical air and countless
tourists got in and removed everything. The paintings illustrated a
dramatic attack on naked white men, navigating yellow boats with
upturned bow and stern. As in the relief from ancient Nineveh, there
is a large crab in the waves and various marine species of fish and
shells, showing that the sailors are either coming from the ocean or
trying to get away to sea. The white-skinned sailors are met on land
by dark-skinned warriors with feathers in their hair, who tie their
hands behind their backs, scalp their blond locks, and lay one of them
on the sacrificial slab. Others dive naked overboard from their
capsized vessel, with long yellow locks floating on the waves among
rays and other salt water fish. Whereas some of the white-skinned
men are dragged helplessly away by their yellow hair, others have
packed up all their possessions and are walking calmly away along
the beach with large packs on their backs.

What legend or historical episode were the Mayas trying to per-
petuate in this way, in a sacred chamber inside one of their most
important pyramids, centuries before the Spaniards landed? No one
knows. The three American archaeologists who copied the wall-
paintings wrote soberly that the temple portraits of light-skinned men
with yellow hair "give rise to much interesting speculation as to their
identity."

We must have speculated more than most, on board the Ra,
where the elements were daily carrying us, as if on a conveyer belt,
toward the Gulf of Mexico, without our having to push or row. We
did not delude ourselves that we could compete in seamanship with
the professional navigators of old. Norman was our only seaman,
but he had never seen a papyrus boat before. Abdullah had, but he
had never seen the ocean. We would never have managed, like people
of old, to navigate a papyrus boat with Egyptian rigging in the
capricious water round Ceylon. Nor could we have sailed Phoenician
vessels between Asia Minor and their colonies at Rio de Oro, a trip
far longer than the distance from Africa to South America. But we
could surely imitate men of old who had been caught by a storm off
the African coast and lost their steering power.

Rain clouds hung about us the length of the horizon and at regular intervals showers came and washed us and the deck so that the papyrus became even more wet and soggy, and the water level on the afterdeck crept slowly but perceptibly farther forward up the narrow strip of deck on the windward side of the cabin, from which we had long since moved the cargo. Sea water now stood in the depression in the papyrus floor caused by the weight of the starboard mast foot, showing how low we were on the windward side, where all the papyrus was now soaking wet. On the lee side, on the other hand, we still had to hang over the edge on our stomachs to reach down to the passing wave caps.

We were now so close to the mainland coast of South America that we were visited by the first sea birds from the other side. Beautiful tropic birds with long, trailing tail feathers flew over the mast. A shark overtook us from the rear and made a savage attack on the life belt we had in tow. Those of the men who had never seen a shark had a startling experience when Carlo shouted that something was fighting the life belt, and soon afterward a two-yard-long dark monster came swimming majestically up with its dorsal fin above the surface. It rose and sank with the waves. When it was level with the *Ra* it turned savage again, rolled its whitish belly upward and thrashed its tail, attacking the underside of the papyrus rolls with gaping jaws. Was it gobbling down some of the long, tasty barnacles? Whatever it was gobbling, the danger to the ropes was serious. With my experience of the low-lying *Kon-Tiki* raft I leaned over the railing and grabbed for the shark's rough tail which I knew was like sandpaper to the touch. Then I saw an open wound on its back and two big pilot fish keeping station close above it. Twice I almost had it, but the lee side was still so high that I would have been dragged overboard unless I could get a better hold. Then big Georges drove his harpoon into the body of the shark. The brute fought for a moment with its steely muscles, until the water foamed about its tail. Georges was left standing with his tough harpoon line, which the brute had snapped in two. It disappeared into the ocean depths with Georges' last harpoon.

We sank back into peaceful daydreams about the unsolved mysteries of antiquity. Norman had been brought up on the doctrine that America was a world apart until his own ancestors came over from

Europe, bringing knowledge and culture with them. The politicians believed that, and most of the ordinary textbooks were written by isolationists. Aztecs, Mayas and Incas had only primitive savages from Alaska and Siberia in their family tree. Europe had received its culture from Asia Minor and Africa via Crete and other islands in the narrow Mediterranean. But America had received nothing across the broad Atlantic until Columbus. Primitive vessels could sail along coasts and reefs, they said, but not on the wide ocean. Now Norman wanted to hear the diffusionists' arguments. Were not the American Indian civilizations in Mexico and Peru completely different from the Afro-Asiatic cultures of the inner Mediterranean that had later laid the foundations of European civilization?

Basically not so terribly different, Santiago and I were able to explain. There are enough dissimilarities for those who are specialists and dwell on details. But if an unspecialized layman, who does not delve into the thickness of potsherds or the motives on the cotton textiles, tried to acquaint himself with the broader common features he would probably be quite amazed.

At a rate unknown to mankind elsewhere in the world, a series of jungle and desert tribes in the central parts of America managed to make up the Old World's cultural lead in the course of a few centuries before Christ, while all the rest of the native population of America, in the more favorable climatic zones north and south of the tropical belt, persisted with the primitive tribal communities of their ancestors until the Europeans arrived. The exact century when the tropical tribes in Mexico and Peru received their record-breaking urge and capacity to take this great leap forward from a primitive way of life to full civilization is known to no one living today. What is certain is that the earliest American civilizations made their real breakthrough before the Christian era and yet after the civilizations of Asia Minor had reached their peak and were busy sending sailors out beyond Gibraltar, with everything carried on board that was needed to establish their important colonies along the Atlantic coast of Africa.

What was the essence of the sudden evolution that began just about simultaneously in the jungle thickets of the Atlantic coast of Mexico and among the sand dunes on the opposite coast of Peru? The sun was suddenly worshiped as a god. It did not matter that, in one place, it was rainy and shady among the dense growths of the

jungle, while in the other the sun burned down unhindered on dry
sand: in both Mexico and Peru the aboriginal Indians suddenly began
to build step pyramids to the sun. They built on the same principles,
each under the command of an omnipotent priest-king claiming divin-
ity and descent from the sun rather than from his own local tribe.
Brother and sister marriage was practiced in the priest-king's family,
just as in Egypt, to keep the divine blood as pure as possible. The
priest-king put an end to the old tribal dance round the totem pole,
to the sacrifices to invisible spirits and other traditional supernaturals.
Hereafter it was the solar disc that was to be studied and worshiped.
Both on the Mexican Gulf and on the Peruvian desert coast the Indians stopped making family huts of branches and leaves. In both
places they began to manufacture adobe brick, using exactly the same
procedure as had been used for thousands of years in the Mediterranean area, from Mesopotamia to Morocco. A special type of earth
was mixed with straw and water and compressed in small rectangular
wooden forms whereupon the contents were turned out and baked
in the sun into adobe bricks of uniform shape and size. While the
neighboring Indians continued to build the wigwams, leaf huts and
plank houses of their forefathers, the sun-worshipers, from Mexico
to Peru, moved into elegant adobe buildings constructed exactly as
in the Old World, often on several floors and with gutters from the
roof, and placed side by side to create organized urban communities
with streets, sewers and aqueducts.

But although the invention or introduction of adobe bricks enabled these particular tribes from Mexico to Peru to build solar
temples whose ruins still stand in jungle and desert like veritable
mountains, they also began to attack the solid rock and hew and
joint together gigantic blocks, with a skill and specialized technique
in masonry to be found nowhere in the world, except in that same
restricted area from the inner Mediterranean and Egypt to the City
of the Sun in Morocco. The Olmecs on the Gulf of Mexico, blessed
with abundant timber, did not content themselves with the manufacture of adobe bricks, but also suddenly started making long journeys across swamps and jungle to find solid rock suitable for quarry-
ing. Almost a thousand years before Christ, they were transporting
stone blocks of up to twenty-five tons each over sixty miles through
jungle and swamp to temple sites near the Gulf, where they had

already manufactured enough adobe bricks to build a sun-oriented step pyramid 103 feet high. Who in Europe almost three thousand years ago had the idea and urge to erect buildings as high as ten-story houses? In Egypt the local custom of building adobe step pyramids to the sun was long dead when the Olmecs hit on the same idea. But in Asia Minor, the back-garden of Phoenicia, the sun was still worshiped from temples on top of stepped ziggurat pyramids, and it was that type, after all, and not the Giza-type of pyramids in Egypt, which shared all the fundamental features of the Olmec and pre-Inca temple pyramids in America.

Before the Christian era the jungle Indians on the Gulf of Mexico had also learned the secrets of a perfect calendar system. In record-breaking time they had assembled a body of astronomical knowledge that had taken several millennia of study in the Old World. The ancient Egyptians, Babylonians and Assyrians, living in open plains and deserts, had the whole starry sky revolving openly above them. The Phoenicians harvested the fruit of this ancient cultural heritage, which enabled them to navigate out of sight of any land. How could the jungle Indians on the coast of Mexico have caught up with them and won the race, living as they did under the dense foliage of the rain forest where visibility was virtually reduced to the range of their own ax handles? Yet these early Indians had a more accurate calendar year than the Spaniards who came and "discovered" them. Even our own Gregorian calendar is not as accurate as the one used by the Maya Indians on the Gulf of Mexico before Columbus. They arrived at an astronomical year of 365.2420 days, which is only one day short in every 5000 years, while our modern calendar is based on a year of 365.2425 days, which is a day and a half too much in every 5000 years. That sort of knowledge was neither quickly nor easily worked out. The Maya estimate of the length of the year was thus 8.64 seconds closer to the truth than our modern calendar. Their earlier neighbors, who entombed their sun king in the dripping stone pyramid we had visited in Palenque, left an inscription stating that 81 months made 2392 days, giving them a month of 29.53086 days, which deviates by only 24 seconds from the true length of the month.

The Mayas had acquired the basis of all their astronomical knowledge from the still older Olmecs down on the coast, who even before the Christian era had been carving precise dates on their beautiful stone monuments. Europe had no chronology at that time. Zero in the Christian calendar is January 1 of the year representing the birth of Christ. Zero in the Mohammedan calendar is the year when Mohammed fled from Mecca to Medina, or A.D. 622 in our calendar. The Buddhist calendar begins with the birth of Buddha, that is about the year 563 B.C. Zero in the ancient Maya calendar would have been August 12, 3113 B.C. in our own time reckoning. What decided this extraordinarily precise starting date? No one knows. Some believe that the Indians snatched this date out of the air, as somewhere to begin their calendar. Others think they may have worked back to some specific astronomical conjunction occurring long before civilization began to flourish in America. In Egypt the first dynasty of the Pharaohs began between 3200 and 3100 B.C.; that is remarkably concurrent with the beginning of the Maya calendar, but as far as we know there was no civilization on the American side of the ocean as early as that. If the jungle Indians came to Mexico at least 15,000 years ago and waited until only a few centuries before our own era before suddenly producing the amazing Olmec civilization, why did they begin their own calendar at a date actually representing the very time when the earliest known civilizations elsewhere in the world began?—precisely when they started to flourish in Mesopotamia, Egypt and Crete?

How did the Mayas inherit a calendar that was accurate to a few seconds, if they began it at random at a time when their own ancestors were barbarians and when, as far as we know, the Olmecs themselves had not begun their astronomical observations in America. We have no answer. We only know that the Maya calendar began at 4 *Ahau* 2 *Cumhu*, that is August 12, 3113 B.C. We also know that the lowland Maya and their Mexican kinsmen, the Aztecs in the highlands, had both written and oral texts stating that civilization came to Mexico when a white, bearded man who claimed descent from the sun landed on the Gulf of Mexico with a large party of sages, astronomers, architects, priests and musicians. The Mayas called him *Kukulkan*, the Aztecs *Quetzalcóatl*; both names mean "Plumed Serpent." We do not know who invented this extraordinary name. A plumed or winged serpent, often of enormous size, is painted on some of the Pharaohs' tombs in Egypt as well, and on a great many of the Egyptian papyrus manuscripts. A mixture of bird and snake is a divine symbol on both sides of the Atlantic. Birds of prey, snakes and felines were the three special symbols for the personalization of the sun and the sun king in Mesopotamia, Egypt, Mexico and Peru. These were the countries in which the sun king's headdress and other emblems were ornamented with the heads and often whole figures of these three particular animals. No less important in Mesopotamia and Egypt were the birdmen, who in symbolic art surround the sun king and the sun-god. They occur again in Mexico, and in super-abundance in Peru, where, just as in Egypt, they are shown as men with beaked bird heads, often helping the sun king on his voyages aboard his crescent-shaped reed boat. From Peru the birdmen reached Easter Island, where they are also depicted with reed boats. But it is not these symbolic, imaginative figures that are credited with bringing civilization to tropical America. This honor is accorded by Mayas, Aztecs and Incas to perfectly normal men. They differ from most Indians only in that they had mustaches, beards and white skins. They did not come on wings, but walking through the forest with cloak, staff and sandals, and they taught the natives to write, build, weave, and worship the sun as the supreme deity. They instituted regular schools with the sacred history of the nation as a principal topic. The earliest American historytellers follow them from their first landing on the Gulf of Mexico up to the Aztec highlands, down to the Mayan jungle peninsula, and on through the tropical forest, southward across Central America. The Indians throughout the vast Inca empire, from Ecuador to Peru and Bolivia, tell a remarkably consistent story: civilization was brought to them by white and bearded men who arrived on reed boats. Under the leadership of the sun king, Con-Tici-Viracocha. They first settled on the Island of the Sun in Lake Titicaca. Later they sailed away from there on a whole fleet of reed boats, to land on the south shore and build the sun pyramid, the megalithic walls, and all the monoliths in human form that can still be seen among the remnants of the ruined city of Tiahuanaco. Hostilities with warlike tribes finally drove these first purveyors of culture north by way of Cuzco to the port of Manta, which lies just where the equator crosses Ecuador. Here they altered course for the west and vanished across the Pacific, like "foam on the water," hence the nickname *Viracocha*, "Sea-foam," which was later given also to the Spanish voyagers and all other white men.

We do not need to believe that there is any truth behind these traditions, even though they are as detailed as they are consistent, but in that case it is a still more remarkable cultural parallel that beardless Indians with raven-black hair decided to carve, paint and describe men with beards, fair skins and blond hair, such as we find on the tombs in Egypt and in historical illustrations both from Morocco and the Canary Islands. We believe in the mastery of masonry and astronomy among Mexican jungle Indians because the ruins cannot be explained away, but we reject their historic traditions, partly because they involve a religion alien to us, and partly because we only believe in the written word. That is, in the word written by Europeans. We forget that the ancient Mexican civilizations had writing. They wrote on paper, wood, clay and stone. And we forget that they illustrated their hieroglyphic accounts with realistic images. The Olmecs, who were erecting monuments with engraved dates before Christ, also pushed themselves to quite inhuman extremes in order to leave for posterity huge stone representations of two widely disparate racial types.

Although their portraits are amazingly realistic in every detail, they do not portray any surviving Indian type. One type is markedly Negroid, with a round face, thick distended lips and a flat, broad, short nose. This type is popularly referred to as "Baby-Face." The other has a well-defined, sharp profile, with a strong aquiline nose, small, thin-lipped mouth and often a mustache and goatee or flowing full beard. The archaeologists have jokingly nicknamed this type "Uncle Sam." "Uncle Sam" is generally portrayed with a majestic headdress, full-length cloak, belt and sandals. This important type, strongly Semitic in appearance and often carrying a wanderer's staff, is illustrated from the Olmec area southward as far as the legends about the white men go. Modern religious sects have often cited this in support of their belief in the "lost tribes of Israel" or the holy "Book of Mormon." A beautiful stone sculpture of the culture-bringer Con-Tici-Virachocha north of Lake Titicaca in Peru was, in fact, confused by the arriving Spaniards with St. Bartholomew, and a monastic order was establish in his honor until the mistake was discovered and the old statue of the culture-bringer, with his ten-inch stone beard, was smashed to pieces.

The "Uncle Sam" type of Olmec is depicted as a peaceful traveler. The Negroid type of Olmec, on the other hand, appears warlike and primitive, often portrayed in grotesque dances, hunchbacked and crooked, or in the form of a spherical stone head lying loose on the ground, and yet so big that it may weigh up to twenty-five tons. Who were "Uncle Sam" and his companion "Baby-Face"? Which of them was the Olmec? Neither. "Olmec" is a name we have coined because we have no idea who either of them was.

The Olmecs could write. Both Aztecs and Mayas learned writing from them, even if they chose to write in quite different systems of hieroglyphs, so that one Mexican people could not understand another. It is easy to learn to write, but not to invent writing. The art is to discover that words and sounds can be converted into inaudible symbols which can be preserved. Having learned that this is possible, it is a simple matter to think of new signs, letters, runes, cuneiform characters or hieroglyphs. In the Mediterranean area one culture acquired the invention of writing from another. Did the Olmecs invent the art of writing all by themselves on the jungle coast of the Gulf of Mexico? Isolationists believe so, arguing that the Olmec symbols do not resemble those of Egypt or Sumer. But why should we expect to find any Old World symbols preserved unaltered in Mexico when, for instance, the Egyptians and Phoenicians, who had such an intimate cultural contact, chose to use mutually unintelligible scripts? And what about Sumer? Its cuneiform script is utterly different from the hieroglyphics of Egypt, yet we know that these two civilizations were in intimate contact with each other for thousands of years.

The invention of paper can hardly be explained as a natural consequence of inventing writing. Yet the original population of Mexico also manufactured genuine paper to write on. Not of wood pulp, as we do, but using the same recipe as the ancient Egyptians and Phoenicians used for papyrus manufacture. They used reeds, hibiscus bark, and other fibrous plants, which they beat and soaked and cleansed of floating cellular tissue before hammering the wet shreds together with special clubs in several layers crisscross manner. The art of producing real paper by this method is so complicated that the

modern Papyrus Institute in Cairo experimented for several years
before Hassan Ragab recently succeeded in duplicating the technique of ancient papyrus manufacture. Mexican Indians, on the other
hand, had learned this art to perfection before the Spaniards came,
and, what is more, like the ancient Phoenicians, they were busy
producing books. Their books, which the Spaniards called *codex*,
did not have cut pages as in Europe, but folded together so that
the whole book could be pulled out in one long, broad strip like
ancient papyrus rolls. The text was written in hieroglyphs and richly
illustrated with colored line drawings, as in the Egyptian papyrus rolls.
Among other records these books contained the story of the bearded
men, in text and illustrations.

While thousands of American Indian tribes to the north and
south were living in the Stone Age until the Europeans came, their
jungle and desert kinsmen along a consecutive belt from Mexico
to Peru began, like Mediterranean voyagers, to look with the experienced eye of the metalworker for mines where they could obtain
gold, silver, copper and tin. They even alloyed copper and tin to
forge themselves bronze tools, just as the ancient civilized people
had done on the other side of the Atlantic. Jewelers all the way from
Mexico via the Isthmus of Panama to Peru made filigree brooches,
pins, rings and bells of gold and silver, often set with precious stones,
and with a stupendous workmanship such as only the elite of the
Old World masters could offer. This goldsmith's craft was, in fact, to
cause their tragic fate, for their vast treasures of precious metals in
Mexico, Central America and Peru were a far more powerful lure
to the greedy conquistadors who followed in Columbus' wake than
were the crude stone and bone products of the Indian tribes elsewhere
in America. These were first collected by peaceful modern ethnologists.

These same Indians who suddenly began to carve in stone, mold
adobe, mine metal, manufacture paper, discover the innermost secrets
of the calendar year, and write down the traditions of their kin—
these same Indians in Mexico and Peru succeeded in crossing two
useless types of cotton to produce a cultivated strain with lint
so long that it could be spun. This done, these Indians started
extensive cotton plantations, carding and spinning the harvest just
as people in the Old World did. When the skeins of yarn were

long enough and had been dyed in all sorts of durable colors, they set up precisely the same two types of horizontal and upright looms as were used in the Mediterranean in ancient times. On these they wove tapestries, which in many cases outstripped in fineness of mesh and exquisite quality the best the rest of the world has ever seen.

Before pottery was invented in the Old World the early civilizations of North Africa had begun to cultivate bottle gourds, which they hollowed out, drying the rinds over a fire to make water containers. This plant became so important and popular that it is used for the same purpose to this very day by the reed boatbuilders from Ethiopia to Chad. By some means or other, this useful African plant fell into the hands of the early cultures of Mexico and Peru, where it was used in exactly the same way and was one of the most important cultivated plants when the Spaniards came. Sharks and other marauding organisms of the sea would have finished a gourd off if it started to drift across the Atlantic alone, or it would have rotted before the Indians found it on the opposite shore and realized how it could be used. Thus, in all likelihood it was brought by boat.

The acquisition of excellent containers from bottle gourds obtained from Africa was not enough for the cotton growers in America; they also managed to duplicate the ceramic art of the ancient Mediterranean. With professional skill they located potters' clay, which they mixed with the correct amount of sand, molded to shape, colored, and fired for containers. They made jars and jugs with all kinds of handles, dishes, vases with and without feet, pots with spouts, spinning wheels, flutes, and ceramic figurines of the same general appearance and often with the same peculiar details as the ancient potters had used in Mesopotamia and Egypt. Even such unique products as thin-walled jars shaped like animals with a spout on the back, produced by the artist first making a two-part negative mold, were made by potters on both sides. So were both flat and cylindrical ceramic seals engraved for stamping and decorating articles by pressing and by rolling respectively. Perhaps the most extraordinary recent discovery is that small ceramic dogs, running on real wheels like modern toys, are found in Olmec graves from the first millennium, b.c., and also in ancient Mesopotamian tombs. This is particularly noteworthy, not least because one of the main arguments of the isolationists had been that the Old World wheel was unknown in America before Columbus. Now, however, we know that it was indeed known, if not by others, at least by those who founded the earliest Mexican civilization. We would not know that pre-Columbian Indians even had wheeled toys had these not been made of enduring ceramic. Paved roads of pre-Columbian origin have been found in the jungles of Mexico, where wheeled transport could have been used. Since iron was unknown and ceramic unsuitable, full-scale Olmec wheels could only have been made of wood. No such perishable material from the Olmec period has survived. Why the wheel was subsequently lost in America is another matter; it was there at the beginning of local civilization, and perhaps the Mexican jungle, almost impenetrable with its dense timber and muddy soil, together with the absence of horses and donkeys, gradually discouraged wheeled transport.

Horses, of course, could scarcely be brought to America on reed boats. Dogs could. The dog was man's earliest companion in the Mediterranean world and followed him on most of his journeys. The Olmecs had dogs, as exemplified in their wheeled models. The Mayas, Aztecs, and Incas continued to keep dogs, as witnessed by their art and by the records of the early Spaniards. Dogs were mummified in pre-Inca Peru, and left with their masters in their desert graves. At least two breeds were kept, neither of them descendant from any wild American progenitor, and both of them quite different from the Eskimo-type dog brought from Siberia by other Indians. Both breeds are strikingly similar to the dogs of ancient Egypt, where the craft and custom of mummifying dogs and birds were as much a part of the culture as in ancient Peru.

No mummies of men or beasts will last in a jungle climate, but we know that important persons were embalmed to attain eternal life by the sun-worshipers of ancient America, because hundreds of carefully embalmed mummies are preserved in desert tombs in Peru. Their grave-goods proclaim their high rank. While some Peruvian mummies have coarse, straight black hair like modern Indians, others have reddish and even blond, wavy and soft hair, and their great body height is in striking contrast to the Indians living in Peru today, who are among the shortest races in the world. Relieved of their internal organs, filled with cotton, massaged with special preparations, sewn up and wrapped in mummy cloths, and finally provided with a mask over their faces, the pre-Inca mummies follow a traditional pattern which in all essential particulars is familiar from Egypt. The tall sun priest, lying full-length among his ornaments under the five-ton lid of the stone sarcophagus inside the Palenque pyramid, also had a mask over his face, and his long body had once been wrapped in a red cloth, of which fragments remain on the bones. But no embalmer's art could save his mortal remains in the climate of the Mexican rain forests.

It was natural that a Mexican priest-king should be wrapped in red cloth and that his sarcophagus should also be painted red inside. Red was the sacred and favorite color in both Mexico and Peru, just as among the Phoenicians. In Peru special expeditions were sent north up the coast on large balsa rafts and reed boats simply to collect and bring home special red shells, just as the Phoenicians sent expeditions—and even founded colonies along the Atlantic coast of Africa mainly to satisfy their fanatical desire for red dye made from the purple mollusk.

In Mexico and Peru the Indians took up many customs that did not occur to the other Indians, and some of them were as strange as they were striking. They began to circumcise boy babies, as was the religious custom among the Jews and others in the eastern Mediterranean. They decided that sun priests of high rank, lacking real beards, must wear artificial ones, a typical custom of high priests in Egypt. Of the myriads of stars available to choose from, they selected the first annual appearance of the constellation of the Pleiades to signal the start of their agricultural year—just as was the custom among some peoples of the inner Mediterranean. And the surgeons in Mexico, and still more expressly in Peru, practiced trepanning of the skull partly as a magical operation and partly to heal fractures. When the Spaniards reached America, the extremely difficult art of trepanning had a most limited distribution elsewhere in the world. It existed exclusively along the narrow Mediterranean belt from Mesopotamia to Morocco, and, strangely enough, among the *Guanches* on the Canary Islands.

The small details of daily life were not so staggeringly different, either, despite the distance from the Mediterranean to the Gulf of Mexico. Family life and community organization, from priest-king to slave and eunuch, followed roughly the same pattern in these hierachic dictatorships; and domestic articles varied mostly in detail. Farmers in Mexico and Peru had begun terrace farming, with aqueducts, artificial irrigation and manuring with animal dung, just as they did in the Mediterranean area; and the isolationists themselves have pointed out remarkable coincidences of detail in types of pick, basket, sickle and ax. Fishermen in both places made the same sort of nets with sinkers and floats, the same sort of traps, and fishhooks with bait and line on the same principles. Their reed boats were the same. The musicians in both areas had drums with skin stretched over the end; horns in a variety of forms; trumpets with mouthpieces; many kinds of flute, including Panpipes; clarinets; and all sorts of bells. The isolationists themselves have pointed out similarities in the structure and organization of the armies, the use of military cloth tents in the field, the custom of giving the soldiers shields with painted designs to indicate their units, and the fact that the sling, unknown to the Indians who came across the Bering Strait, but characteristic of the warriors of the inner Mediterranean, reappeared as one of the most important weapons in the pre-Inca cultural area. Both diffusionists and isolationists have stressed that there are striking similarities in loincloths and men's cloaks, women's garments with belted waists and shoulder pins, and sandals of hide or coiled rope with very specific resemblances in design and manufacture. Personal ornaments, metal mirrors, tweezers, combs, and instruments for tattooing. Fans, parasols and litters with seats for important personages. Wooden headrests. The same sort of beam scales and the same sort of Pan scales. Board games and dice. Stilts and spinning tops; and an unending series of parallels in patterns and designs. All in all, there is not such a fundamental difference between what the people of Asia Minor and Egypt had already created while Europe was still living in barbarism, and what the Spaniards found when they arrived in America a couple of thousand of years later. They came, under the sign of the Cross, to bring a new religion from Asia Minor to the sun-worshiping Indians at the other end of the ocean current.

All this we contemplated and discussed, as that perpetual Atlantic current drove our own reed boat steadily closer to tropical America. Perhaps, after all, the boat we were sitting in constituted one of the most remarkable parallels. The stern was sinking lower and lower. That was our Achilles' heel. Our boatbuilders from central Africa had at first been unwilling to give us any raised stern at all. Unlike the ancient Egyptians and Mesopotamians they were not used to making one; they had never learned how. The Indians in Peru were used to it, however. The art had been passed down unchanged from father to son since the earliest Peruvian potters made models of their own crescent-shaped reed boats. Lake Titicaca in South America was now the only place in the world where reed boats still carried sails, and oddly enough throughout that part of South America the sail is carried on just the same sort of strange, two-legged, straddled mast as in ancient Egypt. Lake Titicaca is also the only place where really compact reed boats are still being built today, peaked and raised at both ends and with rope lashings running from the deck right round the bottom of the boat, all in one piece, just as ancient artists have painted the lashings on tomb walls in Egypt. Our friends from Chad had bound many narrow bundles of reed together in several layers, using numerous short ropes linked in the form of a chain; and although we had finally persuaded them to add an elevated stern it was still only the outward shape that coincided completely with the Egyptian paintings. Apart from the caravan routes, the great ancient civilizations had never penetrated across the continent to Chad in the same way as they had spread by boats bringing organized colonists along the Mediterranean coast to Morocco. Now, for the first time, I began to wonder if I might perhaps have allowed myself to be misled by the map. I had brought my reed boatbuilders from Chad because there were no better to be found in the Old World. But what if the cultures on both sides of the Atlantic had a common heritage? In that case the Indians who lived on Lake Titicaca, the most important and oldest pre-Inca cultural center, could have inherited their boatbuilding craft from the Mediterranean more directly than the remote Buduma tribesmen in the African interior. I remember the isolationists' claim that there was an insuperable distance between the inner Mediterranean and Peru. Had I also allowed myself to be fooled by this dogmatic claim? Had we all forgotten that the Spaniard Francisco Pizarro, who had neither airplanes, roads, nor railway lines to help him across ocean or jungle, had traveled straight from the Mediterranean to Peru with his perfectly ordinary men, just about as fast as Hernán Cortés made his way to the Mexican uplands? The Spaniards colonized the whole area from Mexico to Peru in one generation; there is no reason why earlier voyagers could not have crossed the Isthmus of Panama and reached Peru with the same ease. It is a sound isolationist lesson that history repeats itself. The Spaniards first discovered the islands lying in front of the Mexican Gulf, yet they delayed the establishment of their main settlements until they had pushed on to Mexico and Peru. We seven men from seven nations were there on board a reed boat to prove how alike human beings are, whatever their homeland. And yet we found it so difficult to understand that the same likeness pursues us through time as well, from the days when the ancient Egyptians were writing their love songs, the Assyrians were improving their fighting chariots, and the Phoenicians were laying the foundations of our own writing or struggling with sails and rigging to explore the riches of West Africa.

When the first week of July was past I began, deep down, to feel uneasy. I hoped the photographer's boat would be dispatched in time, before the constant showers that had kept us company for several days coalesced into a real gale. The hurricane season was beginning in the area we had now entered. The men took it all with devastating calm.

On July 8 the wind began to rise and the waves piled up as if a real storm had taken place beyond the horizon. Giant seas flung themselves on our miserable stern, and for the first time washed right over the steering bridge, which stood on long legs behind the cabin. We had a rough night of it. The wind howled in pitch-black darkness, the water rumbled, gurgled, splashed, roared and thundered everywhere. The cases we lay on began to rumble and float up and down in the cabin, with us on top. Those who lay farthest back on the starboard side had to empty the cases under them of all their possessions: they were half full of water. They moved all their things into the other sleeping cases, where the water was only trickling in, rising and falling a few inches where the gaps in the cases were leaking most. Every few seconds waves smashed against the back wall of the cabin, which was now covered with sailcloth. The wicker walls shook and salt water trickled in on all sides—if we were lucky enough not to get a whole deluge straight on our heads. Most of us got used to the ceaseless rhythmic crashes over our heads, though Santiago needed sleeping pills; but now and then there was a sharper, more vicious thunder that had us all shooting out of our sleeping bags—the struggling sail had lashed back against the mast and once again we were joined in battle with the giant which we could scarcely see above us in the lamplight. We stubbed our toes and stumbled over Santiago's jars and Carlo's almost impenetrable network of stays. At about six o'clock the next morning, I was standing on the bridge taking the strong wind on the starboard quarter with the help of a lashed rudder-oar and another under constant handling, when the sea quite unexpectedly rose about me and engulfed everything. A shining stretch of water moved slowly up to my waist and without any appreciable noise the cabin roof in front of my chest was submerged. Some seconds later Ra began to quake violently, while the vessel lay hard over into the wind, so hard that I had to hang on to the tiller of the rudder-oar in order not to skid down the slope and overboard with the water. At every moment I expected the heavy bipod mast to tear the papyrus bundles under it to shreds and topple into the sea. But Ra, shivering, simply rolled on to her beam ends to empty out the water, then righted herself, though never again as fully as before. The starboard mast foot had been pressed deep into the supporting bundle, and the cabin also had become oblique toward starboard. In the days to come the helmsman had to stand with his left knee bent to keep upright on the slanting steering bridge.

With the stern sloping away like a beach, we now had to tie ourselves on securely in order not to be washed out to sea when bathing on board. The waves soared on forward on both sides of the cabin, and on the lee side, aft of the cabin door, we built a screen of empty baskets and ropes, covered with Ra's spare sail for which we had had no use until then. Dead flying fish lay everywhere. Although the stern section acted as a powerful brake, and although we were constantly zigzagging along with no real steering power, the strong wind drove us 63 sea miles closer to America that day. This was only 10 to 20 miles less than the average daily distance for the papyrus ships of old as given by Eratosthenes the librarian. Once again we were visited by white-tailed tropic birds from Brazil or Guiana, which now lay to the south and southwest. All the crew were in the best of spirits. Norman had made radio contact with

Chris in Oslo who confirmed that he was trying to help Yvonne find a cameraman in New York. As soon as the cameraman was ready to leave home they hoped he would be able to come out on some boat or other from the West Indies.

On July 9 we had just discovered that the sea that had gone over the cabin roof had also forced its way through the lid of a cask containing almost two hundred pounds of salted meat, which soon rotted. It was during this morning inspection that an agitated Georges came to report something much worse. All the main ropes that secured the outermost papyrus roll on the windward side to the rest of the *Ra* had been chafed through as the floor of the cabin shifted to and fro under the onslaught of the waves. Georges was pale and almost speechless. In one leap I was on the other side of the cabin with Abdullah. We were met by a sight I shall never forget. The boat was split in two lengthwise. The big starboard bundle, supporting one mast, was moving slowly in and out from the rest of the boat down its entire length. The roll was attached to *Ra* only at bow and stern. Every time the waves lifted the big papyrus roll away from the rest of the boat we stared straight down into the clear blue depths. Never had I seen the Atlantic so clear and so deep as through that cleft in our own little papyrus world. If Abdullah could have turned pale, he would have done so. With stoic calm, and without a tremor in his voice, he said coolly that this was the end. The ropes had worn away. The chain was broken. The rope links would unravel themselves one by one, and in an hour or two the papyrus reeds would be drifting away from each other in all directions.

Abdullah? Abdullah had given up? For a moment Georges and I, too, stood paralyzed, our eyes turning from the rift of sea, which opened and shut rhythmically at our feet, to the lashed top of the straddled mast. With a foot on each side it was really the mast that had been holding the two halves of the boat together so that the ropes remaining fore and aft had not worn away long before. Norman was suddenly standing beside us, glaring like a tiger about to spring:

"Let's not give up, boys," he said through clenched teeth.

Next moment we were all on the go. Carlo and Santiago pulled out coils of rope and measured and chopped up lengths of our thickest cordage. Georges plunged into the waves and swam crosswise under the *Ra* with a thick end of rope. Norman and I crawled all over the boat examining the chafed lashings to find out how long it would be before we fell apart. Papyrus stems were floating in our wake, singly and in sheaves. Abdullah stood with the sledge hammer, driving in *Ra*'s huge sewing needle, a thin iron spike with an eye at the bottom, large enough to take a rope one quarter of an inch thick. With this needle we were going to try to sew the "paper boat" together. Yuri stood the grueling turn at the rudder-oar alone, hour after hour. First Georges swam under the boat four times crosswise with our thickest rope, which we cinched up on deck like four big barrel hoops, in the hope of holding the bundles together so that the straddled mast would not burst open at the top. Then he ducked under the papyrus bundles in the spot where Abdullah's big "sewing needle" had been pushed through. In the depths Georges had to pull the thin rope out of the needle's eye and rethread it a moment later when Abdullah pushed the needle down again empty in another place. In this way we got the fatal gap "sewn" up again to some extent. But we had lost a lot of papyrus and were consequently lying harder over to windward than ever. The straddled mast was askew, but *Ra* was still sailing so fast that Georges had to be held on a rope. We were delighted to be able to haul him on board for the last time without his having been spiked through the head by the sharp point of the giant needle.

Carlo apologized for the meal: waves were constantly washing into the galley box and putting out the fire. A big wicker crate from the *Ra*, contents unknown, was observed at sundown bobbing up and down on the waves behind us. Before nightfall we inspected the resewn papyrus roll, which represented the whole breadth of the *Ra* starboard of the cabin. It was wriggling ominously in the thin ropes we had used to sew it on, and was so depleted and waterlogged that we had to wade waist-deep to pass the cabin on that side. Then it was night again. The last thing I saw was the whites of Abdullah's eyes in the corner just inside the door opening, moving up and down above the mattress as he prayed, all amid the grinding and the whining and the gushing of water. Norman received a radio message that the boat Yvonne was trying to charter might be meeting us in four or five days.

On July 10 we awoke heavy-eyed at sunrise. The cases on which we slept—two under each of us—had been heaving and rolling wildly all night, quite independently of *Ra*'s motion. Norman could not keep his balance on his recalcitrant cases, so he had been lying across the legs of the rest of us. Our first thought was to tighten the four ropes we had secured round the whole boat yesterday. Yet another rope was swum round the place where the mast stood to prevent its legs from doing the splits. All day we went on sewing ourselves together with the long needle that was pushed up and down through the papyrus, from deck to bottom.

That day Norman heard that two American photographers were expected on the island of Martinique and that a little motor yacht called *Shenandoah* was on her way there to pick them up. But Italian television had announced that we were disabled and had taken to the rubber boat. We thought with sardonic humor of the day when we had carved it up. No one missed it. No one would have boarded it if we had had it. We had more than enough papyrus left to float on. While the worst seas were breaking over us, and a yell from Carlo announced that his best saucepans had been carried overboard, Georges suddenly appeared with a dripping red object that he had fished up out of knee-deep water.

"Do we need this, or can I heave it overboard?"

It was a little fire extinguisher from the days when smoking on the starboard side was forbidden. Volleys of laughter followed the apparatus out to sea. Even Safi hung from a mast stay and stared as the fire spray vanished into the depths, baring her teeth and making throaty noises to show that she, too, appreciated the joke.

On July 11 the sea began to compose itself in gentler folds, but even peaceful waves washed a long way in from astern and over the starboard beam. As I stood my evening watch several constellations, and also the Pole Star, appeared for the first time in many nights, and with my nosometer I quickly fixed our position at 15° N.

In the middle of the night some big seas poured in over the submerged starboard beam and drove right through the wickerwork of the cabin wall, so hard that the one case on which Norman had been sleeping up to now, was splintered to matchwood. The case had long been empty, and only broken bits of wood floated about in the seething water inside the cabin. *Ra* had begun to make some particularly disagreeable noises on the side where the papyrus roll was repaired, and that night no one heard Safi's cries for help when her perforated sleeping suitcase was knocked off the wall by the next wave. She sailed about, imprisoned, among the splintered fragments of Norman's case until, incredibly, she managed to open the lid and release herself. Santiago was awakened by her sitting, dripping wet, by his cheek, screeching to be admitted into his warm sleeping bag.

On July 12 birds flew out from the coast again to visit us. Over the radio we heard that the yacht that was to meet us would be delayed, as two of the crew had jumped ship when they got to Martinique. The surprise of the day was a literal wreck of a ship that appeared on the horizon to the south and came yawing toward us. At first we thought it was some adventurers in a home-made boat, but then we saw that it was an old, patched up fishing vessel covered with Chinese characters. Dried fish hung everywhere and the crew stood at the railing silently gazing as the *Noi Young You* staggered past us, some two hundred yards away. There we stood, on our two boats, gazing at each other in commiseration and dismay, and taking photographs on both sides. The Chinese waved nonchalantly, with kindly condescension. No doubt they thought *Ra* was a native *jangada* or primitive balsa raft, out fishing from the Brazilian coast, and they were visibly shaken to see that such a dilapidated heap could still be in use today. The wash from the fishing boat rippled over *Ra*'s afterdeck as it lurched away and then we were left alone with the sea. It began to rain again. The wind rose, and the seas with it. Soon it was pouring down everywhere.

As night began to advance over a pallid, wet, overcast sky, we saw real storm clouds rolling up like a herd of angry black cattle over the horizon to the east and stampeding thunderously after us. We made ready to weather the full gale which came tearing along, flashing lightning, in fiercer and fiercer squalls. There were limits to what the sail could take, but we left it up. We had only a few days left, and we had to hurry. *Ra* shuddered in the squalls. The seas rose. The Egyptian sail was drawing as never before and once again we seemed to be riding on a wild beast's back. The scene had a savage, barbaric beauty. Black seas grew whiter, boiling, streaked with foam; more showers came from the sea than from the clouds. The wave crests were flattened by the wind and *Ra* traveled so fast that the torrents of water overtaking us from astern had less force than usual.

But those that did break over us did it so thoroughly that it was impossible to get more than a few seconds' nap between the shocks.

Dangers lurked everywhere unless we were properly secured to cabin wall or papyrus bundles. Heavy masses of water fell with a crash on the basket roof, which was subsiding, saddle-backed, farther and farther toward our noses. Santiago was washed overboard with the rope in his hands, but grabbed a corner of the sail. Now and then *Ra* heeled so violently that everyone gripped the stays and hung outboard as a counterweight. One of the galley boxes was splintered and Carlo waded around to save the other, which was floating between the masts. The antenna blew off, so the radio was dead. The duck was washed overboard on its line time after time and in the worst of the chaos it broke a leg, which Yuri had to set. Safi was in great form inside the cabin. In the huge wave troughs the biggest schools of flying fish I had ever seen showered to and fro. Just before the watch changed I heard Abdullah trying to sing on the bridge in the darkness. A giant wave fell on the cabin roof from behind, silencing Abdullah; then it was my turn. Abdullah stood roped up, high on the bridge, his hair glistening with sea water in the lamplight.

"How's the weather, Abdullah?" I asked, jokingly.

"Not bad," said Abdullah, undismayed.

The storm raged with varying strength for three long days. It was becoming more and more perilous to have the sail set, but we managed it for the first two days, while *Ra* raced over the stormy seas. The starboard mast danced alone through the semi-detached oscillations of the loosely resewn roll, which had lost so much papyrus that what was left was pinned under the surface. Consequently the straddled mast was leaning steadily farther into the wind, and this helped us to take the squalls better, even though the block in which the starboard mast foot was set was sinking deeper and deeper into the poorly secured bunch of papyrus. Georges and Abdullah sewed as hard as they could under this mast foot, which seemed to be making its way right through the bottom. The masts bounced up and down in the wooden shoes and only their own weight and all the stays pulled them back into their sockets after each leap. Because of the many ropes that had been worn away and worked loose on the starboard side, the papyrus reeds there were able to absorb unlimited water, and in addition the whole bundle became so limp and flabby that we never knew how much we could or should tighten the mast stays. When the bipod mast whipped backward, all the parallel rows of stays on either side of the cabin curved like a jump rope, while the next moment they were jerked taut as bowstrings by a wrench of the mast so violent that only the giant hawser tied right round the boat as a bulwark in the ancient Egyptian style prevented the papyrus reeds from being ripped asunder. The single reeds were as tough and strong as after one day in water, and they floated when we lost them. But with every opportunity to absorb water freely, and with the leaning bipod mast throwing all its weight onto the damaged side, the loosely sewn remnants of the starboard bundles became more and more deeply submerged and the flexible wickerwork floor of the basketwork cabin bent elastically with them, without breaking.

We tried to fill up the empty space left by Norman's broken case, but before we had finished a new wave broke in through the wicker crevices and smashed his second case. One case after another was shattered to matchwood under us in the cabin. As each case went, it became more difficult to control those that were left, for now they had room to sail around two by two like small boats in an overcrowded harbor, each pair, with a heaving straw mattress on top. Socks and underclothes disappeared in the undertow inside and popped up in quite different places. Norman and Carlo moved out and lay on provision baskets under the fringe of roof, forward of the cabin. Yuri's two cases were smashed under him before he had emptied them of his medicines, which resulted in an inferno of broken glass bottles, squashed tubes, cartons, pills, ointment and test tubes, all of which emitted an incredible odor. It became dangerous to fall off cases, and we packed mattresses, sleeping bags and anything we could spare into the empty spaces as padding against the waves bursting through the wall, so that we could lie safely on the cases that were left. Yuri moved out. In the middle the roof was sinking lower and lower over our noses and the jiggling kerosene lantern had to be moved up to a higher corner. Jokes and roars of laughter from the three who had chosen to move out to the other side of the thin wicker wall confirmed that spirits were still high, both inside and out.

Outside the gale raged, the lightning flashed, but we could hardly hear the crashes of thunder above the awful sucking sound of water rushing in on the starboard side and gurgling round us until it disappeared in a backwash through the same starboard wickerwork wall again. The watch aft had a hard stint and we tried to change shifts as often as possible. The stilts under the starboard side of the bridge had sunk with the papyrus rolls, and the platform on which the helmsman stood had become as steep as the sloping roof of a house. We could no longer reach down to the tiller of the starboard rudder-oar. We had to cling to the port corner, where the bridge was highest, and had therefore worked out a system as ingenious as it was laborious. With one rope tied to a foot and another held in the hand, we swung to and fro on the starboard rudder-oar, but only when we could not hold the course with the port oar alone. For brief seconds at a time we made fast all the ropes we could in order not to become completely exhausted. All that mattered was keeping the sail filled, and one tack from each corner of the sail was also secured to the railing of the bridge so that the helmsman could turn the hard-pressed yard if the rudder-oars alone could not cope with the situation. The whole bridge was covered with rope, while the sunken stern behind us acted as a completely unpredictable giant oar, which made steering insanely complicated. If Ra were allowed to thrash helplessly about in the storm, there was an overwhelming danger that the mast would jerk out or force its way down through the papyrus, since our waterlogged raft simply would not capsize.

On July 14 we made radio contact with Shenandoah, now heading east from Barbados. They reported that the storm had reached them too, with waves breaking over the yacht's twenty-foot-high wheelhouse. Their radio ham had sent a signal that they were in danger and they had considered turning back, because the yacht was not built for major gales. Only the thought that we were lying still farther out under the same conditions made them sail on eastward into the storm. The captain gave the maximum speed he could allow as eight knots. That was three or four times as much as Ra could manage, but in the teeth of the storm the yacht would travel much more slowly; at best it might reach us in a day or two, if we were heading straight toward each other on opposite courses. A radio ham had picked up a message that a merchant ship was said to be about thirty miles from our position, in case we needed help. But all of us on board wanted to sail on westward alone.

At one o'clock in the morning Yuri yelled out in the darkness that the yard had broken with a terrific crash. Everybody out. But no one could see anything wrong; the sail was drawing as never before, on a straight yard. But just then steering suddenly became desperately difficult. As we relieved one another through the night we all agreed that steering watches had never been worse; *Ra* simply would not obey the oars. It was not until sunrise that we realized what had happened, when Carlo discovered that we had all been steering with a mere shaft and no blade. The thick, double-shafted rudder-oar had snapped off again as if struck by a giant sledge hammer, and in the darkness the great oar blade had disappeared forever in the waves. That was the crack Yuri had heard, and we had all been working ourselves to death with two round poles while *Ra* held her course alone with her submerged stern as the only rudder.

On July 15 the storm reached a climax. The sail could no longer stand the strain, and in squalls that flung us over so hard that an ordinary boat would have capsized, we lowered the sail, whose frenetic flapping sounded like thunderclaps. Lightning flashed, rain fell. With the sail gone the masts, with their gaping ladder bars, stood swaying alone naked in the lightning flashes like a skeleton. There was a ghastly sense of emptiness and apathy without the sail. The waves seemed to pluck up more courage to attack us as our speed slackened. The rest of the galley boxes disappeared into the sea. For a time broken eggs and powdered lime eddied round Carlo's legs, when one jar smashed. Still the foredeck and port side were covered with food in well-secured jars with tight lids. And the sausages and hams remained hanging from the roof and the steps of the mast. Worse than egg yolks was the sudden arrival of a number of Portuguese men-of-war, sailing round the deck with their long, stinging filaments entangled in everything. I stepped on a bubble body but was not stung. Georges and Abdullah got their legs entwined in stinging threads while they were working waist-deep in water to sew on new ropes where the old had been worn away. Each was thoroughly washed at once with Yuri's improvised natural medicine. Abdullah denied that it hurt. But he also bore the round burn marks of cigarettes which he had stubbed out on his own arm to prove that a man from Chad is indifferent to pain.

Outside, the port side of the cabin was the only place where we could be safe and more or less dry when the gale was at its height. Here, we could sit on a sort of bench formed by jars along the wall with the door opening. All the film and all the valuable equipment were stowed here too, so that there was scarcely any room left for us. The duck and the monkey now lived in their own baskets one above the other on top of all our private possessions. Inside the cabin, the waves bursting through the walls continued to wreak their havoc. Case after case was smashed. By evening, only Abdullah and I were left inside under the roof; all the others had moved out and were sleeping on the galley baskets, in the mast and on the cabin roof, which had become so sway-backed that it could scarcely support the weight of two or three men. There were only three whole cases left of the sixteen that had once made up our beds. Two belonged to Abdullah and one to me. Because our sleeping places were farthest over to port, our cases had lasted longest, but now our turn had come. The case under my legs had already been smashed and clothes and books mixed like pulp in the porridge floating round us. I balanced a case lid on edge with my heels to prop my feet up and clung to roof and wall so that the case under my back would not overturn when the water mess surged over to our side. It was grotesque. Abdullah knelt praying in the door opening. Then he slipped into his sleeping bag on top of his two intact cases and went to sleep. The gurgling sound about us was diabolical in the dark. My pillow skidded down into the maelstrom which revolved from wall to wall letting nothing escape. It was like being in the stomach of a whale, where the wicker wall was the whalebone filtering the food so that only the salt water escaped. I clutched at my floating pillow and fished up something soft. A hand. A rubber hand or some kind of bloated, water-filled glove from Yuri's surgical equipment. This was too grisly. I sat up and turned off the kerosene lantern, but then I bumped my head and a pool of rain water from the canvas on the roof poured down my neck; with that the lid of the case I was balancing under my feet slipped and vanished into the water. My one remaining case capsized. I crawled out to join the others. It was safer out in the rain. On the lee side, Abdullah was left sleeping alone in our once cozy home.

Long before sunrise on July 16 we regained radio contact with

Shenandoah. We cranked and cranked and listened and listened until we heard the metallic voice of the radio ham on board. The captain asked us to send up signal rockets while it was still dark. The wind had dropped. The gale had rushed farther west and had now reached the islands. Apart from Sinbad the duck, with his broken leg, we were all unscathed. Norman got out the signal rockets we had retained when we cut up the life raft. They were so waterlogged we could not even light their fuses with a match. On a scrap of loose label we read: "Keep in a dry place." We asked *Shenandoah* to send up her own rockets. Shortly afterward, the captain replied that they could not light theirs either. Neither of us had a completely accurate position after the storm, but as far as we could judge we were traveling in precisely opposite directions on the same latitude.

The radio voice asked us to keep our hand generator going constantly, transmitting out call signal the whole time, so that they could try to home in on it. For although the wind had died down and the torrential rain had flattened the waves, neither of our vessels was large enough to be visible at long distances. We learned that the motor yacht was an eighty-tonner, seventy-four feet in length. As we sat cranking we noticed that the sea was once again covered with asphalt-like lumps, and we had seen the same thing the day before. They were left stranded on the papyrus while the water filtered through. I collected a few samples to be sent with a brief report to the Norwegian delegation to the United Nations. We had now sailed through this filth on both sides of the Atlantic, and the middle as well.

While Norman worked with knobs and earphones and the rest of us took turns cranking, Carlo served the most delicious cold dishes. He regretted that the galley was not operating as well as before, partly because all the saucepans had floated off and partly because he could not get the Primus stove lit since it was lying at the bottom of the Atlantic Ocean. But if we would like smoked ham and Egyptian fish roe, he still had a knife left. And there was no rationing of "mummy bread," which tasted better than ever, whether we spread it with Berber butter and honey or ate it with peppered sheep's cheese in oil. The storm had dealt kindly with the provision jars, packed down as they were on the soft papyrus reed. It was the wooden cases that had taken the beating. Papyrus and rope, jars and skins, wicker and bamboo went well together. Everywhere, it was the rigid timber that had lost battles with the seas.

Late on the afternoon of July 16 the weather was fine again and we kept a lookout in all directions from cabin roof and masthead. Yuri was cranking and Norman was ceaselessly intoning our call signal into the microphone, when suddenly something inexplicable happened. Norman, who was sitting immovably in the cabin doorway, turning knobs with both hands, suddenly stared strangely straight ahead without looking at any of us and said in a voice full of emotion.

"I see you, I see you; can't you see us?"

A dramatic moment passed for the rest of us, sitting speechlessly round him, before we realized that he was talking to the radio operator on the *Shenandoah. Shenandoah!* We all turned sharply, Georges on the cabin roof, keeping a lookout in the wrong direction and Carlo swinging to and fro on the crazy masthead with his camera on his stomach.

And there she was! She came into view at short intervals, like a white grain of sand on top of the distant crests. As she came closer we saw that she was rolling wildly. What was left of *Ra* took the seas with far more stoic calm. How we found each other is still a miracle to us, but here we were, leaping in turn, up and down, at sea off the West Indies. A big black bird circled above us. Shark fins appeared, cutting the water around the *Ra.* They must have followed the yacht out from the islands. Both sides filmed and photographed, but it was one day too late. The *Ra*'s mainsail had been lowered forever the previous day: the mast would support no more than a shred of sail without being driven straight through the flimsy foothold left to it on the starboard side.

A tiny rubber dinghy was lowered from the yacht and Abdullah cheered delightedly when he saw a man with skin the color of his own come rowing over to meet us. He shouted a greeting, first in Chad Arabic and then in French, and gaped speechlessly when the black man replied in English. Africa met Abdullah in America. An Africa that had become American through and through.

The first thing to be loaded onto the dancing dinghy was all the expedition film. We rowed over in several installments to meet the men on board the yacht—cheerful, straightforward men. With its high superstructure and narrow beam, the pretty vessel rolled so badly that we who had spent eight weeks on *Ra* had difficulty in finding our sea legs on the immaculately scoured deck. She rolled so violently that Carlo and Jim, each trying to film the other from his own vessel agreed that it was much easier to film the yacht from the reed boat than the other way round.

The captain and crew were all young men, most of them hired for the occasion, and all eager for us to come aboard so that they could start for home at once. This was not in accordance with the charter contract, and we continued to keep the *Ra* manned. *Shenandoah* had brought us four oranges each and a box of chocolates for Santiago. But the improvised crew had set off without discovering that the provisions on board consisted mainly of numerous bottles of beer and mineral water. So the captain was insistent on returning before they ran out of food. And before there was another gale. We borrowed *Shenandoah*'s dinghy and returned from *Ra* with several whole hams, cured mutton, sausages and jars of other food. On *Ra*, we had enough food and water for all of us to eat and drink for at least another month.

So *Shenandoah* waited. *Ra* floated with her port side intact, but the starboard side had lost so much papyrus that it was no longer capable of supporting the thirty-foot-high and extremely heavy bipod mast. We decided to cut it down. As our proud mast toppled in the sea Norman erected a light straddled mast from two fifteen-foot rowing oars tied together at the top and provided with a little improvised mainsail. *Ra* sailed on. On July 17 and 18 we ferried all unnecessary cargo over to *Shenandoah* and worked at sewing the bundles together as securely as possible. While Carlo swam over with the straddled mast, Georges worked underneath the *Ra*, Yuri danced alone in the dinghy in a perilous shuttle service between the two boats, and the rest of us waded about on the papyrus bundles with ropes and soaking wet possessions. Visitors crowded in on us from down below. We began to see more and more shark fins slicing through the surface of the water all round us, like sails on toy yachts. If we put our faces under water we could see big fishy forms sailing slowly about, far down in the clear blue depths. The crew of *Shenandoah* began to fish for shark. A white-finned shark six feet long, and another, slightly smaller, were pulled on board and we had Ra's boiled rice served with tasty shark's liver. A blue shark, twelve feet long, was too crafty to be enticed onto the hook, and patrolled about restlessly.

Despite all orders to observe the utmost caution Georges suddenly terrified us all by flinging himself onto the submerged starboard edge of Ra with a huge shark in pursuit close to his legs. Georges had an old shark bite on one leg. I forbade him to swim any more as long as we were surrounded by these man-eaters, and he said that in that case we would have to wait a long time, because he had counted between twenty-five and thirty sharks circling in the blue depths. It was pointless to risk human lives and we quit any further sewing up of the papyrus bundles. Better to let individual papyrus stalks and even entire sheaves of reed afloat away in our wake. We could afford to lose all the starboard side as long as the midships and port side were intact and showed no sign of breaking up.

The weather reports on Shenandoah were ominous, and the captain had good reason to urge our return to harbor. The entire crew of the Ra agreed that if a new gale broke we would be safer on board our own wreck. True, our papyrus boat was no longer navigable, with rudder-oars broken and a steering bridge on which we could scarcely keep our feet, but the remaining bundles were afloat and would continue to drift westward like a giant life buoy until they were washed ashore. Shenandoah was navigable, even though both its pumps and one of its two diesel engines had been put out of operation by the gale. But both her captain and crew were fully aware that in a hurricane, however small, she would spring a leak or capsize, and then the whole metal craft would go straight to the bottom.

I summoned all the men of the Ra to the first really serious "powwow" since we had sawed up the rubber raft off the African coast. I explained that it seemed to me right to end the experiment now. We had lived on board the papyrus rolls for two months, they were still afloat, and without taking our zigzag course into account, we had sailed almost exactly five thousand kilometers—over three thousand statute miles—the distance across the North Atlantic from Africa to Canada. This proved that a papyrus boat was seaworthy. We had the answer. There was no reason to risk human lives pointlessly.

All the men, bearded and weather-beaten, with palms callused from pulling cords and tillers, sat listening gravely. I asked each of them to say what he thought.

"I think we should go on in the *Ra*," said Norman. "We have enough food and water. We can make a platform of wicker baskets and broken cases to sleep on. It will be tough, but in about a week we shall be at the islands, even with the little scrap of sail we have set now."

"I agree with Norman," said Santiago. "If we give up now no one will believe that papyrus boat sailors could have reached America. Even many anthropologists will say that it's not the long voyage behind us that counts, but the little bit left ahead. If there were only one day to go, that would be the one that counted. We must get all the way from coast to coast."

"Santiago," I said, "the few anthropologists who do not realize that the people who had used papyrus boats for generations could handle them better than we won't be convinced, even if we sail right up the Amazon."

"We must go on," said Georges. "Even if the rest of you give up, Abdullah and I will go on. Right, Abdullah?"

Abdullah nodded mutely.

"This is an Egyptian boat. I represent Egypt. I must go on as long as there is a papyrus bundle left to keep my head above water," Georges concluded dramatically.

Carlo gave me an inquiring look.

"If you think we should go on, I'll go on too," said Carlo, stroking his beard. "It's for you to size up the situation."

Yuri had been sitting, staring in front of him, for some time.

"We are seven friends who have shared everything," he said at last. "Either we should all go on, or we should all stop. I am dead against our splitting up."

It was a painful decision for me to make. All the others were willing to go on. It might be all right, but a severe storm could wash one or the other of us overboard. It was not worth it. I had set this experiment in motion because I was looking for an answer. We had the answer. A papyrus boat, with defective stern, wrongly loaded, and badly handled by a group of uninitiated landlubbers, in a time when no one living could give lessons or advice, had ridden off a

major storm with men and animals surviving and all essential cargo
intact, after zigzagging the open ocean for eight weeks. If we drew
a circle centered on the ancient Phoenician port of Safi, where we
had started, taking the distance we had sailed as its radius, the circle
would encompass both Moscow and the northernmost tip of Norway.
It would cut through the middle of Greenland, cross Newfoundland,
Quebec and Nova Scotia in North America and touch the tip of Brazil in South America. If we had not set out from Safi but from
Senegal, down on the west coast of Africa, the distance we had sailed
would have been enough, as the crow flies, to take us right across
the Atlantic and up the Amazon almost to its source. For the Atlantic
is barely one thousand nine hundred miles wide at its narrowest
point, whereas we had covered three thousand. It was better to stop
while the going was good. Here were two boats, each with its particular weaknesses, sailing west together in an ocean region known
as the birthplace of hurricanes. Unknown to us, the first hurricane of
the year, Anna, had just been born in the sea behind us, where
we had recently passed, and was traveling with rising momentum
toward the northernmost of the West Indian Islands ahead. Our
own course was set for Barbados, in the far south of the same
chain. Equally unknown to us was the fact that research planes from
the American BOMEX project (Barbados Oceanographic and Mete-
orological Experiment), which discovered the hurricane at its birth,
had found that the highest layer of air over Barbados was mixed
with fine sand from the Sahara. Sand from the Sahara was raining
over the jungles of Central America. And ahead of us and behind us,
clots of oil were drifting from the coast of Africa toward the beaches
of Central America. It was to become *Ra*'s fate to travel alone with
the elements to the tropical land ahead.

I was alone in making the decision.

Chapter Eleven

RA II. BY PAPYRUS BOAT FROM AFRICA TO AMERICA

Sᴛʀᴀɴɢᴇ ᴀᴘᴘʀᴇʜᴇɴsɪᴏɴ. Uncertainty. I awoke disturbed. Clutched at my support. Rolling. Rolling and pitching and the rush of water. Night. Was I dreaming? Was the voyage in the *Ra* not over? Could it have been just a bad dream that the stern section sank and we cut down the mast? Or was it now that I was having nightmares and dreaming that we had not yet left the precarious wreck? For a moment I was confused, trying to separate dream from reality. The voyage of the *Ra* was over. I had sworn to myself that I would never attempt such a thing again. And here I was. The same wickerwork cabin around me. The same low, wide opening out into the wind and the naked world, where savage waves, streaked black and white, reared up against the night sky. Ahead the same big Egyptian sail stood unchanged, set taut on the straddled mast, which we had cut down, and astern the slender tail of the papyrus boat soared above us in an elegant curve, though we had seen it sinking sluggishly into the foaming seas. I was dead tired, my arms were aching. I sat up when Norman came crawling in, large as life, and shone the flashlight first on me and then on a bushy head with a red beard, sticking out of the sleeping bag close beside me.

"Thor and Carlo, change of watch, your shift."

I picked up my own flashlight and shone it around me. There lay all the others, tightly packed as before, more tightly in fact, so that when Norman tried to dig himself out a modest sleeping space in the opposite corner, they all turned over in unison: Carlo, Santiago, Yuri, Georges. But squeezed between them was a strange head with Asiatic features and stiff raven-black hair. That was Kei. Kei Ohara from Japan. Now, how had he come on board the *Ra?* Of course. I flopped down on my back and began to pull on my trousers. Much too low under the basket roof to stand: we could barely sit up. Lower than on *Ra I.* Of course. It was all clear now. This was *Ra II.* I had started everything all over again. We were right back off Africa once more. We had not even passed Cape Juby. It was not Abdullah waiting to be relieved on the steering bridge out there in the darkness. It was another African whom I scarcely knew yet, a dark-skinned, full-blooded Berber called Madani Ait Ouhanni.

"Get up, Carlo, you have been lying on half my mattress and now you are sitting on my shirt sleeve."

On the bridge it was damnably cold, but peaceful. Madani pulled down his Berber hood and showed me how far it was safe to turn the rudder-oar away from land without risk of the onshore wind twisting the giant sail. Carlo took over the job of look-out for lights from both land and shipping. We felt threatened from all sides now, until we had once again cleared the perilous rocky coast of the Sahara and the constant traffic of the shipping lanes round Africa.

But we had done all that before. This was nothing but a risky repetition. We had already cleared Cape Juby alive, and here we were, sailing into the onshore wind again, in obvious danger of ruining everything we had achieved. Why had we not at least started below Cape Juby this time? Why a second *Ra?* Why was I beginning a thick expedition diary from page one again? Could I answer?

"We've got to make it this time," muttered Carlo from the cabin roof. "We've got to make those last few sea miles to Barbados."

Was it he and the others who had persuaded me to set all the wheels in motion again? Because we were short a few miles to satisfy the skeptics? Or was it continued curiosity? The desire to find out if we could cross the ocean in a better built papyrus boat, now that we had practical experience of a single fumbling attempt to build and navigate a ship whose design we knew only from tomb paintings

thousands of years old? Both, perhaps. Such an unbelievable amount
had happened in barely ten months, between the landing of *Ra I* and
the launching of *Ra II*. I had seen still more reed boats. They
survived just where deep traces remained of ancient civilization on its
way out from the inner Mediterranean into the Atlantic Ocean.

In the large lagoon of the Oristano marshes on the southwest
coast of Sardinia, Carlo Mauri and I had embarked with the fishermen
in their traditional reed boats, *fassoni*, and speared fish on tridents,
while the impressive and ancient Nuraghi towers were silhouetted on
the low hills around us. What an atmosphere of bygone times! The
archaeologists attributed the oldest of these magnificent stone ruins
to inspiration from the inmost Mediterranean basin almost three
thousand years before Christ. But the same type of building was
continued on Sardinia long after that. The fishermen had taken us
into the best preserved of these giant cylindrical stone cairns, whose
moss-grown megalithic walls were intact after millennia of wars and
earthquakes. No sooner had we fumbled our way through the little
opening into the enormous boulder structure and switched on our
flashlights than I seemed to recognize the place. I had seen once
before this whole complex caracole system of narrow but lofty tun-
nels, one running in a ring inside the other, while the big boulder
walls seemed to press in on us as they leaned over to meet in a
pointed false arch high above our heads. And here, just as before, I
followed a low passage that crossed these ring-shaped corridors and
led to a narrow tunnel opening farther in, where it was possible to
scramble up a spiral staircase that wound up through the compact
boulder core to an observation point on the roof.

How strange! An extraordinary composition, but on the very
same plan as the one used by the Mayas when they built their astronomical observatory, the famous "caracole" of Chichén Itzá on the
Yucatan peninsula, before the Spaniards arrived. This was the tower
that stood beside the Maya pyramid that contained the painting of
blond mariners fighting black men on the beach. Was there a missing
link? Had the unknown masters of the Mayan architects, the earlier
Olmecs, also built ceremonial observation towers like the towers of
Sardinia?

From the lookout roof of this ceremonial cairn I could see what
must have met the eyes of its Sardinian architects thousands of

years ago: the distant surf sending white cascades into the lagoon where rows of golden tusk-shaped reed boats were set up on end to dry in the Mediterranean sun. The Mediterranean: the home of man's earliest ventures at sea, the home of deep-sea navigation, with the Straits of Hercules as an ever-open gateway to the world beyond. This water had helped culture to spread. We know that it had spread by sea from the corner where Asia Minor and Egypt meet to the island of Crete. From Crete to Greece. From Greece to Italy. From the original homes of Phoenician sailors to Lixus and other Moroccan colonies outside Gibraltar, at least a thousand years before the birth of Christ.

Reed boats were man's earliest kind of watercraft in the Mediterranean corner where culture was born. Reed boats built like those depicted in ancient Nineveh survived among Greek fishermen on the island of Corfu until the present generation. They were not made of papyrus, but of the stalks of a giant fennel. Their local name is still *papyrella*, although the plant and the term papyrus are unknown on modern Corfu. And we had found them still in use, though made of another kind of reed, among Italian fishermen on Sardinia. We saw them from the roofs of towers built by unknown architects who had come from somewhere in the inner corner of this historic ocean, this breeding pool of culture crisscrossed since the morning of time by unknown navigators. Lost civilizations. Lost ships. No wonder the prophet Isaiah could speak of messengers visiting the Holy Land on boats of reeds that sailed across the sea.

Egypt, Mesopotamia, Corfu, Sardinia, Morocco, yes, even Morocco. No sooner had I found the ancient Sardinian reed boats still in use, than those that had once existed in Morocco began once more to haunt my thoughts. They don't exist; all our boats are built from planks and plastic, was the categorical reply I had got from a telephone call to the district administrator of the Lucus region, where reed boats were reported shortly before the First World War. Returning to Morocco to build *Ra II*, I regretted that I had accepted his "no" for a valid answer. Our good friend, the Pasha of Safi, now lent me his car and an interpreter guide, and on good roads we reached the Atlantic port of Larache near the mouth of the Lucus River. In this modern town, nobody had heard of any reed boats other than a huge one that passed along the highway to Safi on a trailer the previous year. We wasted no more time among the city dwellers, but headed for the fishermen's wharf where some old seamen were sitting on cobblestones mending nets.

Reed boats? Did we mean *madia*? Sure!

With one old Berber as guide we were soon on the trail. For two days we tried to find wheel tracks through the sparse cork forest hiding a tiny Jolot village somewhere near the sea. We found our way at length on foot. Stone Age dwellings, hidden from the sight of nearby modern Africa by the lack of asphalt roads and landing strips. Picturesque huts with walls of mud-covered branches thatched with the boatbuilders' reeds. The bushy reed gables with big storks' nests were scarcely visible behind a labyrinth of impenetrable hedges of giant cactus. Goats, dogs, children, chickens and old people. Whole families were blond with blue eyes. Others were completely Negroid. The Arab migration into Morocco had left no traces here. This was a striking sample of Morocco's mixed indigenous population. They should have been labeled "unidentified." Yet black and blond were for mere convenience mixed together and put in one bag marked "Berber." A black giant chased away the dogs and guided us through the cactus fences that barred the little sunbaked kingdom from view of sea, river or the sparse pastureland with its gnarled cork trees.

Madia? Of course. All the old people, bent graybeards and toothless crones alike, had known both *shafat* and *madia*, the two types of reed boat that had been in use in the Lucus River estuary until only a few decades ago. Two old men hastened to make models: a *shafat* with its flat, sliced off stern, for floating cargoes across the river, and a *madia* with bow and stern curving upward. A *madia* could be used out in the surf, it could be made as large as you liked, because *khab*, the thin flat reed they used, floated for many months. The old men built a bed-size sample with upturned bow and cut end, the five persons jumped into it paddling about just to show us its incredible bearing capacity.

Here at the mouth of the Lucus River, as in Sardinia, colossal ruins of megalithic structures overlook the waters where reed boats survived: the mighty ruins of Lixus. In fact, but for my search for reed boats I would never have stumbled upon Lixus. The ruined city was as unfamiliar to my archaeologist colleagues as to the common citizen of Morocco. An expert on Egypt or Sumer, not to men-tion a specialist on ancient Mexico, knows little about the Atlantic coast of Africa and nothing about the sites on the Lucus River. Only a couple of archaeologists specializing in Morocco have had time and means to open a few small test trenches and disclose the colossal stones forming Lixus' oldest buried walls. I stumbled on these ruins merely because they towered above the modern road from Larache to the cork forest where I was to search for the village of the reed boatbuilders. It was only a few miles from the mighty ruin to the modest surviving village. The difference in magnitude, in proportions and in cultural level opened wide perspectives with regards to the dimensions of the watercraft formerly built in this area. It was on the outlet of the wide Lucus River, just where it wound past the hill where these colossal ruins stood, that reed boats had been in common use into the present century. Warehouses from Roman times emerge from the silt at the foot of the hill, witnessing to times when Lixus was the main Atlantic port for sailors from the Mediterranean world.

Reed boats had lured me to Lixus. Few sights have surprised me more. The Atlantic Ocean in front of us, the unbroken mainland of Africa at our backs, stretching all the way to Egypt, with Phoenicia and Mesopotamia close behind. They had come here, from the innermost corner of the Mediterranean, past Gibraltar and down the west coast of Africa, with women and children, with astronomers and architects, with potters and weavers, those travelers from distant Asia Minor who, when the Romans later came out past Gibraltar, had been living here since the morning of time. This was truly historic ground. Out here on the Atlantic coast lay this ancient town, so old that the Romans called it the Eternal City, connecting it with the giant Hercules, son of their supreme deities Hera (or Hra) and Zeus, and hero of the earliest Greek and Roman mythology.

The oldest walls, now completely or partly covered by the compact detritus of Phoenicians, Romans, Berbers, and Arabs, were sufficiently impressive to stir anyone's imagination. Gigantic blocks had been quarried and transported to the top of this hill in enormous numbers. They were carved in different shapes and sizes but always with vertical and horizontal sides and angles that fitted neatly together like pieces in a gigantic jigsaw puzzle, even when right-angled indentations in some blocks made their façade ten or twelve-sided instead of rectangular. This special technique, unknown and almost inimitable, appeared as a sort of signature carved in stone wherever reed boats had once been in use, from Easter Island back to Peru and Mexico, and from there back to the great civilizations of Africa and the inner Mediterranean. Olmecs and pre-Incas had mastered this technique to perfection, just as the ancient Egyptians and Phoenicians had, but Vikings or Chinese, Negroes or prairie Indians would all be as perplexed as a bunch of modern scholars if they were shown a mountainside and asked to carve blocks and fit a wall together on these principles, even if they were given steel tools and a pattern to copy.

As I wandered among the tumbled and half-buried blocks of the Eternal Sun City and recognized that sophisticated special technique, I felt as if America and the eastern Mediterranean were drawing closer to each other. Lixus seemed to link them and divide the distance in half. This far the eastern Mediterranean civilization had spread its branches—many centuries before Christ. Here well-equipped and well-prepared colonists and traders had been sailing to and fro at a safe distance from the menacing cliffs of Africa here and further down, past the perilous Cape Juby, during just those centuries when bearded Olmecs appeared on the opposite shores of the Atlantic and set about clearing glades in the jungle. Just when Mediterranean stonemasons poured out through the Strait of Gibraltar, the unknown Olmecs began introducing stonemasonry and civilization to the Indian families that had roamed the wilderness for many thousands of years. Here at the river mouth, the classical reed boat had survived, although all sorts of timber were available on the shore. Here it survived, with the same ocean current surging off the coast, that very current that now had us in its grasp for the second time in a year.

I gave the heavy rudder-oar an extra shove outward, to give us the greatest possible chance of steering clear of the rocks round Cape Juby. How many vessels in the early days of Lixus had struggled, like us, to round the dangerous reefs where Africa swung southward to the furthest Phoenician colonies below Cape Bajador.

"This time the rudder-oars will surely hold up," I said laughingly to Carlo and patted the thick log I was steering with on the port side. The other, on the starboard side, was set in a fixed position with stout rope. Those thin shafts we had used last time had broken on their first encounter with the ocean waves and reduced the whole voyage on *Ra I* to a drift voyage.

The papyrus hull itself was also infinitely stronger this time. The papyrus had once again been collected at the source of the Nile, because the sparse papyrus growing in Morocco, where we built *Ra II*, did not cover our requirements. Neither Abdullah nor I could reach Bol on Lake Chad to fetch Mussa and Omar; the rebels had struck again in the desert and French parachute troops had cordoned off the entire area. Nor had the Central African technique proved strong enough in the long run at sea. After two months we had lost the reed on one side because the makeshift tail tacked on behind had gradually subsided and allowed the waves to use the wicker cabin as a saw, until the rope chains raveled like knitting. I had decided to try reed boatbuilders who were still regularly building robust vessels in the ancient Mediterranean style, with a pointed stern soaring as high into the air as the bow. That was how the South American Indians still built their reed boats in Bolivia and Peru. They also followed the illustrations of ancient Nineveh and Egypt in another remarkable detail: their ropes ran continuously from the deck right round the bottom of the reed boat, so that from the side, the vessel consisted of a single compact bundle, while the boats on Lake Chad, apart from having a flat stern, consisted of many small papyrus rolls, held together on top of and beside one another by short, linked loops of rope.

Strange that the Indians in South America should use a method far closer to the ancient Mediterranean technique than the one that had survived in Central Africa. Perhaps the explanation was that the Buduma on Lake Chad had never had any close personal contact with the civilizations of antiquity. But the Quechua and Aymara Indians on Lake Titicaca had. It was the Aymaras' own forefathers who had helped to build the Akapana pyramid and the rest of the megalithic structures in Tiahuanaco, once South America's most important cultural center, which stood in pre-Inca days on the shores of Lake Titicaca. It was they who had transported the colossal building blocks by reed boat across the lake. It was they who told the Spaniards that white men with beards had appeared among their forefathers to direct this stone work, and that when they came they had first appeared in reed boats of this type. The Aymara Indians themselves had never learned to work stone. But they had succeeded, to perfection, in copying reed boats for fishing on the lake, right up to the present day.

All the crew of Ra I had declared their willingness to join in a further experiment. Once again, Santiago left his post at Mexico University, this time to look for reed boatbuilders on Lake Titicaca. In Addis Ababa, my local contact, Mario Buschi, was discreetly asked to send his Ethiopian assistants out on Lake Tana to harvest another twelve tons of papyrus. Reed from Ethiopia and boatbuilders from Bolivia were to be transported covertly to Morocco, where the building had to proceed in all secrecy if I were to be left in peace to write the chapters on Ra I, a piece of work which was an absolute necessity to help me bear the additional expenses of this continuous experiment. Twelve tons of Ethiopian papyrus, shipped around Africa under the cover name of "bamboo," were unloaded in Safi harbor and vanished. Four full-blooded Aymara Indians and their Bolivian interpreter landed at the airfield in Casablanca with Santiago and vanished. Sailcloth from Egypt, a wickerwork cabin woven in Italy, timber for masts and oars, quantities of rope, all arrived unnoticed in Morocco from various directions, and vanished. Nobody but the Pasha of Safi and my closest circle of collaborators knew that a second Ra was being built in Morocco.

On May 6, a section of the high wall around the city nursery garden in Safi collapsed and out from the flowers and palm trees roared a mighty bulldozer, followed by a little frail ship of flower stems, which seemed to have grown naturally from the greenery.

Ra II was born.

She moved slowly through the crumbled masonry like a big paper bird emerging from its egg. With majestic dignity she rolled slowly on wheels down narrow alleyways, where Arabs and Berbers in hooded tunics and veils stood packed together to watch. Police paraded and barefoot children danced along in the procession. Excited gardeners and electricians hung from the trees and posts and on top of a red mobile ladder, to prevent branches and wires from tearing or setting fire to the dry papyrus tips rising fore and aft of the golden showboat. The authorities breathed a sigh of relief when the strange construction had jounced across the railway lines and stopped be-

tween rows of newly painted fishing boats waiting to be launched
for the first sardine fishing of the spring.

"I name you *Ra II*," said Aicha, wife of Pasha Taieb Amara, as
for the second time in the little under a year she splashed goat's milk
over a bone-dry papyrus boat before it slid out on the water.

"Hurrah," yelled the sea of people surging over the quay, ap-
plauding while the strange vessel lay bobbing around on the very
surface of the water exactly like a toy paper boat. Many of the
spectators had felt sure it would capsize or at least lie out of trim,
for it had all been made by hand and eye. We who were to use the
thing felt a tremendous relief in seeing how perfectly she floated on
top of the water. The crew of the waiting tugboat just stood staring,
without moving a muscle.

Hurrah!

But what now? Stop! Help! Ay-ay-ay! A despairing shriek from
the crowd. Panic on the tugboat. A powerful squall came chasing unexpectedly over the mountain, twirled the paper boat round and
whisked it off alone away from the tugboat, at terrifying speed,
straight toward a twelve-foot-high jetty of solid stone. Howls and cries
of distress, orders yelled in French and Arabic, faces buried in hands,
photographers plunging into shallow water with their cameras. And
there was the newly baptized infant, spinning round and high-tailing
it at top speed, straight for the wall. Bang! The elegantly curved new
papyrus tail took the whole shock and bent like a feather. It was heart-
rending. The stern! The very part which must be invulnerable and
perfect this time. The hull turned and danced recklessly on the wavetops right up onto the stones. No one could stop the boat in the gusts
of wind. The experiment with *Ra II* seemed to be over before it had
begun. But no. The harp-shaped tail gave like a spring, and the reed
boat bounced off the wall like a rubber ball. Once. Twice. A wooden
boat would have splintered and gone to the bottom. *Ra* was unscathed. Just a scuffed gray patch on the outer sheath of some of the
golden straws. Then the tugboat captured the rope. Nothing to repair. *Ra II* followed cheerfully on her tow rope, over to the quay
where the bipod mast was to be put on board. Dancing to right and
left in the gusts of wind, she behaved like a paper kite trying to get
air-borne.

I shuddered at the rudder-oar as I thought back to the launching.

But at the same time I thought that if we were now to be cast up on reefs and rocks in the mist over there, we would have a good chance of saving our lives before this ball of hay went to the bottom. It was so compact and solid that it did not bend an inch on the seas. *Ra I* had undulated like a sea serpent. *Ra II* was as rigid as a baseball. Everyone on board was equally impressed with the Indians' brilliant design. Those perfect lines and the incredibly ingenious way in which the difficult construction problems had been solved were quite inconsistent with the style and quality of the Aymara Indians' other earthly possessions. This was inheritance. Even if the real secret of their ancient technique seemed to have gone unnoticed by laymen and scholars alike, our own research and experiments had proved that this Lake Titicaca method is the only one that can produce a vessel with shape and lashings concurring with the details on ancient Mediterranean reliefs. All other methods of binding the papyrus together in the form of a crescent-shaped boat led inevitably to sagging and jerking, with catastrophic results to the ropes. It is easy to construct a makeshift raft of reeds, but not a crescent-shaped reed boat capable of resisting ocean waves. The system employed by our Indians was so simple and yet so ingenious that I know of no living tribe or individual who would be able to duplicate it without instruction and much practice.

The four taciturn Indians, Demetrio, José, Juan and Paulino, and their equally calm Bolivian interpreter, Señor Zeballos, a museum curator from La Paz, organized the building of *Ra II* in masterly fashion with a handful of Moroccan helpers. They were all so silent that I constantly had to put my manuscript aside and look out of the tent, only to see that the building work among the palm trees really was progressing at full speed, with gestures and brief grunts in the Aymara tongue, Spanish and Arabic.

The Indians first stacked up two huge untidy rolls of those papyrus stalks, elegantly wrapped in a thin papyrus mat, which was woven so that all the ends turned inward and were squashed flat. Before the ropes were drawn tight, these two thirty-foot cylinders were so thick that no one could get on top without the help of scaffolding. In the open passageway between these two big rolls, a much thinner roll of the same length was now made, to which both the large ones were to be bound. This was done by first

winding a rope several hundred yards long in a continuous spiral
that at the same time encircled both the thin central roll and one
of the thick outer rolls. A second rope was then run, without
touching the first, in a complementary spiral round the thin roll
and the other thick outer roll. So when these two independent
spiral ropes were drawn tight by the united strength of the Indians,
each of the big rolls was forced closer and closer to the little one
in the middle, until it was jammed between them and ended up
squeezed right into them, forming a completely invisible core. Thus,
only the two big rolls remained visible, pressed tightly together all
along their center line. This resulted in an unshakably compact,
double-cylinder hull, with no knots or crisscross ropes, and all that
remained was to extend the hull on the same principle, to produce
the elegant upswept peaks at bow and stern. A sausage-shaped
bundle was finally bound on either side of the deck to give it
breadth and to break the waves. Then we lashed on ten crossbeams
as a base for the light basket cabin, the steering-bridge poles, and
the foot plates for the heavy bipod mast. Ra II was finished, thirty-
nine feet long, sixteen feet wide at center, six feet deep. The cabin
was thirteen feet long and nine feet wide, tailor-made for eight
people, if we lay four by four, feet together, stretched out like
Egyptian mummies. Not only was Ra II about ten feet shorter
than Ra I, but her cross section was also rounder and thus much
slimmer. I thought with regret of all the buoyant papyrus—almost
a third of it—left lying unused on the buildingsite this time. But
neither rewards nor arguments could persuade our Aymara friends
to add a single stalk or a single day's work to the boat. This was
the absolute limit of their scope, and they wanted to be off posthaste,
home to their abandoned wives on Lake Titicaca.

"A pleasant voyage and welcome to Suriqui Island," Demetrio
had said kindly, pulling off his stocking cap as the garden wall crashed
and their masterpiece disappeared from the buildingsite.

"To Suriqui Isalnd?" we said bemusedly.

"Well, if not actually to our little island, welcome to our side
of Lake Titicaca in any case."

Geography was obviously not the Aymara Indians' strong point.
They did not realize that they themselves had built Ra II on the
other side of the Atlantic and had come down from a lake that

lay twelve thousand feet above sea level. But they knew how to build reed boats with a perfection no engineer, no model-builder, no archaeologist in our modern world could emulate.

"Rigid as a block of wood," said Carlo. We both breathed a sigh of relief after a brightly lit cargo boat had thundered close by us without running us down. "Rigid as a block of wood, but we're sinking," he added.

"The sinking won't last. So far we have been carrying too much load in proportion to the amount of papyrus under water."

"Norman thinks we should have daubed all the papyrus with pitch as it says in the Bible."

"Not necessary," I said. "It's only the cut ends that absorb water. That was why we dipped the last inch of most of the reeds in pitch this time."

But in fact I, too, was beginning to wonder if we should not have covered the whole vessel with a thick layer of pitch. Then we would not have sunk as much as half an inch. Perhaps the ancient Egyptians had done this inside the exposed reed mat for otherwise the wall paintings would certainly have shown the reed boats as black, not green and yellow.

Several clergymen had written to me after Ra I, pointing out that according to the Bible Noah's ark was daubed with pitch, and Moses' mother had explicitly used pitch on the papyrus basket in which she had launched her son on the Nile for Pharaoh's daughter to find drifting among the reeds. The idea had not just come out of thin air. There was surface pitch lying about for the asking in those days and it was in common use in ancient Egypt and Asia Minor. Nevertheless we had seen from Ra I that tightly bound papyrus floated without pitch too, as long as the ropes held.

The ropes. On Ra I we had used much thicker ropes, and Mussa and Omar had knotted together hundreds of short, independent loops, that held even if others were chafed away. At first glance the Indians' rope lashing looked quite absurd. They had used only a single thin rope in a continuous spiral from bow to stern. Moreover, they had blankly refused to use a rope more than half an inch thick. They said that in this way the rope would be subject to a more even strain, and even if it broke the lashings would not fall away, because wet papyrus would grip the rope. Could we rely on

Captions for the following four pages

102. *The starboard side* had not enough papyrus left to keep the cabin above water and numbers of sharks put a stop to all further repairs. Norman and Georges salvage the mainsail. (Above)

103. *The port side* was undamaged and still afloat with the whole cargo. Norman and the author on board, Georges in the yacht's rubber dinghy. (Below)

104 and 105. *Farewell Ra, see you later.* Norman, Santiago and Georges hoist a small sail on two oars on the storm-racked vessel, which sails the last leg of the voyage west alone. The reed bundles had carried us three thousand miles in eight weeks. Inset, from left, Yuri, Santiago, Carlo, the author with monkey, Norman, Abdullah, and Georges with duck.

106. *Thanks for the lift, Ra.* You have proved that even landlubbers can sail thousands of sea miles on papyrus bundles. You have proved that men from east and west and north and south can live and work together for the common good, even in cramped quarters.

107. *Ra II*, built by Indians from Lake Titicaca, was perfectly designed and crossed the Atlantic without loss or damage to a single papyrus stem. (Above)

108. *Madani Ait Ouhanni* from Morocco collected samples of the oil clots floating all over the Atlantic. (Left)

109. *Kei Ohara* from Japan took most of the films of the *Ra II* expedition. (Right)

110. *Ra II* was ten feet shorter than *Ra I* and had a crew of eight instead of seven men.

111. *In fifty-seven days Ra II* crossed the Atlantic from Safi in Morocco to Barbados in the West Indies.

them? On whom else could we rely? Everyone on board was aware that this was a new experiment. We could have used the Chad method again, with the improvements we now knew to be necessary, and then we would not have been exposed to this fresh uncertainty. The fateful bowstring from the curly tail down to the deck behind the cabin was in position now, and wise from experience, we had also concentrated the cargo on the lee side, but otherwise *Ra II* was full of unknown qualities. Not only were we afraid that the very thin long rope, all that held us together, might snap in heavy seas, but while *Ra I* lay on the water as comfortably as a mattress, *Ra II* rolled so that we could neither sit nor stand without hanging on to something. On the very first day we tried in vain to rig hand ropes, because there was nothing to catch us at the edge if we fell. And we were sailing fast.

While the papyrus was still lying high in the water we skimmed over the wavetops with the sea frothing round our bows, and covered 95 nautical miles (or 177 kilometers) on the first day. It was all we could do to hold the big sail. Once both sheets blew out of our hands and another time the wind tore them to shreds, so that the mainsail, twenty-six feet high, twenty-five feet wide at the top by the yard and sixteen at the bottom, hung like a gigantic flag, battering, flapping and slapping until we expected the vessel to disintegrate. On the very first night we had rushed past the islet off Mogador, where one of the Phoenician purple-dye factories had been, at such close quarters that we could see the lights of every single house on the mainland behind it. On the second day the squalls off the Sahara coast were so violent that we had to lower the whole sail at the risk of tearing the high slender papyrus bow to ribbons in the process. On the third day the wind died. It died so completely that sailing was out of the question and in the end we lay yawing helplessly. Now the coast had disappeared in a wall of fog and we twisted and tugged and hauled on heavy rudder-oars and on the ropes to a heavy slack sail, in order to avoid shipwreck. We were aware, with every little gust of onshore wind, that we were only a few hours from the cliff walls. Fortunately, equally feeble puffs of offshore wind, especially at night, carried us safely away from the shore again.

The wind did not return. On the fourth day there was a flat calm.

"We're sinking," said one man after another. It was easy to see in calm water. The whole craft was on its way down, sinking by at least four inches a day. This was quite new to us. Nothing like this had happened on *Ra I*. Had the long spiral rope of the Indians not succeeded in compressing the papyrus sufficiently? Or was it a different kind of papyrus this time?

Santiago went round unobtrusively with pencil and paper, taking an anonymous opinion poll on whether we thought we would cross the Atlantic alive, or fail. Two thought we would get across, six thought we would fail. I don't know who the other optimist was. Perhaps it was Norman, who always said that if only we cleared Cape Juby safely, we could let the craft steer itself, America barred the way ahead in all drections. Or perhaps it was Carlo, who suffered from an incurable devotion to *Ra I* because he thought *Ra II* had become too much the perfect sailboat.

We were sinking frighteningly fast, and if the current had not maintained its hold on the sinking vessel, we would scarcely have stirred from the spot. It was only the fourth day when Georges came to me with an unwontedly solemn expression to say that Santiago the quartermaster and Carlo the chef thought we had far too much food and water and should get rid of everything that was not absolutely indispensable at sea. He picked up a goatskin and began to finger the stopper preparatory to emptying the contents overboard.

"But that's the drinking water!"

"Better to ration the drinking water than sink before we have passed the Canary Islands. This time we have to make it!"

"Let's start dumping things overboard, it's great fun," Santiago tried to joke in an unusually hollow voice.

"We must throw out all the food that needs long cooking." This came in almost cheerful tones from Carlo. "The Primus stoves are lousy this time. One is burnt to pieces and the other doesn't heat properly."

Yuri stuck his head out of the cabin, looking extremely grave, and behind him I could see Madani, speechless, but with anxiously inquiring eyes. Kei stood like an inscrutable china figure on the steering bridge, betraying none of his feelings. Norman was busy fixing our position.

"We're sinking," said Yuri slowly, "and we know from the last time that what goes down never comes up again. We must throw out everything we can, at once."

Norman was following the argument silently. The atmosphere was explosive. No wind, insufficient buoyancy. Why had this not happened last time? Could the home experts, wrong last time, be right now, in giving us two weeks to stay afloat? We had in fact voluntarily spent ten days floating in Safi harbor to allow the bundles to absorb water so that the light, top-heavy boat with its giant sail would not overturn. We had left port four days before, so now the two weeks had passed. The papyrus rolls were already half under water.

"Let's throw out those two reed boats on the foredeck," Norman suggested. "We don't need them as lifeboats and we've got a three-man inflatable raft for filming this time."

We had barely time to attach a message in a bottle to the largest reed boat before eager hands pushed it into the sea. The other vanished overboard so fast that we had no time to tie anything to it. Farewell. They floated sidelong, like balloons, with faint wind toward land. We had no idea then that the message would be found by a lone guard on a barren Sahara beach a few days later. We ourselves lay deep, letting the current carry us parallel to land.

Then a big sack of potatoes went overboard. Potatoes need lengthy cooking. Then two whole jars of rice. Flour. Corn. Two sacks, contents unknown. A wicker basket. Better to starve than sink. Then most of the grain for the chickens went. A big beam, planks and hardwood boards for splicing and repairs. More full jars. Madani looked at me anxiously, big-eyed. Kei exposed his teeth in an inscrutable grin and stared up at the sail. A heavy coil of rope plunged overboard. A whetstone. A hammer. Georges' heavy iron spike for repairing the boat vanished forever in the depths. Books and magazines floated about us in the calm water. Some had only their bindings torn off. Every ounce counted I agreed. And yet I passionately disapproved at the same time. We had thousands of miles ahead of us. We had barely set out from land, and at this rate we would need food and spare materials for months. But they were right. We were sinking. Why? How long would it continue? I tried to convince first myself and then the others that the submersion would stop as soon as there was enough papyrus under water for its buoyancy to offset all the heavy cargo we had stacked hastily on board on the last day before departure on May 17. Now it was May 20. We were still sinking just as fast.

Yuri resolutely started to tear up a little plank deck we had lashed on top of the papyrus in front of the mast. It had been such a pleasant thing to have. Yesterday Santiago and Georges had used it as a stage in a lively display of clog dancing and clowning with which they had entertained the rest of us as we lay drifting on an almost glassy sea. I got him to save a plank or two to walk on so that we would not stumble between the two thick papyrus rolls when we began to roll on high seas again.

But somebody was sitting in the shelter of the cabin, throwing all our almost weightless Egyptian *karkadé* tea into the sea. And the earthenware stove with all our charcoal. Lavatory paper. Spices. Nothing seemed light enough to be safe.

There was a lump in my throat. Some of the crew were smiling joylessly. Others wore a look compounded of shame and misery. Better to let the havoc run its course within controllable limits than to let anyone be inwardly consumed by the dangerous feeling that we had not done everything that could be done, should we continue to sink. The greatest danger would be for anyone's own peace of mind to suffer. But then the chickens began to flutter overboard. Two of the men took hatchets and knives and were about to cut the whole chicken coop loose so that it could be heaved out to sea. Without a proper Primus stove we could not eat poultry. Then it was time to halt the frenzy. The chickens' days were ended, but Georges pleaded for the solitary duck, which to Safi the monkey's indignation was allowed to strut freely about the deck and nip her tailless stern just as the first Sinbad had done on *Ra I*. Safi had added a few inches to her stature, but was still the same carefree scamp as when we first had her as our mascot on the earlier voyage. The empty chicken coop on the foredeck I myself broke up and turned into a light dining table, though there were some who wanted to get rid of both this and the crude benches, arguing that we could eat with plates and cups in our hands. But this brought a unanimous protest from the two of us who regarded meals as real high points in the day's program.

"In any case, morale on board will collapse if we begin to live like pigs," stated Norman, as an experienced naval officer.

Our minds were at peace. The air had been cleared, as though by a lightning rod, and for once there was really room to move about on board without mountaineering. But the wind had not returned.

The next day was equally still, and the next as well. And the next. We simply lay where we were. It did not look as if we were sinking any more for the time being, but neither were we making any visible progress.

"The statistics say 1 per cent calm here in May," said Norman, putting his finger on the navigational chart. "We have had 100 per cent for a full week."

We tried to work the long, heavy rowing oars. No use. But we seemed to be out of immediate danger. We jumped into the sea and enjoyed life. The sun blazed down on us while the Canary Islands and Africa on either side lay hidden in the haze. Cold, refreshing water. Norman swam with the duck in tow. Safi hung by her back legs reaching for the surface of the water. Inviting water. But in heaven's name, could we never get away from those little black oil clots, floating above and below the surface? Madani had actually netted some samples every day since we left. This time we were going to make a more systematic investigation, day by day. Last time we had only noticed the pollution when the water was so filthy that we could not overlook it. But the report and samples we had sent to the Norwegian delegation to the United Nations had aroused so much interest that more thorough observation was clearly worthwhile, now that we had our noses to the surface again. We used the sea from morning to night, as toothbrush glass, washbasin, bidet and bathtub. Fortunately there was enough space between the clots for us not to bump into them. We dived under the papyrus bundles. Crystal clear. Lots of fish. Striped pilot fish and spotted pampano waggled about in Ra's shadow, or kept station close under the papyrus. The papyrus was sleekly firm and sturdy, the whale-belly shape even more stylish than on *Ra I*. Look there, a hulking great grouper, nearly five feet long, fat and heavy. We could not be far from the Canary Islands; these fish do not venture far out to sea. The grouper came right over and poked at Georges' diving mask. An eight-inch, zebra-striped pilot fish came gliding like a little zeppelin toward my fingers. Santiago was right, the fish swam only when they were on the surface. They appeared not to swim, but to fly, free as birds, when seen from down in their own watery element. Two extraordinary creatures resembling footless stockings undulated past my nose. And there, a round disc resembling a rubbery jellyfish. With Portuguese men-of-war fresh in our memories we kept clear of this sort of unknown invertebrates.

"Shark, big shark!"

It was a long way off. Dorsal and tail fins were cutting through the water an uncanny distance apart, so it was really big. It was not bothering about the *Ra*. It continued unperturbed on its course at right angles to our own.

Everyone was in good humor after seeing how perfect *Ra II* looked under water. The tail was as strong and elegant as ever. No list to windward. Not one reed loose. Yuri and Georges even thought the papyrus bundles had lifted themselves out of the water a little in front. Perhaps the tropical sun was steaming off the moisture absorbed above water line during the first days' rolling. The day before, they had thought that not more than two or three men should be before the masts at one time, to prevent the bow from sinking. Now they agreed to our making seats out of the few materials we had left, to provide us with a cozy dining room on the foredeck.

For a week we lay idly yawing to the southeast, with feeble puffs of wind from east and west which did not even lift yard and sail free of the mainmast and with the whole sea drifting slowly under us. The sea was moving. Only we could not see it, because sea and boat were drifting at the same rate. Then the air began to follow suit, slowly at first. We began to nourish hopes of getting enough wind to enable us to steer. When we were bathing or diving to play with the tame fish, we always had a long rope looped round our bodies, so that we would be towed along if the boat began to move in the variable breezes. It would be too bad to lose the boat.

On the last day of calm, Norman, Santiago and Sinbad the duck were all swimming on their ropes when I dived out with mine and swam underneath the boat before coming up to the rippling surface on the other side and lying on my back to drink in the sun. A perfect holiday idyll. Unusual to see the underside of a duck swimming, nothing but a fat belly flanked by paddling feet. I turned over to enjoy the sight of the extraordinary vessel beside us. Noah's ark. Straw and yellow bamboo. Monkey in the stays, dove on the roof, and two bare feet sticking out of the cabin doorway. What a strange sight. The sail was bellying slightly. Small ripples round the rudder-oars, now we were really beginning to move. Strange that I could not feel the tug of the rope. What an astonishingly long rope I had. The rope! Where was it? Nowhere. Gone. I had swum out of the loop and was lying sunning myself alone on the Atlantic while the Ra sailed on. I felt a stab of panic—I was being left behind. Relax, the Ra was still quite close. I was far from being a swimming champion like Georges or Norman, but this I could manage easily. Made it. Jammed my fingers into the tight, thin rope round the smooth papyrus and hoisted myself on board. How safe those sturdy reed bundles felt. Said nothing, but rigged up the bathing net on the lee quarter, a sack-shaped net that I had designed so that we could scramble down into it and bathe overboard as we sailed. We did not know what effect soapsuds would have on the papyrus if we took a shower on board; the soap would remain between the reeds, for there was no planking here to be scrubbed like an ordinary deck.

We got our wind. With the northeast trade wind blowing in on the starboard quarter, we pushed the tillers of both rudder-oars across as far as we could and rushed along with the waves without sighting land in any direction. On May 26 Norman came down from the cabin roof with sextant, pencil and paper and breathed a sigh of relief. We must be past Cape Juby. Hurrah, the coastal cliffs, the Ra's most dangerous enemies, were behind us. Now the sea lay free and open before us once again, and this time we faced it with the Ra's tail still curving skyward and with unbroken oar shafts as thick as telephone poles. Everyone who had seen those exaggeratedly hefty poles before the start had smiled. We could have managed with something much slimmer and lighter, they said; the thin papyrus stems would be torn to pieces a hundred times before such massive logs would snap.

Life was sweeter than we had ever known it on a papyrus deck. From the invisible coasts on both sides of us we had been met by a colorful menagerie which came fluttering wearily out of the sky. One at a time, they had settled on the yardarm, on the cabin roof, on the shaft of the rudder-oar, on the papyrus peaks fore and aft. Carlo's fantasy of living in a floating birds' nest had materialized. There were friends from home, a wild dove, tits, swallows, finches and sparrows, a parrot-colored beauty of a roller with its dazzling blue and green plumage, and a carrier-pigeon with a copper ring on its leg that circled over us, made a half-landing on the mast and sailed down to join the bridge watch under the blue flag of the United Nations. The dove of peace, we all thought. It and the UN flag we were sailing under seemed to belong together. We read "27773–68A–España" on the copper ring. We had become a floating zoo. Mute, wriggling fish of many species kept us company below, and on board twittering birds in bright colors sat everywhere, pecking at water bowls and grain originally intended for the poultry. But as we glided steadily further away from the Canary Islands, without attempting to reach land, the rested birds made their adieus one by one, and left. Only the parrot-colored beauty queen could do no more and gradually wasted away. She was an insect-eater and we had not so much as a fly to offer. But the ring-marked dove took a fancy to Sinbad the duck's grain ration. It grew sleekly fat and tame and had apparently made up its mind to come to America with us.

As the wind returned, *Ra II* seemed to rise a little in the water. It looked as if the mighty, wind-filled sail were lifting the foredeck into the air. We were sailing in a kite a little too heavy to become air-borne. And when *Ra II* came to life in the fresh breeze she rapidly began to make up for lost time. At a speed of 60, 70, or 80 sea miles, that is 110, 130 even 150 kilometers a day, she carried us on across the open Atlantic.

The days quickly settled into a routine. Everyone was happy. Song and laughter. Nothing to repair. Easy watches. Good food from earthenware jars. No rationing. Four superb cooks. Any Pharaoh would have envied us Georges' spiced Egyptian dishes and no geisha could have bettered Kei's cooking. Madani's piquant recipe for salt meat in onions and oil à la Berber and Carlo's tireless capacity for producing something good when the others had not volunteered, all helped to make us feel we were speeding over the waves on a first-papyrus-class ticket.

When the evening shadow of the sail fell across the boat, seven sunburned, bearded, cheerful men sat round the empty poultry coop eating, while the eighth man stood on the steering bridge turning the thick rudder-oar with the setting sun for guide. The compass pointed west. The sun spread its very last rays like a peacock's tail over the sea in front of our own golden paper swan as she forged ahead on the very heels of the immortal *Ra* of past and present. And then the Big Dipper with the Pole Star stepped out on the starboard beam. Good friends. Part of our little world. We knew it all so well from the last time.

A fresh night breeze. On with long trousers and heavy sweaters. Madani in his thick Moroccan caftan with the pointed hood looked like a medieval monk as he kneeled down on the roof, silhouetted against the tropic sky, and bowed his face to the wickerwork in worship. An unusually pleasant and good-natured traveling companion. He had come in Abdullah's place, to represent the colored men of Africa. He was not quite as raven-black as Abdullah, but he was of the darkest type of Berber. Abdullah was the only man from the *Ra I* team whom we had unfortunately lost on the starting line in Safi, three days before departure. For a year he had been a voluntary refugee from Chad, where a bloody conflict was now in progress between his fellow Mohammedan in the north and the Christian Negro government, supported by the French Foreign Legion. Abdullah felt increasingly uneasy, with a wife here and a wife there, and geographical obstacles preventing a normal family life. In one hand a photograph of three charming African children in Chad, in the other a telegram to say that now, just now, his latest, favorite wife had borne him a daughter in Cairo. Who was going to sort out these tangles if Abdullah went to sea again on a papyrus ship? Good-by, Abdullah, we will all miss you. Abdullah was no sooner out of the door than Madani Ait Ouhanni stepped smilingly from behind the reception desk in the hotel where we all lived. Could he come with us? He had been appointed supervisor by the big phosphate factory in Safi, which had recently taken over the hotel. He was carried off from his hotel by seven guests about to set sail, who wanted a genuine African to replace Abdullah on the voyage.

We had known Madani for three days. None of us had ever seen Kei before. A Swedish friend of mine was going to Tokyo to negotiate an exchange of television programs. I had asked him to recommend a Japanese cameraman with a friendly nature and good health. Soon after, stocky little Kei Ohara tumbled in through the hotel doors in Safi, laden with camera equipment, and bursting with *joie de vivre*, music and judo muscles. Experience at sea? One sightseeing trip by water bus in Tokyo Bay. And then he had been on a film assignment on Lake Titicaca and photographed the Indians in reed boats.

"And you, Madani?" asked Norman, rather anxiously.

"I went on a fishing trip off the jetty once, when I first came down to Safi from Marrakesh, but I was seasick and returned to shore."

"Nothing but landlubbers this time too," said Norman, looking at me in mild despair.

"Then they won't load the papyrus boat as sailors would have loaded an ordinary wooden ship," I said, referring to last year's catastrophe. "Safest with those who realize they know nothing about papyrus navigation. A practiced ski jumper is seldom flexible enough to make a good parachutist."

Both the first-trip men suffered the fearful torments of seasickness the first two days, while the slender papyrus boat rolled and pitched like an empty bottle in fierce seas. Then Buddha and Allah seemed to hear their prayers for calm in defiance of all the statistics and the weather chart, and when at last the wind stole up on us again the representatives of Japan and Morocco had slipped quite naturally into the picture. As on *Ra I*, we shared the same trials and the same blessings. Those who were pale turned brown in the sun. Those who were still browner increased their lead, without anyone thinking about family trees, certificates of baptism, membership cards or passports. There was little room on the foredeck, still less on the afterdeck, and only a strip three feet wide along both sides of the thin cabin walls. The basket cabin consisted of a single

room too low for standing—except on top of its roof—and much
too narrow to turn over in bed in a curled-up position without
putting a knee in one's neighbor's stomach or an elbow in his
eye. We knew each other's swear words, snores, table manners and
jokes, even though the shrieks and creaks from mast stays and
lashed steering bridge often made it difficult in the darkness to
decide who was producing what sounds. Only Santiago and Georges
occasionally asked Yuri for sleeping pills. We might have been at
a non-stop party, no room for secrets, at all times of day and in
every situation we were all there, at the closest possible range.

If an American and a Russian seldom get properly acquainted,
two of them were getting thoroughly familiar with each other now.
If Arabs and Jews had been natural enemies, one of them would
have disappeared into the waves behind *Ra*. If the Almighty did
not allow Himself to be worshiped under many names we would
have had a religious war on board. We represented a Babel of
eight different languages, but English, Italian and French were
the ones spoken daily, Arab and Spanish occasionally, Russian,
Norwegian and Japanese only in our sleep. We argued, told funny
stories and sang in chorus whenever we had leisure, especially
after supper, with two or three men sitting at the bottom of the
mast ladder and the rest seated round the poultry coop table, because
inside the cabin there was always someone wanting to sleep. We
discussed politics, and never pulled our punches. For here the arguments for East and West were uncensored; no one was standing
by with loaded pistols. Hand harpoons, hatchets and fishhooks were
the nearest things to weapons on board. They were used for the
common good, for we were all in the same boat. Together, like
other people, we mulled over the Palestinian problem, the tribal
feuds in Africa, the intervention of the Americans in Vietnam and
of the Russians in Czechoslovakia. No one got angry, no one
was offended, no one raised his voice. We most often agreed. We
discussed religion and no one felt a holy wrath. Copt and Catholic, Protestant and Mohammedan, Buddhist, atheist, free-thinker
and half-Christian Jew, there was no space for a greater mixture on
our little ark, where the monkey was Noah and we played the
animal roles. We had no religious feuds on board. But—we dis-

cussed the ownership of a lost-and-found toothbrush and then we heard yells of rage and angry curses in various tongues. In their inmost hearts human beings are amazingly alike, regardless of geographical distance. A toothbrush held close to your nose is bigger than a cannon a thousand miles off. It is easy to find differences between man and man, but still easier to find the highest common denominator of mankind. Whether we tried to understand one another or not, we were packed close enough together on board our papyrus ark to see each other as slices cut from the same loaf. We rejoiced and were angry over the same things, we helped each other all we could, because we were thus helping ourselves. One steered so that others could sleep, cooked so that others could eat, sewed sails and hauled on ropes so that we would all make good progress. We had to keep each other in top form so that we would all be ready for a major effort whenever it was needed to withstand the threat from outside.

Days and nights passed. Weeks passed. A month passed.

"It's getting quite boring," Carlo complained cheerfully as he picked up his fishing rod. "Not like *Ra I*, nothing to repair, no breaking timber, no ropes to splice."

He sat down in the bow with his feet overboard and hooked on a little flying fish as bait. Plenty of them came sailing on board. We had pampano among the pilot fish underneath us that were quite good and bit at once when we wanted them to. But the coveted dolphin, or gold mackerel, the raft sailor's surest prey, was a far from frequent visitor this time, and the tuna fish just flipped their tails or shot into the air at a distance without allowing themselves to be tempted onto the hook. One day Georges swam through a seemingly endless shoal of silver cigars: bonitos. Once, close to Africa, a group of big whales passed quickly by; perhaps it was the same family as last time. A flat manta ray, big as the whole bridge of the *Ra*, shot itself above the waves in a mighty leap and dropped like a pancake with a shattering crash. Busy, resilient porpoises rolled past us, crisscrossing and leaping for joy, and a fat, lazy eel, as long as a man and thick as a thigh, undulated sleepily away in our wake. One afternoon a pink giant of a squid appeared from beneath the *Ra* and climbed, arm over groping arm, from papyrus bundles to rudder-oar before it let go, and stretching all ten tentacles above its head, shot backward down into the depths by built-in jet power.

So there was still some life left in the ocean, but there were far more oil lumps than fish. In the first month there were only three days on which Madani did not spot any of the drifting black clots, but then the sea had been too choppy for proper observation. On June 16, one month after the start, the sea was so filthy that it was uncomfortable to wash in it. Big and small lumps, from the size of a potato to a pea or a grain of rice, covered the water. Only in the current between Morocco and the Canary Islands had we seen worse on this voyage, but then there had been a flat calm when it was easy to see anything afloat. On May 21 I had noted in the logbook:

"The pollution is shocking. Madani is fishing up tarlike lumps as big as prunes and overgrown with little barnacles. Small crabs, worms and many-legged crustacea are living on some of them. In the afternoon the smooth surface of the sea was covered with enormous quantities of brown and black clots of asphalt, floating in something that looked like soap suds, and here and there the surface shimmered in all colors as if covered with gasoline."

In the same area a few of the stocking-like coelenterates were swimming. When alive they were taut like sausage-shaped balloons painted orange and green. However, thousands upon thousands of them floated dead among the oil clots, collapsed and flat as punctured toy balloons. For two days we drifted in this muck of oil and dead coelenterates before sailing beyond it. This polluted surface was traveling on the same course, but more slowly, toward America. Later on the voyage, when the seas began to mount up, big clots, big as a fist, were washed on board and left there when the sea water filtered away through the papyrus stalks as it does through the baleen of a whale. Yet oil pollution was not modern man's only gift to the sea. As we kept a lookout scarcely a day passed without some form of plastic container, beer can, bottle or more perishable materials such as packing cases, cork and other rubbish drifting close by Ra's sides.

We had covered 1725 nautical miles from the starting point and had 1525 left to sail when we ran into an absolute plethora of oil pollution for the second time. The next day the wind was strong. The day after that, June 18, the sea began to pile up in the biggest waves we had seen on either of the *Ra* voyages. The wind which reached us was a moderate gale with fierce squalls approaching full gale strength, but the breakers reared up in parallel ridges, higher and higher, out of proportion to the force of the wind. Perhaps a major storm had passed where they came from in the northeast. At first it was exciting, then one after another we began to feel a little suppressed anxiety, followed by astonishment and a rather dubious relief at how well we were doing. Finally we felt a surge of uninhibited admiration for the masterly way in which our little nutshell took the towering walls of water. I stood alone on watch on the steering bridge behind the cabin, turning the port oar so that we took the seas directly astern, while the starboard oar shaft was lashed securely and thus worked only as a keel. It went unbelievably well, the breaking wave ridges were quite different from breakers in shallow water on a beach. The sloping base of the wave first overtook us from behind, rolled in under the sickle-shaped stern and lifted us high into the air before the crest broke. The comb would usually break while we were perched on top, so that we shot forward in the rush of wind, water and foam, and sped at a mad rate, tail up and nose down, into the deep, blue-green valleys. It was vital then not to swing broadside on.

"Twenty feet, twenty-five feet."

The men were guessing at the height of the wave crests with a mixture of glee and horror.

"Thirty feet." Now the wavetops were towering higher than the masthead.

Thirty feet. Madani was struggling with seasickness. Thick storm clouds and rain on every side. Everything going like clockwork. *Ra II* took those parallel hills of water with incredible elegance. Just a little splash on deck now and then, nothing to speak of. No problem so long as we could keep our fabulous tail to the pursuing water. Fortunately the waves were regular, well spaced, just right for the *Ra's* length and shape, the ranks evenly dressed, one, two, three, lined up behind one another. Best not to turn one's head, to steer straight. Behind, one wall of glass after the other seemed to be toppling forward to bury us as we fled, unable to escape. My companions, off watch, crawled into the cabin one by one. There they could stare up at the basket roof and only listen to the deafening noise of the sea in uproar. But Carlo, the mountaineer, went on sitting in the high papyrus bow, his favorite spot, legs dangling as if he were on horseback.

Once again I felt the boat being lifted high in the air, higher than usual, and rushing forward and downward with the wall of water. Then the same crest rose ahead of us again, smooth and white-streaked, as it swept past.

"That was higher than the top of the mast," yelled Carlo enthusiastically, white teeth flashing in his full red beard.

A little later he unhitched himself from the bows and came teetering aft, dragging his life line to join the others inside. He told us that a gulf of a valley had yawned under him in the bows, so deep that when the Ra tilted and began to rush down, it looked as if we were plunging headlong into a bottomless watery grave. Better not to look.

The change of watch had to be almost due, but I dared not take my attention off the course for a second; the boat must not turn broadside to the waves. It had to be nearly four o'clock in the afternoon. From behind came the sound of the next foaming wave crest, higher above us than any of the others. Every muscle tensed to prevent the oar blade from being swept round. I felt a tremendous wall of water grip hold of the stern and lift us up, up, up. Eyes fixed to the compass so as not to lose the course. Must lie at right angles to the wave. Was there no end to the height we would reach this time before the boiling giant passed under us? Then the crest itself came gushing along our beams, seemed to be passing, the foam seethed, we tipped sharply and were about to career forward and down again at breakneck speed, as if on a surfboard equipped with a giant sail. Then it happened. A mighty crack. The harsh sound of thick timber breaking. A shock through oar shaft and vessel, and Ra II was rushing diagonally forward out of control, port side foremost, into the valley of water.

It was like being stunned with a club. I clung to uncertainty for a moment before forcing myself to turn my head and look catastrophe in the face. The rudder-oar! The thick shaft of the rudder-oar I was holding had snapped right across and the broad blade hung loose, dangling on the safety rope. I caught only a glimpse of it before the masses of water broke over us, rushing unimpeded over the whole starboard beam now that the peaked stern was not breaking the waves and lifting us into the air.

"All hands on deck! Port rudder-oar broken! Out with the sea anchor, Yuri!"

Vessel and bridge together buckled savagely under the pressure of water and I allowed myself to slide sideways down to the lashed oar shaft on the starboard side, to loosen the ropes there. The roar of water surging against the cabin wall and the thunder of the mainsail twisting and slamming against the straddled mast told the seven men in the cabin more than any call from the bridge, and they came swarming out, silent and dogged, knotting loose life lines round their middles.

"Which sea anchor?"

"The biggest."

I had undone the lashing on the undamaged rudder-oar, but the two hardwood forks that held it top and bottom were stuck askew, so that the rudder shaft could not be moved. Another heavy sea broke over us, and another. The mast creaked ominously, while wind and water flung sail and papyrus boat about at will.

"Lower the mainsail!"

To increase our speed Norman had recently hoisted a little topsail on a bamboo pole. That had already splintered and the topsail was flapping and whipping against the mainsail like a punctured balloon.

"Lower the mainsail before it rips!"

Norman took command on the foredeck and clambered up to the masthead himself to cut down the topsail. Then five men grasped the thick halyard to lower the mainsail and soon the twenty-three-foot yard began to move away from the mast top. But instead of allowing itself to be lowered, the heavy yard was lifted forward and up by the big wind-filled sail and the five men on the foredeck could only hang on with ten outstretched arms and all their united weight to stop the mainsail from flying out like a kite over the waves. Another thunderous sea engulfed us.

"Out with the sea anchor, damn it!"

"The waves have tangled the rope!"

"Then throw out the little one before the seas smash us to bits!"

Another sea right over the boat. And an even bigger one. It was lucky that we happened to be twisted starboard onto the torrents. The cabin had no opening on that side and we had covered the long wall with sailcloth, against which the sea was now hammering, up to the height of the roof.

"The little one is out," called Carlo triumphantly.

But its braking power was too little, the small bag we were now streaming in our wake did not hold well enough to turn the stern of the waterlogged papyrus boat back again. Yuri and Carlo stood waist-deep in water on the papyrus aft and regularly disappeared, heads and all, in the tumble of foam as they worked feverishly to sort out the tow rope of the biggest canvas bag, which the waves were continuously tangling up on deck.

"Check your life lines. Everyone must be tied on!"

Then I managed to get the jammed starboard oar turned a few inches, a little more and still a few more inches. But it was no good. The squalls tossed the bottom edge of the huge sail heavily against the top of the peaked papyrus bow. Wild, uncontrolled uppercuts from right and left, then the sail hooked itself over the slender tip and wrenched the papyrus bow to port. Seas and gale crashed and howled, so that shouts and suggestions from every side had to be intercepted and transmitted from bridge to mast and back again.

"Lower the sail before the whole ship is torn to shreds!" I shouted.

Now it was jerking its way down.

"Stop! Get the sail up again before a wave gets hold of it!" screamed Norman.

"If it falls in the sea we'll never get it on board again," yelled Georges.

He was absolutely right. Across the bottom the Egyptian sail was of the same width as the deck, but at the top, the same sail and the heavy yard holding it were very much wider, so to lower it without the wide upper section being swept up by the wild waves on both sides of deck was hardly feasible.

A solution offered itself. The sail was lowered a few inches at a time but never touched the deck, because five men stood secured across the boat, rolling it up from below as it came down. The five were struggling all the time to keep their feet against gusts of wind, the rolling boat and surging floods of water. Tugging and banging on the tiller as well as the shaft of the unbroken starboard rudder-oar, I finally forced it to swing by degrees in uneven jerks, but it did not help at all with the course. The men on the sail managed bit by bit to roll up one third and reefed the roll firmly with a series of rope ends hanging in a line along the sail for this very purpose. It was time to rescue the big loose oar blade, which was still dangling and skipping wildly in tow, and was regularly flung heavily against the stern by the waves. The safety rope attached to the blade, copied from Egyptian tomb paintings, helped us to pull it in. The shaft had broken across just by the lower fork. Six inches thick all the way down, like the average telephone pole, and made of the strongest pitch pine, the timber we had all regarded as invulnerable had snapped like a matchstick, though there was no fault in the wood. Not a single papyrus reed was broken, loose or damaged. The papyrus bundles had withstood more than the wooden log, so once again the strength of Goliath had been forced to yield to the dexterity of David. The accident taught us once and for all that we had used too thick a rope to secure the rudder-oar top and bottom. We should have tied it with thinner rope at the bottom so that the rope would snap, like a safety catch, before the oar shaft. Only upon our return did we learn that this was precisely what the ancient Egyptians had done, but this detail had been overlooked on the ancient design, since everybody had thought that the difference in thickness of the upper and lower ropes had been a mere coincidence in the artist's reproduction. Yet, a re-examination of the old designs showed that this difference in thickness was most consistent.

It was Georges who hauled in the heavy oar blade, overgrown with edible barnacles. He cut off a bunch of short papyrus stubs that Norman had tied to the blade in order to streamline it on the side where we had bound the thick shaft. He threw the short, maltreated papyrus ends into the sea and stood expectantly waiting to see what would happen. They sank. He said not a word to a soul, and had no idea that someone else was watching from the bridge, equally perplexed and with the same sinking feeling in the stomach. What was the matter with the papyrus? Had all the air been squeezed out of it? Yuri and Carlo had their backs turned to him. They had quite enough on their hands, sorting out the rope of the big sea anchor. Then it, too, was in the sea, the little one retrieved, and now the canvas bag held and began to turn the stern slowly back again. But not completely. We were still lying slightly across the wind, taking the sea in huge waves over the starboard quarter, just as on *Ra I.*

The storm raged. The time on board was ten to nine and night was falling when the men on the foredeck managed to reef half the mainsail so that the orange-red sun symbol was left half rolled up from the bottom, like a reflection of the sunset we could not see behind the storm clouds. Had we seen it, it would not have been straight ahead today, as we lay drifting at an angle; it would have been far to the left of the crooked bow.

Tragedy. Catastrophe. No reserve log thick enough or long enough for a few oar shaft. All heavy hardwood pieces suitable for splicing had been dumped overboard at the Canary Islands. If we lay here long enough with the sea anchor out to brake our speed they might come drifting after us! Bad joke. Hopeless situation. No solution. Good-night everybody. We must sleep now and think tomorrow. Useless to steer any more with half a shaft and no blade and another that does not work. The sea can thunder on board and out again, the sea anchor will hold our course so that it does not come gushing in through the cabin door. But we must alternate watches through the night, to avoid being run down by ships in the big waves.

It was hopeless trying to sleep that night. We were on *Ra I* again, on those last nights when the sea was gaining the upper hand. Tons of water smacked against the back wall on the starboard side, surging, seething, sucking, gurgling and clucking all round us. A regular river was running to and fro on board, under the cabin floor, in the broad, deep cleft between the two papyrus rolls that kept us afloat. The water surged along the papyrus, chasing wildly along the cracks between the reeds which could have let it out. But the reeds were swelling more and more and closing up all the fissures so that the water never had time to run out before new torrents surged on board and filled the big bathtub to the brim.

I tossed about in my sleeping bag and did not manage to sleep a wink before it was my turn to crawl out and keep watch. Then, I fell asleep like a log, sitting on the bamboo bench, lashed fast, outside the cabin door. I awoke with a shock, ashamed and bewildered, to see a bat, no, it was a night owl, swerving round and round the *Ra* until it came tumbling in between the lines of stays straight toward me. Swooping to the attack, our nocturnal visitor was flying badly, caught a wing on a guy rope, missed me, and staggered before getting its feet safely under it on the bench close beside me. But it was a pigeon! It was our own ringed traveling companion! It had been scared away from the roof by the mad battle of sail and heavy seas, had missed the usual human company on the steering bridge, which was empty and deserted. Frightened by the loneliness of its own basket nest on the roof, it had searched vainly for another dry spot, and now came exhausted back. It continued to sit close beside successive watches in the doorway until day dawned. Round the corner the Atlantic broke on board unimpeded. It poured overboard again on each side of the cabin, so that we on the lee side only had rivulets running back and forth round our feet before they, too, ran out again into the sea.

Extraordinary vessel. The trouble was that she was beginning to be as watertight as an ordinary boat, so the water no longer ran away fast enough through the hull, which should have had a leaky bottom.

The next day was still an inferno. We were dead tired as we waded in foaming water, moved jars that had to be rescued from the stormy side, threw the cracked ones into the sea, resecured loose cargo, tightened stays and stitched sails and racked our brains trying to work out how to recover our steering ability. Lying as we were, waterlogged and at an angle to the waves, the sea's final victory was only a question of time. Wood and reed were only held together with rope, which we could expect to snap at any time under this enormous strain. The long spiral rope that held the papyrus together was half an inch thick, like a man's little finger. The cabin, the feet of the mast and steering bridge were all lashed in place with a much thinner, third of an inch rope braided in three strands like a pigtail. The Indians would not allow anything thicker to pass between the reed bundles. But we danced ahead like a ball. If all the joints of cabin, bridge and mast had not been completely flexible the sea would have torn us apart as violently as it could splinter timber and bend steel. During the early days the sea got nowhere with the reed ball; it bounded away from all the punches. But the sea had another trick. It slowly boarded us and lay there as useless deck cargo, pushing us under. We were beginning once more to sink at frightening speed, partly because of tons of splashing sea water dammed up as a dead weight in the long deep ditch between our two papyrus rolls, and partly because this water, entering from above, was now penetrating the upper half of the papyrus rolls, which had stayed dry and light hitherto. All the papyrus was busy soaking itself full and heavy, from above and from below. We were really sinking at an uncanny rate again. We all realized that. There was no sign that anyone was seriously afraid; everyone was doggedly determined that we should weather this. We all made suggestions, which were considered and then unanimously rejected. Madani, who had not seen the sea on board Ra I, took me aside and asked warily if it was dangerous. When told that for the time being it was not, he was all smiles from ear to ear again. Kei shook the sea water off his ears and his shining black hair and said with a broad grin that he had had no idea that such waves existed.

Thanks to the sea anchor the stern had turned slightly to meet the waves. If we pulled it in we would be lying broadside on again and get the whole sea over our full breadth. On the other hand, with the sea anchor out we stayed put and made no progress. We were stuck in the middle of the Atlantic, sinking, nineteen hundred nautical miles from the start and thirteen hundred nautical miles from our goal.

For two days we could do nothing but fight to save ourselves and the cargo. To splice the rudder-oar proved impossible. The seas continued to run twenty to twenty-five feet high, with a few thirty to thirty-five feet giants among them. Inside the cabin I cut up the cardboard back of a writing tablet and made a model of the loose oar blade, the two broken pieces of shaft and the gap between the two wooden forks that held the slanting rudder shaft in place top and bottom. The model showed that if we tied the upper and longer portion of the shaft to the upper part of the blade, the top of the shaft would just reach the floor of the bridge. That was how we fixed it, evolving by our united efforts a system that allowed the helmsman to stand on the opposite side of the bridge, twisting the starboard rudder-oar with his right hand, while he turned the curtailed shaft on the port side one way by means of a rope tied to his foot, and the other way by means of a long bamboo pole held in his left hand. This was quite an acrobatic performance, and the maneuvering became still worse because the helmsman also incessantly had to haul on the sheets, which were tied to the railing of the bridge, because the reed boat was now lying so deep that the combined effect of two rudder-oars was not always enough. If the boat did not obey the two rudders, it was necessary to steer with the sail as well, to avoid being caught broadside by wind and wave.

Ra II was lying uncomfortably deep in the water when we were ready to try out the new system late on the second evening. Everyone realized that we had a tough job ahead if we were to complete the second half of the voyage. The position improved a little as soon as we got the crippled oar in place. We immediately managed to turn the stern into the seas, retrieve the sea anchor and speed westward under reefed sail. The day after that we took a chance on unfurling and hoisting the whole mainsail. Once again the big sail seemed to lift us higher out of the water as it drove us forward at a rate of almost three knots, over sixty miles a day. But now the deck was only just above water. Astern the seas continued to wash in one side and out the other. Ahead, heavy seas flung themselves over us at regular intervals if we tried to sit round the poultry coop as before, so we all had to squeeze together and eat on the mast ladder, like birds on a bough.

"We have to make a barrier against the worst breakers so that the water on board has time to run out, otherwise we'll sink," said Yuri, and busied himself hanging up a strip of canvas which he stretched forward from the mast stays on the starboard side, made fast with thick cords top and bottom.

"Relax, Yuri!" Everyone laughed. "The first wave will rip that strip of canvas." But the enterprising Yuri went on resolutely.

The next wave came frothing along the starboard cabin wall, lazily pushed Yuri's canvas wall into a little bulge and poured overboard. Only a little water trickled in on the foreward deck; the canvas had channeled the rest away. Yuri sat down triumphantly at the poultry coop to eat, while the rest of us came down wide-eyed from the mast ladder with our plates when we saw that the next wave did the same, and the next. There we sat at the table, gazing at Yuri the wizard who could stop the sea by hanging up a cloth. The secret was that the papyrus tail aft took the force of the sea and split the wave in two. The sailcloth curtain had only to channel overboard that cross section of the wall of water that came surging along both sides of the boat.

"More canvas!"

With the hunting knife we cut up all the sailcloth that covered the front wall of the cabin, so from then on we could see straight through the wickerwork to the poultry coop, the masts and the sea. Then we cut up the whole of the spare mainsail. Yuri hung up the pieces and soon we were living behind a veritable screen of burgundy, orange, green and yellow. The waves flowed along the screen, giving it a friendly nudge so that the mast stays swung like a clothesline in the wind and only a tiny proportion of the torrents of water found its way on board.

"Hippies! Gypsies!" cried Carlo and Georges, roaring with laughter, next time they launched the little three-man rubber raft to film us from outside. We popped our heads up over Yuri's multicolored screen and looked at the two of them as they vanished and reappeared behind the wave crests.

"Come back," I yelled. "Get yourselves on board a proper ship before you capsize."

We had inflated the little raft and filmed ourselves before, in a flat calm and later on fine seas, but now we were so used to waves and salt water that everyone was beginning to get reckless.

Days and weeks continued to roll on with the waves. In the course of barely a year, the six of us who had been on Ra I had been together on reed rolls for almost four months. After the accident with the rudder-oar we had to start water rationing, two cups per man per day, plus nine quarts jointly for cooking. Several jars had cracked, some had admitted salt water. That we ourselves had poured the contents of most of the goatskins out into the sea when we were becalmed was a delicate subject which it was better not to broach. What a piece of impetuosity! Carlo was plagued with salt water sores in the groin and Yuri prescribed bathing with fresh water twice a day. Poor Carlo used the contents of one cup; he would not allow himself any more. The duck, the dove and the monkey together tippled as much as one man every day. Georges protested violently at innocent animals being rationed like us men. Santiago was not a hundred per cent fit, either. He had been treated for kidney stones before the start and was not supposed to eat salted meat, nuts, dried vegetables, eggs. These were the dishes that dominated our menu. He was fatigued, but performed all his duties on board without a murmur. As long as he was not neglecting a duty he preferred to lie on his back in the inmost corner of the cabin, where Yuri kept him under observation.

One evening we were all tired. Santiago came out of the cabin opening with a dark face and sat down with the rest of us by the poultry coop. He looked from Carlo to Georges.

"I heard some nasty remarks through the cabin wall!"

Carlo blew up! "Drop that professorial face."

"Take on a bit more, like the rest of us," interrupted Georges. "If you volunteer to relieve a tired helmsman you turn up ten minutes before his watch ends."

The accusations began to fly. Hard-working Carlo and playboy Georges had had difficulty in understanding each other on the previous trip, but they were the best of friends now, and for the moment the quiet professor of anthropology had got under both their skins. He was now informed that he lay in the corner psychoanalyzing us while the others worked. Moreover, it was his idiotic idea that we should have food and water in jars this time as well, instead of light cans and water in jerry-cans. On *Ra I* we had proved that it was possible to live without modern food. Why the devil did we have to prove it a second time? And having talked us into bringing more than a hundred ceramic jars this time as well, he as quartermaster should have secured them well enough to prevent them from breaking and forcing us to ration the water.

"The jars are just as light as jerry-cans, and who was it who emptied all the water out of the big goatskins into the sea!"

There was a savage duel of words; angry allegations and all sorts of suppressed irritations poured out and took away the appetite of everyone round the poultry coop. Santiago struck out again, from his soapbox on the mast ladder, but was left sitting almost punch-drunk under the joint assault of the others.

"Carlo," I said. "You are a professional mountaineer, an experienced expedition man. You mustn't expect a university professor to be as good as you at knots and weight-lifting. You are like a priest, so perfect that you want other people to do everything as well as you do."

That was apparently the worst thing I could have said. Carlo rose slowly, his face turning redder than his beard, one hand clutching at his bushy hair.

"Me, a priest!"

For a moment he stood speechless, swallowing. Then he turned away from me to Santiago and suddenly thrust out an open palm, covered with calluses:

"All right. Let's forget all about it, boys!"

Everyone leaned across the poultry coop and shook hands. Norman ran to fetch harmonicas for himself and Kei, and Madani pulled out his Moroccan drum. When I slipped into bed two hours later I fell asleep to the sound of a celebratory orchestra and chorus from the foredeck, with a repertoire from seven different corners of the globe.

The experiment with *Ra I* the year before had been reduced to a mere drift voyage on the very first day at sea, when we broke both rudder-oars. The elements carried us westward in a curve, and we were making straight for Barbados, far south in the West Indian chain, when we broke off the experiment. This time we were still completely seaworthy, and decided to steer for the island to which nature herself would have carried us last time. So, every day, the distance ahead was measured in numbers of sea miles from Barbados. We could not have picked a better course to give us wind and sea dead astern. But it was damnably difficult for the helmsman to prevent the waterlogged reed boat from broaching to and drifting beam on toward Barbados. We were worn out at the end of an average night watch, almost unable to straighten our cramped fingers. And if the boat swung round so that the sail was taken aback and the sea rushed on board, it was as if devils had boarded our ship under cover of the night. Yuri's sailcloth would be torn and angry curses rained down on the poor helmsman as seven half-asleep men had to put on their life belts. Naked bodies tumbled out into the darkness, waist-deep in seething water, to heave and haul at the sail, row or back the oars at the stern, and rescue cargo. Some of the men asked as a precaution not to be left responsible for the bridge alone, so we increased the hard night watch from two to three hours, but with two men on the bridge at once.

We had to think of something if we were to avoid wearing ourselves to death with the laborious steering system.

"If only we could move the masts forward," I mused one night, when Norman and I were keeping watch together on the bridge. "If the sail were right forward in the bow the boat would steer itself down wind."

"We can," said Norman eagerly. And before anyone really knew what was happening next morning we were carrying out an extremely difficult operation. The top of the heavy straddled mast had to be tilted to bring the big sail forward.

Norman began chopping at the base of the masts with a hatchet, so that the footplate began to lean forward. Next we cautiously slackened off all the twelve parallel stays that ran aft, six from each leg of the straddled mast to each side of the reed boat. We could then tilt forward the thirty-foot double mast, which weighed at least six hundred pounds. As we pulled the mast top forward the yardarm followed, and when we fastened the mast stays again the wind-filled mainsail was hanging in a curve down in front of the high papyrus bow. The steering improved at once, as long as our only desire was to follow the wind, nose first.

Ra II sailed westward at dazzling speed. All further sinking soon stopped when there was enough papyrus under water to counteract the new cargo we had shipped in the form of unwanted sea water on deck. Five weeks after the start we were no longer sinking, but we were lying so low that in calm water the deck was scarcely above the surface, and from now on barnacles began to grow on the papyrus deck along the exposed starboard wall of the cabin. Madani continued to fish up lumps of oil every single day.

On a day of rain and savage squalls the sail caught fast on the slender bow and turned it a little more askew, while the sailcloth seam along the bottom tore. The sail was next in importance to us after the hull, and after consultation we decided to sacrifice the fine upswept bow. Carlo sat astride in the bow, sawing away at our proud vessel. For safety's sake we tied a rope firmly round the bow so that the whole reed boat would not split when the two important spiral ropes were cut as we sliced off the entire tip of our vessel. But our Indian builders had been right. The rope was wedged so tightly in its coils round the little built-in central bundle that, even with our combined efforts, we could not pull it loose. The papyrus reeds were so compressed and swollen that the cross section in front looked like a giant sliced onion when the bow fell to the vandal's saw. *Ra II* at once took on a more sober, modern line, and through the wicker of the cabin wall we could suddenly see the whole horizon ahead under the sail. It was as if the shutters of the ark had been set ajar so that we could begin to look out for land ahead.

Not many days later we decided to saw off the stern peak as well. It had been left standing like a close-hauled sail after the bow had fallen and made the course unsteady, besides which we wanted to reduce unnecessary weight. It was with a distinctly shaky feeling that we removed the fatal bowstring from the tip of the curly tail and moved it down on to the flat, broad chicken's tail that was left. But no amount of interference seemed to affect the unrivaled toughness of this vessel. One after another we slipped overboard on a line, emerging relieved and delighted to report to those who had not yet been under the living room floor and seen for themselves that *Ra II* was unchanged under water, just as rigid, just as firm, just as complete. Not a reed, not a rope had shifted, only now it was covered with living barnacles, like little black and white mushrooms, with waving yellow gill fringes.

The little amateur radio set came out of its case less often now than on the previous trip. We thought the families at home were feeling more secure, and we were reluctant to worry them with much more than a simple "all well on board." But in the last half of the second month we were sailing so fast and had traveled so far that we could give an approximate time and place for landing. Yvonne packed her bag at once and flew to Barbados with the children.

Not long afterward Norman made contact with a radio ham on Barbados and we heard my wife's voice. Yvonne produced six unexpectedly technical questions about the marine life that had joined us under the reed bundles and next explained that the answers were of interest to the head of a marine biology project which the United Nations Development Aid Department had stationed on Barbados for the time being. We were able to report on the faithful escort of various small friends swimming with us under the reed floor, a couple of dolphins chasing flying fish round us, and large flocks of sea birds from South America circling like drifting clouds over the horizon to south and west, where glittering tuna exploded like silver rockets out of the blue sea. Next day the radio ham told us to expect a visit from a UN research vessel.

On June 25 a brown, four-winged dragonfly fluttered on board. Were we so close to land? Or had the big insect hitched a ride on some boat that had passed beyond the horizon? There had been an extraordinary dearth of ships since a couple had almost run us down in the traffic off Africa.

We were now sailing at full speed into the area where we had abandoned *Ra I* after the final dramatic days of last year's voyage. We all shuddered when a shout from the steering bridge drew our attention to a fierce shark that was snapping furiously at the red buoy we were towing in case anyone fell overboard. It was just here that we had met all the sharks last year. But this year's solitary wanderer soon abandoned the buoy and disappeared northward. The sharks were apparently uninterested in a craft like *Ra II*, which needed no underwater repairs.

On June 26 the seas began to heave violently again and the waves came racing after us, with white combs frothing like snow from an engine wheel plow. Rain rushed down on us from dense clouds. We let the salt wash off our bodies and licked our arms. We could have collected rain water, but we were sailing so fast that the rations would hold out. The duck waddled round on the roof, sipping at the puddles. Safi wanted to crawl into the cabin. The starboard rudder-oar stuck in its forks and we were afraid it would break, but Kei chipped it loose under water. Next day the tame pigeon had gone. For some time it had seemed restless, flying in big circles over the *Ra*, and yet always fluttering back to the grain bowl on the roof. But on June 27 it took off and was gone for good. The Flood must be nearly over. The ark had lost its dove. We missed it. Had it got wind of land? The nearest coast was French Guiana to the south.

The venturesome dove now bore two rings, one with its Spanish number and another marked "*Ra II.*"

On June 28 the water temperature suddenly rose two degrees and after that we saw no more lumps of oil. Had we passed into another branch of the current? This was strange, for it was just here that we had been wallowing in lumps of oil when we abandoned *Ra I* last year, and the whole sea moves in an incessant circuit between the continents.

On June 29 we found Safi's chain hanging slackly in the sea. It was empty. Chaos on board. Then Safi, free at the top of the mast, was looking triumphantly down at us. Neither coconut nor honey tempted her down, but when Yuri fetched her favorite toy, an ugly green, squeaking, rubber frog with big red eyes, Safi was down on deck like lightning to recover the frog, while Yuri recovered the monkey. Immediately afterward there was a yell from Norman in the cabin. He had made direct contact with a radio ham on the UN research vessel *Calamar*, which was quite close, and which had asked us to send up rockets after nightfall so that she could find us in the choppy seas.

That night we were given a fright of a quite unexpected kind. Norman roused me in a low voice for the change of watch on June 30 at 0.30 hours, and I sat up in my sleeping bag and began to pull on my socks, as the air was raw and cold on the bridge. Then he called again, and this time there was terror in his voice:

"Come quick, quick! Look there!"

I dived out of the opening in the wicker wall with Santiago close at my heels and we hoisted ourselves over the cabin roof where Norman was pointing.

It was like the Day of Judgment. Over the horizon to starboard, in the northwest, rose a pale, round disc, which never completely left the water, but grew and grew like a phantom aluminum-colored moon rising half-hidden by the rim of sea. Like a compact nebula, brighter than the Milky Way and symmetrically circular, it grew in size, a stemless mushroom, and seemed to be rushing straight toward us as it spread farther and farther across the sky. The moon was up on the opposite side, in a starry, cloudless sky. My first thought was a reflection against a veil of humidity from an enormous searchlight over the horizon, my next was an atomic cloud caused by human error, or a phenomenon of the northern lights, but the feeling that a scintillating shower of foreign bodies was descending on us from the cosmos persisted, until the disc of light was covering about thirty degrees of sky. Then it suddenly stopped growing, dissolved almost imperceptibly and disappeared. We were left without an explanation.

We now began to burn flickering red flares and send up rockets of starry rain to show the *Calamar* our position. That was an extraordinary night, with a bizarre atmosphere. We heard the voice from the *Calamar* on the little set again but they could not see the rockets and had not been on deck when the disc of light appeared. Next morning we heard through the radio ham on Barbados that the same phenomenon had been observed from several of the West Indian Islands, but in a northeasterly direction. Was it a section of rocket from Cape Kennedy that had exploded and burned out as it fell into the atmosphere? We never knew. But UFO enthusiasts looking for evidence of flying saucers confused the phenomenon with two previous observations we had made on two successive nights, farther out to sea. We had seen small orange lights on the horizon to the northwest. One was a brief flash, with no sign of a ship, the other was drop-shaped and we saw it just as it sailed diagonally down and vanished into the sea. We had alerted radio hams on land, in case they were emergency rockets from ships in trouble, but no SOS had been sent out so the indications were that they were signals between naval vessels on exercise, perhaps a submarine marking its position on the surface.

While we continued due west, under full sail, the *Calamar* zigzagged about us all night, searching. We were short of rockets, but kept a constant lookout from the mast top. The sun rose, day dawned and Norman, who had his hands full with sextant, abacus and the little hand-powered emergency radio, constantly reported that the *Calamar* must be close by. Now to the north, now to the south. Always hidden behind endless ranks of high waves. We ate lunch. And supper. We gave up the idea that anyone would find us. The tropical sun was about to set again. Local time was only 6 p.m., though our watches stood at 9 p.m., because we had adjusted them only once since leaving Africa. It was then that the lookouts on both boats saw each other simultaneously. They reported sighting a sail and we saw an almost invisible green speck on the horizon—behind us.

Darkness was about to fall when a proud little ship overtook us from behind. It was a great moment.

The big, fast trawler came close up on our beam and saluted by lowering and raising the blue flag of the United Nations that fluttered from the masthead. Norman hurried over to the straddled mast and replied with our own UN flag. Only two-thirds of it were left, the rest had been ripped away in a storm. We were exultant, we all climbed on to the bridge, the roof, the mast, waving and hallooing and blowing our shrill hunting horn. The whole crew of the UN boat—brown, black and white alike—stood along the railing waving and hallooing back. The captain was standing on the bridge. He was Chinese. Beside him stood a man with a megaphone who yelled in Swedish:

"Welcome to the American side of the ocean!"

When Kei saw the Chinese on the bridge his cup of joy overflowed. He crawled over to me on the roof and held out his hand.

"Thank you for letting me come."

There was something unreal about the whole meeting: that a UN boat should actually be the first to meet us on the other side. I had never seen a boat flying the UN flag before, apart from the *Ra*. Darkness closed over the sea, the brightly lighted boat circled round us a few times, then switched off her engines to drift through the night. Her lights quickly disappeared behind us until we were left alone with the waves and our own feeble kerosene lantern. Snug, but lonely.

Late that night we were reminded that the voyage was not yet over. A powerful squall suddenly rushed down from the north and took the sail completely aback before the watchers on the bridge could pull themselves together. The pressure of wind on the big sail was terrific, forcing the whole ship to heel over to port until the deck was under water. It was an unusual sensation for us in the cabin to tumble out on the lee side and immediately finding ourselves thigh-deep in water, water that was no breaker frothing its way overboard, but the actual surface of the sea itself, looking as if it had come to stay. For the first time on any raft I felt that we were now quite definitely on our way to the bottom of the sea. There was no more buoyancy. Yells and shouts and blinking flashlights. Madani waist-deep in water without his life line. Yuri's screen on the lee side torn to ribbons. Then the wind veered back to the east, the direction we

were used to, and eight experienced papyrus sailors finally managed
to turn the sail back into position. *Ra II* righted herself serenely as
the water poured overboard; the deck returned to the level it had
maintained for the last part of the voyage. But three of the many
jars that had hitherto stood safely in the lee on the port side had
been smashed by the masses of water, and wading barefoot I cut
my toes on the fragments, and Yuri had to bandage my foot. The
port side had been infiltrated by a web of the thin, glistening, stinging tentacles of Portuguese men-of-war, and Georges burned himself
while he was answering the call of nature. He had to be bathed with
ammonia.

Next morning the *Calamar*, which had switched off her engines,
took some time to catch up with us again. No one on board the
trawler had expected any great speed from a primitive reed boat. But
in spite of our tribulations we had sailed seventy-five nautical miles in
the last twenty-four hours.

The *Calamar* delivered mail, ointment to soothe Carlo's suffer-
ings, some bags of delicious Barbados fruit and a big carton of ice
cream, which had melted to custard before it reached us in the bobbing rubber boat. The *Calamar* stayed near us for two days, then increased speed and went ahead with fresh greetings for Barbados.
Now we were once again in those waters off the West Indies that are
the birthplace of the Atlantic hurricanes. The weather was unsettled
now, at the beginning of July. Dark walls of rain were falling on all
sides, driven over us almost every day by powerful gusts of wind, often
at gale force. Again and again we had to stream the sea anchor and
struggle to save the sail. But wind and current remained generally in
our favor and in the final days we made the best average speed of
the voyage, covering up to 81 miles in a day. We frequently encountered ships now, plying between North and South America.

On July 8 we were only 200 nautical miles from Barbados, and
the island authorities sent a fast little government boat, the *Culpepper*, to welcome us to this little independent corner of the British
Empire. Yvonne and our eldest daughter, Anette, were the only passengers on board. If they found us on the basis of our position we
should meet late that same night.

The night passed, and the day as well, while the *Culpepper* rolled
about, over and among the waves in our immediate neighborhood,

without finding us. The weather was far from perfect and we intercepted reports from the government boat to the land station describing the big waves and reporting that the raft sailor's wife was suffering from seasickness but bravely insisted on continuing the search. The search went on for the next night and the day too, for two days. It was near nightfall on the second day and we half expected to reach land before the government boat, for there were barely a hundred nautical miles left. Then the *Culpepper* appeared, also on the wrong horizon, overtaking us from astern. Flat and broad and seaworthy, a real man's boat, she maneuvered alongside, with two white women clinging to the railings, surrounded by a waving black crew. While the ladies were obviously having difficulty in sorting out all the sunburned shaggy creatures with full beards, waving wildly from the roof of the wicker cabin, the crew of the *Culpepper* turned their attention to Madani, whom they thought to be a sailor from Barbados. Madani, the landlubber from Marrakesh, impressed the onlookers by throwing out a fishhook baited with salt sausage and immediately pulling in five pampano and an unknown silver-green fish of the same general type. Georges the skindiver crossed to the *Culpepper* just as the sun was setting to negotiate a morally permissible barter: fresh fish, Egyptian bread and the ever-tasty Moroccan *sello* in exchange for unnecessary but very welcome oranges. He was standing on the afterdeck, about to dive for his swim back to *Ra II* with the *Culpepper*'s searchlight playing on the waves to show him the way, when a black man stopped him and asked him if we on the *Ra* were not afraid of sharks.

"No," said George grandly, but swallowed his boast when the man pointed calmly to a large man-eater, gliding slowly out of the ship's wake into the beam of light. Our own rubber raft was so worn by rubbing against the earthenware jars on board that we did not dare to launch it. Georges had to spend the night on the *Culpepper* and return next morning in a little oarless dinghy let out on tow from the *Culpepper*, and hauled back again empty.

The *Culpepper* stayed on our port quarter all night. The day after, July 12, such large flocks of sea birds flew out toward us from the west that we knew land must be just over the horizon. It was Sunday, and Norman and I, who had the five to eight watch, were standing on the bridge looking forward to our relief. Soon Carlo and Kei would be scrambling out and unbedding our last eggs from the lime paste to be fried for the occasion: Sunday breakfast. We still had plenty of provisions, especially sacks of Egyptian mummy bread in the chests we slept on, salt sausage and ham hanging under wicker roof, and jars of *sello*, the honey and almond mixture that contained everything a desert traveler in Morocco needed. We had never gone hungry and were in good form. Then I noticed something and grabbed Norman by the arm.

"Do you smell it?" I said, sniffing up the salt sea air. "Fantastic, a distinct scent of green, fresh-cut grass!"

The two of us stood and sniffed. We had been at sea for fifty-seven days. Santiago, Carlo and the others came out and sniffed with us. The non-smokers among us smelt it distinctly. And damned if I didn't scent cow dung, as well, the smell of farming. It was pitch dark and we could see nothing. But the movement of the waves was strange too, a different rhythm, somehow, which must be the effect of backwash from land. We pushed both rudder-oars hard over to starboard, where the wind was coming from, and held a course as close to the north as we could. It was incredible how well the low-lying reed boat was able to sail close-hauled.

Norman, Carlo and Santiago climbed to the masthead in turn all morning, and at twelve-fifteen our time we heard a wild yell from above our heads:

"Hurrah!"

Norman had sighted land. Safi screamed and the duck flapped across the roof. Like flies we swarmed up the steps of the swaying masts, every man jack of us, for *Ra II* was incredibly stable, now that most of the papyrus was under water. The *Culpepper* blew her siren. Then we all saw land, low and flat on the horizon to the northwest. We had steered too far south the day before, trying to counteract the current that swung north just before the islands. We had succeeded too well. So now we had to turn the mainsail and shove the rudder-oars right over in the opposite direction, otherwise we would sail past Barbados and land somewhere on the dense chain of islands just behind. That was all very well, but family and friends were waiting for us on Barbados. *Ra II* responded to maneuvering like a keeled vessel. The straight deep furrow running right along the bottom between the two reed rolls evidently acted as a negative keel. With the wind almost across our beam the red life buoy was being towed dead astern, showing that we were moving in the direction the bow was pointing, without any side drift, straight toward the low coastline.

When we sat down round the poultry coop for lunch we knew it would be our last meal on board. Late in the afternoon we heard the hum of aircraft. A little private plane circled over us and waggled its wings. Soon after, a bigger, twin-engined plane came out from the islands with the Prime Minister of Barbados, and soon there were four planes circling over our mast top. One of them dived so low that its slip stream threatened to take the mainsail aback. The land mass rose higher and the sun flashed on the glass of distant windows. We saw more and more houses. Dozens of boats were on their way out through the land haze. A speedboat came bucking over the waves with Norman's wife, Mary Ann, and my two youngest daughters, Marian and Bettina on board. Boats of all sorts. Seasick faces, joyful faces, gaping faces. Some were laughing themselves silly, shouting and asking if we had really come from Morocco on "that thing." Seen from outside, we were just a wickerwork cabin floating on the water behind a majestic Egyptian sail, with two shorn-off tufts of reed sticking out of the water at either end.

Yuri's motley rag curtain did not exactly reinforce the impression of an ocean voyager either. Over fifty vessels of every type and size finally escorted Ra II across the finishing line. We were making for Bridgetown, the capital. Sailboats, speedboats, fishing boats, yachts of many kinds, a catamaran, a trimaran, a police boat, a Hollywood-type full-rigger decorated as a pirate ship and packed with tourists, and our old friend the Culpepper, circled round us in a melee that made the peace-loving Carlo long for the solitude of the sea. Georges, on the contrary, felt quite at home; he lit our last red flare and installed himself like the Statute of Liberty on the cabin roof.

So ended the voyages of the Ra. Outside Bridgetown harbor we lowered the bleached mainsail with its round solar orb for the last time, and furled it while the crew of the Culpepper tossed us a tow rope.

The harbor area was swarming like an anthill. Every street was packed with people. It was five minutes to seven P.M. by our watches; we had to adjust them to Barbados time, a long awaited moment, for we had sailed 3270 nautical miles since last we set foot on land.

Before putting into the quay we found an opportunity to shake hands, all eight of us. There was not one of us who failed to realize that it was only thanks to a common effort that we had come safely across the sea.

We threw a last look back at the vanquished ocean. There it lay, seemingly boundless, as in Columbus' day, as in the golden age of mighty Lixus, as in the days of the roving Phoenicians and intrepid Olmecs. How long would whale and fish gambol out there? Would man at the eleventh hour learn to dispose of his modern garbage, would he abandon his war against nature? Would future generations restore early man's respect and veneration for the sea and the earth, humbly worshiped by the Inca as *Mama-Cocha* and *Mama-Alpa*, "Mother-Sea" and "Mother-Earth"? If not, it will be of little use to struggle for peace among nations, and still less to wage war, on board our little space craft.

The ocean is not endless.

We jumped barefoot ashore at the other end.

The ocean current rolled on alone. Fifty-seven days. Fifty-seven thousand years. Has mankind changed? Nature has not. And man is nature.

POSTSCRIPT

Dʀʏ ꜰᴇᴇᴛ. Dry hair. Everything dry. Windows closed. Big trees swaying in the wind. Strong wind. Outside. But the paper on my desk doesn't flutter about, doesn't even move. My armchair doesn't move. All is stable, fixed, and firm. I am safe, back in my own workroom. Blue water is visible between the swaying branches of mighty trees. The Mediterranean. The highway of early cultures. The link between three continents which close it in solidly on all sides, except for a single vent at Gibraltar. The blue sea is white-capped but silent. To hear the surf rumble I must open the window. I don't, for the wind will play havoc with my papers. It feels unbelievably good to be safe in my cozy study again. Surrounded by books on all walls. Books and closed windows. Poor sailors who are at sea in this wind. I pull down a large rolling map in front of the window facing the sea. It shows the mighty Atlantic, the way the map-makers see it. A flat, lifeless impediment dividing a rectangular world in two. Africa to the right, America to the left. North up, and south down. What a shocking misconception of the most dynamic, vigorous, never-resting, ever-rushing conveyer that nature ever set into motion. Perpetual motion, caught in a still picture like an antelope in the air. Motionless as the Sahara. Petrified like the Alps. Only different in color.

Printed blue, while firm land is yellow, green, white. What a perfect game board. Just suited for small markers—small men—to be moved about at the throw of dice. We can throw and move on any color until our men are stopped on blue. If you try to cross blue, you are cheating. The diffusionists couldn't care less. They are cheating. Move on blue in all directions. How amazed all players would be if the blue on the game board began revolving. Like the ocean. Revolving in wide bands, throwing the markers about, sending them from Africa to tropic America. From tropic America to Asia and back again to North America. If the maps had been made dynamic, new rules would have to be invented for the game. White and black men reaching a square off Morocco would gain an extra jump to America on the blue band of the Canary Current. Yellow men off Indonesia would hit the revolving band coming from Polynesia and be sent back there in two throws, by way of the Japan Current and Northwest America. Blue would always mean a long jump in one direction, a loss of turn in the other. Yellow deserts, white ice, green swamps, would be the new impediments in this realistic game.

I snatched at the string that sent my stupid map up like a racing rocket. The Mediterranean moved again between the trees like a meadow combed by wind. I pushed the window open, listened for the living surf, and let the wind play havoc with all my papers, all my speculations. To hell with paper. To hell with "isms," diffusionism as well as isolationism. Open windows. Fresh air. Rain and thunder and reality. If only the rumbling sea could speak. One thing is sure. It would have stories to tell about unrecorded voyages during antiquity that would match any of those duly recorded in the medieval age. The medieval age was a step down, not up. Men of antiquity were not chessmen. Their stupendous creations show they were dynamic, imaginative, inquisitive, courageous, clever. Stronger than men of push-button times and with greater trust in their gods, yet filled with all the vanity, love, hate, and desire embodied in the glands and nerves of men through all ages since Adam. Sailors from ancient Egypt left the Red Sea to visit Mesopotamia and even Asian ports far beyond. From the mouth of the Nile, they crisscrossed the eastern Mediterranean to collect taxes from distant islands forced to pay tribute to the Pharaoh.

The people of Egypt and the people of Mesopotamia, affiliated although speaking different languages and writing different scripts, bred sailors as able as their architects, and caused sea-borne civilizations to bloom, again with different languages and different scripts, on all the distant islands that form stepping stones to the north and to the west. We do not know when the Egyptians began their influence on the islands, but the Phoenicians gradually took over. We hardly know the origins of the Phoenicians and what kind of ships they first constructed. Reed boats were originally used among their nearest neighbors to the east and to the south. Even to the west: an engraved ring from the ancient culture of Crete shows a crescent-shaped reed boat with transversal lashings, mast, and cabin. From Phoenician waters, culture spread beyond Gibraltar. To Lixus, where reed boats survived. Nobody will ever be able to retrace the routes of all these vessels or reconstruct the interrelationships between all these diversified civilizations, intimately interlocked and yet clearly different as they were, partly imposed on earlier local cultures, and nourished by different lines of rulers, in different geographical environments. Who shall ever identify the mariners that carried a jar with Mediterranean gold and copper coins from the fourth century B.C. to Corvo Island in the outer Azores, nearer to North America than to Gibraltar? Seeking fortune, or refuge, thousands upon thousands of ships left their home ports during antiquity, leaving no written logs. Royal artists perpetuated the Egyptian Queen, Hatchepsut's great naval expedition down the Red Sea to Punt, but only chance made the ancient geographer Eratosthenes record the distance between remote Ceylon and the River Ganges in the number of sailing days needed by ordinary papyrus ships with Egyptian sail and rigging. No temple was raised in their honor. Only when King Hanno personally sailed through Gibraltar in the fifth century before Christ, with sixty ships stocked with provisions and thousands of Phoenician colonists of both sexes aboard, was the event immortalized on an inscribed stele raised in his honor in Carthage. Yet, the inscriptions admit that Hanno was no pioneer, for on the fourth day of coastal sailing outside Gibraltar, his fleet reached the megalithic city of Lixus, where he took local pilots onboard who knew the coast and had names for all the capes they subsequently encountered in twenty-eight days of further sailing down Africa. Stocked with provisions to last for two months beyond Lixus, Hanno turned back only when his binational exploring fleet reached well down the jungle and river coast of Equatorial West Africa. The king's inscribed stele, as recorded by later Greeks, refers to the population of Lixus as foreigners among whom the explorers sojourned long enough to obtain friendship and advice. These ancient voyagers were masters of the art of obtaining fruitful relations even with hostile, primitive people. According to their own record, they always landed a tempting gift on the beach to be picked up by local tribes as a friendship token before they dared to leave the ships. This method was used on the jungle coasts of West Africa, and it would have functioned among unorganized jungle tribes anywhere else.

The obvious benefit of international collaboration on voyages to foreign lands was fully understood by man of antiquity. Not least by the Egyptians and Phoenicians. This is why it was quite normal that Egyptians and Phoenicians directly joined hands in the first historically recorded circumnavigation of Africa, nearly two centuries before Hanno's skillfully prepared fleet of emigrants sailed down along the already known west coast. In fact, Pharaoh Necho's circum-African expedition about 600 B.C. was a proper Egyptian enterprise utilizing Phoenician ships and crew. No King or Pharaoh went along on the three-year venture, thus no Egyptian tomb or stele tells the story. It just happened that Herodotus recorded the event before it was forgotten, traveling as he did between the Phoenician coast, Mesopotamia, and Egypt in the fifth century B.C. while preparing his famous world history.

What kind of culture would have begun to flourish among formerly primitive jungle hunters on the other side of the Atlantic if such a mixed expedition of colonists or explorers had been driven there? What kind of pyramids would they have built?

That stupid map with the dead blue that places Mexico centuries or millennia away from Morocco, instead of a few weeks. A few snatches of sleep for a monkey, a duck, or a sailor—even if he did not know the sea was salt. Mere seconds, counted within the frame of history. True, the people of America had not seen ribbed plank ships before Columbus. But the people of Morocco, the entire Mediterranean, and Mesopotamia had seen reed ships.

Like those surviving in America. I had only made a fumbling experiment in building two, with the aid of a scant handful of lake people, and sailed some six thousand nautical miles in four months, the second time landing in America. By building a hundred *Ra*'s, we, too, like Hanno, might have learned to sail safely up and down off the dreaded Cape Juby. But in the meantime, how often would we have run the risk of breaking the rudder-oar and landing in America? And heaven knows what kind of culture pattern we from *Ra* would have agreed upon.

I closed the window. I grabbed my pencil and wrote:

I still don't know. I have no theory but that a reed boat is seaworthy and the Atlantic is a conveyer. But I would hereafter consider it barely short of a miracle if the multitude of active maritime expeditions during the millennia of antiquity never happened to break their rudder-oars off Lixus, or be swept off course while struggling to avoid shipwreck in the dreaded currents around Cape Juby. Did we drift to America because of unprecedented stupidity in handling wooden steering oars, or because of unprecedented skill in sitting on reeds?

Here I do have a theory: Perhaps we got across because we sailed on the ocean and not on a map.